AGEING EQUITABLY WITH CARE
Power, Policy, Practice

Edited by
Tamara Daly and Susan Braedley

P

First published in Great Britain in 2025 by

Policy Press, an imprint of
Bristol University Press
University of Bristol
1–9 Old Park Hill
Bristol
BS2 8BB
UK
t: +44 (0)117 374 6645
e: bup-info@bristol.ac.uk

Details of international sales and distribution partners are available at policy.bristoluniversitypress.co.uk

Editorial selection and matter © the editors 2025; individual chapters © their respective authors 2025

The digital PDF and ePub versions of this title are available open access and distributed under the terms of the Creative Commons Attribution-NonCommercial-NoDerivatives 4.0 International licence (https://creativecommons.org/licenses/by-nc-nd/4.0/) which permits reproduction and distribution for non-commercial use without further permission provided the original work is attributed.

DOI: 10.51952/9781447375067

British Library Cataloguing in Publication Data
A catalogue record for this book is available from the British Library

ISBN 978-1-4473-7504-3 paperback
ISBN 978-1-4473-7505-0 ePub
ISBN 978-1-4473-7506-7 OA PDF

The rights of Tamara Daly and Susan Braedley to be identified as editors of this work have been asserted by them in accordance with the Copyright, Designs and Patents Act 1988.

All rights reserved: no part of this publication may be reproduced, stored in a retrieval system, or transmitted in any form or by any means, electronic, mechanical, photocopying, recording, or otherwise without the prior permission of Bristol University Press.

Every reasonable effort has been made to obtain permission to reproduce copyrighted material. If, however, anyone knows of an oversight, please contact the publisher.

The statements and opinions contained within this publication are solely those of the editors and contributors and not of the University of Bristol or Bristol University Press. The University of Bristol and Bristol University Press disclaim responsibility for any injury to persons or property resulting from any material published in this publication.

Bristol University Press and Policy Press work to counter discrimination on grounds of gender, race, disability, age and sexuality.

Cover design: Bristol University Press
Front cover image: iStock/Boonyachoat

Contents

Series editors' preface v
List of figures and tables vii
Notes on contributors viii
Acknowledgements x

1   Ageing with care: aiming for equity and inclusion   1
       Tamara Daly and Susan Braedley

PART I   Power, knowledge, skills

2   Traversing the cityscape: locating age-friendly, age inclusion   17
       and age equity
       Tamara Daly and Tesia Wood

3   Age-friendly for all? Equality and equity in the changing   37
       landscape of the social democratic welfare state
       Gudmund Ågotnes and Bodil H. Blix

4   Who gets counted? Ageing statistics and advancing age equity   53
       Madeline McCoy and Renate Ysseldyk

5   Counting care workers: when the 'muddle' is the message   68
       Tamara Daly, Sara Charlesworth, Frode F. Jacobsen
       and Katherine Laxer

6   Ageing, intersectionality, social location and identity   94
       Donna Baines and Renate Ysseldyk

PART II   Policies, practices, people

7   Queering age-friendliness: addressing safety, indicating equity   113
       Susan Braedley, Christine Streeter and Oliver Debney

8   Super-invisibility: 'older' care workers in home care and   131
       residential long-term care
       Tamara Daly, Sara Charlesworth and Frode F. Jacobsen

9   Resistance, resilience and relationship: Indigenous older   159
       adults and ageing in the Canadian city
       Lauren Brooks-Cleator and Sean Hillier

10   Triple jeopardy: addressing age equity for older   177
       immigrant women
       Susan Braedley, Karine Côté-Boucher and Renate Ysseldyk

11   'East' meets 'West': trans-national ageing in a space of   195
       'cultural liminality'
       Elias Chaccour and Tamara Daly

12   The promise of dementia-friendly approaches: addressing stigma   212
       Sienna Caspar and Kelsey Berg

13	Addressing social barriers to age-equitable public transportation: don't miss the bus!	223
	Madeline McCoy, Susan Braedley and Renate Ysseldyk	
14	Your days are numbered: active ageing, wearable technologies and surveillance capitalism	239
	Albert Banerjee, Jacqueline Choiniere and Martha MacDonald	
15	The longevity divide in a globalised climate – a forward conclusion	256
	Tamara Daly	
Index		279

Series editors' preface

*Chris Phillipson (University of Manchester, UK),
Toni Calasanti (Virginia, Tech, USA) and Anna Wanka
(Goethe-Universität, Frankfurt am Main, Germany)*

As the older population continues to expand across the global North and South, new issues and concerns arise for consideration by academics, policy makers and practitioners worldwide. *Ageing in a Global Context* is a series of books, published by Policy Press in association with the British Society of Gerontology, which aims to influence and transform debates in what has become a fast-moving field in research and policy. The series seeks to achieve this in three main ways: first, through publishing books which re-think key questions shaping debates in the study of ageing. This has become especially important given the pressures on health and social care systems, alongside the complex nature of population change, both of these elements opening up the need to explore themes which go beyond traditional perspectives in social gerontology. Second, the series represents a response to the impact of globalization and related processes, these contributing to the erosion of the national boundaries which originally framed the study of ageing. From this has come the emergence of new concerns explored in various contributions to the series, for example: the impact of cultural diversity, changing patterns of working life, patterns of inequality through the life course, the role of ethnicity in later life and building age-friendly communities. Third, a key theme of the series is to explore interdisciplinary connections in gerontology. The various books provide a critical assessment of the disciplinary boundaries and territories influencing later life, creating, in the process, new perspectives and approaches relevant to the development of gerontology in the 21st century.

Ageing Equitably, with Care: Power, Policy, Practice provides a major advance in our thinking about how to achieve equity in supporting and empowering different groups within the older population. The volume has a particular focus on issues around the devaluation of care work in a neo-liberal society, but it covers a wider range of concerns relating to developing strategies for ageing well across the life course. The book is especially important in advancing a feminist political economy, drawing upon contributions from critical gerontology, intersectionality theory and related perspectives. The approach taken in the book is especially significant for the *Ageing in a Global Context* series as it continues a debate about the challenges associated with ageing in urban environments, providing a critical perspective on the 'age-friendly' paradigm advanced by the World Health Organization. The book highlights the contradictions in attempts to develop this approach in the context of economic austerity, and the priority attached to market-based solutions in respect of health and social care. At the same time, cities also offer exciting opportunities for fulfilling the potential of ageing populations and advancing new forms of collective support. The book represents a major contribution to the literature on advancing age equity and social inclusion, drawing on the voices and experiences of care workers, diverse groups of older people and an extensive and inter-disciplinary research team. The editors have put together an exciting collection of papers which highlight the urgency of recognising the centrality of care work in society, the social and cultural differences within ageing populations and the significance of a feminist political economy in taking forward theoretical and policy debates. The book should attract a wide readership across a broad academic, policy and professional audience, and is a valuable contribution to the *Ageing in a Global Context* series.

List of figures and tables

Figures

2.1	A scoping search and selection process	18
4.1	Canadian surveys: where and how are older adults included?	56
4.2	International surveys: where and how are older adults included?	58
4.3	Comparison of variables related to gender, sex, 2SLGBTQI identity, culture/ethnicity, religion, and indigeneity in Canadian and international surveys	60
5.1	Residential LTC nursing workforce, Canada 2014–23	78
8.1	Income sources aged 65+, 2020 or latest available year, as a percentage of income	136
8.2	Workforce by sex and age, percentage of total workforce, Australia, Canada and Norway (2023)	139

Tables

5.1	Mapping cross-jurisdictional categories by roles and job titles	72
5.2	Assessment of workforce data gaps	74
5.3	Sex of residential Aged Care and Home Care Packages Programme workforce (2023)	75
5.4	Residential Aged Care and Home Care Packages Programme workforce 55+ (2023)	76
5.5	Size of workforce 55+, by National Occupational Categories (NOC), nursing and assisting occupations, across settings, by sex (2021)	81
5.6	All Norwegian municipal care services 2016–20, by FTE and total employees	84
5.7	All Norwegian municipal home care workers (2016–20), by FTE	85
5.8	All Norwegian municipal institution-based care workers (2016–20), by FTE	86
5.9	Proportion aged 55+, by job category and number of Norwegian employees, of all employees in municipal health and care services (2016–20)	87
5.10	Share and number of employees with an immigration background in municipal health and care services (2016–20)	88
5.11	Summary of care workforce characteristics	89
8.1	Income below the median rates, 65+, by gender, 2020 or latest year	137
8.2	Pension conditions, by country, years as specified	138
8.3	Workers aged 55+ as percentage of all workers, by category, most recent data available	140
8.4	Comparative attributes of LTC, Australia, Canada and Norway	144

Notes on contributors

Gudmund Ågotnes is Professor in the Department of Welfare and Participation at the Western Norway University of Applied Sciences in Bergen, Norway.

Donna Baines is Professor in the School of Social Work at the University of British Columbia in Vancouver, Canada.

Albert Banerjee is Associate Professor and an NBHRF Research Chair in Community Health and Ageing in the Department of Gerontology at Saint Thomas University, Fredericton, Canada.

Kelsey Berg is a research specialist in the Alberta Health Services and a trainee at University of Lethbridge, Lethbridge, Canada.

Bodil H. Blix is Professor in the Department of Health and Care Sciences at the Arctic University of Norway.

Susan Braedley is Professor in the School of Social Work and the Institute of Political Economy at Carleton University, Ottawa, Canada. She is Associate Director of the Imagine Aging partnership grant.

Lauren Brooks-Cleator is a researcher with the Social Research and Demonstration Corporation in Ottawa, Canada.

Sienna Caspar is Associate Professor of Recreation Therapy at the University of Lethbridge, Lethbridge, Canada.

Elias Chaccour is a doctoral candidate in the Graduate Programme in Health, field of Health Policy and Equity, at York University, Toronto, Canada.

Sara Charlesworth is Professor Emerita at RMIT, Melbourne, Australia.

Jacqueline Choiniere is Associate Professor in the School of Nursing at York University, Toronto, Canada.

Karine Côté-Boucher is Associate Professor in the Faculté des Arts et des Sciences, École de Criminology at the Université de Montreal.

Tamara Daly is Professor of Health Policy and Equity at the School of Health Policy and Management, York University, and Director of the York

University Centre for Aging Research and Education. She is Director of the Imagine Aging partnership grant.

Oliver Debney holds a Masters in Social Work and is a Trans-2SLGBTQ+ counsellor in Ontario, Canada.

Sean Hillier is Associate Professor in the School of Health Policy and Management at York University, Toronto, Canada, and a research chair in Indigenous Health Policy and One Health.

Frode F. Jacobsen is Professor and Research Director at the Centre for Care Research, Western Norway University of Applied Sciences.

Katherine Laxer teaches at York University, Toronto, Canada.

Martha MacDonald is Professor Emerita of Economics at Saint Mary's University, Nova Scotia, Canada.

Madeline McCoy completed her MSc at Carleton University and is a researcher at Bruyere Institute in Ottawa, Canada.

Christine Streeter holds a Masters in Social Work and a PhD in the School of Social Work and the Institute of Political Economy, Carleton University, Ottawa, Canada.

Tesia Wood completed her Master of Arts in the School of Health Policy and Management, York University, Toronto, Canada.

Renate Ysseldyk is Associate Professor and social psychologist in Health Sciences at Carleton University, Ottawa, Canada.

Acknowledgements

This book, like most projects of its kind, relies on a cast of thousands.

First, there is our incredible 'Imagine Aging' interdisciplinary, international research team that has worked together and individually through challenging conditions involving global pandemics and political and personal upheavals. While most of the team continues together, others, including both graduate students and faculty, have joined us for just one or two sites and then moved on to other related work. But across the team, we have relied on all researchers' high motivation to do this research and contribute to debates, policies and practices that advance together both age equity and decent work for care workers in ways that take context into account.

Second, this book is indebted to hundreds of older adults, paid and unpaid carers, and other workers in services important to older adults who trusted us with their stories, engaged in analysis with us, and provided us with information and feedback that shaped much of this volume. We hope this book meets their hopes and affirms their trust.

Third, our research partners and collaborating organizations across many cities, including government partners, unions, community non-profit organizations, public services, activist groups and advocates for older adults and equity-seeking groups, have continuously informed our work, provided critique and engaged us to consider their priorities, problems and hopes.

Fourth, funding from the Social Sciences and Humanities Research Council of Canada, from our various universities and generous contributions from research partners make it possible for us to do this work, and to share it within and beyond our academic worlds.

Fifth, in each of our sites and across the team, our access to sites, our data, our schedules and our day-to-day accommodation, transportation and food arrangements rely on teams of administrative support people and graduate student trainees, including Negeen Pak's constant and consistent support from the very beginning of this project and Elias Chaccour's invaluable support in preparing this manuscript.

Sixth, we are indebted to Policy Press and the editors of the Ageing in a Global Context series for their continued support and patience in getting this book into the hands of the public.

Finally, thank you to all our families, who have managed the demands of care at home while we've been away (even when in our own cities) conducting our extensive field research. The editors especially thank Chris and Ron, who have listened to us, debated the merits of various points and been truly wise counsel.

1

Ageing with care: aiming for equity and inclusion

Tamara Daly and Susan Braedley

Introduction

Ageing is a privilege, one that is not equally enjoyed, nor equitably distributed. Further, the ways in which ageing is 'policy-ed' and practiced do not usually produce age-inclusion or age equity and often promote their opposite. Wealthy democratic welfare states with both the economic resources and political capacity to ensure political, economic and social security in later life have the potential to offer the most promising conditions for ageing well. However, concerns about economic growth and productivity often restrict ageing-related policies to ones that reduce and constrain state costs associated with rapidly increasing older populations, and facilitate markets for services provision (Armstrong and Armstrong, 2020). Policy debates and discussion papers focus on how to improve dependency ratios, adjust old age pension age, eligibility and rates to reduce state liabilities, and promote ageing-in-place policies that can minimise health-care and long-term care costs by shifting costs and care to older people and their families. Meanwhile, nation states are impacted by globalisation, and the crises like climate change that result.

Contradictions abound. At the same time as states are committing to the proliferation of various global ageing paradigms, including the World Health Organizations' decades of development work to promote 'Age-friendly Communities' and the United Nation's 'Decade on Healthy Aging', states are considering and enacting policies that permit people living with dementia to provide advance directives for euthanasia while failing to offer safe, accessible, affordable, quality dementia care. In many jurisdictions the conditions for ageing well are declining, resulting in rapidly rising numbers of homeless and precariously housed older people, growing poverty rates particularly affecting older women, long waiting lists and unmet needs for public health-care and long-term care support, and fragmented, under-funded and over-worked long-term care staff. Equity-seeking groups are the most disadvantaged: women, racialised people, immigrants, 2SLGBTQI[1] older adults, Indigenous peoples, people with disabilities and those living on low incomes. The gap between rich, well-resourced older people and poor, under-resourced people is growing, a condition that repeated research has shown reduces health and well-being for everyone in a given society (Marmot, 2010, 2015; Wilkinson and Pickett, 2010). As Chapter 15 of this volume points out, there is a growing 'longevity divide'. These inequities are increasing across many jurisdictions where governments are removing policies and practices that support them and attacking and suppressing equity-seeking groups.

These facts drive our research and writing. Like others, we believe that progressive change is possible. Beyond describing problems, our research and this volume focus on identifying the opportunities and conditions that can advance age equity and inclusion, and how policies and practices at many levels of scale can contribute to these aims. Our vision, however, goes beyond these ends, to imagine emancipatory conditions that make ageing well a realistic possibility for all.

To advance this project, we argue that addressing the inequitable conditions of ageing without attending to the inequitable conditions for caring is to fail before we start. This book is entitled *Ageing Equitably with Care* to emphasise that all of us rely on others to reproduce our daily lives, no matter our age. In later life, age-related impairments can be minimised through changes in physical design, technologies and more, but living well across the life course requires support and care from others, whether through regular social interaction and creating celebrations and fun, health care and social care, help with household chores and meals, or support to bathe, dress, toilet, move and eat. We argue that care workers, both paid and unpaid, must be included in studies that aim to advance age equity and inclusion. We recognise that many older people are carers, providing for their spouses, parents, children, communities, and more, sometimes as paid workers, but more often as unpaid and under-recognised carers. There are also many other volunteer, family and friend carers who provide and exchange unpaid care with older people. Then, there are the many paid care workers, from migrant domestic workers in people's homes, to care aides who provide home care and long-term care home support, to professional nurses, doctors, social workers and dentists. There is a considerable group of food services workers, laundry workers and housekeepers who offer specific services to support the needs of older adults in meal programs, senior's organisations, day programs, home care and long-term care homes and institutions.

In pursuing our research, we have been frustrated by a disconnect between debates and analyses of ageing equitably and care labour concerns, that, while bridged by some authors, permeate much of the work on age-friendliness and age equity. In our teaching on ageing across professional, social science and humanities programs, in our involvement with many community advocacy and activist groups who work on questions of social justice, age-friendliness and/or care labour, and in our engagement with policy makers at the municipal, federal, and supranational levels, there has been consistent, high interest in this intersection.

Consequently, and across the chapters, this volume puts age equity and care labour considerations into dialogue to takes up questions about equity, access, safety and inclusion for diverse groups of older people and for diverse groups of care workers. In doing so we consider how age equity and inclusion are being approached, who is included and who is left aside or oppressed in the process. A considerable international literature on care work demonstrates repeatedly and consistently that most care work is undervalued, feminised work that is taken-for-granted or assumed in much age-related policy and practice (Daly et al, 2011; Baines, 2015; Banerjee et al, 2015; Charlesworth et al, 2015; Daly et al, 2016). Even with a long-standing care labour shortage around the world that intensified with the COVID-19 pandemic and has not recovered, care work issues are usually considered separately from age-friendly, age-inclusive and age-equity policy initiatives. The time is ripe to change this approach. Ageing well depends on conditions for providing quality care, recognising that carers, whether paid or unpaid, deserve conditions that support their caring and allow them to age well, too.

Our research project

In the context of global socio-demographic ageing, austerity budgets, escalating political polarities and economic globalisation, our international team of scholars has been investigating whether, when, and how conditions that shape the lives of older people and carers in cities are advancing age equity and inclusion, and for whom. In our large scale, multi-year research partnership, Imagining Age-friendly Communities within Communities: International Promising Practices,[2] we work together to identify promising practices that produce more equitable conditions, not as universal best practices, but as 'ideas worth sharing' (Baines and Armstrong, 2015), that keep context in mind.

Our project's overarching feminist political economy perspective is put into dialogue with other epistemologies and theory, including Indigenous knowledges, and critical approaches from social work, critical gerontology and across ageing studies. We draw on theoretically grounding texts in the political economy of ageing (Estes, 1979, 1984, 2000, 2001, 2004; Phillipson, 1982; Estes et al, 1984, 2003), and the feminist political economy of health and care work (Connelly and Armstrong, 1992; Doyal and Pennell, 1994; Doyal, 1995; Folbre, 2001; Braedley and Luxton, 2010; Armstrong and Braedley, 2023). We share spaces and dialogue with critical gerontology (Laws, 1995; Baars et al, 2006; Calasanti and Slevin, 2007; Katz, 2019;

Grenier et al, 2020; Buffel, 2024) and poststructuralist debates within feminism (Bacchi, 2009, 2017; Connell, 2021).

Our methods include scoping review, statistical analysis, team ethnographic investigations, media analysis, autoethnography and more. Our work is team based, with researchers of all ages and stages – from trainees, to new assistant professors, through to 'retired' professor emeriti – working together on deep dives into statistical datasets and policy and planning documents to prepare for team-based rapid ethnographically-informed 'field' case studies that include local researchers (Imagine Aging, nd) and building upon previous work we have done collectively (Baines and Cunningham, 2011; Armstrong and Lowndes, 2018).

In our field studies, we use our distinct version of rapid team ethnography methods to focus on specific cities. We identify potential promising practices that have potential to advance age equity across the city, including in housing, care, recreational and social services, governance, transportation and more. We make observations, do interviews and take expert-led tours. We talk with activists, advocates, older people, policymakers and workers. Together, these activities yield important insights into the way power is exercised and resisted. In some cases, we have worked closely with research partners, including equity advocates, unions, community workers, policymakers, services for older adults, carers and older adults, to take up related research questions important to them in sub-studies, or to involve them in shaping our research studies and analyses.

Our team members, many who are authors in this book, include feminist political economists, health and social policy analysts, sociologists, a psychologist, an economist, legal scholars and anthropologists as well as professionals from care labour occupations, including social workers, a nurse and an occupational therapist. They are international scholars and students located in Canada, Australia, New Zealand, Taiwan and Norway who are women and men, queer and straight, white, racialised and Indigenous. Some of us have worked together for over 20 years on a host of international projects, bringing with us experiences, perspectives, theory and method that inspired this collaboration. Others are newer to this team and/or to large-scale international research. Some have focused primarily on care work, others on ageing, and a significant group have consistently focused on their intersections.

At its core, our project situates 'ageing' as a 'whole' site that is both contested and contextual. It is 'whole' in the political economy sense, comprised of states, markets, households and the voluntary sector interacting in relations of power that define those who benefit, those who don't and the conditions producing these distributions (Armstrong et al, 2001). The policies and practices that structure these materialist 'relations of ruling' as they affect ageing and care, or social reproduction more generally, also reveal how people's social locations are hierarchically 'ordered', producing inequities and exclusions. As a contested and constructed site, we argue that ageing exposes power relations, and the ways in which collective struggles and resistance are waged.

Thinking about 'communities *within* communities' frames our 'way in' to studying how ageing is understood, governed and experienced. Global paradigms and various national and local policies provide the context and reveal important 'relations of ruling', within policies and practices shaping the conditions of ageing (Smith, 1993). Within welfare states, cities are our cases of community, while various communities *within* the city comprise important sub-units that reveal inequities and exclusions as well as resistance and struggle. We take up cities, not only because they are home to the majority of older people in most welfare states, but because they are places in which evidence of equality and equity shows most vividly.[3] Our comparative approach reveals not only how the countries compare, but also how some of the planet's most super diverse cities (Toronto, Vancouver and Melbourne) compare with smaller ones, including one of its most equitable (Bergen), are aiming for age equity and age inclusion differently, with different pressures and with varying results. Focused on ageing in urban contexts in a global world that is rapidly urbanising, we omit consideration of specific conditions of ageing or care in rural, remote and Canadian on-reserve contexts. Nonetheless, we note that cities are also places where health and social care are accessed by older adults living outside of cities, including Indigenous peoples. Like others, we see cities as an important spatial boundary marker (Buffel et al, 2024), set within the politics and policies of nation states and the processes of economic globalisation.

Thus, we explore the city-as-a-whole and its many communities linked and cleaved by gender and sex, sexuality, ethnicity, language, Indigeneity, disease, disability, income and poverty, addiction and homelessness. We identify and explore the most promising policy approaches – from global, to national and local – always attending to the implications and the experiences of those running, providing and receiving care in them. Further, we build on the insight that cumulative advantages and disadvantages accrue to manifest in later life (Crystal and Shea, 1990; Crystal et al, 2017), extending this construct to explore the multiple, intersecting, overlapping and accumulating loci of oppression and dominance that play out in the life chances and experiences of those in later life and those who care for them.

This book

This volume both reflects and builds on our project's theoretical and methodological approaches. The first section of the book takes up power relations as demonstrated in the research knowledge and official data collection on older people and on care workers. Authors note who and what is present and missing in these forms of knowledge to consider the implications for the conditions of ageing and caring, and how researchers and advocates can develop the knowledge base and skills to advance equity. In the second section, the chapters focus on policies, practices and people to consider a wide range of perspectives on advancing age equity. Each chapter is situated within an explicit political, economic and social context that highlights the longevity 'win' implicated in global socio-demographic ageing amidst the challenges that come from declining birth rates, migration flows, care work invisibility, climate change, austerity-oriented health and social care policies, economic globalisation, political movements and polarisations, care labour shortages and fault lines heightened and highlighted by the COVID pandemic.

The contributions in this book are based on our completed theoretical and empirical work to date. We draw examples from the first three of our five welfare states we have studied: Canada, Australia and Norway.[4] Many of the examples are from our research in Canada, an early adopter of the World Health Organization's age-friendly framework partly due to Canadians' involvement in developing it (Plouffe et al, 2013). Our examples highlight challenges and promising approaches, amidst some differences in governance; comprehensiveness and approaches to health and social care; geographic size and ageing demographics; type and level of support for migration; and histories with respect to Indigenous populations.

While the examples are drawn mostly from Canada (one of the most super-diverse nations on earth and a charter contributor to the 'Age-Friendly' movement), other examples from Norway (a very different welfare state, and one of the most equitable countries), and Australia (a quite similar country comprised of Indigenous peoples and immigrants and 'equally inequitable' to Canada), underscore the broader importance of the questions we ask and the examples we provide. In other words, the countries are all advanced, albeit different, welfare states, and the examples highlight how this is not a book about any one country, city or group per se, but one that uses these examples to advance critically important questions for the overall study of ageing.

Across the chapters, authors draw from among a wide array of critical gerontological considerations of age-friendliness and healthy ageing, studies that take up questions related to age equity and age inclusion, while also filling an important gap in this literature with its focus on critical insights from studies of care labour, both paid and unpaid. Considering social reproduction is central, including research on: the conditions for care; the social relations of workers who are an ageing, gendered, often migrant and racialised workforce; policies and practices to support care labour; and the availability and willingness of unpaid family care.

In sum, this book accomplishes two aims. First, it identifies knowledge gaps and problems that impede advancing age equity. Second, it provides a range of theory and evidence to advance equity for older people and those who provide the care labour. Using an interdisciplinary, collaborative research approach, we address timely, important questions about the conditions of ageing alongside care work in the context of global and national level developments that are producing and reproducing inequities, and pose others. The book has two sections. Part I: 'Power, knowledge, skills', is a series of chapters that consider the knowledge bases for age-equity movements and aged care work. The concluding chapter considers interdisciplinarity and different takes on knowledge, including the skills needed to put knowledge into action. Part II: 'Policies, practices, people', focuses on age equity and care work in a series of chapters that take up age equity in the context of policy and practice, always rooting analysis in data that conveys the perspectives and experiences of those most affected. The section ends by reaching ahead with a 'forward conclusion', examining the implications of the latest features of globalisation for the study and experience of ageing and by taking action and resistance into account.

Across the chapters, readers will note both continuities and conflict among the perspectives, topics and positions taken by the various authors. We hope you learn as much from these analyses as we have learned from each other while the research was being conducted and debated among us.

Part I: Power, knowledge, skills

Chapters in this section offer an assessment of the research knowledge that informs and shapes age-friendly, age-inclusive and age-equity movements and developments, the ways that jurisdictional context shapes these movements and understandings of what might count as equity, as well as the ways that disciplinary understandings and theories shape research and advocacy. In sum, this section takes up the power of knowledge, context, perspective and skills in advancing and impeding age equity.

Setting the frame for the volume, in Chapter 2, 'Traversing the cityscape: locating age-friendly, age inclusion and age equity', Tamara Daly and Tesia Wood consider the power of knowledge by reviewing available English language academic journal literature to identify whether and how equity, inclusion and care have been approached in research related to the Age-Friendly movement. While their scoping review shows a range of research studies that provide useful evidence that supports some or all of WHO's Age-Friendly Communities indicators, few city-based analyses assessed for or considered equity, inclusion or care work, and even fewer attended to issues related to older adults from equity-seeking groups, setting the stage for topics addressed by later chapters in the volume.

Chapter 3, 'Age-friendly for all? Equality and equity in the changing landscape of the social democratic welfare state', by Gudmund Ågotnes and Bodil H. Blix, shows that context matters in shaping how age-friendly and age-equitable objectives are understood and developed. The authors critically examine developments in Norway to assess how 'age-friendliness' is perceived and articulated through official and political discourses within this context. They argue that the generous and universal welfare state is based on a notion of 'equality' in which 'sameness' is a core value. This value permeates understandings and presentations of 'age-friendliness' in Norway and other Nordic States, leaving aside other interpretations of equity, while also promoting notions of individual responsibility and choice often used in arguments about welfare state unsustainability in the face of socio-demographic ageing and even rejections of the welfare state altogether. This chapter explores the possibilities and limits to age-friendliness that coexist with the power inherent in jurisdictional ideologies and structures.

Chapter 4 takes up the power of statistical measurement and its relationship to age-friendly policies through examples from national data collection in Canada and from a group of international statistical instruments. Given that the Age-Friendly Cities framework was developed to improve health and well-being among older populations, Madeline McCoy and Renate Ysseldyk explore how statistics reflect and shape related policy and practice, to assess whether and how older adults are included. 'Who gets counted? Ageing statistics and advancing age equity' goes further, to explore which older adults are included and what dimensions of their lives and identities are measured. The authors argue that statistics are considered and used as a reliable measurement tool for policy and practice, yet many statistical instruments fail to include or sufficiently distinguish older adults as a group. Even fewer instruments allow for intra-group comparisons. These omissions are likely to limit the evidence needed to support the impact of 'age-friendly' policies and practices, while hindering age-equity aims.

Offering a parallel analysis that examines public statistical datasets in Australia, Canada and Norway, Chapter 5, 'Counting care workers: when the 'muddle' is the message', by Tamara Daly, Sara Charlesworth, Frode F. Jacobsen and Katherine Laxer points out statistical failures across Australia, Canada and Norway to count the carers who do the work of care for older people. The data are particularly weak for those in assisting occupations, who form the bulk of the long-term care workforce in residential aged care and home care settings. They argue that datasets are largely weak, unclear and hidden, hampering aged care workforce planning and government accountability for their public stewardship in this important policy area. Pointing out that age equity requires care security for older people that does not imperil the health and well-being of care workers, the chapter calls for careful, publicly available 'counting' of care workers.

Part I concludes with Chapter 6, 'Ageing, intersectionality, social location and identity'. Donna Baines and Renate Ysseldyk demonstrate the power and value of interdisciplinarity as they bring contrasting and sometimes conflicting perspectives of anti-oppressive social work and social psychology to questions of ageing, identity and oppression. Proposing a melding of dissonant concepts, they argue that the resulting analytic tools offer ways to understand the intersections in the struggles for care experienced by diverse older people for age-friendly social fairness and equity. Further, they call for critical reflection and other intersectional-competent skills useful in not only understanding the complex lives of older people but in mobilising for anti-oppressive change.

Part II: Policies, practices, people

In Part II, chapters draw from statistical work, our literature reviews, our rapid ethnographies and from related research studies in wealthy welfare states. We consider age equity including its relationship to care work, with perspectives from older adults and/or care workers, especially those from equity-seeking groups.

Chapter 7, 'Queering age-friendliness: addressing safety, indicating equity', by Susan Braedley, Christine Streeter and Oliver Debney, reports on Canadian empirical research with queer older adults and queer workers in services important to older adults. In 2020, Canada had the strongest legal protections for 2SLGBTQI people among OECD countries, suggesting that it was among the safest, most inclusive and welcoming of welfare states for queer folks. While showing that Canada still has a long way to go to advance queer age equity, the chapter offers a path forward for policy and practice by identifying six indicators for age-equitable institutions, organisations and services that offer safety, accessibility and inclusion for queer older adults and the workers on whom they depend.

Chapter 8, 'Super-invisibility: "older" care workers in home care and residential long-term care', takes up paid care work in three countries, Australia, Canada and Norway, to focus on age equity considerations for the many older workers who do it. Long-term care and home care are included in one of the eight age-friendly domains, 'community supports and health services'. Tamara Daly, Sara Charlesworth and Frode F. Jacobsen argue that poor conditions within long-term care work produce poor health, safety and financial security outcomes for older care workers, a group of care workers who are the least visible, as their chapter in Part I discusses. They argue that the under-valuing of care work that pervades many societies, exacerbates the invisibility of ageing care workers' working and retirement conditions, even while they do work for older people. The result is their positioning of 'super-invisibility' within policy and planning.

In Chapter 9, our book switches gears to consider: what is age equity for Indigenous older adults living in cities in Canada? In 'Resistance, resilience, and relationship: indigenous older adults and ageing in the Canadian city', Lauren Brooks-Cleator and Sean Hillier conclude that Indigenous older adults' experiences of ageing in a city are defined simultaneously by exclusions shaped by ongoing settler colonialism that permeates Canadian society, and by inclusions shaped by their Indigeneity, their relationships and their resiliency. Throughout, they highlight the significance of culture, agency, equity and connections to care systems, working to reimagine age-friendly communities for Indigenous older adults.

Extending our consideration of age equity from yet another perspective in Chapter 10, 'Triple jeopardy: age equity for older immigrant women' draws on data from three empirical research projects with older immigrants to Canada, to focus on older immigrant women's experiences, in the context of Canada's reliance on immigration to maintain its labour force. This chapter highlights Canada's reliance on mothers of immigrants and their unpaid work. Susan Braedley, Karine Côté-Boucher and Renate Ysseldyk show that older immigrant women are caught in a web of inequities as they contribute significantly to (unpaid) familial and household care work. While research has revealed the conditions and struggles of immigrant workers in paid care work, this analysis shows the conditions of unpaid care work involved in the immigrant-care nexus.

In Chapter 11, '"East" meets "West": trans-national ageing in a space of 'cultural liminality', Elias Chaccour and Tamara Daly reveal further dimensions affecting immigrant older adults. They develop and explore the concept of 'cultural liminality' as it applies to older adults in transnational families living between Canada and Lebanon as they navigate between Eastern and Western cultural norms. The authors examine how political and economic conditions, state support systems, family dynamics and perspectives on ageing shape older adults' experiences across transnational borders to show the impact on caregiving and intergenerational relationships. The chapter concludes by highlighting research gaps and offering recommendations for inclusive policies that address the needs of older transnational migrants in multicultural societies.

Dementia is among older adults' greatest concerns, affected by widely-held social stigma. In Chapter 12, Sienna Caspar and Kelsey Berg argue for extending age-friendliness to include all those who live with dementia. 'The promise of dementia-friendly approaches: addressing stigma', argues for inclusive and integrated systems of support that recognise people with dementia as equals, honouring their experiences and capabilities, and enabling them to live with meaning and purpose in societies. It asks us to recognise stigma as a barrier for those with dementia, who deserve to live fully within the wider community, and notes the benefits for caregivers that could result.

Bringing together many of the equity considerations raised in other chapters, Chapter 13, 'Addressing social barriers to age-equitable public transportation: don't miss the bus!' by Madeline McCoy, Susan Braedley and Renate Ysseldyk takes up one of the age-friendly city indicators – transportation – to consider public transportation through a social determinants of health and age equity lens. Drawing on findings from ethnographic and interview research with older adults, seniors' services workers and transportation services workers and managers in Ottawa, Canada, they consider and identify promising practices that can address transportation barriers and advance age equitable public transportation for diverse populations of older adults.

Technological advances are often a policy and practice tool to advance social change. Chapter 14, 'Your days are numbered: a critical look at active ageing and self-monitoring', takes up the question of technology via an autoethnography of fitness tracker technology, and its relationship to notions of healthy active ageing and its affiliate terms 'successful' or 'positive' ageing. Albert Banerjee, Jacqueline Choiniere and Martha MacDonald problematise the theoretical assumptions around individual choice and lifestyle and illustrate the biases in the active ageing approach by linking individual self-monitoring and digital technology with the growth of surveillance as a tool for employers, marketers, insurance companies, health providers and, indeed, families. Posing the feminist political economy questions of who benefits, and who pays, the authors complement the book's other chapters on quantitative measurement, showing how data can be both helpful and dangerous.

The book's forward-looking conclusion, written by research project Director, Tamara Daly, explores the impact of economic globalisation for nation states and for ageing, with a focus on shifts over time. Drawing attention to the inequality of the 'longevity divide', the chapter explores the ways in which economic freedoms have gained ascendency over political ones, affecting nation states' capacities to address big challenges, maintain solidarity and handle political struggles. The chapter proffers the example of the 'Swiss Grannies', who, amidst documented threats to their own longevity, took their politicians to court for doing too little to protect their lives and won in a landmark case in the European Court of Human Rights Grand Chamber. Chapter 15, 'The longevity divide in a globalised climate - a forward conclusion', acknowledges that we need to know more about how globalisation accelerates crises like climate change with impacts for ageing, particularly given the reality of the longevity divide.

Notes

1. In this volume, we use the acronym preferred by our community partners, 2SLGBTQI: two-spirit, lesbian, gay, bi, trans, queer, intersex. We recognize that different acronyms may be used by different groups.
2. 'Imagining Age-Friendly Communities within Communities: International Promising Practices', Director: Tamara Daly, Social Sciences and Humanities Partnership Grant, 2018–2027, #895-2018-1013.
3. To date, the team has conducted field studies in Canada (Toronto, Ottawa, Halifax, Vancouver); Norway (Bergen); Australia (Melbourne); New Zealand (Auckland) and Taiwan (Taipei).
4. The countries in the project include: Canada, Norway, Denmark, Australia, New Zealand and Taiwan.

References

Armstrong, H., Armstrong, P. and Coburn, D. (2001) *Unhealthy Times: Political Economy Perspectives on Health and Care*, Oxford University Press.

Armstrong, P. and Armstrong, H. (2020) Contracting-out care: nursing homes in Canada, in F. Collyer and K. Willis (eds) *Navigating Private and Public Healthcare*, Palgrave Macmillan.

Armstrong, P. and Braedley, S. (eds) (2023) *Care Homes in a Turbulent Era: Do They Have a Future?*, Edward Elgar Publishing.

Armstrong, P. and Lowndes, R. (eds) (2018) *Creative Teamwork: Developing Rapid, Site-Switching Ethnography*, Oxford University Press.

Baars, J., Dannefer, D., Phillipson, C. and Walker, A. (eds) (2006) *Aging, Globalization and Inequality: The New Critical Gerontology*, Routledge.

Bacchi, C.L. (2009) *Analysing Policy: What's the Problem Represented to Be?* Pearson.

Bacchi, C.L. (2017) Policies as gendering practices: re-viewing categorical distinctions, *Journal of Women, Politics & Policy*, 38(1): 20–41.

Baines, D. (2015) Neoliberalism and the convergence of nonprofit care work in Canada, *Competition & Change*, 19(3): 194–209.

Baines, D. and Armstrong, P. (2015) *Promising Practices in Long Term Care: Ideas Worth Sharing*, Canadian Centre for Policy Alternatives.

Baines, D. and Cunningham, I. (2011) Using comparative perspective rapid ethnography in international case studies: strengths and challenges, *Qualitative Social Work*, 12(1): 73–88.

Banerjee, A., Armstrong, P., Daly, T., Armstrong, H. and Braedley, S. (2015) Careworkers don't have a voice': epistemological violence in residential care for older people, *Journal of Aging Studies*, 33: 28–36.

Braedley, S. and Luxton, M. (eds) (2010) *Neoliberalism and Everyday Life*, McGill-Queen's University Press.

Buffel, T., Doran, P. and Yarker, S. (2024) *Reimagining Age-Friendly Communities: Urban Ageing and Spatial Justice*, Policy Press.

Calasanti, T.M. and Slevin, K.F. (2007) *Age Matters: Re-Aligning Feminist Thinking*, Routledge.

Charlesworth, S., Baines, D. and Cunningham, I. (2015) If I had a family, there is no way that I could afford to work here': juggling paid and unpaid care work in social services, *Gender, Work and Organization*, 22(6): 596–613.

Connell, R. (2021) *Gender in World Perspective* (4th edn), Polity Press.

Connelly, M.P. and Armstrong, P. (1992) *Feminism in Action: Studies in Political Economy*, Canadian Scholars' Press.

Crystal, S. and Shea, D. (1990) Cumulative advantage, cumulative disadvantage, and inequality among elderly people, *The Gerontologist*, 30(4): 437–43.

Crystal, S., Shea, D.G. and Reyes, A.M. (2017) Cumulative advantage, cumulative disadvantage, and evolving patterns of late-life inequality, *The Gerontologist*, 57(5): 910–20.

Daly, T., Banerjee, A., Armstrong, P., Armstrong, H. and Szebehely, M. (2011) Lifting the 'violence veil': examining working conditions in long-term care facilities using iterative mixed methods, *Canadian Journal on Aging*, 30(2): 271–84.

Daly, T., Struthers, J., Müller, B., Taylor, D., Goldmann, M., Doupe, M. et al (2016) Prescriptive or interpretive regulation at the frontlines of care work in the 'three worlds' of Canada, Germany and Norway, *Labour*, 77: 37–71.

Doyal, L. (1995) *What Makes Women Sick: Gender and the Political Economy of Health*, Macmillan Press Ltd.

Doyal, L. and Pennell, I. (1994) *The Political Economy of Health*, Pluto Press.

Estes, C.L. (1979) *The Aging Enterprise*, Jossey-Bass Publishers.

Estes, C.L. (1984) *Political Economy, Health, and Aging*, Little Brown.

Estes, C.L. (2000) From gender to the political economy of ageing, *European Journal of Social Quality*, 2(1): 28–46.

Estes, C.L. (ed) (2001) *Social Policy and Aging: A Critical Perspective*, Sage.

Estes, C.L. (2004) 'Social security privatization and older women: a feminist political economy perspective', *Journal of Aging Studies*, 18(1): 9–26.

Estes, C.L., Gerard, L., Zones, J.S. and Swan, J. (1984) *Political Economy, Health, and Aging*, Little Brown.

Estes, C.L., Biggs, S. and Phillipson, C. (2003) *Social Theory, Social Policy and Ageing: A Critical Introduction*, Open University Press.

Folbre, N. (2001) *The Invisible Heart: Economics and Family Values*, New Press.

Grenier, A., Phillipson, C. and Settersten, T.A. Jr. (eds) (2020) *Precarity and Ageing: Understanding Insecurity and Risk in Later Life*, Policy Press.

Imagine Aging (nd) Imagining Age-Friendly 'Communities within Communities': International Promising Practices [online], Available from: https://imagine-aging.ca/

Katz, S. (ed) (2019) *Ageing in Everyday Life: Materialities and Embodiments*, Policy Press.

Laws, G. (1995) Understanding ageism: lessons from feminism and postmodernism, *The Gerontologist*, 35(1): 112–18.

Marmot, M.G. (2010) *Fair Society, Healthy Lives: The Marmot Review*, The Marmot Review.

Marmot, M.G. (2015) The health gap: the challenge of an unequal world, *The Lancet*, 386(10011): 2442–4.

Phillipson, C. (1982) *Capitalism and the Construction of Old Age*, Macmillan.

Plouffe, L.A. Garon, S., Brownoff, J., Eve, D., Foucault, M., Lawrence, R., Lessard-Beaupré, J. and Toews, V. (2013) Advancing age-friendly communities in Canada. *Canadian Review of Social Policy*, 68/69: 24–38.

Smith, D.E. (1993) *Texts, Facts, and Femininity: Exploring the Relations of Ruling*, Routledge.

Wilkinson, R.G. and Pickett, K. (2010) *The Spirit Level: Why Equality is Better for Everyone*, Penguin.

PART I

Power, knowledge, skills

2

Traversing the cityscape: locating age-friendly, age inclusion and age equity

Tamara Daly and Tesia Wood

Introduction

A cornerstone of policy and practice on ageing is the Age-Friendly Cities and Communities movement (Fitzgerald and Caro, 2014; Beard and Montawi, 2015), with more than 1,000 cities taking part as of 2024. Likewise, 'healthy ageing', advanced by the United Nations and the World Health Organization (WHO), is today's dominant global ageing paradigm, represented by the Decade of Healthy Ageing. Despite over 3,000 'healthy ageing' articles that Sadana and colleagues (2016) identify, few combine analyses of healthy ageing with an equity analysis or the social determinants of health. With an aim to better understand how equity and inclusion are being addressed by those studying 'age-friendly', we conducted a scoping review of English language academic studies and grey literature of the 'age-friendly' domains across advanced welfare states. We had two main objectives: to map dominant themes in studies of age-friendly cities and communities and to assess the extent to which equity (WHO, nd) and inclusion have been taken up in studies of age-friendly initiatives.

As with reading any map, traversing begins with understanding location. In this chapter, we traversed the 'cityscape' of the age-friendly literature using a scoping review method. We highlight major landmarks, changes in direction, key intersections, and what may be absent. Ultimately, our findings call for an expanded evidence base and a shift in perspective that builds on age-friendly approaches to integrate an age-equity vision that, importantly, includes care. Overall, these literatures identify important areas for policy and future research. In addition, they highlight gaps that exist in our current knowledge.

In the first section, we outline our review method. In the second, we present the main thematic foci from the literature on age-friendly cities and communities, the most recent, widespread, and praxis-based example of enacting the global healthy ageing paradigm. Specifically, we explore whether and how concepts of 'friendly', 'inclusion', and 'equitable' are addressed. We report the main themes that emerged and discuss notable gaps in the second section. Further, we draw attention to studies that examine diverse communities of older adults and conclude with some suggestions for mapping the path of age-friendly to equity – with care – moving forward.

Our approach

We conducted a scoping review (Arksey and O'Malley, 2005) of English-language studies focused on age-friendly cities, looking for ways in which aspects of equity and inclusion might be addressed.[1] Our process is outlined in Figure 2.1.

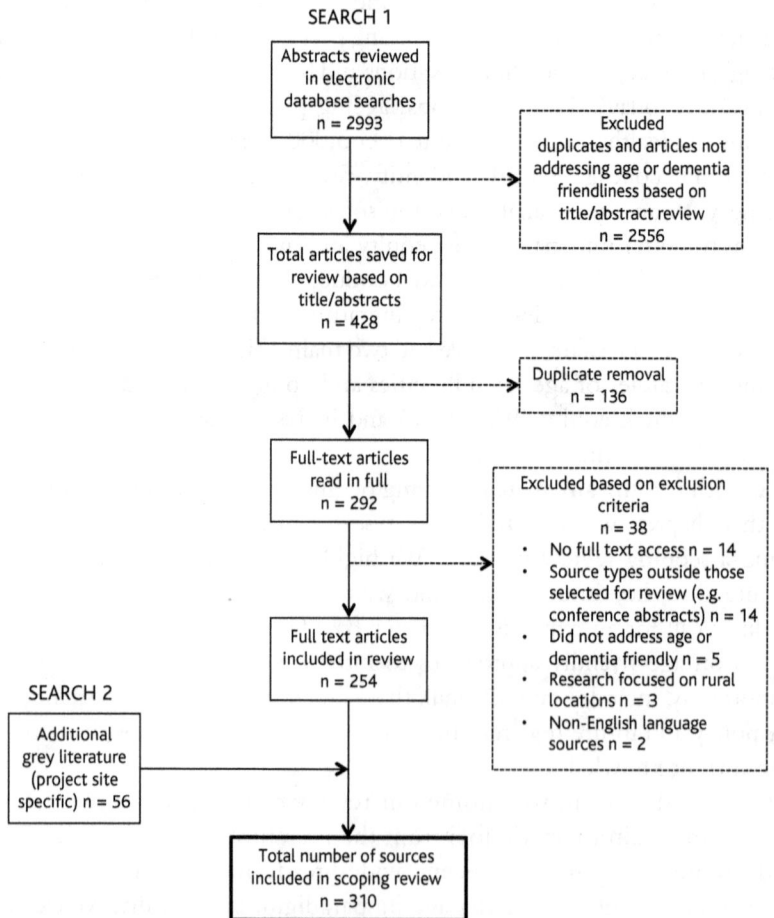

Figure 2.1: A scoping search and selection process

We organised articles by main focus: 'age-friendly', 'age inclusive' or 'age equity'. Overall, articles categorised as 'age-friendly' assessed the WHO age-friendly framework but homogenised the experiences and needs of ageing people. 'Age-inclusive' articles often emphasised belonging and acknowledged a range of experiences of ageing, while still operating predominantly within the WHO age-friendly domains. 'Age-equity' articles recognised the heterogeneity in experiences of ageing and ageing needs and offered critical appraisal of the WHO age-friendly framework in ways that further develop it. To map the categories, themes were charted for each journal article or report.[2] The 310 reviewed sources were aligned to categories as follows: age 'friendly' (n = 200), age 'inclusive' (n = 88) and age 'equitable' (n = 22). We will now highlight key articles and sub-themes. Given search limits, the review includes the most salient sources and findings.

Traversing the cityscape from age-friendly towards age equity and age inclusion

In what follows, we identify themes and gaps in the scholarly and grey literature assessing age-friendly cities and communities, including attention to the eight original WHO 'age-friendly domains': outdoor spaces and buildings, transportation, housing, social participation, respect and social inclusion, civic participation and employment, communication and information, and community and health services (WHO, 2007). Next, we identify how inclusion and equity have been taken up in the literature on studies of age-friendly practices.

Age-friendly

We found that 'age-friendly' articles primarily locate their analysis within only one or more of the original domains, even when they indicate they are assessing all or most domains (Keefe and Hattie, 2007; Burton et al, 2011; Friedman et al, 2012; Scharlach, 2012; Lehning, 2014; Scharlach et al, 2014; Elsawahli et al, 2017; Lehning and Greenfield, 2017; Buckner et al, 2018; Ellis et al, 2018; Lin et al, 2019a Lin et al, 2019b). Often, articles pay minimal attention to ageing issues beyond these domains. While many cities have targeted one or a few WHO domains, only a few cities address all eight (Jackisch et al, 2015). The two most prevalent WHO domains studied are outdoor spaces and buildings, and health and community services (n = 109). The former focuses on mobility, transportation and physical accessibility or 'walkability' of public spaces. It includes issues such as pleasant and clean environments, the importance of green spaces, having somewhere to rest, age-friendly pavements, safe pedestrian crossings, [physical] accessibility, a secure environment, walkways and cycle paths, age-friendly buildings, adequate public toilets and acknowledging the customer service needs of older adults (Rosenbloom, 2009; Shiau and Huang, 2014; Winters et al, 2015; Almeida, 2016; Hwang, 2017; Mah and Mitra, 2017; McAdam and Williams, 2017; Lee and Dean, 2018). These focal areas are frequently reflected in age-friendly policy documents (such as Government of Alberta, 2017; City of Toronto, 2018). Often studied are buildings' physical accessibility, particularly for health and community services (Huang et al, 2011; Kelley et al, 2011; Fitzpatrick, 2018).

Some studies map services to highlight needs for more supports for ageing populations (Lowen et al, 2015) or the approaches health systems or hospitals take, such as in Riyadh (Alhamdan et al, 2015), the United States (Allen and Ouslander, 2018; Mate et al, 2018) and Taipei (Lin et al, 2010). Making acute care settings more dementia- or age-friendly was also a theme (Borbasi et al, 2006; Galvin et al, 2010; Handley et al, 2015; Handley et al, 2017; Brooke and Semlyen, 2019).

A notable number of sources (n = 42) address governance and policies to promote age-friendliness, including how local government can implement or measure age-friendly initiatives (Ontario Seniors' Secretariat, 2013; Glicksman et al, 2014; McGarry, 2015; Sun et al, 2017; Gibney and Shannon, 2018; Ontario Seniors' Secretariat and Accessibility Directorate, 2018). Case studies describe how the local government(s) facilitate or hinder age-friendly developments (Menec et al, 2014; van Hoof et al, 2018). Other studies are directed to community as action guides to support grassroots change (McGarry and Morris, 2011; Garon et al, 2014; Heward et al, 2017; Hewson et al, 2018; Lin et al, 2019); or involve researchers who provide evidence in support of age-friendly initiatives (Neal et al, 2014; Ozanne et al, 2014; Moulaert and Garon, 2015).

Some articles focus on design in different ways, such as dementia-friendly housing (Bligh, 2016) or co-producing knowledge about neighbourhood interventions (Doran and Buffel, 2018). Others identify and describe places or specific communities as offering promising ways forward (Antonucci, 2016), ways to scale promising initiatives (Ball and Lawlor, 2014), or ways to direct communities' attention to ethno-cultural needs (Chan et al, 2015). Less often, but importantly, social connection, isolation, spirituality, ageism and meaningful interaction are addressed (Manheimer, 2009; Emlet and Moceri, 2012; Vitman et al, 2014; Lindenberg and Westendorp, 2015; Fields et al, 2016; Lai et al, 2016; Plunkett and Chen, 2016; Ronzi et al, 2018).

That most of the mainstream age-friendly scholarly and grey literature tends to focus on aspects of the physical environment or governance issues reveals much about the less frequently noticed dynamics of ageing. Diversity was considered, but only as follows: living with frailty (Cramm et al, 2018), living with dementia (Crampton and Eley, 2013), and how age- and dementia-friendly strategies are aligned (Turner and Cannon, 2018). Older adults living with dementia were the most often cited specific population 'group', mentioned by nearly one-quarter (23 per cent) of 'age-friendly' articles. As noted in the following sections on equity and inclusion, few articles addressed other social locations with ageing. Apart from dementia, and with a few exceptions, the needs and experiences of a few other specific communities (such as family carers, care workers, ethnocultural groups, Indigenous, gender, 2SLGBTQI, people living with disabilities, or those living in poverty) are discussed within this literature. Indeed, taken as a whole, the literature presumes homogeneous experiences of ageing with little consideration of social location. In some instances, diversity was not defined in terms of the social locations and identities of older adults, but by the perspectives of policymakers, planners and researchers (Clark and Glicksman, 2012). Some notable studies focus on frontline workers' attitudes and beliefs about dementia-friendly services (Alden et al, 2019) and environments (Cassarino and Setti, 2016), including long-term care (Castle et al, 2009).

Age inclusive

Few articles about age-friendly initiatives overtly consider issues of age inclusion. When inclusion is addressed, the focus is mostly on health and social services, social inclusion and buildings/outdoor spaces. In many articles, social inclusion is assessed as part of reporting the results of a particular intervention, such as one study describing a documentary theatre program for people with dementia and their caregivers to build community and enable creative expression (Black and Lipscomb, 2017). Other articles described inclusion in theatre performance (Taylor, 2019), community gardening (Wang and Glicksman, 2013), and at-home creative activities (Eades et al, 2018). Often inclusion is considered through the lens of social isolation. For instance, Courtney-Pratt and colleagues (2018) explore how a reduction of stigma and dementia education are critical to addressing social isolation and increasing social inclusion among people with dementia and their carers. Austin and colleagues (2005), describe the success of an elder-friendly pilot project in Calgary that has developed ethno-specific community services. In their study of inactive ageing in Liverpool, Barrett and McGoldrick (2013) report that exclusion in older age is related to barriers of poverty and deprivation. Buffel (2018) describes the success of a co-researcher, community-based research study to design an age-friendly community that considers the needs of people living in social isolation. Experiences of poverty are highlighted by Lehning and colleagues (2015), who compare lower and higher-income seniors and their ability to age in place. Investigating US neighbourhoods, Moorman and colleagues (2016) note that social segregation along lines of age, race and socio-economic status produce homogeneity within two-thirds of American neighbourhoods, threatening implementation of age-friendly principles.

Immigrant groups' representation in local government planning is important when developing age-friendly initiatives that are inclusive to newcomers (Neville et al, 2018). One conceptual article argues that the international Age-Friendly Cities project requires an ecological model, with 'fit' between older adults and their environmental conditions, such that the eight domains must be considered alongside intra-personal 'factors' including age, gender, income and functional status (Menec et al, 2011). Building on this ecological approach, Ring and colleagues (2017) find that neighbourhood-level poverty is associated with poor self-rated health and should be addressed in any age-friendly policy. Further, when considering how to build age-friendly communities, Parekh and colleagues (2018) – in their study of social cohesion and social capital conducted in the Southern US – find that age-friendly communities must build social capital for the individual and social cohesion that benefits the community. The latter is predicated on having opportunities for civic engagement and building connection with others. Importantly, they point out that barriers, including language, culture, poverty, and importantly, transportation, prevent older adults' engagement. For instance, marginalised Hispanic older adults' experiences of language barriers, low-income and immigrant status prevented social cohesion and reduced opportunities for civic engagement when compared to both Caucasian and African American older adults.

Another study notes that as people aged, their abilities to walk and otherwise traverse the city were reduced (Turrell et al, 2014). The authors argue that designing targeted interventions to support walking should be a priority in building age-friendly neighbourhoods. A study of life satisfaction among vulnerable South Korean older adults showed that higher levels of support in their physical and social environments were highly correlated, while better levels of service were correlated to lower life satisfaction (Park and Lee, 2017). The study highlights the importance of considering ways to design support services to target different groups between and within societies (Park and Lee, 2017). A Chinese study (Xie, 2018) highlights that perceptions of housing conditions, local amenities and social inclusion were important to life satisfaction, but as in other studies, this was moderated by socio-economic status with participants with lower status giving the lowest assessment of age-friendliness.

Several studies suggest additions or changes to the eight age-friendly domains. One study argues that partnership building – in the form of democratised committee meetings between low-income older people, service providers and non-profit housing – was an important factor in the success of ageing-in-place strategies for older people transitioning to affordable housing (Sixsmith et al, 2017). Smith and colleagues (2013) query the Age-Friendly

Cities framework and the Environmental Protection Agency framework in their study, finding that socio-economic disadvantage is an oversight in the original eight domains and that six additional factors contribute to older adults' experiences of their communities: access to businesses and leisure activities, opportunities for social interaction, access to health care, the absence of neighbourhood problems, social support and opportunities for community engagement. Using photovoice, Novek and Menec (2014) show that in Manitoba, Canada, the eight domains resonate with older adults, but independence, affordability and accessibility were also key factors identified by participants.

Many articles analyse the needs of people living with dementia, with discussion centred on health services (Handley et al, 2017; Hanson et al, 2017; Brooke and Semlyen, 2019), neighbourliness (Cho and Kim, 2016) or the design of physical environments (Davis et al, 2009; Charras et al, 2016). Silverman (2019) focuses on family carers of people living with dementia, finding that walking alone or with the person with dementia facilitates caregivers' connections to nature, the built environment, to the social life of the community. Only a few articles attend to age-friendliness and unpaid family care (Johnson et al, 2016). More attention to older people living with low income (Lili, 2018) is needed; many articles identify social isolation, ageism, stigma and care work conditions as important considerations for age-friendliness. One study by Bell and Menec (2015) argues that the high value attributed to independence in many societies undermines inclusion, due to the stigma associated with relying on others or being perceived as old. Soilemezi and colleagues (2017) report that family carers' meaning of home changes and can become contradictory when caring for a person with dementia. While familiar home environments help a person living with dementia to maintain their functioning, carers' homes become environments in which they are seldom alone and always alert. To promote inclusivity, age-friendly policies must support the range of living conditions – from public housing to single family dwellings – and services they need, such as home care to residential long-term care.

A few articles focused on technology as a means to improve the experiences of urban ageing (van Hoof et al, 2018) and advance inclusion in age-friendly communities, but noted that affordability, access and education must be addressed (Gudowsky et al, 2017). An article by Biggs and Carr (2015) focuses on intergenerational relations to advance inclusion. Puhakka and colleagues (2015) concur, emphasising that opportunities for intergenerational relations should be cultivated and promoted, while van Vliet (2011) calls for 'intergenerational cities' that make cities livable for all. A protocol to study the Canadian Longitudinal Study on Aging dataset (Levasseur et al, 2017) aimed to study which components of age-friendly communities and their mechanisms foster outcomes of positive health, social participation and health equity in ageing Canadians. They later reported that higher social participation at the individual level was associated with better outdoor spaces and buildings, better communication and information, as well as with not having material deprivation (Levasseur et al, 2023).

Significantly, only a few 'inclusive' articles attended to gender (n = 6), sexuality (n = 3), or people with disabilities (n = 1), while ethnicity, race and Indigeneity were absent.

Age equity

Our scoping review surfaced few articles that take up the topic of age-friendly cities with a view to age equity for older adults. Of those that do, Buffel and colleagues (2014) indicate that Manchester has been better at implementing active ageing policies because of its inclusion of ethnic minority groups in its programming. Furthermore, Buffel et al (2012) raise questions about whether age-friendly city 'ideal types' can adequately address the heterogeneity of urban ageing experiences. They argue that rather than identifying ideal age-friendly cities, a shift towards 'material conditions of city life' and 'how age-friendly is a particular city' are more suitable foci. Buffel and Philipson (2016) note that age-friendly city initiatives are challenged by other directions in government policy including austerity-related cuts to social programs, urban development pressures and the increasing privatisation of urban space. Buffel and colleagues (2014) point out that citizenship rights, so often denied to ethnic minority older adults, are key to advancing age-friendly cities. To ameliorate social inequalities and to counteract the impacts of economic austerity, Buffel and Phillipson (2018) provide a manifesto for the Age-Friendly movement, insisting that this movement must challenge inequalities, enhance older adults' participation, include older adults in the production and design of age-friendly communities, ensure that participation includes all political, economic and social sectors, involves people with multi-disciplinary expertise and brings research evidence into policy decision-making.

Dalmer (2019) notes that age-friendly policies rarely acknowledge care networks/partners, especially family/household members who care, even though the home environment is 'pivotal' to peoples' lives. When family is mentioned in this literature, it is typically considered as a source of social connection or as an information resource for older adults. Family care of and by older adults is infrequently addressed in the age-friendly literature with some exceptions (see Bookman and Kimbrel, 2011 as one example). While the care work literature addresses unpaid family care and paid care for older adults, there are too few links between it and the age-friendly literature.

Equity considerations include attention to issues of isolation, exclusion, or marginalisation. Phillipson (2018) outlines important tensions and challenges that prevent the Age-Friendly movement from succeeding, noting particularly local and state contexts of economic austerity. His analysis points to the need to reach out to socially and economically marginalised groups, including those older people who cannot fit into 'active ageing' frameworks, and marginalised/understudied groups, to respond to the pressures of rapid urban development and to address the generational divisions in housing and urban neighbourhoods. Likewise, Syed and colleagues (2017) find that the age-friendly framework has the potential to address issues of social isolation among ethnic minority older people; however, there is a need for more research on age-friendliness among different cultural and ethnic groups as it is 'glaringly understudied' (239). They state that a standardised age-friendly framework is a potential challenge within the context of diverse urban landscapes. They also find a significant gap in literature addressing older social isolation and gender, indicating that the issues are 'glaringly understudied'. Furthermore, Wang and colleagues (2017) captured ageing experiences in developing countries that are not addressed in the WHO framework. These are missed themes, include questions about basic living conditions, welfare benefits, migration and migrant workers. All these articles highlight groups that are missed or excluded.

Using a post-colonial theoretical lens, Brooks-Cleator and colleagues (2019) highlight ways that age-friendly policies can both support and hinder ageing urban Indigenous people in Ottawa, Canada. Based on qualitative interviews, they argue that the urban physical and social environments do not support ageing Indigenous people in Ottawa. Research on ageing for Māori elders in New Zealand notes that a strengths-based approach emphasising autonomy, identity and self-actualisation is critical for later-stage life transitions (Oetzel et al, 2019).

Greenfield (2018) argues that the Age-Friendly movement can address social justice and social inequalities; however, Lehning and colleagues (2017) are critical, arguing that all 'friendly' initiatives – whether targeted at older adults, children or immigrants – are unable to reduce groups' vulnerabilities because of an underlying contradiction between collective rights and individualism within these strategies. In some ways supporting this argument, Joy (2018) focuses on Toronto, finding that its age-friendly city approach aims to reduce public costs associated with ageing populations by responsibilising older adults to care for themselves, rather than increase accessibility. Modlich (2010), who reviewed international examples of age-friendly initiatives, notes both that many neo-liberal policy directions run counter to age-friendly initiatives and that women's issues and gender have been left aside in the Age-Friendly movement, including the issue of unpaid care work.

Conclusion

In this chapter, we report on a scoping review of journal articles and selected grey literature to consider the extent to which equity and inclusion were considered in research on 'age-friendly cities'. We found that most research considered one or two of the eight age-friendly domains: outdoor spaces and buildings and health services. We noted critiques that argued for greater research emphasis on inclusion and equity, including the perspectives and experiences of marginalised, subordinated and oppressed older people to inform policy and practice that can address exclusions and inequities.

For instance, what specific services and supports are needed by women, men and gender diverse people whose gender experience affects their experiences of ageing? How can we understand the needs of migrants and Indigenous peoples, who have specific linguistic, ethnocultural and spirituality or faith needs, and who may have family spread between remote and urban settings or even across continents? In addition, those who provide care as family and friends as well as who do so for pay, many of whom are in new countries but are themselves ageing but in jobs without adequate labour force protections to enable planning for retirement? What is needed for those who experience accelerated ageing due to an accumulation of social, economic and political disadvantages – for instance, for seniors living in poverty, without homes, or on or off Indigenous land but in ways that are disconnected from their past or their relations? How can communities appropriately address the needs of 2SLGBTQI communities, many of whom describe returning to the closet in older age? Finally, how can we design systems that can wrap services around some individuals, such as those with chronic and degenerative diseases associated with ageing, such as Dementia, Parkinson's and Multiple Sclerosis, and some mental and cognitive health conditions, or some families who require more financial, social, service, health and emotional supports?

Other recent age-friendliness scholarship has extended the utility of the concept in multiple ways. For instance, Repetti and colleagues (2024) consider age-friendliness for those who migrate for retirement. Others consider ways to elevate age-friendly to the level of an 'ecosystem' that including facets of community, the social determinants of health, health-care systems and public health systems (Fulmer et al, 2020). In their recent edited volume, Buffel et al (2024) consider how to better design inclusive urban environments that can meet the needs of diverse older adults living in cities. They consider the needs of specific ethnocultural and linguistic groups, as well as those living precariously and in marginalisation. The salience of 'age-friendly' communities remains intact, but with increasing calls to elevate it, to advance goals of access and justice.

The WHO defines *health* equity as 'the absence of avoidable, unfair, or remediable differences among groups of people, whether those groups are defined socially, economically, demographically or geographically or by other means of stratification' (WHO, nd). Health equity assesses the extent to which people are afforded fair chances to attain their full health potential with unfair disadvantages removed or minimised. Like health equity, we see age equity as an achievable goal. What is needed is the design and delivery of policy, services and supports to enable people to enjoy a full life with access to social, physical, emotional, spiritual and economic supports that are consistent with their needs. It may require that some groups get more services and supports when their barriers to participation are greater. Age equity should address cumulative disadvantage earlier in life as well as the cumulative disadvantages that accrue by older age to enable people to experience health, joy, mobility, meaning and engagement in later life.

Notes

[1] This chapter selectively presents the most salient articles and findings. In terms of our method, first, academic sources were identified from Proquest, Ebsco and Scholar's Portal through keyword searches. Journal articles, dissertations and theses, trade magazines, reports, white papers, strategy and policy documents were all considered relevant for review, while edited and solo authored books were excluded. Inclusion and exclusion criteria were kept intentionally broad to capture a wide range of literature from across the age-friendly literatures, to also include dementia-friendly literatures. As Figure 2.1 identifies, 428 sources were initially saved based on title and abstract scanning. After duplicate removal and full-text reading, 254 sources were deemed relevant and included in the final review. Second, to find grey literature and policy documents, searches were conducted on the Canadian Electronic Collection – Health Research database and Google. Keyword combinations were developed to identify site-specific (municipal, regional or federal) age- and dementia- friendly grey literatures. As in the first search, exclusion and inclusion criteria were kept broad although here focused on project specific sites; 56 additional sources were identified through this process, resulting in a total of 310 sources included.

[2] This data included: source type, research type, location, how many WHO domains or other identified themes were addressed, whether specific communities or marginalised groups were acknowledged, and whether sources aligned with a particular ageing paradigm. This charting framework provided a visual aid to help support analysis across a large quantity of data.

References

Alden, S., Wigfield, A., Kispeter, E. and Karania, V. (2019) Changing the narrative: the role of frontline worker attitudes and beliefs in shaping dementia-friendly services in England, *Disability & Society*, 34(5): 775–96.

Alhamdan, A.A., Alshammari, S.A., Al-Amoud, M.M., Hameed, T.A., Al-Muammar, M.N., Bindawas, S.M. et al (2015) Evaluation of health care services provided for older adults in primary health care centers and its internal environment: a step towards age-friendly health centers, *Saudi Medical Journal*, 36(9): 1091–6.

Allen, K. and Ouslander, J.G. (2018) Age-friendly health systems: their time has come, *Journal of the American Geriatrics Society*, 66(1): 19–21.

Almeida, M.F. (2016) Age-friendly walkable urban spaces: a participatory assessment tool, *Journal of Housing for the Elderly*, 30(4): 396–411.

Antonucci, J.A. (2016) Designing an Elder-Friendly Senior Living Community: A Longitudinal Study of the Village Vitality Program with Implications for the Built Environment, Doctoral dissertation, University of Florida, ProQuest Dissertations & Theses Global [online], Available from: https://www.proquest.com/docview/1847568678?pq-origsite=gscholar&fromopenview=true&sourcetype=Dissertations%20&%20Theses

Arksey, H. and O'Malley, L. (2005) Scoping studies: towards a methodological framework, *International Journal of Social Research Methodology*, 8(1): 19–32.

Austin, C.D., Camp, E.D., Flux, D., McClelland, R.W. and Sieppert, J. (2005) Community development with older adults in their neighborhoods: the Elder Friendly Communities Program, *Families in Society*, 86(3): 401–9.

Ball, M.S. and Lawler, K. (2014) Changing practice and policy to move to scale: a framework for age-friendly communities across the United States, *Journal of Aging & Social Policy*, 26(1–2): 19–32.

Barrett, G. and McGoldrick, C. (2013) Narratives of (in)active ageing in poor deprived areas of Liverpool, UK, *International Journal of Sociology and Social Policy; Bingley*, 33(5/6): 347–66.

Beard, J.R. and Montawi, B. (2015) Age and the environment: the global movement towards age-friendly cities and communities, *Journal of Social Work Practice*, 29(1): 5–11.

Bell, S. and Menec, V. (2015) 'You don't want to ask for the help': the imperative of independence – is it related to social exclusion?, *Journal of Applied Gerontology*, 34(3): NP1–21.

Biggs, S. and Carr, A. (2015) Age- and child-friendly cities and the promise of intergenerational space, *Journal of Social Work Practice*, 29(1): 99–112.

Black, K. and Lipscomb, V.B. (2017) The promise of documentary theatre to counter ageism in age-friendly communities, *Journal of Aging Studies*, 42: 32–7.

Bligh, J. (2016) A mainstream social housing response to dementia, *Working with Older People*, 20(3): 144–50.

Bookman, A. and Kimbrel, D. (2011) Families and elder care in the twenty-first century, *The Future of Children*, 21(2): 117–40.

Borbasi, S., Jones, J., Lockwood, C. and Emden, C. (2006) Health professionals' perspectives of providing care to people with dementia in the acute setting: toward better practice, *Geriatric Nursing*, 27(5): 300–8.

Brooke, J. and Semlyen, J. (2019) Exploring the impact of dementia-friendly ward environments on the provision of care: a qualitative thematic analysis, *Dementia*, 18(2): 685–700.

Brooks-Cleator, L.A., Giles, A.R. and Flaherty, M. (2019) Community-level factors that contribute to First Nations and Inuit older adults feeling supported to age well in a Canadian city, *Journal of Aging Studies*, 48: 50–9.

Buckner, S., Mattocks, C., Rimmer, M. and Lafortune, L. (2018) An evaluation tool for age-friendly and dementia-friendly communities, *Working with Older People*, 22(1): 48–58.

Buffel, T. (2018) Social research and co-production with older people: developing age-friendly communities, *Journal of Aging Studies*, 44: 52–60.

Buffel, T. and Phillipson, C. (2016) Can global cities be 'age-friendly cities'? Urban development and ageing populations, *Cities*, 55: 94–100.

Buffel, T. and Phillipson, C. (2018) A manifesto for the age-friendly movement: developing a new urban agenda, *Journal of Aging & Social Policy*, 30(2): 173–92.

Buffel, T., Phillipson, C. and Scharf, T. (2012) Ageing in urban environments: developing 'age-friendly' cities, *Critical Social Policy*, 32(4): 597–617.

Buffel, T., McGarry, P., Phillipson, C., De Donder, L., Dury, S., De Witte, N. et al (2014) Developing age-friendly cities: case studies from Brussels and Manchester and implications for policy and practice, *Journal of Aging & Social Policy*, 26(1–2): 52–72.

Buffel, T., Doran, P. and Yarker, S. (2024) *Reimagining Age-Friendly Communities: Urban Ageing and Spatial Justice*, Policy Press.

Burton, E.J., Mitchell, L. and Stride, C.B. (2011) Good places for ageing in place: development of objective built environment measures for investigating links with older people's wellbeing, *BMC Public Health*, 11(1): 839.

Cassarino, M. and Setti, A. (2016) Complexity as key to designing cognitive-friendly environments for older people, *Frontiers in Psychology*, 7: 1329.

Castle, N.G., Ferguson, J.C. and Schulz, R. (2009) Aging-friendly health and long-term-care services: innovation in elders' homes, in ambulatory settings, in institutions, *Generations*, 33(2): 44–50.

Chan, A.C.-M. and Cao, T. (2015) Age-friendly neighbourhoods as civic participation: implementation of an active ageing policy in Hong Kong, *Journal of Social Work Practice*, 29(1): 53–68.

Charras, K., Eynard, C. and Viatour, G. (2016) Use of space and human rights: planning dementia-friendly settings, *Journal of Gerontological Social Work*, 59(3): 181–204.

Cho, M. and Kim, J. (2016) Coupling urban regeneration with age-friendliness: neighborhood regeneration in Jangsu Village, Seoul, *Cities*, 58: 107–14.

City of Toronto (2018) *Toronto Seniors Strategy Version 2.0*, City of Toronto [online], Available from: https://www.toronto.ca/legdocs/mmis/2018/ex/bgrd/backgroundfile-114780.pdf

Clark, K. and Glicksman, A. (2012) Age-friendly Philadelphia: bringing diverse networks together around aging issues, *Journal of Housing for the Elderly*, 26(1–3): 121–36.

Courtney-Pratt, H., Mathison, K. and Doherty, K. (2018) Distilling authentic community-led strategies to support people with dementia to live well, *Community Development*, 49(4): 432–49.

Cramm, J.M., van Dijk, H.M. and Nieboer, A.P. (2018) The creation of age-friendly environments is especially important to frail older people, *Ageing and Society*, 38(4): 700–20.

Crampton, J. and Eley, R. (2013) Dementia-friendly communities: what the project 'Creating a dementia-friendly York' can tell us, *Working with Older People*, 17(2): 49–57.

Dalmer, N.K. (2019) A logic of choice: problematizing the documentary reality of Canadian aging in place policies, *Journal of Aging Studies*, 48: 40–9.

Davis, S., Byers, S., Nay, R. and Koch, S. (2009) Guiding design of dementia-friendly environments in residential care settings: considering the living experiences, *Dementia*, 8(2): 185–203.

Doran, P. and Buffel, T. (2018) Translating research into action: involving older people in co-producing knowledge about age-friendly neighbourhood interventions, *Working with Older People*, 22(1): 39–47.

Eades, M., Lord, K. and Cooper, C. (2018) 'Festival in a box': development and qualitative evaluation of an outreach programme to engage socially isolated people with dementia, *Dementia*, 17(7): 896–908.

Ellis, G., Hunter, R.F., Hino, A.A.F., Cleland, C.L., Ferguson, S., Murtagh, B. et al (2018) Study protocol: Healthy urban living and ageing in place (HULAP): an international, mixed methods study examining the associations between physical activity, built and social environments for older adults the UK and Brazil, *BMC Public Health*, 18(1): 1135.

Elsawahli, H., Shah Ali, A., Ahmad, F. and Al-Obaidi, K.M. (2017) Evaluating potential environmental variables and active aging in older adults for age-friendly neighborhoods in Malaysia, *Journal of Housing for the Elderly*, 31(1): 74–92.

Emlet, C.A. and Moceri, J.T. (2012) The importance of social connectedness in building age-friendly communities, *Journal of Aging Research*, 2012: 132–40.

Fields, N.L., Adorno, G., Magruder, K., Parekh, R. and Felderhoff, B.J. (2016) Age-friendly cities: the role of churches, *Journal of Religion, Spirituality & Aging*, 28(3): 264–78.

Fitzgerald, K.G. and Caro, F.G. (2014) An overview of age-friendly cities and communities around the world, *Journal of Aging & Social Policy*, 26(1–2): 1–18.

Fitzpatrick, L. (2018) Practical strategies to help develop dementia-friendly hospital wards, *Nursing Older People*, 30(2): 30–4.

Friedman, D., Parikh, N.S., Giunta, N., Fahs, M.C. and Gallo, W.T. (2012) The influence of neighborhood factors on the quality of life of older adults attending New York City senior centers: results from the Health Indicators Project, *Quality of Life Research*, 21(1): 123–31.

Fulmer, T., Patel, P., Levy, N., Mate, K., Berman, A., Pelton, L. et al (2020) Moving toward a global age-friendly ecosystem, *Journal of the American Geriatrics Society*, 68(9): 1936–40.

Galvin, J.E., Kuntemeier, B., Al-Hammadi, N., Germino, J., Murphy-White, M. and McGillick, J. (2010) Dementia-friendly hospitals: Care not crisis: an educational program designed to improve the care of the hospitalized patient with dementia, *Alzheimer Disease & Associated Disorders*, 24(4): 372–9.

Garon, S., Paris, M., Beaulieu, M., Veil, A. and Laliberté, A. (2014) Collaborative partnership in age-friendly cities: two case studies from Quebec, Canada, *Journal of Aging & Social Policy*, 26(1–2): 73–87.

Gibney, S. and Shannon, S. (2018) Developing indicators for the Age-Friendly Cities and Counties Programme in Ireland, *Working with Older People*, 22(1): 59–67.

Glicksman, A., Clark, K., Kleban, M.H., Ring, L. and Hoffman, C. (2014) Building an integrated research/policy planning age-friendly agenda, *Journal of Aging & Social Policy*, 26(1–2): 131–46.

Government of Alberta (2017) *Alberta Dementia Strategy and Action Plan*, Government of Alberta [online], Available from: https://open.alberta.ca/dataset/772005d6-94f8-4a62-a39b-cc91265f3fca/resource/40959fbb-ca1d-4b44-8864-f05e8d1c6d0f/download/alberta-dementia-strategy-and-action-plan.pdf

Greenfield, E.A. (2018) Getting started: an empirically derived logic model for age-friendly community initiatives in the early planning phase, *Journal of Gerontological Social Work*, 61(3), 295–312.

Gudowsky, N., Sotoudeh, M., Capari, L. and Wilfing, H. (2017) Transdisciplinary forward-looking agenda setting for age-friendly, human-centered cities, *Futures: The Journal of Policy, Planning and Futures Studies*, 90: 16–30.

Handley, M., Bunn, F. and Goodman, C. (2015) Interventions that support the creation of dementia-friendly environments in health care: protocol for a realist review, *Systematic Reviews*, 4(1): 180.

Handley, M., Bunn, F. and Goodman, C. (2017) Dementia-friendly interventions to improve the care of people living with dementia admitted to hospitals: a realist review, *BMJ Open*, 7(7): e015257.

Hanson, H.M., Warkentin, L., Wilson, R., Sandhu, N., Slaughter, S.E. and Khadaroo, R.G. (2017) Facilitators and barriers of change toward an elder-friendly surgical environment: perspectives of clinician stakeholder groups, *BMC Health Services Research*, 17(1): 596.

Heward, M., Innes, A., Cutler, C. and Hambidge, S. (2017) Dementia-friendly communities: challenges and strategies for achieving stakeholder involvement, *Health & Social Care in the Community*, 25(3): 858–67.

Hewson, J.A., Kwan, C., Shaw, M. and Lai, D.W.L. (2018) Developing age-friendly social participation strategies: service providers' perspectives about organizational and sector readiness for aging baby boomers, *Activities, Adaptation, & Aging*, 42(3): 225–49.

Huang, A.R., Larente, N. and Morais, J.A. (2011) Moving towards the age-friendly hospital: a paradigm shift for the hospital-based care of the elderly, *Canadian Geriatrics Journal CGJ*, 14(4): 100–3.

Hwang, E. (2017) Impacts of objective neighborhood built environment on older adults' walking: literature review, *Housing and Society*, 44(1–2): 141–55.

Jackisch, J., Zamaro, G., Green, G. and Huber, M. (2015) Is a healthy city also an age-friendly city?, *Health Promotion International*, 30(suppl 1): i108–17.

Johnson, R., Hofacker, J., Boyken, L. and Eisenstein, A. (2016) Sustaining Chicago's informal caregivers: an age-friendly approach, *Journal of Urban Health*, 93(4): 639–51.

Joy, M. (2018) Problematizing the age-friendly cities and communities program in Toronto, *Journal of Aging Studies*, 47: 49–56.

Keefe, J. and Hattie, B. (2007) *Age-Friendly Cities Project: Halifax Site*, Province of Nova Scotia [online], Available from: https://novascotia.ca/seniors/pub/2007_AgeFriendlyCitiesReport.pdf

Kelley, M.L., Parke, B., Jokinen, N., Stones, M. and Renaud, D. (2011) Senior-friendly emergency department care: an environmental assessment, *Journal of Health Services Research & Policy*, 16(1): 6–12.

Lai, M.-L., Lau, S.-H., Lein, S.-Y. and Lai, M.-M. (2016) Modeling age-friendly environment, active aging, and social connectedness in an emerging Asian economy, *Journal of Aging Research*, 2016: 13–26.

Lee, E. and Dean, J. (2018) Perceptions of walkability and determinants of walking behavior among urban seniors in Toronto, Canada, *Journal of Transport & Health*, 9: 309–20.

Lehning, A.J. (2014) Local and regional governments and age-friendly communities: a case study of the San Francisco Bay Area, *Journal of Aging & Social Policy*, 26(1–2): 102–16.

Lehning, A.J. and Greenfield, E.A. (2017) Research on age-friendly community initiatives: taking stock and moving forward, *Journal of Housing for the Elderly*, 31(2): 178–92.

Lehning, A.J., Smith, R.J. and Dunkle, R.E. (2015) Do age-friendly characteristics influence the expectation to age in place? A comparison of low-income and higher income Detroit elders, *Journal of Applied Gerontology*, 34(2): 158–80.

Levasseur, M., Dubois, M.-F., Généreux, M., Menec, V., Raina, P., Roy, M. et al (2017) Capturing how age-friendly communities foster positive health, social participation and health equity: a study protocol of key components and processes that promote population health in aging Canadians, *BMC Public Health*, 17(1): 502.

Levasseur, M., Dubois, M.-F., Généreux, M., Naud, D., Trottier, L., Menec, V. et al (2023) Key age-friendly components of municipalities that foster social participation of aging Canadians: results from the Canadian longitudinal study on aging, *Journal of Urban Health*, 100(5): 1032–42.

Lili, X. (2018) Age-friendly communities and life satisfaction among the elderly in urban China, *Research on Aging; Thousand Oaks*, 40(9): 883–905.

Lin, L.-J., Hsu, Y.-C. and Kuo, H.-W. (2019a) The prospects and opportunities of age-friendly Taiwan, *Journal of the Formosan Medical Association*, 118(3): 655–6.

Lin, L.-J., Hsu, Y.-C., Scharlach, A.E. and Kuo, H.-W. (2019b) Examining stakeholder perspectives: process, performance and progress of the age-friendly Taiwan program, *International Journal of Environmental Research and Public Health*, 16(4): 608.

Lin, M.-H., Chou, M.-Y., Liang, C.-K., Peng, L.-N. and Chen, L.-K. (2010) Population aging and its impacts: strategies of the health-care system in Taipei, *Ageing Research Reviews*, 9: S23–7.

Lindenberg, J. and Westendorp, R.G.J. (2015) Overcoming old in age-friendliness, *Journal of Social Work Practice*, 29(1): 85–98.

Lowen, T., Davern, M.T., Mavoa, S. and Brasher, K. (2015) Age-friendly cities and communities: access to services for older people, *Australian Planner*, 52(4): 255–65.

Mah, S. and Mitra, R. (2017) The effects of a free bus program on older adults' travel behavior: a case study of a Canadian suburban municipality, *Case Studies on Transport Policy*, 5(3): 460–6.

Manheimer, R.J. (2009) Creating meaningful senior-friendly spaces: a way of being at home in the world, *Generations*, 33(2): 60–5.

Mate, K.S., Berman, A., Laderman, M., Kabcenell, A. and Fulmer, T. (2018) Creating age-friendly health systems: a vision for better care of older adults, *Healthcare: The Journal of Delivery Science and Innovation*, 6(1): 4–6.

McAdam, K. and Williams, S. (2017) *Dementia-Friendly Design Features for Walking Paths: A Focused Practice Question*, Region of Peel Public Health [online], Available from: https://happy-cities.squarespace.com/s/FINAL_demscape_appendices_pages_041423.pdf

McGarry, P. (2015) Local government, ageing and social inclusion: past, present and future, *The Journal of Poverty and Social Justice*, 23(1): 71–6.

McGarry, P. and Morris, J. (2011) A great place to grow older: a case study of how Manchester is developing an age-friendly city, *Working with Older People*, 15(1): 38–46.

Menec, V.H., Means, R., Keating, N., Parkhurst, G. and Eales, J. (2011) Conceptualizing age-friendly communities, *Canadian Journal on Aging*, 30(3): 479–93.

Menec, V.H., Novek, S., Veselyuk, D. and McArthur, J. (2014) Lessons learned from a Canadian province-wide age-friendly initiative: the age-friendly Manitoba initiative, *Journal of Aging & Social Policy*, 26(1–2): 33–51.

Modlich, R. (2010) Age-friendly communities – a women's issue, *Women & Environments International Magazine*, 84/85: 28–31.

Moorman, S.M., Stokes, J.E. and Robbins, S.C. (2016) The age composition of U.S. neighborhoods, *Journal of Population Ageing*, 9(4): 375–83.

Moulaert, T. and Garon, S. (2015) Researchers behind policy development: comparing 'age-friendly cities' models in Quebec and Wallonia, *Journal of Social Work Practice*, 29(1): 23–35.

Neal, M.B., DeLaTorre, A.K. and Carder, P.C. (2014) Age-friendly Portland: a university-city-community partnership, *Journal of Aging & Social Policy*, 26(1–2): 88–101.

Neville, S., Wright-St Clair, V., Montayre, J., Adams, J. and Larmer, P. (2018) Promoting age-friendly communities: an integrative review of inclusion for older immigrants, *Journal of Cross-Cultural Gerontology*, 33(4): 427–40.

Novek, S. and Menec, V.H. (2014) Older adults' perceptions of age-friendly communities in Canada: a photovoice study, *Ageing and Society*, 34(6): 1052–72.

Oetzel, J.G., Hokowhitu, B., Simpson, M., Reddy, R., Nock, S., Greensill, H. et al (2019) Kaumātua mana motuhake: a study protocol for a peer education intervention to help Māori elders work through later-stage life transitions, *BMC Geriatrics*, 19(1): 36.

Ontario Seniors' Secretariat (2013) *Independence, Activity and Good Health: Ontario's Action Plan for Seniors*, Queen's Printer for Ontario [online], Available from: https://dr6j45jk9xcmk.cloudfront.net/documents/215/ontarioseniorsactionplan-en-20130204.pdf

Ontario Seniors' Secretariat and Accessibility Directorate of Ontario (2018) *Finding the Right Fit: Age-Friendly Community Planning*, Ontario Ministry of Seniors and Accessibility [online], Available from: https://www.ontario.ca/document/finding-right-fit-age-friendly-community-planning

Ozanne, E., Biggs, S. and Kurowski, W. (2014) Competing frameworks in planning for the aged in the growth corridors of Melbourne, *Journal of Aging & Social Policy*, 26(1–2): 147–65.

Parekh, R., Maleku, A., Fields, N., Adorno, G., Schuman, D. and Felderhoff, B. (2018) Pathways to age-friendly communities in diverse urban neighborhoods: do social capital and social cohesion matter?, *Journal of Gerontological Social Work*, 61(5): 492–512.

Park, S. and Lee, S. (2017) Age-friendly environments and life satisfaction among South Korean elders: person-environment fit perspective, *Aging & Mental Health*, 21(7): 693–702.

Phillipson, C. (2018) Developing age-friendly work in the twenty-first century: new challenges and agendas, *Working with Older People*, 22(1): 3–8.

Plunkett, R. and Chen, P. (2016) Supporting healthy dementia culture: an exploratory study of the church, *Journal of Religion and Health*, 55(6): 1917–28.

Puhakka, R., Poikolainen, J. and Karisto, A. (2015) Spatial practices and preferences of older and younger people: findings from the Finnish studies, *Journal of Social Work Practice*, 29(1): 69–83.

Repetti, M., Calasanti, T. and Phillipson, C. (2024) Developing 'age-friendly' communities: the experience of international retired migrants, *Sociological Research Online*, 29(4): 981–97.

Ring, L., Glicksman, A., Kleban, M. and Norstrand, J. (2017) The future of age-friendly: building a more inclusive model using principles of ecology and social capital, *Journal of Housing for the Elderly*, 31(2): 117–29.

Ronzi, S., Orton, L., Pope, D., Valtorta, N.K. and Bruce, N.G. (2018) What is the impact on health and wellbeing of interventions that foster respect and social inclusion in community-residing older adults? A systematic review of quantitative and qualitative studies, *Systematic Reviews*, 7(1): 26.

Rosenbloom, S. (2009) Meeting transportation needs in an aging-friendly community: surprisingly, the most promising focus may be on keeping older people driving longer, *Generations*, 33(2): 33–43.

Sadana, R., Blas, E., Budhwani, S., Koller, T. and Paraje, G. (2016) Healthy ageing: raising awareness of inequalities, determinants, and what could be done to improve health equity, *The Gerontologist*, 56(Suppl 2): S178–93.

Scharlach, A.E. (2012) Creating aging-friendly communities in the United States, *Ageing International*, 37(1): 25–38.

Scharlach, A.E., Davitt, J.K., Lehning, A.J., Greenfield, E.A. and Graham, C.L. (2014) Does the village model help to foster age-friendly communities?, *Journal of Aging & Social Policy*, 26(1–2): 181–96.

Shiau, T.-A. and Huang, W.-K. (2014) User perspective of age-friendly transportation: a case study of Taipei City, *Transport Policy*, 36: 184–91.

Silverman, M. (2019) 'We have different routes for different reasons': exploring the purpose of walks for carers of people with dementia, *Dementia*, 18(2): 630–43.

Sixsmith, J., Fang, M.L., Woolrych, R., Canham, S.L., Battersby, L. and Sixsmith, A. (2017) Ageing well in the right place: partnership working with older people, *Working with Older People*, 21(1): 40–8.

Smith, R.J., Lehning, A.J. and Dunkle, R.E. (2013) Conceptualizing age-friendly community characteristics in a sample of urban elders: an exploratory factor analysis, *Journal of Gerontological Social Work*, 56(2): 90–111.

Soilemezi, D., Drahota, A., Crossland, J., Stores, R. and Costall, A. (2017) Exploring the meaning of home for family caregivers of people with dementia, *Journal of Environmental Psychology*, 51: 70–81.

Sun, Y., Chao, T.-Y., Woo, J. and Au, D.W.H. (2017) An institutional perspective of 'Glocalization' in two Asian tigers: the 'Structure–Agent–Strategy' of building an age-friendly city, *Habitat International*, 59: 101–9.

Syed, M.A., McDonald, L., Smirle, C., Lau, K., Mirza, R.M. and Hitzig, S.L. (2017) Social isolation in Chinese older adults: scoping review for age-friendly community planning, *Canadian Journal on Aging*, 36(2): 223–45.

Taylor, N. (2019) The origin of dementia-friendly theatre performances and the role of people living with dementia as creative consultants, *Research in Drama Education*, 24(1): 90–5.

Turner, N. and Cannon, S. (2018) Aligning age-friendly and dementia-friendly communities in the UK, *Working with Older People*, 22(1): 9–19.

Turrell, G., Hewitt, B., Haynes, M., Nathan, A. and Giles-Corti, B. (2014) Change in walking for transport: a longitudinal study of the influence of neighbourhood disadvantage and individual-level socioeconomic position in mid-aged adults, *The International Journal of Behavioral Nutrition and Physical Activity*, 11(1): 151.

van Hoof, J., Kazak, J.K., Perek-Białas, J.M. and Peek, S.T.M. (2018) The challenges of urban ageing: making cities age-friendly in Europe, *International Journal of Environmental Research and Public Health*, 15(11): 2473.

van Vliet, W. (2011) Intergenerational cities: a framework for policies and programs, *Journal of Intergenerational Relationships*, 9(4): 348–65.

Vitman, A., Iecovich, E. and Alfasi, N. (2014) Ageism and social integration of older adults in their neighborhoods in Israel, *The Gerontologist*, 54(2): 177–89.

Wang, D. and Glicksman, A. (2013) 'Being grounded': benefits of gardening for older adults in low-income housing, *Journal of Housing for the Elderly*, 27(1–2): 89–104.

Wang, Y., Gonzales, E. and Morrow-Howell, N. (2017) Applying WHO's age-friendly communities framework to a national survey in China, *Journal of Gerontological Social Work*, 60(3): 215–31.

Winters, M., Voss, C., Ashe, M.C., Gutteridge, K., McKay, H. and Sims-Gould, J. (2015) Where do they go and how do they get there? Older adults' travel behaviour in a highly walkable environment, *Social Science & Medicine*, 133: 304–12.

World Health Organization (2007) *Global Age-Friendly Cities: A Guide*, World Health Organization [online], Available from: https://iris.who.int/handle/10665/43755

World Health Organization (nd) Health equity, World Health Organization [online], Available from: https://www.who.int/health-topics/health-equity#tab=tab_1

Xie, L. (2018) Age-friendly communities and life satisfaction among the elderly in urban China, *Research on Aging*, 40(9): 883–905.

3

Age-friendly for all? Equality and equity in the changing landscape of the social democratic welfare state

Gudmund Ågotnes and Bodil H. Blix

Introduction

Like all the authors in this volume, we engage with the question: How can we create societies in which older adult populations are valued and experience belonging and meaning? We consider this question in the context of the social democratic welfare state as it has developed in the Nordic national states and, more specifically, in Norway. While there are many differences among Nordic jurisdictions, their social welfare programs rest on a common assumption of a relatively homogeneous majority population. Social welfare programs are designed to address socio-economic and gender-related inequities, usually through 'universal' policy frameworks that function as a form of lever to even out differences. In this chapter, we critically examine how 'age-friendliness' is perceived within this context and how it is articulated through official or political discourses. We argue that the generous and universal welfare state is based on a notion of equality in which sameness is a core value and that this value permeates understandings and presentations of age-friendliness.

An understanding of 'equality as sameness' might, we further argue, be at odds with variation and diversity within the large and increasingly heterogeneous older adult population. Older adult populations are diverse in terms of socio-economic status, culture, religion, gender, sexuality and ethnicity, but also in interests and preferences. In Norway, older adult populations include ethnic Norwegians, Indigenous Sami, other Europeans and large migrant and refugee cohorts from around the world (Dzamarija et al, 2022) who are now reaching old age and experiencing 'ageing in a second homeland'.

The presentation of age-friendliness in a Norwegian context is a particular representation of the World Health Organization's delineation of age-friendliness (WHO, 2007, 2015). Diversity and variation in this context are understood as differences in functional abilities and health (WHO,

2015: 7), thus perhaps not living up to the movement's initial ambition to create age-friendly communities that are 'accessible to and inclusive of older people with varying needs and capabilities' (WHO, 2007: 1). We believe that the Norwegian understanding of age-friendliness represents a limited and limiting conceptualisation of the older adult populations, restricting the potential of age-friendly policies and initiatives.

Age-friendliness, both as a policy and in implementation is still at an early stage in Norway. The primary aim of this chapter is to inquire into its position, both as a political project and an ideal, in the context of the Norwegian welfare state.

Background

Historically, Nordic welfare systems have developed similarly, with similar major reforms instituted within the same periods (Christiansen and Markkola, 2006; Pedersen and Kuhnle, 2017). A common denominator within the Nordic countries is a historical welfare policy shift from prioritising a smaller segment of the population (the poor) to prioritising all, giving rise to the claim of being a *universal* welfare model. Within the Nordic welfare model, rights are determined through citizenship, based on the postulate of equal rights to all citizens.

Compared to other welfare states, the Nordic welfare model is described as generous and characterised by significant levels of public spending (Christensen and Wærness, 2018; OECD, 2021). Through relatively high levels of taxation, the state redistributes a sizeable portion of its annual budget back to its citizens through the umbrella of services known as the welfare state. The role of the state is not only to safeguard its citizens with a certain degree of services and rights but to actively *provide* services for them, particularly for the older adult population (Ågotnes, 2017). Long-term residential care and home care services, for instance, are delivered primarily by publicly funded organisations.

A central element of the Nordic welfare model is its relationship to the issue of inequality. Nordic countries are considered less stratified regarding both health and social differences, including gender and social class, compared to most other countries (Esping-Andersen, 2015). Not only economic but also cultural and social capital is considered more evenly distributed in Norway and Scandinavia in general than, for instance, in other European countries (see, for example, Chan et al, 2011). The welfare model is intended to elevate those considered less fortunate; an aim widely considered 'fair' by not only those less fortunate but by the majority. It is widely accepted as the preferred model.

Another significant characteristic of the Nordic welfare model is the emphasis on employment and its inherent systems for incentivising the employment of its citizens, leading to a relatively high level of employment and a high level of tax income for the state (Pedersen and Kuhnle, 2017). This, in turn, secures welfare state services funding, allowing for the system's continuation. This self-sustaining eco-system has also been widely accepted as the preferred model. Only minor revisions, rather than considerable reforms, have been initiated by the shifting governments throughout the post-Second World War period. Therefore, political battles over welfare services have not been a battle over the very existence of the welfare state or its overarching function, but rather over how it should be organized and which areas to prioritize.

Care for the older adult population is considered a core responsibility of the Nordic welfare states. Many of the services offered by the welfare system are either directed toward, or relevant to, the older adult population, such as the pension system, disability support and health and care services. In Norway, the responsibility for public welfare services is divided among the state, the counties and the municipalities. Overall public expenditures in the health and care sector are considered high in Norway (OECD, 2021) compared to other sectors and compared to other countries, particularly when considering per capita proportions of GDP. Although efforts have been made to implement for-profit care and user-pay services in the Nordic model, Norway has been less affected by these changes compared to Finland and Sweden (Szebehely and Meagher, 2013; Ågotnes et al, 2020). In the older adult care sector, levels of staffing remains high in Norway both in terms of the overall level (staff:patient ratio) and skill level (registered nurse:patient ratio, for instance) (Harrington et al, 2012). Considering both cost and number of service recipients, the municipalities are responsible for providing most primary health and care services, whereas the specialist health-care services are a state responsibility. Older adult care, primarily provided in nursing homes, assisted living facilities and home care services, is a municipal responsibility (Lovdata, 2011). Consequently, municipal health and care services are an important employer in Norway, with 157,076 full-time equivalent employees in 2024 (Statistics Norway, 2024a), a majority of whom are women (see Chapters 5 and 8 in this volume for a comparative analysis of Norwegian care work).

Despite a significant and relatively robust public sector, austerity measures are under discussion in the Norwegian context that follow the example of other European countries. In popular outlets, academia, and, most prominently, political discussions, the future of the welfare state is debated (Ågotnes et al, 2021), with an emphasis on how service provision should be organised and by whom. Health and welfare services for the older adult population are particularly susceptible to scrutiny, partly because they are a significant budget item, and partly because, in their current form, their costs are likely to increase in future. As such, discussions of services for the older adult population are draped in a 'sustainability discourse' (Blix and

Hamran, 2018), in which the underlying assumption, and sometimes explicit argument, is that health and welfare services cannot continue 'per usual'.

Related to this discourse, we recognise three major policy shifts shaping services organisation and delivery for the older adult population in the last decade. First, following a larger national reform called the 'Coordination Reform', responsibility for the provision of most health and care services for the older adult population has further shifted from the state to the municipalities (Norwegian Ministry of Health and Care Services, 2008). Second, there has been a noticeable shift from residential care services for older adults to home care services (Norwegian Ministry of Health and Care Services, 2015; 2023), following 'ageing in place' policies and ideologies seen elsewhere (Buffel and Phillipson, 2024). A gradual increase in overall spending on home care services relative to institutional care has accompanied this shift, stagnating the number of institutional beds (Gautun and Hermansen, 2011). Consequentially, those receiving care and services at long-term care institutions are typically frailer, older, and in need of more advanced health and social services than the long-term care residents of yesteryear (Ågotnes, 2017). Notably, these shifts towards local (municipal) responsibility and services in the home have remained *within* the framework of the public sector, in contrast to developments elsewhere (Ågotnes et al, 2020). However, parallel with these processes, a third and less explicit shift has occurred in health and care policies, seeing a (subtle) change in responsibility for the provision of care for the older adult population from the public sector to families and volunteers (Ågotnes et al, 2021). This third, albeit less explicit, shift signifies a potential movement away from public provision of responsibility for older populations, and is, as we will return to, related to what has been termed 'individualisation' of responsibility (Christensen and Fluge, 2016; Askheim, 2017; Jenhaug, 2018).

In summary, recent developments and policies in Norway can be described as a process of decentralisation of responsibility; from the state to the municipalities, from institutional care to the home; and from public health and care services to families and volunteers. With the introduction of 'age-friendliness', we suggest that this latest shift might also include a further shift in responsibility towards the older adults themselves.

A changing welfare state?

Critiques of the welfare model, including rejections of the very idea of a state-run universal welfare platform, have taken several forms, most noticeably by criticising the welfare state as omniscient and paternalistic and/or by questioning the sustainability of the welfare system in its current form. In other words, critiques tend toward ideological or pragmatic standpoints, although the two are highly intertwined. A primary argument within the ideologically based opposition, proposed primarily by right-wing or liberalist political parties and organisations, is that the state-run welfare system does not adequately allow for 'choice' and 'alternatives' (see, for example, Norwegian Ministry of Health and Care Services, 2018: 10), leading the recipients of services, conceptualised as 'users', with few options and with little freedom of choice and autonomy. Although familiar in an international context, this perspective is relatively new in Norwegian discourses, inspired perhaps by external and geopolitical forces of de-regulation (see, for example, Stolt and Winblad, 2009; Szebehely and Meagher, 2013).

The second, related critique, voiced by a wide array of political factions, organisations, media and academia, is more pragmatic: the welfare state as it is now cannot last, primarily because of the expected increase in the older adult population. Such a critique is widespread and has elsewhere been described as too strictly focusing on the downside of potential demographic changes (Daatland, 2012). The proposed remedy is to revise the general scale of services to the older adult population: new and less costly solutions must be found. The premise of this critique – the expected change in the relative portion of taxpayers (and thus the income of the state) vis-à-vis the welfare state's expenditure on the older adult population – is not questioned or problematized. Welfare services directed at the older adult population are, in other words, increasingly presented as a scarce resource (Blix and Hamran, 2018). Ongoing tensions within this discourse are concerned with how to revise the limits or borders of welfare services and balance economic sustainability with new or innovative solutions, while maintaining a high level of 'dignity' or dignified services (Norwegian Ministry of Health and Care Services, 2018).

The question of how to recalibrate welfare services is an ongoing public and political debate, about ideas involving innovation, welfare technology, and, to some extent, marketisation (see, for example, Norwegian Ministry of Health and Care Services, 2013, 2015, 2018). Meanwhile, one aspect remains largely undebated and unchallenged: that is, age-friendliness. But what is age-friendliness in the context of Norway; is it a solution to the problem of demographic changes or a different matter altogether?

Age-friendliness in the changing Nordic welfare state

While the very concept of age-friendliness as well as specific initiatives under its umbrella, have gained political and popular attention internationally, the concept has received less attention in Norwegian political discourses. However, following the launching of a national strategy for creating an age-friendly society in 2016 (Norwegian Ministry of Health and Care Services, 2016), and the subsequent national older adult reform entitled 'A full life all your life' (Norwegian Ministry of Health and Care Services, 2018), and a later reform titled "Community and coping. Living safely at home" (Norwegian Ministry of Health and Care Services, 2023), age-friendliness as a policy direction quickly gained traction and was firmly incorporated into political discussions concerning the older adult population. In the latest reform/white paper, an 'age-friendly program' was launched as one of three target areas to be addressed until 2030, with a main aim of "creating a more age-friendly and inclusive society" (Norwegian Ministry of Health and Care Services, 2023: 62).

Building on WHO's global strategy for age-friendly cities (WHO, 2015), the overarching aim of the official Norwegian policy for an age-friendly society is to create a society in which 'all Norwegians should be able to lead long and meaningful lives, and experience active and healthy ageing' (Norwegian Ministry of Health and Care Services, 2016: 8). Several prominent themes are covered in the strategy, including technology, innovation, the volunteer sector and prolonged work lives, and they relate to challenges and possibilities for an older population. By addressing these aspects, the strategy has links to other governmental white papers (see, for example, Norwegian Ministry of Finance, 2013; Norwegian Ministry of Health and Care Services, 2013, 2015, 2019) that discuss future challenges for the care sector, questions of public health, and the economic implications of anticipated demographic changes, and thus situates age-friendliness within a wider national political discourse. As such, the plan can be seen as a political instrument shaping both the Norwegian welfare services and the master narratives about ageing (Jacobsen, 2015).

Following this strategy, national and local age-friendly initiatives have been created and implemented within a relatively short timeframe. Several larger cities have made their own municipal age-friendly plan. The three largest Norwegian cities, Oslo, Bergen and Trondheim, have some form of comprehensive, municipal-wide plan for becoming an age-friendly city, while other cities and smaller municipalities soon followed suit. As of December 2024, 235 of Norway's 357 municipalities are members of a "Network for age-friendly local communities". Additionally, since 2018, all municipalities have been obliged to have 'senior councils' within the political organisations of the respective municipalities, advising decisionmakers on all matters concerning the older adult population. These councils are presented as a device to secure representation of an underrepresented group in political-democratic processes, interestingly mentioned in the same vein as people with disabilities (Norwegian Ministry of Health and Care Services, 2023: 28). The municipal senior councils are part of a regional and a national structure, with administrative councils on both these levels. While varying regarding their degree of political capital with their respective councils, the overarching implementation and organisation of the system of councils has been reasonably effective, leading to a more recent focus on training programs for members (Norwegian Ministry of Health and Care Services, 2023: 12). Following these changes, a "Center for an Age-friendly Norway" was established in 2021, categorized as a 'national competence center'. The center is "founded on collaboration with various community actors through a network of cities and communities and partnerships with businesses, organisations and researchers" (Senteret for et aldersvennlig Norge, nd; authors' translation), while being formally organized under the Norwegian Directorate of Health, perhaps indicative of the (still) relative prominence of the public sector in Norway. By relating *both* to the geo-political discourse on age-friendliness *and* to a broader national political discourse, the official Norwegian age-friendly policy has unique characteristics and qualities that diverge from both. In the strategy and subsequent reform, and in contrast to the potential we believe age-friendliness can entail for age inclusivity in various ways, Norwegian age-friendliness has emphasised, first, judicial and formal rights limited to the political sphere (through the senior councils), second, the younger parts of the older population, and third, 'active and healthy ageing'. Its strategy explicitly states that efforts are to be directed at 'people aged 60–70 who are in the phase between working life and retirement, and who have the health, capabilities and desire to participate in society' (Norwegian Ministry of Health and Care Services, 2016: 13). A primary focus is directed towards how this group can stay 'active and healthy' for a longer period, thus contributing more to society. The aim is that this segment of the older population should remain independent for a longer period, implying, and sometimes explicitly stating, that they should be less of a welfare state burden. Further, this independence includes autonomy and choice, as noted in following reform:

> A Full Life All Your Life is a reform intended to provide greater freedom to choose. It should give each individual better opportunities to choose service providers (who), be involved in the content of the services provided (what), determine the manner in which services are provided (how), and the time and place for the provision of services (where and when). (Norwegian Ministry of Health and Care Services, 2018: 14)

Independence and autonomy are presented as related to responsibility, more specifically *individual responsibility*. This reform encourages older adults to take 'responsibility for maintaining their functional level through active lives' (Norwegian Ministry of Health and Care Services, 2018: 72), and to 'take greater responsibility in planning for their own senior years' (Norwegian Ministry of Health and Care Services, 2018: 19), for example through 'adapting one's own home' and 'investing in friends and social networks' (Norwegian Ministry of Health and Care Services, 2018: 20). In the latter reform, the adjective 'active' is mentioned 282 times, referring to the ways older adults can contribute to their local communities (Norwegian Ministry of Health and Care Services, 2023: 9), social and physical activities they can partake in (Norwegian Ministry of Health and Care Services, 2023: 19), how they can contribute to the volunteer sector (Norwegian Ministry of Health and Care Services. 2023: 30), and being more involved in the treatment of their own health (Norwegian Ministry of Health and Care Services, 2023: 42), in addition to the need to retain and recruit older people for paid employment (Norwegian Ministry of Health and Care Services, 2023: 61–2). Also in this reform, responsibility for one's own old age is central: 'There is a need to find new solutions that can contribute to more people taking active choices to prepare for old age, and the society must become shaped and changed according to the large increase in the number of older adults' (Norwegian Ministry of Health and Care Services, 2023: 9–10; authors' translation).

Age-friendly policies fuse together the rights *and* duties of the older adult population, representing an interesting and significant shift in how the older adult population is considered in the Norwegian political context. On the one hand, policy suggests that the older adult population should be taken care of by the welfare system. On the other hand, the older adult population should also contribute to maintaining the welfare system. With this perspective, age-friendly policies echo the previously mentioned discourse on sustainability, and can be understood, at least in part, as an answer to the problem it presents; age-friendliness will reduce welfare state burdens related to population ageing. It promises that older adults should be able to live long, prosperous and meaningful lives well after entering retirement, and be able to do so based on their own preference. At the same time, the older adult population is perceived as an untapped resource: 'To date, we have failed to build societal structures that adequately exploit the opportunities provided by a growing population of older people' (Norwegian Ministry of Health and Care Services, 2016: 8). In summary, older adults could and should contribute more and contribute differently, for their own benefit and to benefit society as a whole. These contributions include both paid work within the labour force and unpaid work as volunteers (see also Ågotnes et al, 2021). When reaching the pensionable age of 67 years old, for instance, citizens should be allowed to continue regular paid employment, and thus, 'stimulate the silver economy' (Norwegian Ministry of Health and Care Services, 2016: 9), and/or contribute to their local voluntary sector and communities. Thus, older adults' contributions are presented to appeal to both individual self-interest and altruism. In this discourse the government role is shifted from provider to facilitator. 'It is the Government's goal to make society more age-friendly, and to better harness the resources offered by older people in terms of participation and contribution' (Norwegian Ministry of Health and Care Services, 2016: 8).

While viewing instrumentally the older adult population as a resource to be harnessed is problematic, we believe that Norwegian policy moves towards age-friendly societies is also a relevant, much-needed counter-balance both to what has been characterised as the medicalisation of old age (see for example, Zola, 2009) and to apocalyptic notions of ageing in which 'the age wave' is considered a threat to welfare state sustainability. Age-friendliness counters representations of the older adult population as an economic challenge and demographic with severe health issues to which the health services must attend. Instead, it presumes that older populations present opportunities, abilities and potential. In this sense, the policy is a counterbalance to dominant perspectives on older populations and offers opportunities for older people to contribute in ways they, and society, find meaningful. Still, some critical questions can and should be raised regarding who is included in this policy, and, more importantly, who are left on the margins. This question spurs others, including whether and how Norwegian age-friendly policy takes up or shifts embedded ideals of the Norwegian welfare state, and whether the Norwegian version of age-friendliness represents a turn away from significant ideals of the Age-Friendly movement itself.

Equality and equity in the changing welfare state

The Norwegian welfare state is rooted in a form of universalism from which all citizens should benefit. Citizens who are perceived as less fortunate than others have the right to receive some form of support from the state as an effort to 'even out the score' and aim for 'equality'. According to Esping-Andersen (1990), the standard of what is considered an adequate level of services is higher within the social democratic model than within other models, suggesting that this form of welfare state has not only aimed at but also devised a comparatively efficient mechanism of levelling out differences, particularly socio-economic ones. The success narrative associated with the Norwegian welfare state suggests that it is fair, supportive, inclusive and, first and foremost, promotes equality.

The predominant conceptualisation of age-friendliness is, we argue, a continuation of this ideology: it is intended to include all (of a certain age), by not discriminating or creating barriers to access, and, perhaps most importantly, elevating older adults' significance and capability in the eyes of other generations. The older population is portrayed as able to contribute to society if only society facilitates their contributions. As such, age-friendliness aims towards *intergenerational equality*.

However, in this conceptualisation of age-friendliness, there remains an inherent risk of exclusion, almost by default. The older adult population is presented as a homogeneous mass: an entity without variation, nuance, or differences, as *the* older adult population. This is done, we believe, not so much by dismissing questions of diversity and variation within older adult populations but rather by leaving such questions unaddressed. This implicit homogeneity is further enhanced by juxtaposing 'the older generation' against other generations, seeing welfare realignments to address 'difference' between generations rather than also *among* older adult populations. The diversity of older adult populations is thus masked or under-communicated, perhaps most explicitly through silences about ethnic minorities. Yet, immigrants to Norway have increased from 57,000 people arriving in 1970 to 931,081 in 2024 (Statistics Norway, 2024b).

Thus, Norwegian age-friendly policy addresses questions of how health and welfare services for older adults should be organised, what they should include, and who should be responsible from the perspective of the various service providers and the older adult population themselves. Less emphasis is placed on who older people are and will be in the future. Consequently, the composition and characteristics of the older adult population – the intended target group of the policies – is, paradoxically, rarely mentioned in the policies, in contrast to the societal challenges they represent.

An exception is the prominent portrayal of the future care recipient as more independent, more technologically savvy and more cosmopolitan compared to the older person of yesterday. The new senior is also represented as more affluent and resourceful, and implicitly, as someone with higher demands (Norwegian Ministry of Health and Care Services, 2018: 53). A disclaimer to this generalisation is included, however, 'Being older is not an attribute in itself; there is enormous variation within and between age groups' (Norwegian Ministry of Health and Care Services, 2016: 9), but what this variation is comprised of and what it entails remains unaddressed. Elsewhere, 'variation' among older adults is limited to different physical attributes (Norwegian Ministry of Health and Care Services, 2023: 21). Consequently, the variation and diversity within and among older adult populations remains largely silenced. Apparently, the objective is to illustrate and argue for the need for change in services, costs and society, rather than to understand older adults and differences within this population.

There are a few exceptions to this Norwegian policy tendency to consider older adult populations as a homogenous whole that should be mentioned. First, some policy documents have recognised religion and beliefs as an area to which the welfare state should be cognisant: various forms of spiritual and existential needs should be taken into consideration by health and care providers (Norwegian Ministry of Health and Care Services, 2018: 24). Religion is, however, represented as a service user's right, detached from broader understandings of 'culture' and/or 'ethnicity'. Another exception is the mention of ethnic variation in health status and functioning ability (Norwegian Ministry of Health and Care Services, 2016: 13, Norwegian Ministry of Health and Care Services, 2023: 22). Certain ailments have, for example, higher prevalence in certain migrant groups compared to the majority population (Norwegian Ministry of Health and Care Services, 2018: 34). Consequently, it is implied that service provision must adapt accordingly. In the latest white paper, this is somewhat nuanced, alluding to the older Sami population, older migrant populations, and queer older adults, while maintaining a focus on the health-care needs of these groups and that their family constellations and relationships differ from the majority populations (Norwegian Ministry of Health and Care Services, 2023: 22–3, 27)

We believe that the general silence around diversity is rooted not only in the form and function of the welfare model, as previously mentioned, but also in dominant cultural values and norms. De-emphasising diversity can be part of what Gullestad (2002) has described as a shift from an idea of equality as 'equal worth' to one of equality understood as 'sameness'. In this shift, a collective identity based on generalised kinship and territoriality is identified and communicated, leading to the domination of a majority version, in this case recognisable in the articulation of *the* older adult population in Norwegian age-friendly policies. According to Gullestad, a shared culture, ancestry and origin, rather than citizenship takes over as the core of being Norwegian (2002: 54). A form of 'egalitarian individualism' is proposed, in which the quest for 'sameness' is central in everyday interaction and identity negotiation. Gullestad further argues that there is a peculiar Norwegian version of equality in which the pursuit of 'sameness' is connected to finding and relating to relevant others – those who are seen as 'the same' – to achieve a recognition of oneself and our part of the collective identity. This pursuit culminates in an interactional style in which similar traits are emphasised, for instance, in everyday encounters among Norwegians, while differences are under-communicated.

We argue, likewise, that Norwegian age-friendly policy is underpinned with an ideal of sameness, similarity and homogeneity in a well-intended attempt to include all. Alternatives to and nuances within the generic conceptualisation of '*the* older adult population' are simply not mentioned, leaving only a representation of a majority version by default. This majority version is, we believe, not attuned to the diversification of modern societies in which 'relationships among those who once shared the same structural condition [are] more unstable and fragmentary' (della Porta and Diani, 2020: 42), leading to 'multiple pathways' for different and varied individuals and groups of older adults (Biggs and Daatland, 2006: 3).

While the silencing of diversity is both a generalisation and reductionistic, it becomes particularly paradoxical within the framework of age-friendliness. The notion that age-friendliness is connected to *varying* needs, ambitions, resources and capacities, is, along with diversity and variation, under-communicated. Just as ideals of 'active' and 'successful ageing' have been criticised for their potentially oppressive aspects, especially for those without access to resources or good health (Kostecki and Macfarlane, 2019; Blix and Ågotnes, 2023), the ideal of age-friendliness, presented in its current form, can be a better fit for some than others. The emphasis on older adults' right and duty to contribute is problematic when considering that inequities among and within older adult populations are increasing while the welfare states' social protection is decreasing (Grenier et al, 2020). The *ability* to contribute to society, one of the underlying assumptions of the policy, is not evenly distributed, thus reinforcing rather than combatting differences among older adults.

What we see as a representation of *the* older adult population in the Norwegian age-friendly policy rest on a false premise: 'This means that at best associated narratives only apply to majority populations and at worst, they are grossly inaccurate, because they are based only on data from, and analyses of, part of the ageing population' (Westwood, 2019: 3).

Conclusion

Age-friendliness, as laid out in its Norwegian form, can be viewed as a political attempt to see the older adult population as more than a problem. It offers new avenues for contribution, both allowing and expecting older adult citizens to contribute more and receive less. As such, the age-friendly policy also becomes an instrument in tackling the expected disparity between working, tax-paying citizens and those who are not, in part by incentivising the latter to 'contribute more'. Advocates of the universal welfare system should be cognisant of this mechanism; that age-friendliness can, among other possibilities, become an instrument with which the welfare state downsizes itself.

We have also pointed out a more pressing problematic aspect of age-friendly policies: failures to recognise variation and diversity among and within older adult populations. Based on a rather peculiar notion of equality, sameness is emphasised, while diversity and variation are under-communicated. Perhaps an ideological battle is being waged between ideas of sameness and equality, on one side, and diversity and equity on the other. This conflict in ideologies is potentially relevant to the rapidly increasing attention to age-friendliness in Norway. The age-friendly policy is, in its current form, firmly poised within the former ideological framework, in which sameness is the ideal.

References

Ågotnes, G. (2017) *The Institutional Practice: On Nursing Homes and Hospitalizations*, Cappelen Damm Akademisk/NOASP (Nordic Open Access Scholarly Publishing).

Ågotnes, G., Jacobsen, F.F. and Szebehely, M. (2020) The growth of the for-profit nursing home sector in Norway and Sweden: driving forces and resistance, in B. Meagher and M. Szebehely (eds) *The Privatization of Care*, Routledge, pp 38–50.

Ågotnes, G., Moholt, J.-M. and Blix, B.H. (2021) From volunteer work to informal care by stealth: a 'new voluntarism' in social democratic health and welfare services for older adults, *Ageing and Society*, 43(9): 2173–89.

Askheim, O.P. (2017) Brukermedvirkningsdiskurser i den norske velferdspolitikken, *Tidsskrift for Velferdsforskning*, 20(2): 134–49.

Biggs, S. and Daatland, S.O. (2006) Ageing and diversity: a critical introduction, in S.O. Daatland and S. Biggs (eds) *Ageing and Diversity*, Policy Press.

Blix, B.H. and Ågotnes, G. (2023) Aging successfully in the changing Norwegian welfare state: a policy analysis framed by critical gerontology, *The Gerontologist*, 63(7), 1228–1237.

Blix, B.H. and Hamran, T. (2018) 'When the saints go marching in': constructions of senior volunteering in Norwegian government white papers, and in Norwegian senior volunteers' and health-care professionals' stories, *Ageing & Society*, 38(7): 1399–428.

Buffel, T. and Phillipson, C. (2024) *Ageing in Place in Urban Environments: Critical Perspectives*, Taylor & Francis.

Chan, T.W., Birkelund, G.E., Aas, A.K. and Wiborg, Ø. (2011) Social status in Norway, *European Sociological Review*, 27(4): 451–68.

Christensen, K. and Fluge, S. (2016) Brukermedvirkning i norsk eldreomsorgspolitikk – om utviklingen av retorikken om individuelt ansvar [User participation in Norwegian elderly care policy – the development of rhetoric about individual responsibility], *Tidsskrift for Velferdsforskning*, 19(3): 261–77.

Christensen, K. and Wærness, K. (2018) Long-term care services in Norway: a historical sociological perspective, in L. Fine, J. Davidson and X. Zhang (eds) *The Routledge Handbook of Social Care Work Around the World*, Routledge, pp 15–28.

Christiansen, N.F. and Markkola, P. (2006) Introduction, in N.F. Christiansen, K. Petersen, N. Edling and P. Haave (eds) *The Nordic Model of Welfare: A Historical Reappraisal*, Museum Tusculanum Press, pp 9–29.

Daatland, S.O. (2012) Aldringen av befolkningen og eldreomsorgen – hensikten og problemstillingene, in S.O. Daatland and M. Veenstra (eds) *Bærekraftig omsorg. Familien, velferdsstaten og aldringen av befolkningen (NOVA rapport 2/12)*, Norsk institutt for forskning om oppvekst, velferd og aldring (NOVA).

Della Porta, D. and Diani, M. (2020) *Social Movements: An Introduction* (3rd edn), Wiley-Blackwell.

Esping-Andersen, G. (1990) *The Three Worlds of Welfare Capitalism*, Polity Press.

Esping-Andersen, G. (2015) Welfare regimes and social stratification, *Journal of European Social Policy*, 25(1): 124–34.

Gautun, H. and Hermansen, Å. (2011) *Eldreomsorgen Under Press: Kommunenes Helse- og Omsorgstilbud til Elder*, Fafo-rapport 2011:12, Fafo.

Grenier, A., Phillipson, C. and Setterson, R.A. Jr. (2020) Precarity and ageing: new perspectives for social gerontology, in A. Grenier, C. Phillipson and R.A. Setterson Jr. (eds) *Precarity and Ageing: Understanding Insecurity and Risk in Later Life*, Policy Press, pp 1–15.

Gullestad, M. (2002) Invisible fences: egalitarianism, nationalism and racism, *The Journal of the Royal Anthropological Institute*, 8(1): 45–63.

Harrington, C., Choiniere, J., Goldmann, M., Jacobsen, F.F., Lloyd, L., McGregor, M., Stamatopoulos, V. and Szebehely, M. (2012) Nursing home staffing standards and staffing levels in six countries, *Journal of Nursing Scholarship*, 44(1): 88–98.

Jacobsen, F.F. (2015) Understanding public elderly care policy in Norway: a narrative analysis of governmental White Papers, *Journal of Aging Studies*, 34: 199–205.

Jenhaug, L.M. (2018) Myndighetenes forventninger til pårørende som samprodusenter i omsorgstjenester [The authorities' expectations of family carers as co-producers of care service], *Tidsskrift for Velferdsforskning*, 21: 39–58.

Kostecki, T. and Macfarlane, S. (2019) Women and older age: exploring the intersections of privilege and oppression across lifetimes, in D. Baines, B. Bennett, S. Goodwin and M. Rawsthorne (eds) *Working Across Differences: Social Work, Social Policy and Social Justice*, Bristol University Press, pp 120–36.

Lovdata (2011) *Lov om kommunale helse- og omsorgstjenester m.m. Act on Municipal Health and Care Services* [online], Available from: https://lovdata.no/dokument/NL/lov/2011-06-24-30/KAPITTEL_3#KAPITTEL_3

Norwegian Ministry of Finance (2013) *Long-term Perspectives on the Norwegian Economy 2013 – A Summary (Meld. St. 12 (2012–2013) Perspektivmeldingen), Report to the Storting (white paper) Summary*, Norwegian Government [online], Available from: https://www.regjeringen.no/contentassets/0825e498ab40465ea3836b06bebd6b93/en-gb/pdfs/stm201220130012000engpdfs.pdf

Norwegian Ministry of Health and Care Services (2008) *The Coordination Reform: Proper Treatment – At the Right Place and Right Time (Summary in English: Report No. 47 (2008–2009) to the Storting)*, Norwegian Government [online], Available from: https://www.regjeringen.no/contentassets/d4f0e16ad32e4bbd8d8ab5c21445a5dc/en-gb/pdfs/stm200820090047000en_pdfs.pdf

Norwegian Ministry of Health and Care Services (2013) *Future are (Meld. St. 29 (2012–2013), Report to the Storting (White Paper) Chapter 1–3)*, Norwegian Government [online], Available from: https://www.regjeringen.no/contentassets/34c8183cc5cd43e2bd341e34e326dbd8/en-gb/pdfs/stm201220130029000engpdfs.pdf

Norwegian Ministry of Health and Care Services (2015) *The Primary Health and Care Services of Tomorrow – Localised and Integrated (Meld. St. 26 (2014–2015), Report to the Storting (White Paper) Summary*, Norwegian Government [online], Available from: https://www.regjeringen.no/contentassets/d30685b2829b41bf99edf3e3a7e95d97/en-gb/pdfs/stm201420150026000engpdfs.pdf

Norwegian Ministry of Health and Care Services (2016) *The Norwegian Government's Strategy for an Age-Friendly Society* [online], Available from: https://www.dataplan.info/img_upload/5c84ed46aa0abfec4ac40610dde11285/strategy_age-friendly_society.pdf

Norwegian Ministry of Health and Care Services (2018) *A Full Life – All Your Life: A Quality Reform for Older Persons*, Meld. St. 15 (2017–2018). Report to the Storting (white paper) [online], Available from: https://www.regjeringen.no/contentassets/196f99e63aa14f849c4e4b9b9906a3f8/en-gb/pdfs/stm201720180015000engpdfs.pdf

Norwegian Ministry of Health and Care Services (2019) *Public Health Report – Good Lives in a Safe Society*, Meld. St. 19 (2018–2019). Report to the Storting (white paper) [online], Available from: https://www.regjeringen.no/no/dokumenter/meld.-st.-19-20182019/id2639770/

Norwegian Ministry of Health and Care Services (2023) *Community and Mastery: Stay Safe at Home*, St. Meld. 24 (2022–2023). Report to the Storting (white paper) [online], Available from: https://www.regjeringen.no/no/dokumenter/meld.-st.-24-20222023/id2984417

OECD (2021) *Health at a Glance 2021* [online], Available from: https://www.oecd.org/en/publications/health-at-a-glance-2021_ae3016b9-en/full-report.html

Pedersen, A.W. and Kuhnle, S. (2017) The Nordic welfare state model. Introduction: The concept of a 'Nordic model', in O.P. Knutsen (ed) *The Nordic Models in Political Science: Challenged, but Still Viable?*, Bristol University Press, pp 249–72.

Senterret for et aldersvennlug Norge (nd) *Sammen for et aldersvennlig Norge* (Together for an age-friendly Norway) [online], Available from: https://www.aldersvennlig.no/

Statistics Norway (2024a) *Sjukeheimar, heimetenester og andre omsorgstenester* (Nursing homes, home care services and other care services) [online], Available from: https://www.ssb.no/helse/helsetjenester/statistikk/sjukeheimar-heimetenester-og-andre-omsorgstenester

Statistics Norway (2024b) *Innvandrere og norskfødte med innvandrerforeldre* (Immigrants and their children – a diverse group) [online], Available from: https://www.ssb.no/befolkning/innvandrere/artikler/innvandrerne-og-deres-barn--en-mangfoldig-gruppe#:~:text=I%201970%20bodde%20det%2057,til%202023%20bodde%20877%20000

Stolt, R. and Winblad, U. (2009) Mechanisms behind privatization: a case study of private growth in Swedish elderly care, *Social Science & Medicine*, 68(5): 903–11.

Szebehely, M. and Meagher, G. (2013) Four Nordic countries – four responses to the international trend of marketisation, in G. Meagher and M. Szebehely (eds) *Marketisation in Nordic Eldercare*, Stockholm University.

Westwood, S. (2019) Introduction, in S. Westwood (ed) *Ageing, Diversity and Equality: Social Justice Perspectives*, Bristol University Press, pp 1–21.

World Health Organization (2007) *Global Age-Friendly Cities: A Guide*, World Health Organization.

World Health Organization (2015) *World Report on Ageing and Health*, World Health Organization.

Zola, I.K. (2009) The medicalization of aging and disability, in M.L. Levine (ed) *The Elderly*, Bristol University Press, pp 37–53.

4

Who gets counted? Ageing statistics and advancing age equity

Madeline McCoy and Renate Ysseldyk

Introduction

In considering policies and practices that aim to advance age equity and improve health outcomes for older people, national statistics collected by governments are typically assumed to be a reliable basis for problem identification, evaluation and planning. But are they as reliable as policy makers, researchers and advocates expect? How can age equity be addressed if the available data – whether quantitative or qualitative – are insufficient to understanding the issues and their extent, or to assessing change over time? In this chapter, we consider national statistical data collection about older adults to ask, who gets included and how, who is excluded and how, and with what effects? In this chapter, we will show not only who is left out, but how these absences may undermine 'age-friendly' policies and practices aimed to advance more age-equitable cities by analysing English language survey instruments internationally, and with specific attention to Canada. The Canadian example is useful, as Canada is well-known for its extensive statistical health data collection and analysis, its attention to health equity, and for its high level of Age-Friendly movement uptake. However, in the shadow of the COVID-19 pandemic, Canada has undertaken a review of problems in its health data collection and analysis, identifying many gaps (Public Health Agency of Canada, 2021). Our findings reveal much room for improvement, in Canada and around the world.

Getting the data right about older people is a pressing policy issue. The world is getting older, fast. By 2050, the number of people aged 60 and older is expected to double – this projected increase will result in the population of those 60 and older rising from 962 million in 2017 (or approximately 13 per cent of the world population) to '1.4 billion in 2030 and 2.1 billion in 2050' (United Nations, 2017: xxxiii). As life expectancy increases, addressing long-term health conditions and well-being in older age have become increasingly important aims for public health policy and health-care systems (WHO, 2015). Over the past decades, the WHO's framework for age-friendly communities has promoted policies, services and structures that support active ageing as a 'process of optimizing opportunities for health, participation and security in order to enhance quality of life as people age' (WHO, 2007: 5). From this perspective, policies that support active ageing allow people to achieve good health throughout their life, participate in their community and society at large, and enjoy higher quality of life. However, poor health is associated with social isolation or dependency on care systems (Levasseur et al, 2017; WHO, 2020). Healthy ageing is defined as not merely the absence of disease. It involves the ability to do the things that we value, live a meaningful life, and feel a sense of dignity (WHO, 2020).

The intersection of equity and the social determinants of health (SDoH) has therefore become an area of focus in policy research (Marmot, 1999; Raphael, 2016; Dover and Belon, 2019; Hoyer et al, 2022). SDoH are the social, political, and economic conditions that disproportionately influence health outcomes and well-being for different groups of people (WHO, 2024). Health inequity can stem from the 'unequal allocation or distribution of power and resources, which manifest in unequal SDoH' (WHO, 2024: 2). Although each SDoH can have impacts on health, and the WHO (2007) age-friendly framework has attempted to integrate many of them (for example, housing), some SDoH are particularly cross-cutting in their effects on health and well-being. In this regard, health disparities based on gender and culture that emerge to affect diverse groups and identities – and although acknowledged as important within age-friendly practice and policy – may be overlooked. Yet, 'owing to their overriding influence, these determinants merit specially focused initiatives' (WHO, 2007: 9).

Large-scale surveys can capture health outcomes such as life expectancy and morbidity and mortality rates. They can also capture health disparities and measure progress towards addressing the SDoH which impact health equity (Dover and Belon, 2019; Hoyer et al, 2022; WHO, 2024). Furthermore, surveys can track how disadvantages are compounded over the life course. Surveys that include and measure the SDoH can help to evaluate how health inequities accumulate and shape health outcomes (WHO, 2024). There is a need for public health policies to 'consider the heterogeneity of experiences in older age and be relevant to all older people, regardless of their health status; address the inequities that underlie this diversity; [and] avoid ageist stereotypes and preconceptions' (WHO, 2015: 27; Mikton et al, 2021). However, when health policies and practices are based on statistics that ignore or miss many of these factors, they are unlikely to promote age equity in health.

Creating or building health policy and practice for all means knowing where current policies and practices fall short. However, statistical data collection on older adults has many absences. Attempting to identify steps needed to address gaps, the WHO's Decade of Healthy Ageing 2020–2030 report (2020) suggests distinguishing older people from other age groups when collecting data on health indicators. Further, older adults must be included in the collection of health statistics in ways that allow for an understanding of health status and trajectories (WHO, 2015). When data collection does include older adults, often data comes from those who are healthy or healthier (WHO, 2015), suggesting better data collection methods are needed. Further, promoting health equity 'may sometimes require unequal attention to some population groups to ensure the greatest benefit to the least advantaged, most vulnerable or marginalized members of society' (WHO, 2020). For example, although older adults are not a homogeneous group (Menec et al, 2011), large-scale survey research often overlooks the diversity within national and international populations and thus fails to identify potential relationships among identity factors, SDoH and health outcomes.

In this chapter, we focus on two main questions. Are older adults included in survey sampling strategies and, if so, do analyses distinguish older adults as a group, or analyse them only with the rest of the population? For this question, we took up a wide age range for later life, rather than 65+, to acknowledge that ageing is not a linear process that happens at a certain point in life – acute and chronic health conditions affect different populations at different points across the lifespan (WHO, 2015).

Our second question asks, do Canadian and international health surveys include (and analyse) variables related to gender and culture, such as sex, gender, sexual orientation/2SLGBTQI identity, ethnicity, religion and Indigeneity? The inclusion or exclusion of such variables provides insight into which older adults may or may *not* be included in national statistics and shed light on whether and how health equity can be assessed.

Canadian and international health surveys

We begin by analysing large-scale surveys that focused on health outcomes. These large-scale surveys tended to fall into two categories: those that focus on older adults, ageing and health outcomes, and surveys that collect health data from the entire population. We assumed that population-level surveys that include the 65+ age group would collect data on health outcomes that facilitate plans and policies to improve health outcomes across the entire population and performed a content analysis to consider the sample age ranges included. While we acknowledge that a survey may use a sampling strategy for specific reasons, when the goal of the survey is to collect information on a topic that, for example, impacts 'all Canadians', it is important to assess whether and how older adults were included or excluded.

To identify survey instruments for this analysis, we created a custom Google search to find both Canadian and international surveys using search terms such as 'older adults'/'seniors' and 'health'/'health survey'.

Additionally, World Health Organization, United Nations, and Statistics Canada publications were reviewed to find additional surveys that focused on (or at least claimed to focus on) older adults and health. Often, the term 'seniors' was used in these surveys to refer to the 65+ age group, especially when collecting statistics on health and ageing (examples are Turcotte and Schellenberg, 2007; CDC, 2015). Therefore, the terms 'older adult' and 'senior' are used interchangeably in this chapter. Our search yielded a rich variety of surveys from Canada and internationally.

Canadian surveys

A total of 39 Canadian surveys were identified. In Figure 4.1, provided later in this chapter, in the leftmost pie chart, the light grey section represents the six surveys that focused solely on older adults, or 15 per cent ($n = 6$) of Canadian surveys that focused on seniors and did not include younger adults. Two surveys included people over age 45, one survey included seniors aged 65 and over, one survey included 'seniors' (without further detail), one survey specified including people aged 45–85, and one survey specified including people aged 50–75. Therefore, younger adults below these age cut-offs were excluded to focus on topics relevant specifically to older adults.

Conversely, two surveys, represented by the dark grey section in the leftmost pie chart, used sampling strategies that excluded older adults. The Programme for the International Assessment of Adult Competencies examined the population aged 16–65 but excluded those 66 years and older. Likewise, while the *Survey of Persons Not in the Labour Force* included questions about retirement, it included only those aged 15–69, excluding many (working) seniors.

Figure 4.1: Canadian surveys: where and how are older adults included?

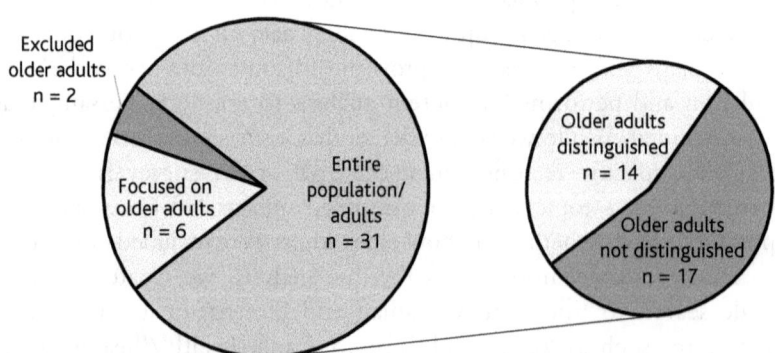

Thirty-one surveys sampled from the entire Canadian adult population; these surveys are represented by the medium grey section of the leftmost pie chart in Figure 4.1. These surveys used a sampling strategy that included all Canadians in the Canadian census or all adults over the age of either 15 or 18, including older adults 65+. We further divided these 31 surveys into two categories: first, surveys that distinguished older adults from the rest of the age groups, giving older adults' health outcomes specific attention, and second, surveys that did not. This breakdown is represented in the smaller pie chart on the right.

Older adults were distinguished from younger adults in 14 of the 31 surveys (see the light grey section of the rightmost pie chart). That is, attention was given to older adults' specific health issues, even when the survey was focused on the entire population. Of these 14 surveys, some included subsections that specifically collected data on 'seniors'. For example, the *Health Services Access Survey* examined waiting times for health care, access to specialist health care, and access to general physicians, but they also included a subsection to specifically examine seniors' health and disability. Some of these 14 surveys included all Canadians but also distinguished older adults from the rest of the adult population via themes relevant to older adults within their health survey focus, such as retirement, pension and long-term care.

In contrast, 17 of the 31 surveys did *not* distinguish older adults from the younger population (dark grey section of the rightmost pie chart, Figure 4.1). These surveys did not include a specific subsection to focus on older adults and themes did not include those relevant to older adults specifically. For example, in the *Hospital Morbidity Database and the Labour Force Survey*, one might expect to see subsections that focus specifically on older adults, given that morbidity or labour force participation might look different for older adults compared to younger adults; however, there is no special attention paid to older adults on these topics.

International surveys

Our search for international health surveys – that is, surveys that either captured responses from multiple countries or focused on a specific country other than Canada, yielded 29 surveys that focused on (or at least purported to focus on) older adults and health. The custom Google search used to find English language international surveys included search terms such as 'older adults'/'seniors' and 'health'/'health survey' (similar to the terms used to find Canadian surveys). We identified 29 surveys that included data collected in Indonesia, India, England and the United States, or across multiple countries. Of course, this is not an exhaustive list. However, this selection offers an indication of whether, which, and how older adults are included or excluded in international health survey data.

Figure 4.2: International surveys: where and how are older adults included?

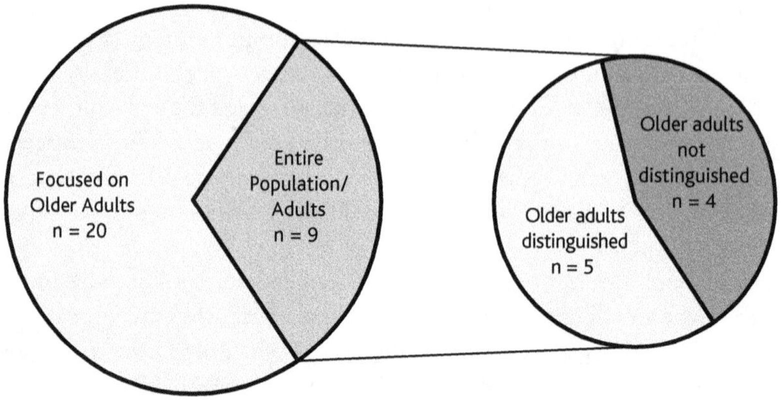

[Figure 4.2: Two linked pie charts. Left chart: "Focused on Older Adults n = 20" and "Entire Population/Adults n = 9". Right chart (expansion of the Entire Population/Adults segment): "Older adults not distinguished n = 4" and "Older adults distinguished n = 5".]

Of these 29 surveys, 20 focused on older adults specifically, including the English Longitudinal Study of Ageing (UK), the *Survey of Health, Ageing, and Retirement in Europe*, and the *Health and Retirement Study* (US). These 20 surveys are represented by the light grey section of the leftmost pie chart in Figure 4.2, found later in this chapter. Like the Canadian surveys in this category, the samples for these surveys included people aged 45, 50, 60 or 65 and over. There were no surveys that excluded older adults.

The remaining nine surveys focused on the overall population within a specific country or multiple countries, represented by the medium grey section of the leftmost pie chart (Figure 4.2). As with our analyses of the Canadian surveys, these nine surveys were then further divided into first, surveys that distinguished older adults from the rest of the age groups, giving older adults' health outcomes specific attention, and second, surveys that did not. This breakdown is represented by the pie chart on the right. Older adults were distinguished in five of the nine surveys (light grey section of the rightmost pie chart). As in the previous description, these surveys showed attention to older adults, even when the survey was focused on the entire population. In comparison, four of the nine surveys did *not* distinguish older adults (dark grey section of the rightmost pie chart). These surveys did not include a specific subsection to focus on older adults or themes specifically relevant to older adults.

Gender and culture: who is included and excluded?

Older adults experience different health challenges when compared to other age groups, but it is also important to consider differences among older people when collecting data. Although the summary of survey data indicates that at least some surveys acknowledge the unique needs and experiences of older adults compared to younger groups, we had questions about whether these surveys considered differences and inequities among older adults, including their relationships to the SDoH. Therefore, we considered whether and how each of the surveys included data that could allow analysis of the health and conditions of older adults based on gender, ethnicity or religion, as three examples. An initial scan of the demographic variables revealed that age, sex, race/ethnicity, income, education and geographic location were included in most of the surveys. Given this finding, and considering the WHO (2007) acknowledgment that their age-friendly framework does not capture inequities in health and quality of life related to gender and culture, our focus included an analysis of which older adults were included in national statistics based on demographic categories relating to gender or culture (broadly defined) including: sex and gender, sexual orientation, culture and ethnicity, religion and Indigeneity. To this end, we analysed the surveys' demographic questions/indicators and performed a qualitative content analysis to understand the themes included in each survey. For this inquiry, our search terms were used to scan both the survey questions used to collect demographic information as well as the description of the survey goals or focus, as a survey is more likely to collect data that can reflect relevant differences within the population if data is collected from diverse social groups.

We examined sex and gender separately. Sex and gender are often used synonymously; however, we define sex to refer to assigned biological sex (generally categorised as male or female), whereas gender refers to gender identity (Lindqvist et al, 2021). In surveys, gender is often considered a binary variable that does not always align with biological sex, but rather the socially constructed roles and expressions of women, men and gender-diverse people (Lindqvist et al, 2021). Therefore, in our content analysis, we used search terms to find sex and/or gender in the surveys, but we also determined how sex and gender were defined and measured. When the only options were to identify as male or female, we considered this to be a measurement of sex. If a survey measured gender by providing participants options to reflect wider categories of gender identity (including, for example, male, female, man, woman, non-binary, other and/or a text box), then we considered it to be a measurement of gender (Lindqvist et al, 2021). Furthermore, we also examined sexuality, sexual identity and sexual orientation, searching for terms such as sexuality and 2SLGBTQI (Morgan, 2013). Sexual orientation is a term used to describe a person's sexuality or to whom an individual is sexually attracted (van Anders, 2015). We recognise that 2SLGBTQI is a term used to refer to gender identity and sexual orientation; therefore, we included it as a search term to find how both concepts of gender identity and sexual orientation are included in (or excluded from) surveys.

For this analysis, ethnicity and culture were grouped to refer to both 'the attributional dimension [that] describes the unique sociocultural characteristics (such as culture, diet) of groups [and] the relational dimension [that] captures characteristics of the relationship between an ethnically defined group and the society in which it is situated' (Ford and Harawa, 2010: 2–3). Moreover, although there are overlaps among the categories of culture, ethnicity and religion, there are also differences (Ford and Harawa, 2010). Thus, religion was separated into its own category to account for groups that might share religion but not ethnicities or cultures. Finally, we considered whether and how surveys include Indigenous populations and how they addressed Indigeneity. Figure 4.3 summarises the frequency of the aforementioned categories appearing in the 39 Canadian surveys and 29 international surveys, keeping in mind that more than one category could appear in each of the surveys.

Sex and gender identity

As seen in Figure 4.3, measurement or discussion of sex was included in over half of the surveys. Meanwhile, gender was under-represented in the Canadian surveys and considered more often in the identified international surveys. However, 2SLGBTQI populations were poorly represented in all

Figure 4.3: Comparison of variables related to gender, sex, 2SLGBTQI identity, culture/ethnicity, religion, and indigeneity in Canadian and international surveys

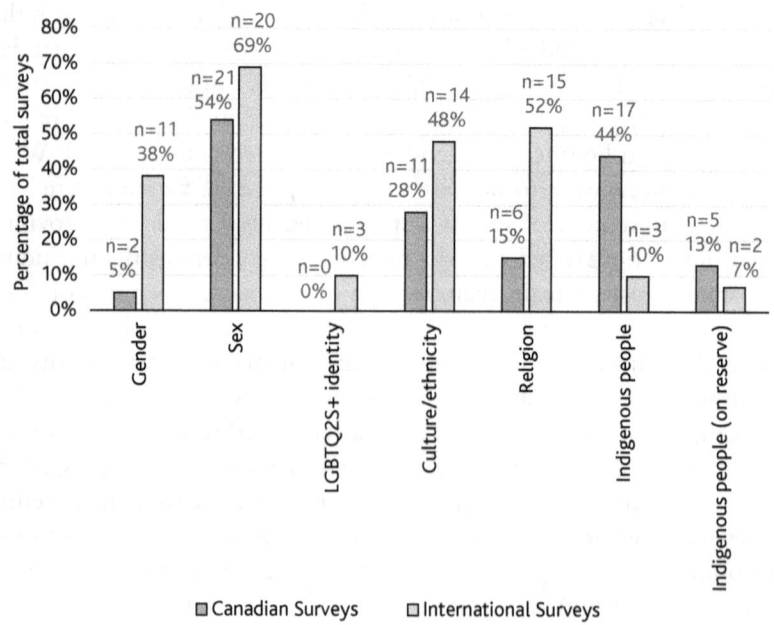

surveys. No Canadian surveys asked questions or discussed themes related to sexuality or sexual orientation. Both gender and sexuality were often left out of these surveys, which tended to collect only data on sex, using binary questions. In many cases, surveys claimed to measure gender but used a binary scale and measured sex instead of gender, for example, asking participants to identify if they were male or female.

Culture, ethnicity, religion, and indigeneity

As noted in Figure 4.3, more international surveys included a discussion of culture and ethnicity compared to the Canadian surveys. This ranged from surveys that collected demographic information on culture/ethnicity and language to subsections of surveys that aimed to capture ethnic and cultural diversity. This is in comparison to the remaining surveys that examined older adults solely as a homogeneous group rather than a group comprised of diverse individuals. Likewise, religious beliefs and activities were considered more often in the international surveys than by the Canadian surveys.

There were, however, more Canadian surveys that included demographic data collection on Indigenous peoples compared to international surveys, no doubt owing to the increasing recognition of Indigenous peoples in Canadian history and society (see Castleden et al, 2015; McBride, 2017; Trevethan, 2019). A similar number of Canadian and international surveys included data on Indigenous on-reserve populations. However, when comparing the inclusion of Indigenous populations more broadly to Indigenous populations living on reserve, many Canadian and international surveys specifically excluded Indigenous populations living on reserve.

Overall, it is critical to note that while the international surveys appeared to more adequately include diverse populations than did Canadian surveys, less than half of both the Canadian and international surveys included these categories. Importantly, while gender, sex, 2SLGBTQI identity, culture/ ethnicity, religion and Indigenous populations/Indigeneity were included in some surveys as demographic variables, very few surveys included these categories as areas of focus, for example, by sampling these population groups or focusing on survey topics related to one or more of these populations (Allen, 2017).

Another issue arising from our analysis is whether surveys offer one snapshot in time or a longitudinal view. Some population-level surveys can use one-time or limited-time ageing-focused surveys to fill gaps in data collection. For example, of the six Canadian surveys that included only older adults, the *Canadian Community Health Survey – Healthy Aging* and the *Canadian Health Survey on Seniors* are occasional surveys conducted most recently in 2010 and 2020, respectively. The *Survey of Ageing and Independence* and the *Survey of Older Workers* (part of the *Labour Force Survey*) were one-time surveys conducted in 1995 and 2008, respectively. These surveys provide a time-limited analysis of conditions, but do not offer policy makers or advocates feedback on the results of policy change. Conversely, the *Canadian Longitudinal Study on Aging* (CLSA) and the *Nursing and Residential Care Facilities – Public* are ongoing surveys conducted since 2009 and annually since 2015, respectively. In comparison, the remaining 33 Canadian surveys focusing on the entire population were conducted to collect health data each of 1, 2, or 5 years, although some were inactive at the time of our analysis. Very few of these surveys were one-time surveys. These repeated surveys offer needed feedback and evaluation of the impact of policy change, as well as helping to identify emerging challenges to health equity.

Promising practices in data collection

Given the findings from our analysis of health and related surveys, we return to our questions about the relationship between health policies and statistical data collection that monitors health outcomes and well-being. The surveys analysed here were designed explicitly so that the collected data can inform policy and programs. Policy makers use these statistics to inform health policies that aim to improve health outcomes for a given population and thus a population-level survey is an opportunity to implement subsections that acknowledge diversity, including among older adults. As we conducted our analysis, we worked to identify promising survey designs that offered direction and examples that include older adults and reflect their diversity.

An example of a population-level survey with focused subsections that take up issues specific to older adults is Canada's *General Social Survey* (Statistics Canada, 2019). The *General Social Survey* focuses on the following seven themes: Canadians at Work and Home, Family, Caregiving and Care Receiving, Education, Work and Retirement, Victimisation, Social Identity, and Time Use (Statistics Canada, 2019). Three of the seven themes (Caregiving and Care Receiving, Education, Work and Retirement, and Victimisation) mention seniors as a special population group (Statistics Canada, 2019).

In our analysis of themes related to culture and gender in data collection we found a general lack of focus on diversity among older adults. However, the *Canadian Longitudinal Study on Aging (CLSA)* promotes an understanding of how social factors impact health and well-being for groups of diverse older adults. In the Baseline stage of the CLSA, data was collected on sex, sexual orientation, ethnicity, culture and religion (CLSA, 2021). Later on, the Follow-Up 1 data collection included gender identity as well. Neither the Baseline nor Follow-Up 1 data collection included the Indigenous identity of participants (CLSA, 2021); however, the COVID-19 Seroprevalence Study Waves have collected data on Indigenous identity and whether Indigenous

Peoples live on or off reserve (CLSA, 2020a). Thus, over time, the CLSA has been revised to integrate more categories for data collection and to weight the data accordingly (CLSA, 2020b), notwithstanding its largely white, Protestant sample when compared to national estimates (Statistics Canada, 2020; Statistics Canada, 2022).

Discussion and implications for age-equity

Since the development of the WHO (2007) age-friendly strategy, many jurisdictions and levels of government have taken policy action to address the SDoH with the aim of advancing health equity (NCCDH, 2015; NCCDH, 2018). However, inadequate data collection strategies can contribute to gaps in the evaluation of interventions and measurement of progress towards health equity (NCCDH, 2015; NCCDH, 2018). The way health statistics are collected, can 'shape what is done, and what is left undone' (Armstrong, 2013: 199). Thus, the sampling strategy and the variables included in large-scale surveys, can contribute to 'understanding … the causes of health inequities and effective interventions' (NCCDH, 2015: 10; NCCDH, 2018). Reliable, comprehensive data collection provides policy makers and advocates with the information they need to monitor health outcomes and advance health equity (WHO, 2015; WHO, 2020; WHO, 2024). Our findings underline the risk that even well-intentioned, evidence-informed policy decisions and directions based on inadequate data will leave behind groups of people who are unaccounted for or not well defined in statistical data and analysis.

Returning to our questions from the beginning of this chapter, our findings demonstrate that while older adults are largely included in surveys, these surveys do not always distinguish older adults from the rest of the population. Moreover, in many cases, less than half of all surveys included variables related to gender, sexual orientation/2SLGBTQI identity, culture/ethnicity, religion and Indigenous populations/Indigeneity. Given that older adults from marginalised groups disproportionately experience health disparities, not only when compared to other age groups but also within their age group, many surveys appear short-sighted and problematic if used in formulating policies and practices affecting older people. While we note that while most surveys did not exclude the wide range of older adults from their samples, many survey designs did not allow the stratification and data analysis using characteristics that distinguish specific groups of older people. The result is that health inequities among and across groups cannot be identified or explored (CIHI, 2018; WHO, 2024).

To promote age equity, data should be collected in a way that allows for data stratification by age and is collected from all ages relevant to the inquiry (CIHI, 2018; WHO, 2024). Further, we call for recognition of the diversity within the older adult age group, including identity, health risks and experiences (Menec et al, 2011; WHO, 2015), in national and international surveys related to health and well-being (Public Health Agency of Canada, 2021). There is a need to recognise the relationships between and among groups within the older adult population as it continues to expand (Goll et al, 2015; United Nations, 2017; Parekh et al, 2018). A one-size-fits-all approach to survey design and analyses will not capture the diversity and range of social groups and identities that are vital to facilitating the creation of policy that meets the needs of all older adults. Attention given to these factors can prevent stereotypical, problematic views or misrepresentations of older adults' health needs (WHO, 2015; Mikton et al, 2021), and, in turn, advance age equity in health policy and practice.

References

Allen, M. (ed) (2017) *The SAGE Encyclopedia of Communication Research Methods*, SAGE Publications.

Armstrong, A. (2013) Neoliberalism and official health statistics: towards a research agenda, in P. Armstrong and S. Braedley (eds) *Troubling Care: Critical Perspectives on Research and Practices*, Canadian Scholars' Press Inc, pp 187–200.

Canadian Institute for Health Information (CIHI) (2018) *In Pursuit of Health Equity: Defining Stratifiers for Measuring Health Inequality: A Focus on Age, Sex, Gender, Income, Education and Geographic Location*, Canadian Institute for Health Information [online], Available from: https://www.cihi.ca/sites/default/files/document/defining-stratifiers-measuring-health-inequalities-2018-en-web.pdf

Canadian Longitudinal Study on Aging (2020a) CLSA COVID-19 Seroprevalence Study Questionnaire: Waves 2 and 3 [online], Available from: https://www.clsa-elcv.ca/our-resources/clsa-covid-19-seroprevalence-study-questionnaire-waves-2-and-3/clsa_seroprevalenceq_v2-0_2021jan12/

Canadian Longitudinal Study on Aging (2020b) CLSA Technical Document 2020: Sampling and Computation of Response Rates and Sample Weights for the Tracking (Telephone Interview) Participants and Comprehensive Participants [online], Available from: https://www.clsa-elcv.ca/our-resources/2020-baseline-sampling-and-computation-of-response-rates-and-sample-weights-for-the-tracking-telephone-interview-participants-and-comprehensive-participants-version-1-2/datasuppdoc_sampwgts_bl_v1-2_2020nov10/

Canadian Longitudinal Study on Aging (2021) CLSA Data Availability Table/Disponibilité des Données de l'ÉLCV [online], Available from: https://www.clsa-elcv.ca/wp-content/uploads/2024/01/CLSA_DataAvailabilityTable_v5.2_2024Dec17.pdf

Castleden, H., Sylvestre, P., Martin, D. and McNally, M. (2015) 'I don't think that any peer review committee ... would ever "get" what I currently do': how institutional metrics for success and merit risk perpetuating the (re)production of colonial relationships in community-based participatory research involving Indigenous peoples in Canada, *International Indigenous Policy Journal*, 6(4): pp 1–23.

Dover, D.C. and Belon, A.P. (2019) The health equity measurement framework: A comprehensive model to measure social inequities in health, *International Journal for Equity in Health*, 18: 1–12.

Ford, C.L. and Harawa, N.T. (2010) A new conceptualization of ethnicity for social epidemiologic and health equity research, *Social Science & Medicine*, 71(2): 251–8.

Goll, J.C., Charlesworth, G., Scior, K. and Stott, J. (2015) Barriers to social participation among lonely older adults: the influence of social fears and identity, *PLoS ONE*, 10(2): e0116664.

Hoyer, D., Dee, E., O'Leary, M.S., Heffernan, M., Gelfand, K., Kappel, R. et al (2022) How do we define and measure health equity? The state of current practice and tools to advance health equity, *Journal of Public Health Management and Practice*, 28(5): 570–7.

Levasseur, M., Dubois, M.F., Généreux, M., Menec, V., Raina, P., Roy, M. et al (2017) Capturing how age-friendly communities foster positive health, social participation and health equity: a study protocol of key components and processes that promote population health in aging Canadians, *BMC Public Health*, 17: 1–12.

Lindqvist, A., Sendén, M.G. and Renström, E.A. (2021) What is gender, anyway? A review of the options for operationalising gender, *Psychology and Sexuality*, 12(4): 332–44.

Marmot, M. (1999) The solid facts: the social determinants of health, *Health Promotion Journal of Australia*, 9(2): 133–9.

McBride, K. (2017) *Data Resources and Challenges for First Nations Communities*, Alberta First Nations Information Governance Centre [online], Available from: https://afnigc.ca/wp-content/uploads/2024/01/Data_Resources_Report.pdf

Menec, V.H., Means, R., Keating, N., Parkhurst, G. and Eales, J. (2011) Conceptualizing age-friendly communities, *Canadian Journal on Aging*, 30(3): 479–93.

Mikton, C., de la Fuente-Núñez, V., Officer, A. and Krug, E. (2021) Ageism: a social determinant of health that has come of age, *The Lancet*, 397(10282): 1333–4.

Morgan, E.M. (2013) Contemporary issues in sexual orientation and identity development in emerging adulthood, *Emerging Adulthood*, 1(1): 52–66.

National Center for Chronic Disease Prevention and Health Promotion (CDC) (2015) Indicator Definitions – Older Adults [online], Available from: https://www.cdc.gov/cdi/indicator-definitions/older-adults.html

National Collaborating Centre for Determinants of Health (NCCDH) (2015) *Equity-Integrated Population Health Status Reporting: Action Framework*, National Collaborating Centre for Determinants of Health, St. Francis Xavier University [online], Available from: https://nccph.s3.amazonaws.com/uploads/2022/06/PHSR_Action_Framework_EN_final.pdf

National Collaborating Centre for Determinants of Health (NCCDH) (2018) *A Gaps Analysis to Improve Health Equity Knowledge and Practices*, National Collaborating Centre for Determinants of Health, St. Francis Xavier University [online], Available from: https://nccdh.ca/images/uploads/comments/A_gaps_analysis_to_improve_health_equity_knowledge_and_practices_EN_Final.pdf

Parekh, R., Maleku, A., Fields, N., Adorno, G., Schuman, D. and Felderhoff, B. (2018) Pathways to age-friendly communities in diverse urban neighborhoods: do social capital and social cohesion matter?, *Journal of Gerontological Social Work*, 61(5): 492–512.

Public Health Agency of Canada (2021) *Expert Advisory Group Report 2: Building Canada's Health Data Foundation*, Government of Canada [online], Available from: https://www.canada.ca/en/public-health/corporate/mandate/about-agency/external-advisory-bodies/list/pan-canadian-health-data-strategy-reports-summaries/expert-advisory-group-report-02-building-canada-health-data-foundation.html

Raphael, D. (ed) (2016) *Social Determinants of Health: Canadian Perspectives* (3rd edn), Canadian Scholars' Press.

Statistics Canada (2019) *General Social Survey: An Overview, 2019*, Statistics Canada, Available from: https://www150.statcan.gc.ca/n1/en/pub/89f0115x/89f0115x2019001-eng.pdf

Statistics Canada (2020) Data Tables, 2016 Census [online], Available from: https://www12.statcan.gc.ca/census-recensement/2016/dp-pd/dt-td/index-eng.cfm

Statistics Canada (2022) Data Tables, 2021 Census of Population [online], Available from: https://www12.statcan.gc.ca/census-recensement/2021/dp-pd/dt-td/index-eng.cfm

Trevethan, S. (2019) *Strengthening the Availability of First Nations Data* (Prepared for Indigenous Services Canada & The Assembly of First Nations), QMR Consulting [online], Available from: https://www.afn.ca/wp-content/uploads/2019/05/NCR-11176060-v1-STRENGTHENING_THE_AVAILABILITY_OF_FIRST_NATIONS_DATA-MAR_25_2019-FINAL_E.pdf

Turcotte, M. and Schellenberg, G. (2007) *A Portrait of Seniors in Canada, 2006*, Statistics Canada [online], Available from: https://www150.statcan.gc.ca/n1/en/pub/89-519-x/89-519-x2006001-eng.pdf

United Nations, Department of Economic and Social Affairs, Population Division (2017) *World Population Prospects: The 2017 Revision, Volume II: Demographic Profiles*, United Nations [online], Available from: https://www.un.org/development/desa/pd/content/world-population-prospects-2017-revision-volume-ii-demographic-profiles

van Anders, S.M. (2015) Beyond sexual orientation: integrating gender/sex and diverse sexualities via sexual configurations theory, *Archives of Sexual Behavior*, 44(5): 1177–213.

World Health Organization (2007) *Global Age-Friendly Cities: A Guide*, World Health Organization [online], Available from: https://www.who.int/publications/i/item/9789241547307

World Health Organization (2015) *World Report on Ageing and Health*, World Health Organization [online], Available from: https://www.afro.who.int/sites/default/files/2017-06/9789240694811_eng.pdf

World Health Organization (2020) *Decade of Healthy Aging 2020–2030*, World Health Organization [online], Available from: https://www.who.int/publications/m/item/decade-of-healthy-ageing-plan-of-action

World Health Organization (2024) *Operational Framework for Monitoring Social Determinants of Health Equity*, World Health Organization [online], Available from: https://www.who.int/publications/i/item/9789240088320

5

Counting care workers: when the 'muddle' is the message

*Tamara Daly, Sara Charlesworth,
Frode F. Jacobsen and Katherine Laxer*

Introduction

There is power in numbers. Consequently, counting is central to modern bureaucracies and when, how and about whom counting is done matters greatly for who gets what, under what conditions and when. Answering these 'counting' questions has taken on urgency as we proceed at pace to enable decision-making by Artificial Intelligence (AI), with 'big' data, large language models and algorithms problem-solving for us (see Chapters 4 and 14 to consider big data on ageing). Increasingly, data will power who and what are visible, while data silences will oppress who and what are not.

Care work is often invisible work, as it is work completed behind closed doors and by women workers who are paid too little and recognised less than most others (Baines et al, 2016). Accurately counting the number of care workers is important for advancing equity by enabling workforce planning and critique, yet it is very difficult to do given what current public datasets report and what data are not collected.

We are, as Caroline Criado Perez (2019: 24) argues, living within a 'gender data gap', riddled with 'data bias', 'big silences' and 'half-truths', a position from which 'women become invisible'. While Criado Perez documents the data gap for women's *unpaid* care burden, this chapter explores care work data gaps using the example of the *paid* care workers, also mostly women. Like Criado Perez, we see the capacity to count – with rigorous and publicly available workforce statistics – to be an important country level indicator of equity. To count care workers accurately, data collected and publicly reported about the workforce must at least be on a level available in other sectors. We argue that accurate data can address data bias, and support accountability for the government's public stewardship responsibility for long-term care (LTC) – particularly given state responsibilities to fund, manage and meet the LTC systems' structural quality and capacity for decent working conditions for paid care workers.

Income security and care for older adults have been important state responsibilities since at least the 1960s; welfare states were birthed by the struggle for equality and the introduction of public pensions were an important cornerstone of that struggle. In addition, access to LTC – whether provided in homes or communally in residential settings – is part of the basket of state responsibility in advanced nations. The chapter examines LTC dataset examples from Australia, Canada and Norway, three jurisdictions where there is public stewardship of LTC that ensures governments 'robustly monitor, assess and enforce good quality care and decent work at the system and organisational level' (Charlesworth et al, 2024). Another aspect of public stewardship is ensuring accountability by collecting and publishing good quality administrative data for services delivered with public funds and making them available to the public and for independent scrutiny (Daly, 2019). This public availability facilitates independent analysis by those outside of the sector who do not have the constraints of material ties to industry or the state. Some governments will make data available for a fee, which can limit the capacity to conduct analysis, even for other public sector groups.

Accurate counts of LTC care workers would enable better workforce planning and draw needed attention to care gaps, shaped by the longevity boon with more people living longer. 'Ageing' and the needs of vulnerable, older people living with disabilities and frailties have become central concerns, including in age-friendly frameworks. Yet, too few paid care workers are available, which pushes more care onto family and friends. In the context of policy and practice problem-solving, and especially with AI, the significant care workforce data gaps threaten policy and planning capacity while reinforcing the current state of care workers' invisibility and the corresponding super-invisibility of older care workers, discussed in Chapter 8. Further, systems that fail to house, protect, clean and publicly release the data result in public accountability challenges.

With examples from Australia, Canada and Norway, this chapter assesses the strength, clarity and public availability of national level data about the composition of the care workforce, including nurses and care assistants who, collectively, comprise the major groups in the LTC sector. Our approach is comparative, to reveal possibilities and challenges that extend beyond a single jurisdiction. In reviewing these public datasets, our goal is to surface some of the data gaps, given the evidence needed to advance the decent work and quality care necessary to advance equity. For instance, evidence for one of the most important quality metrics in LTC services is 'staffing level', as understaffing is common in LTC and is associated with poor outcomes in both care quality and working conditions. Counting the number of carers by role is important to assess, because skill mix and staff ratios matter when aiming for quality care conditions. Another quality metric is 'continuity', that is, the ability to receive care from the same workers over a period of time, because knowing someone portends good outcomes for both the workers and the clients. Evidence about whether there are too few or too many casual or part-time workers, when compared with full-time workers, raises red flags about the system's ability to support continuity of care.

With these considerations in mind, we queried the datasets to compare the care work data regimes across the three countries. We ask four straightforward questions of the publicly available datasets specific to the care workforce in residential LTC and home care. How many care workers are employed, by role, over time? What is the age profile, by role? What are the proportions of each role, by sex? What is the overall proportion of migrants in the care workforce? We present our findings and discuss promising and problematic features, highlighting what data gaps need to be redressed to ensure public stewardship and independent scrutiny.

The chapter is organised as follows. The first section outlines the parameters of our query, highlighting various attributes and dimensions. The next section applies these parameters to analyse our case of 'counting care workers', using public LTC data regimes across the three jurisdictions. We show that the data regimes are messy and muddled, with aspects of weak, 'noisy' and hidden data. We found significant confounders in all, requiring qualifiers that preclude proper analysis of care work for older people.

Marshall McLuhan (1965) argued that '[i]n a culture like ours, long accustomed to splitting and dividing all things as a means of control, it is sometimes a bit of a shock to be reminded that, in operational and practical fact, the medium is the message'. In the final section, we argue that the 'muddle' in these datasets *is* the message, that is, by maintaining datasets about care workers that are weak, noisy and/or hidden, governments shield themselves from critique of their public stewardship obligations to be open to independent, public scrutiny. Without rigorous and publicly reported data, governments can avoid the messiness of managing or can manage with impunity, hidden from public view. We conclude by highlighting how, in an algorithmic world increasingly powered by AI, data privatisation and ageing care systems that may be influenced by 'surveillance capitalism' principles (Zuboff, 2019), it is imperative that national statistics agencies and governments not only count care work carefully but make publicly visible care work data, especially for publicly funded care. Taking care work out of the shadows – to address bias, silence and half-truths – requires publicly available data. Making the data public enables independent monitoring and measuring of who works in care for older adults, both for comparison and planning, contributing to decent work and good care outcomes necessary to equity, while countering surveillance and data privatisation.

Defining data gaps

Publicly reported data about the care workforce is sub-optimal in all jurisdictions studied. There are several discrepancies – within and between countries and between groups of workers – along the following attributes: data strength (strong/weak), data clarity (clear/noisy) and public availability (available/hidden). Each attribute has several dimensions.

Data strength

For data strength, 'professional privileging' describes when publicly reported statistics are only about professional (for example, nurses), but not para-professional care work (such as care assistants), creating challenges for workforce analysis, particularly as the latter is the largest worker group in Canada and Australia and perform most of the hands on care, while Licensed Practical Nurses, part of the nurse workforce, are the largest group in Norway. Professional privileging can obscure analysis of under-staffing and retention challenges, especially if para-professional data calculations are weak to start.

Even though there are a variety of direct and ancillary workers in home care and residential LTC services, in this analysis, we take up just two groups: nurses, considered professionals with a variety of educational qualifications, and those who assist with care in para-professional roles. We use the terms, 'care worker' and 'care workforce' generically to refer to all, 'nurse' for all types of nurses and 'care assistant' for those who are paraprofessionals. Within each jurisdiction, we employ its specific nomenclature. Table 5.1 maps nomenclature used across the three countries and in this chapter.

Beyond professional privileging, issues with data strength can also emerge when datasets do not account for multiple job holding, for instance, counting a person twice if they work part-time in two places, a common circumstance for care assistants, or anyone in part-time or contract roles. 'Unaddressed bias' in workforce surveys – either due to selection or response-based problems – or 'errors' in weighting methods that don't account for the real-world lives of care workers, including part-time work and multiple job holding, produce findings that misrepresent the size or stability of the workforce.

'Under-estimates' are more likely in jurisdictions and organisations in which an undetermined number of private companions, employed by older people or their families and not the formal employer where they perform the work, do the same work as frontline staff in LTC homes (Daly et al, 2015; Daly and Armstrong, 2016). While paid companions do not work in the LTC context in Norway, evidence suggests that in some Canadian and Australian urban settings, and for the financially well-off and older adults with challenging needs, paid companion numbers rival those of officially

Table 5.1: Mapping cross-jurisdictional categories by roles and job titles

Categories used in this chapter	Role	Job titles		
		Australia	Canada	Norway
Nurse	Nurses with advanced education	Nurse practitioner; registered nurse	Nurse practitioner; registered nurse; registered psychiatric nurse	'Sykepleier': advanced practice registered nurses; registered nurses
	Nurses without advanced education	Enrolled nurse	Licensed practical nurse	Licensed practical nurses; 'Hjelpepleir':auxiliary nurse; 'Helsefagarbeider': health worker
Care assistants	Care assistants (varying education)	Personal care worker also, assistant in nursing and 'home care workers'	Personal support worker + 22 other titles	'Pleiemendhjeler'/ 'Pleieassistent': care worker

'counted' care workers in some LTC homes. No data exists to support these types of under-estimates.

Data clarity

In terms of data clarity, there are 'definitional challenges' when comparing jurisdictions because each country or sub-national jurisdiction uses different job classifications and terminology to capture who does what work. These classifications may or may not reflect levels of training or job sites. These differences mean that comparative analyses must include multiple qualifiers and risk 'apples to oranges' comparisons. There are also 'conflation challenges' that make it impossible to disaggregate labour force data to determine, for example, how many workers are working in different settings, such as community, home and LTC homes, or to identify whether workers with different qualifications are doing similar tasks. Further, a 'lack of disaggregation' along important indicators such as work setting, age, gender, race/ethnicity and immigration status obscures analysis of the composition of this often under-valued, over-worked labour force. Finally, data discrepancies between available census data and other databases mean that workforce planning is really a guessing game, underscored by the challenges reported in terms of understaffed working conditions and difficulty accessing care. In contrast with clear data, 'noisy' data have broad definitional boundaries. For instance, with care workers, it would be difficult to discern who works primarily in care for older adults, because everyone in receipt of care would be included in the data calculations. Across all three countries, another key challenge in workforce monitoring and planning is not being able to get any data at the level of a single LTC home or home care organisation. Grasping statistically the relationship between staffing composition and levels and resident/client outcomes is not possible with current datasets.

Public availability

Public availability of data is important as it relates to public accountability. We consider data to be hidden in the following instances. First, hidden data occurs when data are publicly available but provided in ways that are very difficult to interpret, might require expert knowledge, or when one of the other data problems – such as conflation or definition differences – changes the meaning and comparability of the data. We consider hidden data to include: those datasets that are collected but not publicly released; data are made available to only select groups and behind firewalls; data releases that are carefully controlled in terms of aggregation; and data that have delayed release and/or are old and not updated, limiting timely public discussion. We also consider data to be hidden if they are captured but not released or are very expensive to access.

Comparing the care work data regimes

In this section, we highlight available and missing attributes in the Canadian, Australian and Norwegian public workforce datasets by showing the proportion of workers employed in home care and LTC homes by role and disaggregated by sex, age and migrant status. Based on our analysis, we compare each country's dataset attributes. Our findings are summarised in Table 5.2. Italics denote attributes that contribute to invisibility for all care workers, and super-invisibility for older care workers, as we discuss in detail in Chapter 8. Along with the chart, the detailed analysis is presented for each country.

Australia

Australia, with a national 'Aged Care Program', publicly reports more robust data about care workers than Canada and Norway; however, the dataset is beset with 'weakness' and 'noise' limitations. Up until 2016, the national government contracted an independent research institute to undertake the National Aged Care Census and Survey (NACWS) using a census design, to be completed by aged care provider organisations, with surveys distributed directly to their employees. Both the census and survey require data about worker socio-demographics and experiences in residential and community-based settings (Mavromaras et al, 2017). In 2021, the *Aged Care Provider Workforce Survey* (ACPWS) replaced the NACWS with a sample

Table 5.2: Assessment of workforce data gaps

LTC workforce data	Australia	Canada	Norway
Nurses – residential LTC		Weak Clear Publicly available	
Nurses – home care	Weak Noisy Publicly available	Weak Noisy Hidden	Weak Noisy Hidden
Care assistants – residential LTC		Weak Noisy Hidden	
Care assistants – home care		Weak Noisy Hidden	

survey approach. The Australian government conducted this survey, and provider organisations were tasked with its completion. Two rounds have been conducted to date (2021, 2023). Like the previous census and survey, the ACPWS (2021, 2023) includes the work of Nurse Practitioners (NPs), Registered Nurses (RNs), Enrolled Nurses (ENs), Personal Care Workers (PCWs) (by certification and by training, and including 'Assistant in Nursing' who are the same as PCWs) and clinical managers in each of five nationally funded aged care programs: the *Residential Aged Care* (RAC), the *Commonwealth Home Support Program* (CHSP), the *Home Care Packages Program* (HCPP), *Multi-Purpose Services* (MPS), and *National Aboriginal and Torres Strait Islander Flexible Aged Care* (NATSIFAC). Usefully, data are reported by program and disaggregated into 'direct care', and 'administrative, ancillary care or other' to enable estimates of the capacity on the frontline. In terms of advances, data from NATSIFAC and MPS were unreported before 2020, a weakness now corrected and another promising practice when compared with Canada and Norway.

Here we report Australian RAC and HCPP data, showing how introduced changes nonetheless present challenges for understanding the workforce socio-demographic composition. For instance, recent 'age' reporting for the RAC workforce appears to underestimate its ageing profile when compared with 2021 Census data (ABS, 2022). Overall headcounts are weighted data, not actual number counts, and are subject to 'double counts' of workers who work for more than one provider, or with workers doing work funded out of two separate aged care programs, such as the HCPP and the CHSP. Notably, staff working in multiple settings, or for the same provider under different aged care programs, may be counted more than once, resulting in potential overestimates. Finally, and most concerningly, there is high proportion of 'unknown' selected, as a legitimate response to some questions. For instance, unknown responses to the question of 'age' for RAC directly employed workers across all roles was 24,212 (13 per cent), while for HCPP it was 9,973 (9.7 per cent) of responses. Because it is the organisations that complete the survey, not the workers, there may be reporting inaccuracies. Further, 'age' data tabulates only 'directly employed workers', leaving out at least 7 per cent of the workforce who are agency or self-employed workers. These design changes mean that the data available to aid in workforce planning has become less reliable. This limitation must be considered when using data for workforce planning, even with weighting, as estimates risk over-counting and overestimating the number of workers. Consequently, the data provide basic but limited estimates of the Australian LTC workforce composition.

Approximately 549,000 workers were employed across aged care programs, with three quarters (75.4 per cent) in 'direct care' (AIWH, 2024). In RAC, there was a decline in total staff from 2020 (n ~ 277,671) to 2023 (n ~ 273,000); the numbers are higher than the total number of staff working in HCPP (n ~ 170,000), of whom, 76 per cent (n = 128,000) are direct care (AIHW, 2024). As shown in Table 5.3, the total percentage by sex confirms that most 'directly employed direct care' are women.

The proportion of those aged 55+ working in RAC is lower than those 55+ in HCPP across all categories of nurses, except Nurse Practitioners (Table 5.4). Of the 87 per cent of directly employed RAC workers (nurses and care assistants combined) whose age was reported by their employer, 20,389 are 55–64, and 6,063 are 65+, together representing 16.1 per cent

Table 5.3: Sex of residential Aged Care and Home Care Packages Programme workforce (2023)

Roles		RAC			HCPP		
		Men (%)	Women (%)	'Other' (%)	Men (%)	Women (%)	'Other' (%)
Nurse	Nurse practitioner	20.30	79.70	0.00	–	–	–
	Registered nurse	16.50	83.50	0.10	13.90	86.10	0.00
	Enrolled nurse	11.70	88.30	0.00	16.00	84.00	0.00
	Total % by sex	*14.90*	*85.00*	*0.05*	*14.40*	*85.60*	*0.00*
Care assistant	Personal care worker (*)	14.70	85.20	0.00	12.30	87.70	0.00
	Personal care worker traineeship	14.50	85.30	0.20	18.20	81.80	0.03
	Total % by sex	*14.70*	*85.20*	*0.03*	*12.70*	*87.30*	*0.03*

Source: Analysis of ACPWS, AIHW (2023); unknown responses excluded; (*) includes title of 'Assistant in Nursing'

Table 5.4: Residential Aged Care and Home Care Packages Programme workforce 55+ (2023)

Roles		Residential Aged Care				Home Care Package			
		55–64 (%)	65+ (%)	Aged 55+/ role (%)	Total aged 55+ (%)	55–64 (%)	65+ (%)	Aged 55+/ role (%)	Total aged 55+ (%)
Nurse	Nurse practitioner	17.1	13.7	30.8	16.4	0.0	0.0	0.0	25.6
	Registered nurse	8.6	3.4	12.1		18.6	4.5	23.1	
	Enrolled nurse	19.3	6.4	25.7		25.2	8.4	33.6	
Care assistant	Personal care worker (*)	12.6	3.5	16.1	16.0	25.0	7.3	32.3	32.5
	Personal care worker traineeship	4.8	1.7	6.6		25.4	11.1	36.5	

Source: Analysis of Aged Care Provider Workforce Survey, AIHW (2024); unknown responses excluded; (*) includes title of 'Assistant in Nursing'

of the RAC nursing workforce. In home care, over one-quarter of nurses (n = 1,512) and over one-third of care assistants (n = 27,438) are aged 55+. More than one third of the home care workforce is aged 55+.

Of concern, ACPWS and census data do not correspond. The 2021 Census data for the residential aged care industry reveals a much older age profile for nurses and personal care workers: among nursing staff (RNs and ENs) and PCWs, one in five (20 per cent, n = 32,231) are aged 55–64 years, while one in 20 care workers (5 per cent, n = 7,740) are 65+. Of this latter cohort, some 1,778 workers (23 per cent) were aged 70+ (ABS, 2022). Australian Census data are unavailable for the home care sector, and like the Canadian Census, relevant industry employment data are aggregated within a category that lumps together workers under an 'other social assistance' label. This data gap makes triangulation between ACPWS and NACSCS impossible and renders home care workers and their pattern of ageing less visible. Discrepancies between the census and the NACSCS data raise further questions about the new ACPWS data collection methods and data accuracy, with significant implications for workforce planning.

In Australia, half of residential aged care workers are born in Australia, while half are migrant workers. The composition of the migrant workforce also creates age related data confounders, since analyses of 2016 Census and 2016 NACWCS data suggest that migrant aged care workers, who are a growing proportion of the aged care workforce, are younger on average than Australian-born workers (Eastman et al, 2018; Charlesworth and Isherwood, 2021). The largest migrant group are from Southern and Central Asia

(18 per cent), with others from Southeast Asia (11 per cent), Northwest Europe (5 per cent), 4 per cent from each of Oceania, Northeast Asia, Sub-Saharan Africa, 2 per cent from Southern and Eastern Europe, and 1 per cent each from the Americas, North Africa, and the Middle East (AIHW, 2024).

Canada

Some Canadian health-care workforce trends are publicly reported by the Canadian Institute for Health Information (CIHI), using administrative provincial/territorial data, but it is almost exclusively limited to reporting on professionals. CIHI reports on nurses across four categories, depending on educational levels and provincial licensing (NPs, RNs, Registered Psychiatric Nurses (RPNs) and Licensed Practical Nurses (LPNs)). In 2023, ~48,278 nurses were working in LTC in Canada (CIHI, 2024). Figure 5.1 shows the LTC nursing workforce trends since 2014. CIHI datasets are hampered by reporting weaknesses, as data gaps abound. For instance, RN figures were unreported by three out of 13 Canadian provinces and territories: Manitoba (2019–23), Prince Edward Island (2021–22), and Quebec (2022–23). British Columbia did not report RPNs from 2019–23. LPNs were unreported in Nunavut (2014–23), Yukon (2019–23), and New Brunswick (2019 and 2021) (CIHI, 2024). Of note, more than 2,500 nurses stopped working in LTC in 2021. Moreover, 3,300 nurses across categories moved to community health agencies and another 2,300 moved to private nursing agencies or self-employment (CIHI, 2024). If we extrapolate RN numbers from Manitoba's and Quebec's last report year, the overall proportions of RNs working in LTC dropped by at least 3.6 per cent (2017–23). Among LPNs, it appears that overall numbers of nurses are increasing, but it is noteworthy that between 2018 and 2022, the number of New Brunswick nurses dropped from 1,225 to 910, representing a loss of about one-third of this workforce in that province alone (27.1 per cent).

Looking at overall nursing workforce trends, a drop in RNs working in LTC may have been addressed by an increase in the numbers of LPNs, a worrying trend given higher LTC acuity levels and LPNs' lower skills mix. CIHI data show that nurses move around; however, without understanding shifts within the profession and between provinces, there is little ability for policymakers to plan, re-balance, and incentivise workers to remain, shift into LTC as needed, or to encourage upskilling where and when need arises.

While CIHI houses definitionally clear and publicly available data for residential LTC nurses, this is not the case for home care nurses, who are grouped in with community care nurses and often work across multiple sites. Despite limits, CIHI nurse workforce data are more granular than publicly reported Statistics Canada (StatsCan) nurse and care workers datasets, which are riddled with loud noise. StatsCan uses the National Occupational

Figure 5.1: Residential LTC nursing workforce, Canada 2014–23

LTC Nurse Practitioners	
2014	86
2015	113
2016	138
2017	167
2018	196
2019	201
2020	205
2021	238
2022	198
2023	216

LTC Registered Nurses	
2014	21731
2015	23224
2016	23467
2017	23572
2018	23399
2019	22304
2020	22450
2021	21776
2022	14146
2023	14596

LTC Registered Psychiatric Nurses	
2014	635
2015	619
2016	529
2017	518
2018	492
2019	338
2020	323
2021	313
2022	281
2023	278

LTC Licensed Practical Nurses	
2014	30268
2015	31638
2016	33069
2017	33265
2018	33843
2019	33761
2020	35458
2021	34545
2022	33689
2023	33188

Classification's (NOCs) nine broad sector categorisations (Government of Canada, nd). Within health, frontline nursing work is in 'professional occupations in health'. Nurses are divided by roles and professional qualifications. Still, they are lumped together across the following sites of care: 'nursing homes, extended care facilities, rehabilitation centres, doctors' offices, clinics, community agencies, companies, private homes and public and private organisations or they may be self-employed'. The data gaps in Canada are even more pronounced for Personal Support Workers (PSWs); all PSW datasets are weak, noisy, and hidden. CIHI uses 'personal support worker' as a representative title (CIHI, 2023) and we follow suit.

Noisy data can result from job classifications with unclear boundaries based on the site of care or the client population. For instance, in Canada, how 'personal care' work is designated involves a dizzying array of 22+ job titles, with administrative data not necessarily tied to the place of employment (such as long-term care, hospital, home), and without indication of whether the care is for older people or younger people with disabilities, because LTC and home care program eligibility is not normally age-restricted in Canada. This means that both younger people with disabilities and older people reside in LTC homes; home care is delivered for all ages in homes, in retirement homes and for children, in schools. PSWs work across client groups in Canadian health settings.

With professional privileging, there are marked differences between what Canada collects, reports and analyses about nurses compared to PSWs. As an 'unregulated' health profession, the exact number of PSWs providing care in Canada is unknown (CIHI, 2024). 'Definitional differences' across Canadian sub-national governments, and 'conflations' based on which workers are captured in the data, make it difficult to discern the number of workers across LTC settings, and which workers mostly care for older adults or other groups. As health and social care are provincial/territorial matters, PSW workforce data may be collected by provincial ministries but are not always publicly reported and are not provided to a national body or aggregated nationally (Daly, 2019). Counting PSW numbers is marred by poor definitional and terminological clarity, particularly with title/role changes over time. Most data about the PSW workforce remain hidden; any available data is noisy.

At a policy level, lacking a reliable PSW dataset means that there is too little evidence-based workforce planning and reporting (CIHI, 2023), hindering appropriate policy measures to redress growing shortfalls or pressure governments to raise the minimum required care hours in provinces/territories where that is mandated. To redress gaps, CIHI reports some public sector employees' data for the province of Alberta, the sole province with a functional Health Care Aide Directory (HCAD) owned by the College of Licensed Practical Nurses of Alberta (CLPNA) and operational since 2017. But the dataset is a workaround. CIHI and CLPNA started a data-sharing agreement in 2022; after data cleaning and applying assumptions, CIHI reports that while RNs are the largest tabulated group of health-care workers in Alberta, Care Aides (PSWs) are probably the largest group (CIHI, 2023). Further, it included only public sector workers, so it misses 30 per cent of the province's LTC workplaces. It lumps together public Alberta Health Services sites (hospital, home, residential LTC and community), making it impossible to identify PSW multiple job holding or transfers between sites, or whether there is a retention problem in LTC. CLPNA conducts some workforce analysis of its HCAD, with obvious limitations. Alberta public sector PSWs are reportedly mostly either younger or older workers and are ethno-racially diverse. Almost half (46.8 per cent) of this sub-set of PSWs speak English and one or more of 100 other languages (CIHI, 2024). The data gaps limit analytical power for planning purposes because we are unable to report with confidence even about the Alberta PSW workforce. This data is somewhat helpful to Alberta, but any findings cannot be extrapolated to other provinces or territories, as each has their own systems and labour markets. Further, workers migrate from one area of Canada to another, as well as from other countries, and intra-Canadian labour migration is impossible to capture. The limits of this workaround serve to highlight and exemplify the wider invisibility of this workforce.

A further issue is that dataset discrepancies are unresolved by Canada's StatsCan National Occupational Classification (NOC) system, which categorises all occupations. Canada's data remain extremely noisy for the care workforce. PSWs working in residential and home care are counted in (at least) two places in the dataset, but grouped with other kinds of workers, and across a wide array of sites (Government of Canada, nd). First, they are included in the category, 'assisting occupations in support of health services', sub-categorised as 'nurse aides, orderlies, and patient service associates', and 'employed in hospitals, nursing homes, assisted care facilities for the elderly and other health care establishments', but this category also includes 'emergency medical care attendants employed by private ambulance services, urgent care centers or other health facilities.' Other PSWS are counted in a work category that lumps together 'occupations in education, law, and social, community and government services', into the category: 'Home support workers, caregivers and related occupations' include those doing personal care, companionship for seniors, persons with disabilities and those who are convalescing'. This cohort of workers may be employed in a variety of sites, including private homes, supportive housing, assisted living and retirement homes, and in schools for children, and includes providers who may also reside in the home. Employers include agencies, private households and self-employment. These workers are also lumped in with others who work in private homes, such as doulas, or birthing helpers. The main criteria guiding the categorisation seems to be whether work is located in 'health settings' or 'home settings' and it is tied to workers' minimum level of education rather than which groups are cared for, or what tasks, skills or experience are needed to do the job. Further confounding analysis, in some provinces, family members with little or no formal health-care training can be paid by some government programs to do the work, and their labour is captured in 'home care provider occupations', even though they are not care workers for anyone other than family member(s). This categorisation reinforces sexist assumptions about the skill required to perform 'home care', and assumes any women's work in the home is the same, and related to gendered instincts and preferences rather than acquired skill and inequitable divisions of labour (Armstrong and Laxer, 2006).

Further, the data architecture makes understanding trends over time tricky, as NOC categories change. An older version (NOC 2016 version 1.3) includes 24 groups for nurses, personal support workers and care aides that don't completely map onto the new five-digit version (NOC 2021, version 1.0) (StatsCan, 2023). Granular analysis is further limited by the significant aggregation in the NOC public data categories reported by StatsCan (2023). For instance, the 'home care' category lumps together those providing care to children with carers of older adults, people with disabilities and convalescent care.

Despite significant limits, a fuzzy picture emerges (Table 5.5). Among these workers, most are women, including 90.2 per cent of nurses and allied health-care professionals. In addition, this group of health workers is ageing. Our data analysis shows that those who are 55+ comprise nearly one-fifth (18.8 per cent) of the nurse and allied health-care workforce – across all health

Table 5.5: Size of workforce 55+, by National Occupational Categories (NOC), nursing and assisting occupations, across settings, by sex (2021)

		Nurse +		Care assistant			
		Nursing + allied health professionals (NOC 3130)		Assisting occupations in support of health services (NOC 3310)		Home care provider occupations (NOC 4410)	
		n	% of all workers	n	% of all workers	n	% of all workers
All ages 15+	Male	34,200	9.8	66,695	14.1	8,770	8.1
	Female	315,310	90.2	406,525	85.9	99,020	91.9
	Total	349,510		473,220		107,795	
Only 55–64 years	Male	4,290	1.2	10,960	2.3	1,745	1.6
	Female	49,275	14.1	75,900	16.0	22,460	20.8
	Total	53,565	15.3	86,860	18.4	24,205	22.5
Only 65+ years	Male	805	0.2	2,635	0.6	1,215	1.1
	Female	11,320	3.2	15,230	3.2	7,985	7.4
	Total	12,125	3.5	17,865	3.8	9,200	8.5

Source: Analysis of StatsCan (2023) Table 98-10-0591-01 (2021); note the category 'Nurses' also includes allied health

settings, including LTC. Most of those who are 55+ are women, making up 17.3 per cent of the nurse and allied health workforce. Canadian studies report that PSWs are an increasing share of workers working beyond the usual Canadian retirement age of 65 years (Armstrong and Laxer, 2006), even though it is usually men who work beyond the age of 65 in Canada. Likewise, most workers in 'assisting occupations', including PSWs, are women (85.9 per cent), and about one-fifth (22.2 per cent) of these workers are 55+, with older women workers making up 19.2 per cent and older men making up 2.9 per cent of the workforce for this group of workers. 'Home care provider occupations' are also mostly females (91.9 per cent), about one-third (31 per cent) of whom are 55+; of those workers, the vast majority are women (StatsCan, 2023). CIHI does not collect provincial administrative data about PSWs like it does for nurses. StatsCan labour force data categories make it impossible to disaggregate nurses and PSWs from other workers to discern a LTC workforce apart from other sites. This weak, hidden and noisy Canadian data seriously hampers LTC workforce planning. With noisy data, analysts are forced to make weak assumptions to assess workforce trends, and we know the least about what is likely the largest group within the health-care workforce, PSWs.

Like in Australia, the Canadian workforce is also highly gendered and increasingly racialised; however, the StatsCan groupings make 'race' analysis as challenging as 'age'. Looking at LTC, Lightman and Baay (2021) group LPNs, 'nurse aides', and 'orderlies and patient service associates', using 2016 Census microdata. Among their groupings, migrants are 36.8 per cent, and racialised members are 35.2 per cent. Lightman and Baay's groupings add some and miss other workers we include in our StatsCan analysis. Milan and Gagnon (2020) present 2016 Census microdata with categories that overlap those we present in this chapter. They indicate that 11.5 per cent of nurses, 15.7 per cent of 'assisting occupations in support of health services' and 10.5 per cent of 'home care providers and educational support occupations' workers are South Asian, Chinese or Black. Importantly, they show that there are more racialised workers who are younger than 55 among these groups in the care workforce. Proportionally fewer female nurses are 55 and older and either black (19 per cent), Chinese (15 per cent) or South Asian (9 per cent). In contrast, all other groups of female nurses aged 55 and older make up 21 per cent of the workforce. We have already noted that it is impossible to discern the workers who work only with older adults in residential LTC and home care settings using public use data. Owing to StatsCan data limitations related to locating LTC within the larger workforce, no studies provide sufficient analysis of Canadian care workers' 'age' and 'race' and this remains an important area for further research and data clarity. Owing to data limitations, no studies provide detailed analysis of Canadian care workers' age and other characteristics at a population level, or specific to LTC.

Norway

Only some of Norway's care workforce data are publicly available, and unfortunately, data are most frequently found in secondary source reports. Examples of national publicly available workforce data are the educational background of LTC workers (Statistics Norway data), data on the gender of workers in LTC and home-based care (the PAI-registry, published by the Norwegian Association of Local and Regional Authorities, KS) and the share of part-time and full-time employment. However, these data are not disaggregated, so only report the whole health-care workforce (PAI, KS). Further, for the LTC workforce, the reporting is not timely, as it is only available when analysed in reports. Further, most data are not subject to public manipulation of the datasets. Notably, the local municipalities have excellent data on the care workforce, but it remains mostly hidden from public oversight. As a result, we consider the Norwegian care work data to be hidden and less useful for planning and public accountability than we consider optimal.

Both in Statistics Norway databases and the KS data (PAI-data), some datasets are made available for public manipulation. However, such data represents a sub-set of administrative data that could have been made available for public manipulation but is not. Some Norwegian LTC national data covers both public and private (non-profit and for-profit) services and is reported by FaFo, an independent Norwegian social science research foundation originally established and funded by the major Norwegian peak union called LO or the Norwegian Confederation of Trade Unions. FaFo is committed to labour market research and publishes reports on the Norwegian labour market situation and working conditions, including for workers in the care sector. According to this data, the number of employees in LTC, both home and residential, increased from ~170,000 (2010) to 197,000+ (2019) (Midtsundstad and Nielsen, 2021); the number of older workers increased from 60,000 to 67,000, but older workers' overall share of the total Norwegian workforce declined slightly from 35.3 per cent to 34 per cent.

Norwegian care services are delivered locally, and municipal (public sector) work is a major part of it. The municipal work is captured in KOSTRA (KOmmune-STat-RApportering); the functional and sub-service codes for LTC are included in the 'care services' (codes: 234, 253, 254, 261), specifically home including day care centers (234, 254), and institution-based services (253) and municipal health and care services (261). These care work data categories do not suffer from the challenge of double counting like the Australian case, but these data are noisy, like Canadian data, due to not separating out care provided to older adults and lumping together public sector workers who are working across different sites of care. Further, distinguishing care for older adults as a category is impossible. Using the 'site' of care, but not the client population, makes it difficult to discern the total number of workers providing care services for older adults. Furthermore, statistics group together LTC homes and day programs workers, since municipal health and care services, where most care workers are employed, bundle workers into 'home-based' and 'institution-based' categories. Moreover, home-based services include outreach services in which health and care services personnel meet people in their homes for many reasons, whether within municipal housing or other locations. The institution-based services category captures the largest group of workers, including those working in nursing homes, in municipal acute inpatient units, and in 24-hour staffed housing used by different groups who have extensive care needs.

The Norwegian Helsedirektoratet (Health Directorate) reports that 'care services' collectively have 146,059 'man-years' or full-time equivalents (FTEs). This accounts for 86.9 per cent of all fulltime equivalents (FTEs) in the broad

Table 5.6: All Norwegian municipal care services 2016–20, by FTE and total employees

Category	Roles	n	2016	2017	2018	2019	2020	% change 2016–20	% change 2019–20
Nurse	Nurse without further education	FTE	25,204	26,240	26,546	27,347	27,636	9.7	1.1
		Total	29,206	30,155	30,235	30,890	30,988	6.1	0.3
	Nurse with further education (*)	FTE	4,389	4,533	4,690	4,778	4,771	8.7	−0.2
		Total	4,909	5,048	5,214	5,290	5,256	7.1	−0.6
	Health worker, auxiliary nurse, care worker	FTE	45,879	46,927	47,070	48,392	48,854	6.5	1.0
		Total	61,356	62,201	61,949	62,554	62,663	2.1	0.2
Care assistant	Nursing assistant/ nursing assistant without other health education	FTE	3,891	4,321	5,036	5,410	5,651	45.2	4.4
		Total	6,809	7,400	8,275	8,586	8,985	32.0	4.6

Source: Analysis of Helsedirektoratet (2021); (*) includes midwives and health-care providers

category of 'municipal health and care services'; this percentage excludes psychologists, doctors, and physiotherapists employed by municipalities (Helsedirektoratet, 2021). As Table 5.6 shows, among nursing aide/nursing assistants who possess other health education there has been a significant FTE growth of 45.2 per cent from 2016 to 2020 with 1,760 new FTEs, or 2,176 employees. Of this increase, nearly half (46 per cent, n = 1,001) were immigrants. Only the main employment condition is counted in the data, to avoid double-counting; however, this means that if someone has a main job outside of the municipality, and secondary employment in it, they are not even counted as employed. This raises questions about whether some part-time workers who consider another job their main one are missed.

Across home and institutional settings, comparing the data reported for 2019 between FaFo (~197,000) and Helsedirektoratet (n = 146,059), 74.1 per cent (n = 107,320) care services workers are public sector employees, with the remaining 26.9 per cent (n = 50,941) employed in mostly non-profit and some for-profit providers. While job titles are used relatively consistently across different data sources in Norway, the limited factors collected and reported reflect a government oversight regime that is less strict and extensive, with lower reporting demands for service providers than in many other jurisdictions (Choiniere et al, 2016). This relatively lenient system of oversight – leading to a dearth of administrative data on both staff and service users – may reflect an overall relatively high level of trust in Norwegian society, including mutual trust between the government and service providers (Jacobsen and Ågotnes, 2019), with an interpretive rather than a restrictive approach to regulation (Choiniere et al, 2016; Daly et al, 2016). Moreover, data reported about workers are categorised in different ways in different data registries, where for example, residential LTC can include a broad range of institutions (albeit residential LTC homes are the majority), and where home-based care services and residential long-term care services are frequently lumped together. Usefully, the Helsedirektoratet (2021) disaggregates home care and institution-based workers, but as noted, these categories aggregate many 'sites' of care.

As Table 5.7 shows, among 'home care' workers there was significant growth in the labour force between 2016 and 2020 of 12.6 per cent to 51.2 per cent across all roles; the highest growth occurred with 'nursing assistants without other health education', and may reflect efforts to increase the number of men working in care, as nearly half of the men working in municipal and care services (49 per cent) lack health and social work education (Helsedirektoratet, 2021). It also could reflect the growth in the proportion of immigrants, as described further on. Unfortunately, without refined data or the capacity to independently manipulate it, it is not possible to assess. Consequently, these trends remain hidden from independent scrutiny.

Table 5.7: All Norwegian municipal home care workers (2016–20), by FTE

Category	Role	2016	2017	2018	2019	2020	% change 2016–20	% change 2019–20
Nurse	Nurse *without* further education	11,519	12,141	12,639	13,123	13,517	17.3	3.0
	Nurse with further education (*)	2,222	2,380	2,501	2,588	2,656	19.6	2.6
	Health worker, auxiliary nurse, care worker	23,804	24,782	25,399	26,168	26,802	12.6	2.4
Care assistant	Nursing assistant/nursing assistant *without* other health education	2,200	2,472	2,930	3,205	3,325	51.2	3.8

Source: Analysis of Helsedirektoratet (2021); (*) includes midwives and health-care providers

Table 5.8: All Norwegian municipal institution-based care workers (2016–20), by FTE

Category	Role	2016	2017	2018	2019	2020	% change 2016–20	% change 2019–20
Nurse	Nurse *without* further education	13,685	14,099	13,906	14,225	14,119	3.2	−0.7
	Nurse with further education (*)	2,167	2,153	2,189	2,190	2,115	−2.4	−3.5
	Health worker, auxiliary nurse, care worker	22,075	22,145	21,672	22,224	22,052	−0.1	−0.8
Care assistant	Nursing assistant/ nursing assistant without other health education	1,692	1,849	2,106	2,205	2,326	37.5	5.5

Source: Analysis of Helsedirektoratet (2021); (*) includes midwives and health-care providers

Growth in institution-based care employment occurred for groups without additional education (Table 5.8). Within the 'nursing assistant' category, this may reflect better staff-to-resident ratios to produce decent working conditions or represent de-skilling, created by hiring more workers who have fewer qualifications to complete some of the work. It may also suggest that some types of institutions are moving towards more of a social care model, in comparison with an emphasis on health professional qualifications. Again, without more refined data, no additional trend analysis is possible.

The publicly available Norwegian data make it impossible to understand how the age of the workforce has shifted since 2020. The FaFo report shows that there is an increasing share of older people who remain working in LTC until they leave the labour market for retirement. Of concern, they indicate that almost one-quarter of 50-year-old RNs were expected to retire before turning 62 years old, compared to 20 per cent of care workers holding less education (Midtsundstad and Nielsen, 2021). Overall, there has been a notable decline in early retirements, but it continues to happen more among RNs than among care workers with less formal education. Although ill-health and physically demanding work seem to be the main reasons for leaving work in the care services ahead of the mandatory pension age of 67, only 7 per cent of workers surveyed reported that inadequate working conditions influenced their decision to leave (Midtsundstad and Nielsen, 2021). Regulatory bodies, such as the *Norwegian Directorate of Health* and the *Norwegian Board of Health Supervision*, oversee the licensing, quality assurance, and monitoring of residential LTC providers to ensure compliance with established standards (Helsedirektoratet, 2021). The share of LTC workers for every 100 people aged 65+ in 2021 is 12.0 per cent in Norway compared with Australia (7.3), Canada (3.8) and an OECD (2020) average of 5.7 per cent (OECD, 2020), which may be an indicator of relatively better working conditions for LTC workers in Norway or reflect the older age of national retirement of 67. Another government report shows the share of LTC workers 55+ has not changed much, from 31.1 per cent (2016) to 31 per cent (2020) (Helsedirektoratet, 2021). For instance, as Table 5.9 shows, across municipal health and care services, double the percentage of nurses with more education are 55+ (36.4 per cent) than those without it (18.3 per cent) in 2020. The former group excludes midwives and health-care providers, although what this means is unexplained. The age of those in assisting roles are not reported. What has happened since the pandemic remains unreported in 2025, adding to the invisibility faced by this workforce, especially for older workers, as we note in Chapter 8.

Like the other countries, in Norway, care work is highly gendered. The proportion of women is high, although it has declined somewhat from 89 per cent in 2010 to 85 per cent by 2019 (Midtsundstad and Nielsen, 2021). Owing to special initiatives to increase the number of men in health care, analysis of data from Statistics Norway about municipal health and care services show that by 2020 there was a slight growth of 7.5 per cent of men in LTC nursing and 9.2 per cent of men in care work occupations (Helsedirektoratet, 2021).

Table 5.9: Proportion aged 55+, by job category and number of Norwegian employees, of all employees in municipal health and care services (2016–20)

Category	Role		2016	2017	2018	2019	2020	Change in %	
								2016–20	2019–20
Nurse	Nurse *without* further education	%	17.5	17.7	17.8	18.0	18.3	0.8	0.3
		n	5,787	6,044	6,162	6,345	6,533	12.9	3.0
	Nurse with further education (*)	%	34.8	35.0	35.1	36.1	36.4	1.6	0.3
		n	2,076	2,180	2,273	2,385	2,441	17.6	2.3
	Health worker, auxiliary nurse, care worker	%	34.8	34.8	34.8	34.5	33.7	–1.0	–0.8
		n	21,848	22,113	22,058	22,101	21,668	–0.8	–2.0
Care assistant	Nursing assistant/ nursing assistant *without* other health education				Unreported				

Source: Analysis of Helsedirektoratet (2021); (*) excludes midwives and health-care providers

Table 5.10: Share and number of employees with an immigration background in municipal health and care services (2016–20)

Category	Role		2016	2017	2018	2019	2020	Change in % 2016-20	Change in % 2019-20
Nurse	Nurse *without further education*	%	16.2	16.5	16.2	16.8	17.0	0.8	0.2
		n	5,353	5,649	5,613	5,924	6,043	−12.9	−2.0
	Nurse with further education (*)	%	5.9	5.9	6.1	6.3	6.4	0.6	0.2
		n	350	368	393	415	432	−23.4	−4.1
	Health worker, auxiliary nurse, care worker	%	16.2	17.6	17.8	19.3	20.7	4.5	1.4.
		n	10,178	11,168	11,326	12,338	13,274	−30.4	−7.6
Care assistant	Nursing assistant/ nursing assistant *without other health education*	%	21.9	22.3	24.6	24.7	26.4	4.5	1.7
		n	1,723	1,885	2,323	2,420	2,724	−58.1	−12.6

Source: Analysis of Helsedirektoratet (2021); (*) excludes midwives and health-care providers

Care workers in Norway are largely Norwegian-born, although an increasing number are migrants, defined as being born abroad to two non-Norwegian parents. The figure for the share of migrant workers was 18.1 per cent in 2020 (Helsedirektoratet, 2021), but as Table 5.10 shows, the proportion of migrant workers in the LTC sector has increased from 15.7 per cent in 2016 to 18.1 per cent in 2020 (Helsedirektoratet, 2021).

Conclusion

Care work datasets in Australia, Canada and Norway must be fixed to address gendered data bias, improve the accountability of governments' public stewardship role in LTC, and increase the visibility of care work. Analysis of the datasets, though beset by the problems outlined, show that this is highly gendered work, and confirm that the care workforce, especially in home care, is ageing. This significant age and gender stratification across the care workforce reinforces the need to plan with ageing, gendered ageing, and increasingly with gendered and racialised ageing in mind, to prevent poor outcomes for all care workers, including older workers, and to ensure that there is sufficient future capacity in the care workforce across each of the countries examined.

If, as McLuhan (1965) argues, the medium is indeed the message, then the 'muddle' in the care work data speaks volumes about the silences shrouding care work. It also confirms that Criado Perez's (2019) claims about 'gender bias' in *unpaid* care can be extended to the *paid* care workforce. Whether deliberate or as an unintended consequence of poor systems, most certainly, the muddle makes workforce planning extremely difficult and calls public stewardship of publicly funded care into question. Furthermore, these muddled data raise serious doubts about any OECD reports that claim to describe the care workforce comparatively. As McCoy and Ysseldyk delineate, regarding older adults in Chapter 3 of this volume, data gaps such as those about the paid care workforce present barriers to understanding and advancing age equity. Reliable, accessible data collection on the care labour force is required to plan for and ensure care security for older adults and decent work for care workers so they can provide quality care and enjoy good working and retiring conditions in later life. Based on our analysis, we can only make broad generalisations about care workers caring for older adults in Canada and Norway. While we can more accurately identify those working in aged care in Australia, we are nonetheless hampered by data contradictions between Census and AIHW datasets. In all countries, the data suffer from inexcusable weaknesses and noise. Australia does a better job of reporting publicly, though the other attributes call these data into question.

In summary, given the lack of disaggregation in Canada and Norway, and the lack of timely reporting in Norway, we can only report on some broad trends. As Table 5.11 shows, a higher proportion of women work in care in Canada (85.9–92 per cent), while more men work in care in Australia and Norway where the rates of female care workers are 85–87.3 per cent and 85 per cent respectively. More than triple the total number of nurses are directly employed in residential LTC in Australia (~188,332) compared with Canada (~48,278) in 2023. In Norway (2020), 36,244 nurses were working in care work in the public municipal sector.

Table 5.11: Summary of care workforce characteristics

	Australia (%)	Canada (%)	Norway (%)
Sex (female)	85–87.3	~85.9–92	85
Nurses 55+	16.4–25.6 (**)	~18.8 (*)	31 (***)
Assisting occupations 55+	16.0–32.5 (**)	~22.2–31.0	Unreported
Migrants as % of care workforce	51	~38.6 (*****)	18.1 (***)

Source: Analysis of: Helsedirektoratet (2021); StatsCan (2023) Table 98-10-0591-01 (2021) Analysis of Aged Care Provider Workforce Survey, AIHW (2024); unknown responses excluded. (*) includes nurses + allied health professionals, working across all institutional health sites; (**) includes residential and home care but only for aged care sites; (***) includes municipal workers across institutional and home care sites; (****) includes all health-care sites; (*****) Lightman and Baay (2021).

The care sector workforce is ageing, but in various ways. In Australia, 16.4 per cent of RAC nurses are 55+, with fewer older RNs, but there is a larger proportion of older ENs and NPs. In HCPP, an estimated 25.6 per cent of nurses are older, which includes more than one-third (32.5 per cent) of ENs who are older. Among PCWs, an estimated 16 per cent in RAC and 32.5 per cent in HCPP are 55 and older, showing big discrepancies in the age profiles between RAC and home care. Similar broad patterns show up in Canada, but the data are too noisy to get an accurate picture: among a broad swath of workers (nurses, PSWs and other health and home workers across hospital, LTC and community settings) 18.8 per cent of all nursing and 31 per cent of 'assisting' and 'home care provider' occupations are filled by those who are 55+ years and older. Norwegian nurses in municipal work appear to have the oldest workforce, with 'older workers' making up 24.3 per cent of the public sector care workforce in Norway, overall. More refined data are needed to understand what this looks like between residential and home care settings, and among different groups of care workers.

Across each of the jurisdictions, data discrepancies, lapses and gaps are significant, producing outcomes of collective invisibility of LTC workers, and super-invisibility for older LTC workers, as we document in Chapter 8. These outcomes raise urgent questions about workforce retention and recruitment strategies. Further, weak, 'noisy' and/or hidden data produce poor system-level and organisational workforce planning relative to an ageing population's needs. This muddle hampers possibilities to compare within and between jurisdictions so that promising practices can be identified, and problems can be confronted or avoided. When combined with poor working conditions, discrepancies can also result in a mismatch between recruitment over retention. Furthermore, in the overarching contexts of AI and population ageing, knowing the characteristics of paid care workers, including when workers are leaving the sector, is crucial, as a lack of paid care for older adults places pressure on all other parts of the health and social care systems, as well as threatening the labour market participation of women more generally, who bear the greatest burden of unpaid care.

To conclude, ageing equitably with care requires attention to the care services on which older adults depend, and the workers who provide these services, both paid and unpaid. Further, age equity means that the health and well-being of older adults does not come at the expense of poor health outcomes for care workers. To ensure older adults have the care they need, and workers experience decent work, LTC workforce planning is necessary but is hampered by data problems across and within jurisdictions. Further, as governments fund and regulate these services, public data reporting is important in ensuring public accountability and public stewardship. As governments fund the LTC services in all three countries, but are normally not delivering care, governments can compel this information from providers to submit their data for public scrutiny. As Stone (2000: 89) notes, '[m]uch caring is now "produced" by organisations that manage workforces, clienteles, and the "delivery" of care. In these organisations, care is measured, allocated, and monitored by accounting systems, which fragment it into countable components'. Daly (2019) concurs: public funds for care should not result in data that remain private.

References

Armstrong, P. and Laxer, K. (2006) Precarious work, privatization, and the health-care industry: the case of ancillary workers, in L.F. Vosko (ed) *Precarious Employment: Understanding Labour Market Insecurity in Canada*, McGill-Queen's University Press.

Australian Bureau of Statistics (ABS) (2022) Census of Population and Housing 2021, Table Builder ANZSCO Industry (4 digit): Aged Care Residential Services Analysis by ABS for the Aged Care Work Value Case [online], Available from: https://www.fwc.gov.au/hearings-decisions/major-cases/work-value-case-aged-care-industry/research-and-information-work

Australian Institute of Health and Welfare (AIHW) (2024) 2023 Aged Care Provider Workforce Survey Summary Report: August 2024 [online], Available from: https://www.gen-agedcaredata.gov.au/resources/publications/2024/august/2023-aged-care-provider-workforce-survey

Baines, D., Charlesworth, S. and Daly, T. (2016) Underpaid, unpaid, unseen, unheard, and unhappy? Care work in the context of constraint, *Journal of Industrial Relations*, 58(4): 449–54.

Canadian Institute for Health Information (CIHI) (2023) *Recommendations for Advancing pan-Canadian Data Capture for Personal Support Workers*, CIHI.

Canadian Institute for Health Information (CIHI) (2024) Supply and Distribution [online], Available from: https://www.cihi.ca/en/the-state-of-the-health-workforce-in-canada-2022/supply-and-distribution

Charlesworth, S. and Isherwood, L. (2021) Migrant aged-care workers in Australia: do they have poorer-quality jobs than their locally born counterparts?, *Ageing & Society*, 41(12): 2702–22.

Charlesworth, S., Cunningham, I. and Daly, T. (2024) *Decent Work and Quality Long-term Care Systems*, Independent report, Public Services International [online], Available from: https://publicservices.international/resources/digital-publication/decent-work-and-quality-long-term-care-systems?id=14383&lang=en

Choiniere, J., Doupe, M., Goldmann, M., Harrington, C., Jacobsen, F.F., Lloyd, L. et al (2016) Mapping nursing home inspections and audits in six countries, *Ageing International*, 41(1): 40–61.

Criado Perez, C. (2019) *Invisible Women: Exposing Data Bias in a World Designed for Men*, Abrams.

Daly, T. (2019) Public funds, private data: a Canadian example, in *The Privatization of Care: The Case of Nursing Homes*, Routledge, pp 1–16.

Daly, T. and Armstrong, P. (2016) Liminal and invisible long-term care labour: precarity in the face of austerity, *Journal of Industrial Relations*, 58(4): 473–90.

Daly, T., Armstrong, P. and Lowndes, R. (2015) Liminality in Ontario's long-term care facilities: private companions' care work in the space 'betwixt and between', *Competition & Change*, 19(3): 246–63.

Daly, T., Struthers, J., Müller, B., Taylor, D., Goldmann, M., Doupe, M. et al (2016) Prescriptive or interpretive regulation at the frontlines of care work in the 'three worlds' of Canada, Germany, and Norway, *Labour-Le Travail*, 77(77): 37–71.

Government of Canada (nd) National Occupational Classification Hierarchy and Structure [online], Available from: https://noc.esdc.gc.ca/Structure/Hierarchy?objectid=%2Fd0IGA6qD8JPRfoj5UCjpg%3D%3D

Helsedirektoratet [Norwegian Health Directorate] (2021) Personell og Kompetanse i den Kommunale helse- og Omsorgstjenesten [Staff and Expertise in the Municipal Health and Care Services] [online], Available from: https://www-helsedirektoratet-no.translate.goog/rapporter/personell-og-kompetanse-i-den-kommunale-helse-og-omsorgstjenesten?_x_tr_sl=no&_x_tr_tl=en&_x_tr_hl=en-US&_x_tr_pto=wapp

Jacobsen, F. and Ågotnes, G. (2019) Accountable for-profits in nursing home services, in P. Armstrong and H. Armstrong (eds) *The Privatization of Care*, Routledge.

Lightman, N. and Baay, C. (2021) Will COVID-19 finally force us to address the devaluation of long-term care workers?, *Policy Options*, Institute for Research on Public Policy [online], Available from: https://policyoptions.irpp.org/magazines/march-2021/will-covid-19-finally-force-us-to-address-the-devaluation-of-long-term-care-workers/

Mavromaras, K., Knight, G., Isherwood, L., Crettenden, A., Flavel, J., Karmel, T., Moskos, M., Smith, L., Walton, H. and Wei, Z. (2017) *The Aged Care Workforce 2016*, Department of Health.

McLuhan, M. (1965) *Understanding Media: The Extensions of Man*, McGraw-Hill.

Midtsundstad, T. and Nielsen, R. (2021) *Det erfarne blicket Seniorer I plei- og omsorgssektoren* (The experienced perspective Seniors in the care sector), FAFO [online], Available from: https://lengrearbeidsliv.no/kunnskap/forskning-og-utvikling/det-erfarne-blikket/

Milan, A. and Gagnon, V. (2020) *Labour Statistics Research Papers: Occupations of South Asian, Chinese, and Black Women: Prevalence and Age Composition*, Statistics Canada [online], Available from: https://www150.statcan.gc.ca/n1/pub/75-004-m/75-004-m2020002-eng.htm

OECD (2020) *Who Cares? Attracting and Retaining Care Workers for the Elderly*, OECD Publishing [online], Available from: https://doi.org/10.1787/92c0ef68-en

StatsCan (Statistics Canada) (2023) Class of Worker Including Job Permanency by Occupation Minor Group, Labour Force Status, Age and Gender: Canada, Provinces, and Territories and Census Divisions [online], Available from: https://www150.statcan.gc.ca/t1/tbl1/en/tv.action?pid=9810059101

Stone, D. (2000) Caring by the book, in H.M. Meyer (ed) *Care Work: Gender, Labour and the Welfare State*, Routledge.

Zuboff, S. (2019) *The Age of Surveillance Capitalism: The Fight For the Future at The New Frontier of Power*, Profile Books.

6

Ageing, intersectionality, social location and identity

Donna Baines and Renate Ysseldyk

Introduction

In this era of reconciliation with Indigenous peoples and decolonisation, Black Lives Matter (#BLM), and the deep inequities surfaced by the global COVID-19 pandemic, alliances between and among groups that experience systemic racism and other forms of inequity have multiplied and generated new inclusive terminology including BIPOC (Black, Indigenous and People of Colour). These alliances and struggles are necessarily intersectional, with a variety of marginalised and oppressed people finding increased traction by collaborating in the activism and demands of other groups. However, for the most part, age and ageism have not been central to the current surge in anti-racist activism or the intersectional debate. At the level of activism and everyday life, intersectionality is a lived experience of overlapping social locations and identities; at the level of theory and research, intersectionality is complicated and somewhat limited as it evolves to meet the demands of various contexts and populations, including in analyses of ageing and age-friendly communities.

In this chapter, two scholars with different approaches to identity and social location focus on age as first, a social location/identity and second, as a set of social relations that shape life opportunities and choices in interaction with race/ethnicity, religion, gender, class, (dis)ability and more. Reflecting the perspective of a social psychologist, some of the literature and arguments presented reflect the tenets of this tradition and its focus on identity. Reflecting the perspective of social work, some of the literature and arguments reflect a critical, anti-oppressive theory approach to social relations and social location. Sometimes presenting the literature separately but always presenting the analysis jointly, the chapter contributes to intersectional theorising on age and argues that critical reflection and other intersectional-competent skills are required to meet the challenges facing those living and working in diverse urban contexts.

This chapter views ageing as a site of innovation and struggle in the city and seeks analytic tools and theoretical practices that can contribute to efforts for equitable social care and social justice. The analysis also engages with the tensions in social understandings of ageing and the complexity with which ageing intersects with other identities. We propose that a melding of apparently dissonant concepts such as identity and social location is useful for understanding the intersections that form the backdrop for struggles of diverse older people for age-friendly social fairness and equity. The chapter asks, first, what is an intersectional, age-friendly analysis and second, how are critical reflection and other intersectional-competent skills useful in understanding age-friendliness and mobilising anti-oppressive change?

This chapter first analyses selected literature on intersectionality, social location and identity. Next, drawing on examples found in our field notes from our various studies involving older people, the chapter moves on to a brief discussion of how these concepts are useful in understanding equitable and diverse age-friendly cities. We identify analytic tools that highlight intersectional dynamics and may provide insights for activists, practitioners and researchers. The chapter then argues that more equitable, age-friendly outcomes require skills such as activism, advocacy, social analysis, community organising and mobilisation, and policy critique/development that supports those seeking to be allies and activists in the contemporary intersectional struggles facing humankind. Finally, we reflect on some of the pressing social issues and dynamics that intersect with ageing in our times.

A brief review: intersectional literature

Black feminists have long worked to theorise the diversity within singular social categories, such as 'women', and to explore the lived experiences, multiple and mixed identities and social relations shaping people's lives, including in Sojourner Truth's famous 1851 suffragist address, 'Ain't I a Woman?' (Davis, 1981; Hartmann and Sargent, 1981). Drawing on the work of the Combahee River Collective (1977) statement, in 1989, African American legal scholar Kimberlé Crenshaw (1989) is credited with coining the term 'intersectional' to capture the multiple axes of identity and inequity that shape the experiences of Black women in contact with the law. Crenshaw (1991) argued that single-strand theories of discrimination failed to account for multiple forms of inequity that 'relegated the identity of women of color to a location that resists telling' (p 1242). The term, intersectionality, quickly found resonance across many disciplines, particularly among those seeking to understand the overlapping and mutually reinforcing social forces generating subordination and dominance, oppression and privilege, opportunities and inequities.

Reflecting the various strands of academic feminism, intersectional theorising was soon influenced by postmodernism and post-structuralism and emphasised diffuse, fluid and manifold identities (Dhamoon, 2011;

Cho et al, 2013). More materialist approaches such as feminist political economy (FPE) (Armstrong, 2013) and anti-oppressive theory (Hulko, 2009; Baines, 2017; Parada and Wehbi, 2017) emphasised the many connections between larger social structures, and the political and embodied, every day social location and experience (Baines, 2017; Braedley, 2019; Collins, 2020; Collins and Bilge, 2020). This theorising aims to inform the scholarly purposes of theory and analysis, as well as concrete social change efforts and social justice activism. For example, in addition to many articles and books, intersectionality was also central to mobilising diverse groups of women and allies for the women's marches that followed in the wake of Donald Trump's first presidential inauguration in January 2017 and subsequent mass women's marches worldwide (Desmond-Harris, 2017).

Though many theorists recognise the closely aligned dynamics of dominance and subordination (Amiot and Bourhis, 2010; Levine-Rasky, 2011), intersectional theory has largely focused on the experiences of those oppressed and disadvantaged (Collins, 2020). These analyses frequently draw on Young's (1990) argument that there are five faces of oppression that cannot be reduced to redistributive (economic) injustice: exploitation, marginalisation, powerlessness, cultural domination and violence. She argues further that oppression refers to:

> the vast and deep injustices some groups suffer as a consequence of often unconscious assumptions and reactions of well-meaning people in ordinary interactions, media, and cultural stereotypes, and structural features of bureaucratic hierarchies and market mechanisms – in short, the normal processes of everyday life. (Young, 1990: 21)

Often influenced by Young, more materialist intersectional analyses emphasise the links between structural forces and everyday experience. As Braedley (2019: 305) argues:

> [r]ather than beginning with concerns about identity and related inequalities, feminist political economy ... traces the connections between and among relations of domination and oppression, including the dynamics of global capitalism, to reveal how these relations penetrate our most intimate, daily lives ... how peoples' different problems and struggles for emancipation around the world are connected.

Perhaps due to its especially fluid nature, age is rarely analysed as a privileged or powerful identity, however, it is also often ignored as an axis of oppression and discrimination. In terms of a psychological use of the concept of identity, an ageing identity is also often understood in contradictory terms (Biggs, 2003) – as the accumulation of one's personal subjective experiences in contrast to the social portrayal of older adults as 'a strange and utterly problematic species ... needing care' (Baars, 2012: 3). This can give rise to what has been termed 'compassionate ageism', or a patronising perspective on older people as exclusively in need of care and often burdensome (Baars, 2012: 4). In this way, ageing can be interpreted simultaneously in terms of cumulative advantage, for example, of life experiences and wisdom (Baars, 2012), and disadvantage, including, for example, physical deterioration and ageism (Barrett and Gumber, 2020; Mikton et al, 2021) as both personal and social understandings of the self collide (Biggs, 2003). Moreover, fluid and dynamic identities also apply when it is considered that the categories of gender, race, class or age alone do not shape the positionality and experience of older people but rather exist as 'gendered ageism' (Moore, 2009: 656) and the like, which differentially shape the life experiences of people living with multiple social locations/identities.

Individual-based and singular analyses of identity

Identity is a contested concept, with some disciplines adopting individual-based formulations and defining identity as something that 'relates to awareness of self, self-image, self-reflection and self-esteem ... a quality that enables the expression of the individual's authentic sense of self' (Shields, 2008: 301). In this regard, identity is largely defined as personal, referring to that which determines one's uniqueness as an individual and differentiates one from others (Turner et al, 1994; Olson, 2019). Although this conceptualisation of identity has some utility in understanding the individual as an introspective entity, identity is also understood as collective, providing support for material and epistemic needs alike (see Mavor and Ysseldyk, 2020 for an example of the dual nature of religious identity).

Some understandings of identity include an intersectional analysis of personal identity as inherently social – that is, as a 'relational concept that links an individual to the social world' (Byrd, 2014: 516) and therefore the 'pivot between the individual and society' (Reicher et al, 2010: 45). Similarly, social psychologists often acknowledge the dynamics of power and status across social groups (an example is Sidanius et al, 2016). However, the influences of early research in the social identity tradition, including the 'minimal group paradigm', which demonstrated the minimal and arbitrary conditions under which people are inclined to display ingroup favouritism and outgroup discrimination (Tajfel, 1970; Tajfel and Turner, 1979), are evident in work that seeks to generalise from one social identity to others or homogenises all members of a particular identity group. Instead, the meaning and content of each identity must be explicitly recognised (Livingstone and Haslam, 2008; Ysseldyk et al, 2010; Ysseldyk et al, 2014).

Finally, even while considering the uniqueness, centrality and/or salience of social categories (see for example, Settles, 2004; Kachanoff et al, 2016; Wang and Dovidio, 2016), some conceptualisations of social identity fail to acknowledge the co-existence and/or interplay among identities, often formulated as social identity complexity, diversity or compatibility (see the now classic Roccas and Brewer, 2002; Byrd, 2014; Sønderlund et al, 2017). Moreover, still others fail to account for broader social structures of advantage/disadvantage, and privilege/oppression in which identities are embedded. As Byrd (2014: 516) notes, 'intersectionality can be a complex and messy concept'. Nonetheless, when considering the inevitable interactions among the multiple identities from which our overarching social positions are derived, 'intersectionality as a framework is fruitful, in that it troubles tendencies to essentialise identities and troubles the assumptions that experiences can be generalised across identities' (Warner and Sheilds, 2013: 807).

Alternatives to individually-based, singular analyses of identity

Critiquing the individualistic framing of identity as essentialist and limiting, intersectional analyses tend to view identities as features of the self in relation to other people, social structures and power relations. This conglomerate of interwoven and hierarchical social relations is frequently referred to as social location, social positionality, subject position, subject formation, social groups or categories of difference (Naples, 2009; Anthias, 2013; Hopkins, 2019; Collins, 2020). More materialist analyses such as FPE explore the interplay of 'social locations' to understand individuals' social positioning within interlocking systemic inequities at the level of social structures and institutions, as well as within the multiplicity of social, historical and cultural discourses (Azzopardi, 2020). Influenced by postmodern notions of fluidity and multiple perspectives (Mullaly and West, 2018; Almeida et al, 2019), social location is theorised to operate as an imagined space in which various social relations, social categories and social forces come together to shape the expression and experience of a person within the social fabric (Baines, 2017; Almeida et al, 2019). Thus, social location in anti-oppressive and FPE theory is a relational, contextual concept that views social categories or identities as complex and frequently contradictory as well as elected and emergent in relation to power. In other words, we have some agency in what social categories we embody and identify with, though long-term patterns of injustice also exist beyond our identities. As Levine-Rasky (2011: 245) notes, the 'problem is not who has power but how power is practiced so as to effect political and social advantage/disadvantage'. We attempt to highlight contradictory social positioning in relation to power in the examples discussed further on.

Intersectionality theory and the concept of social location (and identity) have been critiqued as determinist and additive – that is, axes of identity are simply added to each other generating a sum total of oppressions rather than an interactive, conflictual and complex web of sometimes contesting, sometimes amalgamating and sometimes disparate expressions of power and oppression (Sønderlund et al, 2017). To avoid rigid formulations, Naples (2009: 569) cites McCall (2001: 6) who uses the construct, 'configurations of inequality' to highlight the frequent and varying intersections between race, class, age and gender depending on underlying economic conditions. To further avoid determinism, Naples (2009: 574) also cites Grewal and Kaplan (1994) who use the term 'scattered hegemonies' to analyse the complex processes, relationships and structural conditions that shape everyday life, relations of ruling and the resistance strategies of diverse actors.

Further intersectional analysis and theory drawing on field note examples

The following section extends our intersectional analysis by drawing on examples from the authors' research projects in Australia and Canada to highlight the complicated interplay between social and individual aspects of power, identity and social location and how they interlink with ageing in webs of privilege and oppression.

> Linnea is a well-respected, two-spirited, Indigenous Executive Director of a major First Nations community agency in Canada. She is well past retirement age but continues to enjoy her work and is widely regarded as very effective. Standing at the bus stop one dark, winter evening after a Board meeting, some young men yell sexist and anti-Indigenous insults at her as they speed by in their car. One young man hurls his disposable coffee cup out the window at her and though she dodges it, coffee sprays over her legs, instantly chilling her legs in the cold night air. Linnea is shaken and suddenly feels alone, vulnerable, and furious.

In this vignette, Linnea has power and experiences respect and satisfaction as an older, two-spirited, female Executive Director in one space in her life, and faces oppression and the jeopardy of anti-Indigenous racism, misogyny and ageism in another related space. Linnea has not changed herself or her identity in either situation; however, at the bus stop she is socially located as victimisable within racist, anti-Indigenous, colonialist, gendered, ageist and cultural social systems of power. Peeling back the intersections of these aspects of identity/social location and power/oppression provides the opportunity to analyse the complex and scattered hegemonies (Grewal and Kaplan, 1994) of oppression and privilege shaping Linnea's experience of marginalisation and violence in one instance, and respect and empowerment in another. At work, the matrices of oppression and privilege (Collins, 2000) that form her identity/social location involve a configuration of power and advantage and she is respected as Indigenous, two-spirited, female and older. However, on the street right outside her office these same identities/social locations form a configuration of inequity (McCall, 2001: 6) and are understood by the young men in this scenario to justify oppression and violence.

As noted, intersectional analyses often draw on identities that are presented to be essentialist, rigid, additive, ahistorical and decontextualised. O'Connor et al (2010) assert that essentialising can be avoided within intersectionality by closely attending to the complex and contradictory dynamics inherent in inhabiting multiple identities/social locations and contexts simultaneously.

This entry in one of the author's fieldnotes highlights some of these fluid complexities:

> Gene has an advantage as an ageing, white person when applying for an apartment in a tight, urban rental market. However, it is essentialist and superficial to leave the analysis at this single-strand level as it is likely that Gene will be disadvantaged by their low income, advanced age and (dis)ability, and may experience explicit hatred as a transgendered person. However, if Gene applies to a queer housing co-op, the oppression relations that impacted them in the private market can be mitigated and they may move up the wait list based on income, age and (dis)ability.

As seen in the example, identities/social locations often hold different meanings and power positions in different contexts and cannot be understood in isolation of each other or the context. Advantage and disadvantage in this scenario are not merely additive, with Gene experiencing one big point of advantage as a white person and four small points of disadvantage as a low-income, very old, transgender person with (dis)abilities. In the context of the private real estate market, ageism, ableism and transphobia interlock to generate a matrix of disadvantage, while the queer housing co-op acts as a form of resistance to the private market and an alternate configuration of power by providing affirmative action along axes of identity/social location such as queerness, (dis)ability and age. An aspect of age-friendly cities, housing co-ops are often found in urban environments where diverse groups of people develop alternatives to the private housing market. In the case of the queer housing co-op, and many other social housing strategies, diverse groups of people come together to meet social needs in ways that actually take housing out of the private market and provide a power base for the intersectional logics of equity and social justice.

At the level of everyday experience, intersectionality can be seen to provide important insights to the operation of advantage and oppression in everyday life, and it can contribute positively to improved practice and analysis. However, at the level of theory, melding concepts from postmodernism and post-structuralism with materialist analyses, such as bringing together the concept of multiple, fluid identities with the concept of global social structures is ontologically and epistemologically unstable (Baines, 2017; Mullaly and West, 2018). That is, postmodernism and post-structuralism have a fluid and norm-eschewing epistemology, while materialism is normative and based on the knowing of oppressed groups. Analyses based on a materialist ontology are similarly grounded in the experience and knowledge of, and for, oppressed groups, while to guard against totalising discourse and practice, postmodernism and post-structuralism are based on fluid and impermanent ontologies. Despite this instability at the level of theory, at the level of practice and social activism, postmodern, post-structural and materialist concepts can be applied and blended in ways that capture the intricacy of global and local forces, cultures, norms and ideologies that shape the dimensions of oppression and domination (Baines, 2017; Azzopardi, 2020). As Fraser (1997) notes, the ultimate test of social justice theories is in social movements and struggles for social justice.

Age-friendly cities and conceptual tools for intersectional analyses

When considering age-friendly cities, the city can be thought of as an incubator for highly collective and socially responsible behaviour, as well as the opposite. Cities are complex environments in which virtuous practices thrive, often alongside or in opposition to more oppressive and harmful practices (Harvey, 2007). As Baines (2016: 78) notes, 'cities have often proven to be places that attract those in need of care and provide innovative solutions to many care needs'. This myriad of care services incorporates the diverse populations who comprise modern metropolises and reflect the complexity of global care chains (Sassen, 2012). As Moore (2009: 669) argues, age-friendly communities must take an intersectional approach to advocate for individuals who have been historically oppressed, even if such efforts 'cannot reverse the legacy of disadvantage accumulated over the life course'.

One such tool can be found in the use of intersectional analysis in conjunction with counter-storytelling or counter-narrative construction for social justice (Brown and MacDonald, 2020). O'Connor et al (2010) argue that an intersectional analysis is key to understanding the complexity of older people's lives and the ways that they talk about them. They assert that 'when social location and positioning is considered, alternative discourses – or storylines – for making sense of the experience emerge'

(37). Using an intersectional analysis to analyse the transcript of a lesbian, Indigenous woman with early onset dementia, O'Connor et al produce a nuanced and compelling account of a complex person seeking and making meaning in her life despite racialised, gendered, heteronormative and class-based obstructions and oppressions. Their analysis identifies ways to improve practice and support for diverse populations living with dementia and other aspects of ageing, and provides conceptual tools aimed at avoiding essentialism and determinism.

Critical reflexivity provides a second strong analytic tool that can be used in intersectional research, knowledge building and everyday activism and social change efforts. Ferguson (2018) argues that this involves reflecting by elevating one's mind above the interactions in which one is involved so that one can think critically about what they are doing and adjust. Though many professions and other groups undertake reflection on their practice and knowledge, critical reflection involves a focus on individual experience as well as on theory, power and the ways that larger social structures shape and delimit thought and possibilities for more socially just ways of being and thinking (Mattsson, 2014). As Fook and Gardner (2007) argue, imbalances of power between workers and service users arising from social class, gender, race, sexualities and (dis)ability need to be reflected upon, with unethical uses of power avoided and oppressive structures and relations challenged.

Morley (2013, 2014) explains further that critical reflection is a skill set that closely aligns the person undertaking critical reflection with the continuous and pressing need for systemic change by peeling back the layers of thought and practice that keep inequities in place. Critical reflection twins effectively with the multi-layered analysis integral to intersectional theory, as they both utilise a systematic analysis of lived experience, complex practices of power, and larger social structures. While critical reflection encourages a deep analysis of everyday life and its connections to larger social systems and structures, intersectional theory ensures that this critical reflection delineates not only the interweaving of identities/social locations that are integral to experience but also analyses the power, privilege, oppression and resistance inherent in the coming together of multiple social relations (Mattsson, 2014; Azzopardi, 2020).

The following field note illustrates some of the concepts already discussed:

> Ruthie lives in a nursing home in a large city. Though she is a child survivor of the Holocaust she has lived a non-religious life, nominally identifies as Jewish, and did not list this axis of identity on her nursing home application. As her dementia increases, she frequently speaks in Yiddish and ruminates about terrifying memories from her childhood. Unlike some of the other residents, Ruthie is of limited financial means and has no family to help pay for a private companion to provide her

with additional support and distraction from the pain of her memories. Ruthie becomes increasingly depressed and withdrawn. The nursing home staff are sympathetic but have heavy workloads and cannot spend enough time with Ruthie to address her suffering. A social work student guesses that Ruthie may be speaking Yiddish and suffering from long-term post-traumatic stress. She asks if she can refer her for trauma counselling. The nursing home does not have a budget for specialist counselling and refers her to the M.D. who has no skills in this area. The student advocates for Ruthie and finds a trauma-survivors community group that will support her and her depression eases.

In this scenario, the axes of age, class, gender, race, ethnicity and religion intersect to shape Ruthie's experience. In Nazi Poland, she was a victim of the Holocaust because of the social construction of Jewishness as a race that should be destroyed. Like many older women, Ruthie has limited finances and cannot afford a personal assistant to extend the care she receives in the nursing home. The nursing home is also at the crossroads of a highly classed social care system in which public and non-profit organisations struggle with constrained and inadequate funding and heavy workloads for care staff, who frequently cannot meet the all the needs of the residents. Ruthie's specific and complex social location makes her vulnerable in a system in which care is provided in a one-size fits all, standardised model. Fortunately, she lives in a big city where the social work student has been exposed to many cultures and languages and makes an educated guess that Ruthie may be speaking Yiddish and that she is about the right age to be a child survivor of the Holocaust. The convergence of skills and diverse people in the city also means that expertise exists in trauma counselling and support, and skilled volunteers are willing to provide care to those in need. Also, fortunately for Ruthie, as part of the conflux of organisations and systems in large cities, the nursing home accepts social work placement students and their student is resourceful and advocates for a lonely and depressed elder.

Other critical skills

Just as cities are incubators for social movements and actions aimed at expanding social justice and equity, cities can also be sites where age-friendly, intersectional services and social change efforts can be fostered and flourish. In light of BLM and other movements for social change and social justice, those committed to intersectional analyses need to build skills in advocacy, activism, social organising, community mobilisation and policy critique/development.

As part of these efforts, Fazzi (2015) argues that people of goodwill need to be well-educated in arguments against racism, right-wing populism and xenophobia, and in how to involve themselves in social change efforts and activism to defend and ally with those targeted by racism, violence and other forms of inequity. Social activism tends to be based on specific incidents or problems in specific communities and populations, which means that it is vulnerable to arguments that put local concerns ahead of international ones. Turtiainen (2017: 12) warns that this may unintentionally perpetuate xenophobic 'processes of othering, which can exclude those who do not fit into national ideals'. Intersectional approaches and ongoing critical reflection can help ensure that this public education and activism do not fall into new forms of oppression and social harm by keeping both the immediate crises and the bigger, global picture in mind.

The need for this balance has also strongly emerged through both the BLM movement and the crisis in long-term care that have overlapped and intersected with the COVID-19 pandemic (Fraser et al, 2020; Crooks et al, 2021), bringing to light the need to remedy long-standing inequities with both immediate and lasting implications at local and global levels. Indeed, the pandemic has exposed age inequities alongside those following racial, socio-economic and geographic lines, in which those who are already most vulnerable and oppressed have faced increased illness and death (Horton, 2020). Moreover, when these identities intersect (such as in the case of an older, ethnic minority woman with low socio-economic status), 'intersectional invisibility', or the perceived group non-prototypicality based on having multiple marginalised identities (Purdie-Vaughns and Eibach, 2008) can result. As BLM brought worldwide attention to ongoing police violence against Black and Indigenous people and other people of colour as well as other forms of systemic racism and inequity, and the ongoing COVID-19 pandemic surfaced inequities based on race, age and other aspects of social location, it is crucial that we develop and teach critically reflexive skills to engage with the complexity of people's experiences over their life spans. Indeed, along with the inherently changing nature of identity based on advancing age, 'all life courses are conditioned by the historical patterns of social change (patriarchy, imperialism, capitalism and chronologisation) which have differential impacts on different groups ... the "life course" links all these forms of inequality' (Moore, 2009: 660).

Though these skills may seem challenging and unfamiliar, like other skills, the only way to get better at organising, advocating and activism is by participating wholeheartedly. More than 40 years of neo-liberalism have left communities with fewer resources, social organisations and solidarity between people, and thus are far more individualised and fragmented. The only way to re-weave the social justice-based social fabric is to start working on it and to hone our skills in the development of new initiatives and optimism.

Discussion and conclusions

In this chapter, we bring intersectional theory to an analysis of field note examples that depict ageing in the city, to illustrate how intersectionality can be useful in analysing the pressing social issues underlying urban ageing, including the work of BLM activism and other struggles of BIPOC people for social justice. We began by arguing that age and ageism have not been central to this surge of anti-racist activism or to intersectional debates, but an analysis of overlapping and interweaving identities/social locations is of central importance to those seeking a clearer understanding of ageing in the contemporary context. We showed various ways that these theorisations can be used to illuminate the complexity of social relations and structures that knit a complex web of oppression and advantage for those who are ageing. Our field note vignettes showed how this analysis can be deployed within the contemporary, diverse, urban context. As a contribution to intersectional theorising on age and age-friendly cities, we argued that critical reflection and other intersectional-compatible skills, such as advocacy, activism, policy development and critique and community mobilisation are required to overcome the challenges facing those living, working and ageing in diverse urban contexts. Indeed, alongside promising strategies that have been suggested by others (such as educational interventions, intergenerational contact, see Mikton et al, 2021), we argue that understanding ageing through an intersectional lens is vital to recognising and addressing the complex experiences of ageing and ageism in the city and beyond.

References

Almeida, R.V., Werkmeister Rozas, L.M., Cross-Denny, B., Lee, K.K. and Yamada, A.-M. (2019) Coloniality and intersectionality in social work education and practice, *Journal of Progressive Human Services*, 30(2): 148–64.

Amiot, C.E. and Bourhis, R.Y. (2010) Discrimination between dominant and subordinate groups: the positive–negative asymmetry effect and normative processes, *British Journal of Social Psychology*, 44(2): 289–308.

Anthias, F. (2013) Hierarchies of social location, class and intersectionality: towards a translocational frame, *International Sociology*, 28(1): 121–38.

Armstrong, P. (2013) Puzzling skills: feminist political economy approaches, *The Canadian Review of Sociology*, 50(3): 256–83.

Azzopardi, C. (2020) Cross-cultural social work: a critical approach to teaching and learning to work effectively across intersectional identities, *The British Journal of Social Work*, 50(2): 464–82.

Baars, J. (2012) *Aging and the Art of Living*, Johns Hopkins University Press.

Baines, D. (2016) Care, austerity and resistance, in C. Williams (ed) *Social Work and the City*, Palgrave Macmillan, pp 193–214.

Baines, D. (ed) (2017) *Doing Anti-Oppressive Practice: Social Justice Social Work* (3rd edn), Fernwood Publishing.

Barrett, A.E. and Gumber, C. (2020) Feeling old, body and soul: the effect of aging body reminders on age identity, *The Journals of Gerontology. Series B, Psychological Sciences and Social Sciences*, 75(3): 625–9.

Biggs, S. (2003) Negotiating aging identity: surface, depth, and masquerade, in S. Biggs, A. Lowenstein and J. Hendricks (eds) *The Need for Theory: Critical Approaches to Social Gerontology*, Baywood Publishing Company, pp 145–59.

Braedley, S. (2019) Equity shifts in firefighting: challenging gendered and racialized norms, in J. Nichols and V. Tyyska (eds) *Working Women in Canada: An Intersectional Approach*, Canadian Scholars Press, pp 620–50.

Brown, C. and MacDonald, J. (2020) *Critical Clinical Social Work: Counterstorying for Social Justice*, Canadian Scholars Press.

Byrd, M.Y. (2014) Diversity issues: exploring 'critical' through multiple lenses, *Advances in Developing Human Resources*, 16(4): 515–28.

Cho, S., Crenshaw, K.W. and McCall, L. (2013) Toward a field of intersectionality studies: theory, applications, and praxis, *Signs: Journal of Women in Culture and Society*, 38(4): 785–810.

Collins, P.H. (2000) *Black Feminist Thought: Knowledge, Consciousness, and the Politics of Empowerment*, Routledge.

Collins, P.H. (2020) *Intersectionality as Critical Social Theory*, Duke University Press.

Collins, P.H. and Bilge, S. (2020) *Intersectionality*, John Wiley & Sons.

Combahee River Collective (1977) The Combahee River Collective Statement, Blackpast [online], Available from: https://www.blackpast.org/african-american-history/combahee-river-collective-statement-1977/

Crenshaw, K. (1989) Demarginalizing the intersection of race and sex: a Black feminist critique of politics, *University of Chicago Legal Forum*, 1989(1): 139–67.

Crenshaw, K. (1991) Mapping the margins: intersectionality, identity politics, and violence against women of color, *Stanford Law Review*, 43(6): 1241–99.

Crooks, N., Donenberg, G. and Matthews, A. (2021) Ethics of research at the intersection of COVID-19 and Black Lives Matter: a call to action, *Journal of Medical Ethics*, 47(4): 205–7.

Dhamoon, R.K. (2011) Considerations on mainstreaming intersectionality, *Political Research Quarterly*, 64(1): 230–43.

Davis, A. (1981) *Women, Race and Class*, Random House (UK).

Desmond-Harris, J. (2017) To understand the Women's March on Washington, you need to understand intersectional feminism, *Vox* 21 January [online], Available from: https://www.vox.com/identities/2017/1/17/14267766/womens-march-on-washington-inauguration-trump-feminism-intersectionaltiy-race-class

Fazzi, L. (2015) Social work, exclusionary populism and xenophobia in Italy, *International Social Work*, 58(4): 595–605.

Ferguson, H. (2018) How social workers reflect in action and when and why they don't: the possibilities and limits to reflective practice in social work, *Social Work Education*, 37(4): 415–27.

Fook, J. and Gardner, F. (2007) *Practicing Critical Reflection: A Resource Handbook*, McGraw-Hill Education.

Fraser, N. (1997) *Justice Interruptus: Critical Reflections on the 'Postsocialist' Condition*, Routledge.

Fraser, S., Lagacé, M., Bongué, B., Ndeye, N., Guyot, J., Bechard, L. et al (2020) Ageism and COVID-19: what does our society's response say about us?, *Age and Ageing*, 49(5): 692–5.

Grewal, I. and Kaplan, C. (1994) *Scattered Hegemonies: Postmodernity and Transnational Feminist Practices*, University of Minnesota Press.

Hartmann, H. and Sargent, L. (1981) *The Unhappy Marriage of Marxism and Feminism: A Debate on Class and Patriarchy*, Pluto.

Harvey, D. (2007) *A Brief History of Neoliberalism*, Oxford University Press.

Hopkins, P. (2019) Social geography I: intersectionality, *Progress in Human Geography*, 43(5): 937–7.

Horton, R. (2020) Offline: COVID-19 is not a pandemic, *The Lancet*, 396(10255): 874.

Hulko, W. (2009) The time- and context-contingent nature of intersectionality and interlocking oppressions, *Affilia*, 24(1): 44–55.

Kachanoff, F.J., Ysseldyk, R., Taylor, D.M., de la Sablonnière, R. and Crush, J. (2016) The good, the bad and the central of group identification: evidence of a U-shaped quadratic relation between in-group affect and identity centrality, *European Journal of Social Psychology*, 46(5): 563–80.

Levine-Rasky, C. (2011) Intersectionality theory applied to whiteness and middle-classness, *Social Identities*, 17(2): 239–53.

Livingstone, A. and Haslam, S.A. (2008) The importance of social identity content in a setting of chronic social conflict: understanding intergroup relations in Northern Ireland, *British Journal of Social Psychology*, 47(1): 1–21.

Mattsson, T. (2014) Intersectionality as a useful tool: anti-oppressive social work and critical reflection, *Affilia*, 29(1): 8–17.

Mavor, K. and Ysseldyk, R. (2020) A social identity approach to religion: religiosity at the nexus of personal and collective self, in K. Vail and C. Routledge (eds) *The Science of Religion, Spirituality, and Existentialism*, Elsevier Academic Press, pp 187–206.

McCall, L. (2001) *Complex Inequality: Gender, Class, and Race in the New Economy*, Routledge.

Mikton, C., de la Fuente-Núñez, V., Officer, A., and Krug, E. (2021) Ageism: a social determinant of health that has come of age, *The Lancet*, 397(10282): 1333–4.

Moore, S. (2009) 'No matter what I did I would still end up in the same position': age as a factor defining older women's experience of labour market participation, *Work, Employment and Society*, 23(4): 655–71.

Morley, C. (2014) Using critical reflection to research possibilities for change, *The British Journal of Social Work*, 44(6): 1419–35.

Morley, C. and Dunstan, J. (2013) Critical reflection: a response to neoliberal challenges to field education?, *Social Work Education*, 32(2): 141–56.

Mullaly, B. and West, J. (2018) *Challenging Oppression and Confronting Privlege: A Critical Approach to Anti-Oppressive and Anti-Privedge Theory and Practice*, Oxford University Press.

Naples, N.A. (2009) Teaching intersectionality intersectionally, *International Feminist Journal of Politics*, 11(4): 566–77.

O'Connor, D., Phinney, A. and Hulko, W. (2010) Dementia at the intersections: a unique case study exploring social location, *Journal of Aging Studies*, 24(1): 30–9.

Olson, E.T. (2019) Personal identity, in E.N. Zalta (ed) *The Stanford Encyclopedia of Philosophy* (Fall 2019 edn) [online], Available from: https://plato.stanford.edu/entries/identity-personal/

Parada, H. and Wehbi, S. (2017) *Reimagining Anti-Oppression Social Work Practice*, Canadian Scholars Press.

Purdie-Vaughns, V. and Eibach, R.P. (2008) Intersectional invisibility: the distinctive advantages and disadvantages of multiple subordinate-group identities, *Sex Roles*, 59(5–6): 377–91.

Reicher, S., Spears, R. and Haslam, S.A. (2010) The social identity approach in social psychology, in M. Wetherell and C. Mohanty (eds) *The SAGE Handbook of Identities*, SAGE, pp 45–63.

Roccas, S. and Brewer, M.B. (2002) Social identity complexity, *Personality and Social Psychology Review*, 6(2): 88–106.

Sassen, S. (2012) *Cities in a World Economy* (4th edn), Pine Forge Press.

Settles, I.H. (2004) When multiple identities interfere: the role of identity centrality, *Personality & Social Psychology Bulletin*, 30(4): 487–500.

Shields, S.A. (2008) Gender: an intersectionality perspective, *Sex Roles*, 59(5–6): 301–11.

Sidanius, J., Cotterill, S., Sheehy-Skeffington, J., Kteily, N. and Carvacho, H. (2016) Social dominance theory: explorations in the psychology of oppression, in C.G. Sibley and F.K. Barlow (eds) *The Cambridge Handbook of the Psychology of Prejudice*, Cambridge University Press, pp 149–87.

Sønderlund, A.L., Morton, T.A. and Ryan, M.K. (2017) Multiple group membership and well-being: is there always strength in numbers?, *Frontiers in Psychology*, 8: 1038.

Tajfel, H. (1970) Experiments in intergroup discrimination, *Scientific American*, 223(5): 96–103.

Tajfel, H. and Turner, J.C. (1979) An integrative theory of intergroup conflict, in W.G. Austin and S. Worchel (eds) *The Social Psychology of Intergroup Relations*, Brooks/Cole, pp 33–47.

Turner, J.C., Oakes, P.J., Haslam, S.A. and McGarty, C. (1994) Self and collective: cognition and social context, *Personality & Social Psychology Bulletin*, 20(5): 454–63.

Turtiainen, K. (2017) Recognition as a moral yardstick against nationalistic social work practice, *Social Dialogue*, 17: 12–13.

Wang, K. and Dovidio, J.F. (2016) Perceiving and confronting sexism: the causal role of gender identity salience, *Psychology of Women Quarterly*, 41(1): 65–76.

Warner, L.R. and Shields, S.A. (2013) The intersections of sexuality, gender, and race: identity research at the crossroads, *Sex Roles*, 68(11–12): 803–10.

Young, I.M. (1990) *Justice and the Politics of Difference*, Princeton University Press.

Ysseldyk, R., Matheson, K. and Anisman, H. (2010) Religiosity as identity: toward an understanding of religion from a social identity perspective, *Personality and Social Psychology Review*, 14(1): 60–71.

Ysseldyk, R., Talebi, M., Matheson, K., Bloemraad, I. and Anisman, H. (2014) Religious and ethnic discrimination: differential implications for social support engagement, civic involvement, and political consciousness, *Journal of Social and Political Psychology*, 2(1): 347–76.

PART II

Policies, practices, people

7

Queering age-friendliness: addressing safety, indicating equity

Susan Braedley, Christine Streeter and Oliver Debney

Introduction

Do age-friendly and age-equity movements, policies, and practices promote conditions of respect and dignity for queer older adults? The relationship between movements to advance age friendliness and other equity struggles – in this case, for two-spirit, gay, lesbian, bi-sexual, trans, queer and intersex, or 2SLGBTQI[1] recognition, rights and redistributions – is both important and complex. To imagine and improve the conditions for good queer ageing, this relationship is critical.

In this chapter, we take up the case of Canada, a country recognised internationally for its efforts to address 2SLGBTQI rights. Canada has decriminalised same sex relations, legalised same sex marriages and adoptions, and enacted legislation to prevent discrimination in employment due to sexuality and gender identity. These policy shifts provide the strongest legal protections for 2SLGBTQI people among OECD countries in 2020 (OECD, 2020).[2] Yet, Canadian 2SLGBTQI older adults told us that while they highly value this legal protection, it is not sufficient to ensure them an age-equitable future. This position is supported by findings from the existing academic research (Wilson, 2021).

These legal protections are also challenged in both law and discourse. The rise of right-wing politics around the world has produced anti-queer politics and policy reversals that threaten to undo decades of 2SLGBTQI progress toward equity, including in Canada. These contradictory political shifts evoke uncertainty about 2SLGBTQI lives in even progressive jurisdictions. As a Canadian queer older adult told us, 'The right being emboldened, and the reestablishment and strengthening and burgeoning of right-wing hate groups, is a problem for us and a problem for older persons in our community ... On the other positive side, there are really good programs happening at a micro level.' Will 2SLGBTQI older adults be able to access quality health and social services, live safely in their communities-of-choice, and care for and be cared by their chosen families? Will their sexuality and/or gender identity be respected by health-care and social services workers, and will respect continue if they experience dementia or other health conditions that erode their self-determination and agency? Queer older adults' assessment overall is hopeful but not confident. As a Senior Pride activist remarked when discussing a right-wing policy reversal affecting 2SLGBTQI folks: 'Holy shit. It didn't stick. It worked out so well, but it didn't last.'

In the context of this uncertainty, this chapter reports on findings from research with queer older adults and queer workers in services important to older adults in Canada, including libraries, transportation, long-term care, health care, recreation, public housing and a wide range of municipal services.[3] Our research partners included a national 2SLGBTQI rights organisation and a national public sector union[4] that worked with us to identify the conditions that support good queer ageing. We held interviews and focus groups with Senior Pride[5] activists, queer older adults, regional 2SLGBTQI action groups, and with queer-identified workers in community services serving older adults.

Throughout the chapter, we advance two main arguments. First, queering age friendliness does not mean squeezing sexuality and gender identity into existing frameworks and policy directions. Instead, it requires attention to the conditions of queer ageing, and how these conditions reframe assumptions about ageing well that are embedded in policies, practices and social life. Second, and implicit in our research process, we argue that services workers and other care providers, both paid and unpaid, must be involved in developing age-friendly and age-equity principles, policies and practices. Age friendliness and age-equity movements have been built on grassroots community development, consultations and research with older adults. But these successes rely on and take for granted the workers who make these changes possible; changes that also affect these workers' health, well-being, and incomes, in turn shaping the conditions for their ageing. As others have pointed out when discussing long-term care, 'the conditions of work are the conditions of care' (Armstrong and Braedley, 2023). To develop age-equitable cities and communities, workers, whether unpaid family members and volunteers, or paid homecare, long-term care, library, transportation, health care, recreation and social services workers, need a voice at the table.

With these two arguments, we work to shift the ground on which we struggle for age equity. Our research findings suggest potential indicators that can help to direct and assess progress on age equity for older adults and workers that include queer people, both illustrating a vision for change and policy and practice moves that can help cities, communities and services to move toward it.

Why queer age-friendly movements?

Despite success in attracting activist attention and policy action to improve the conditions of ageing, the original WHO Age-Friendly Cities Framework

(WHO, 2007) failed to mention or address many equity issues affecting older adults' health and well-being. It ducked issues of income inequality and low income in later life, left to one side issues of gender and culture and ignored issues of sexuality, gender identity, race, ethnicity, immigration status and more (Menec, 2011; Buffel, 2018). While aiming to improve the conditions of ageing, it addresses only indirectly some aspects of structural inequities, including those that produce age-related disabilities, frailties and more. Subsequent international developments in age friendliness have worked to include equity more explicitly. The WHO National programmes for age-friendly cities and communities (2023), a guide for policymakers and other stakeholders responsible for developing and supporting age-friendly cities and communities programs nationally, states:

> Our physical and social environments, including family structure, social norms, and cultural traditions, influence people differently, due to gender, ethnicity, sexual orientation, level of education, or disability. When age-friendly activities address social exclusion and barriers to opportunity, building and maintaining functional ability can also overcome inequity among older adults. (8)

In this articulation, age-friendly initiatives are perceived as potentially contributing to equity, but addressing inequity is not a necessary condition for age-friendliness – an important distinction. However, the WHO *Measuring the Age-friendliness of Cities: A Guide to Using Core Indicators* (2015) is more progressive. This document presents a framework of indicators to assess age-friendliness in physical and social environments that 'places equity at the core, as a cross-cutting principle, to highlight the importance of ensuring equity in the distribution of inputs, outputs, outcomes and impact' (12).

Many cities' policy and practice documents that build on international Age-Friendly movements in jurisdictions across Canada and other high-income countries,[6] tend to reflect the assumptions of these WHO documents. Commendably, cities have relied on consultations with older adults and with some service provider managers and experts. The underlying logic is that older people are most implicated in and affected by ageism and policies and practices affecting later life. However, these consultations do not involve the many paid and unpaid workers, including spouses, families, friends, volunteers and the many paid workers who provide the services to older people that support their active ageing, and who care for them when they experience age-related disabilities and frailty. These policy documents implicitly assume that these workers exist in sufficient numbers and with sufficient skill to do the work, an assumption that the pandemic deeply undermined and that queer community members have long recognised. Further, these documents ignore that working conditions can take a physical, emotional, and financial toll that damages workers' current and future health and income in ways that disable their old age.

As others have pointed out, a second problematic assumption underlying policy and practice developments to support older people is an unarticulated normative life course perspective, or what Elizabeth Freeman (2010) describes as 'chrononormativity': an often-unarticulated understanding that people's lives follow a linear procession of life choices aimed to maximise productivity and wealth in capitalist terms. This birth-to-death ordering of life stages and events produces a concept of the life course as a coherent, value-maximising series of milestones, including efforts to ward off disability, poverty and loneliness, and to age 'successfully' and healthfully. Implicit are assumptions of heterosexual dyads and family formation, suggesting that most older people will have spouses, extended family and especially children who can be called on to care for and support their parents in later life. Also assumed is that most older adults have stable, safe places to live and can access available community supports, including families, to sustain them to 'age-in-place'.

Queer lives are less likely to be lived within these chrononormative boundaries. Many of the queer older adults and queer workers who participated in our research lived alone and did not have biological children. Some had strained relationships with siblings, children and other extended family. These older adults' life course trajectories, affected by discrimination and/or periods of living closeted or partly closeted, meant that some had not developed wealth and/or a wide range of supportive relationships to conform to these assumptions. An older 2SLGBTQI activist told us:

> The messaging we're hearing from the health sector is that more and more is being pushed down into the community to provide. And yet for queer people, we have a lot of problems. We often don't have children, we often don't have extended family around. And there are all kinds of divisions within the queer community. We're not as united together as we advertise. So, this is a problem when things get downloaded to that community.

What then, is an alternative approach to developing a vision of ageing well? Sandberg and Marshall (2017: 7) 'reject the turn to negativity or no futures but also reject an unproblematic incorporation of "Others" into current models of success'. The implication is that age-friendly and age-equitable movements, frameworks and plans must examine the normative underpinnings of their visions of ageing. Revising Sandberg and Marshall's language to fit our project, we call for queering age-friendly cities and communities as a 'project of ... actively imagining radically different aging futures that might account for difference and challenge normativity and structural inequality' (8).

To queer age-friendliness, then, is to imagine a good later life – one that optimises health and well-being, participation, safety and security to enhance quality of life as people age, and embraces notions of homo- and trans-happiness, chrono-diversity, and diverse bodies and minds. Further, a queer age-friendliness means to consider equity not only for older people but for those on whom they rely to provide services, supports and care in ways that support these workers' ageing, rather than undermine them, and to build solidarities between diverse groups of carers and older adults that could advance age equity for all.

In what follows, we briefly outline our research with queer older adults and workers and discuss our most significant finding. We then describe indicators of queer age-equity emerging from our analysis. Our hope is these indicators can contribute to guiding organisations and services for seniors to move toward an age-friendliness that puts 'equity at the core, as a cross-cutting principle' (WHO, 2015).

Our research

This chapter draws on: focus groups and interviews with Senior Pride activists and older 2SLGBTQI identified adults in Ottawa, Toronto and Halifax; interviews and focus groups with older 2SLGBTQI adults and 2SLGBTQI public services workers from five provinces in Canada who work in libraries, senior's centres, long-term care homes, municipal offices, transportation and other services that serve a large population of older adults[7]; and a national environmental scan of services that have made strides to meet the needs of queer older adults and are considered 'promising'. These studies were conducted within the research partnership, 'Imagining Age-Friendly Communities within Communities: International Promising Practices' (see Introduction). The first author was a lead researcher across these studies, the second author led the environmental scan, interviews with the cross-Canada sub-study, and the report that inspired this chapter (Streeter et al, 2020). They were also a trainee on our studies in Ottawa and Toronto. The third author conducted literature reviews on 2SLGBTQI older adult-related matters and has conducted research with trans adults (Debney, 2021).

Taking a community-engaged feminist political economy approach to both data collection and analysis, many of our research participants and collaborators from partner organisations have contributed to the analysis offered here, attending presentations on initial findings and offering feedback, providing comments on draft publications and suggesting alternative framings. As the lead author is straight, white and older, and other authors are a mix of straight and queer, younger, emerging authors, this community-engaged research analysis has been an important component of our methods.

Our respondents included 44 older adults, 27 workers, and ten respondents who were both. Their social locations and backgrounds varied, from activists who have struggled hard for decades, to others who had lived most of their lives closeted, only coming out and/or transitioning later in life. It is important to keep in mind that '[t]here are not just generic queer seniors', as one participant emphasised. In addition to many distinctions of sexualities and gender identities, we met with queer older adults and workers who were Black, racialised, white, Indigenous, Muslim, Jewish, Christian, persons with disabilities and more. People belong to multiple communities, and their social locations influenced their conditions for ageing. One older adult told us, 'As an Indigenous person … it is rare for us to live [long lives], you know we maybe have a handful who are in their eighties and seventies.' Across these communities, income was a determinant of health and well-being. A worker in seniors' services noted, 'One thing … that I have sort of noticed is that we have two LGBT communities. Those who have been professionals in health, pensions and stuff. And those who … have lived on the poverty line.'

Throughout our research, we worked to include women and men equally, and while we did not ask all participants about their gender identity, at least six participants identified as trans and two identified as gender queer. Participants told us about gender and its operations within 2SLGBTQI community groups, indicating that gay men are often the most visible representatives of the gay community while lesbians are often less visible and trans folks are sometimes shunned or excluded within gay and lesbian groups. As one participant told us about attending queer community organising events:

> I come from a family with nine sisters, black activists, women from the community … who definitely would not shut up … I'm looking around and I'm saying, something's off here. You know … there aren't very many women. And the ones who are here are not saying anything … and so then I start talking to the guys like, you know, you have lesbian friends. I assume they did. Well, no.

In this analysis, we have worked to consider and reflect the similarities and differences across and among 2SLGBTQI social locations.

Queering age-friendliness: it's about safety

As we have noted, policy analysis suggests many changes that could strengthen age-equity frameworks by considering the conditions of queer lives, but when we asked 2SLGBTQI older adults and workers what might address and support conditions of dignity and respect for queer older people in Canada, we heard one consistent, basic requirement: safety. While there were other significant findings (see Streeter et al, 2020), no matter the jurisdiction or participant social location: 'Its about safety, right? If you are afraid and if you are going back in the closet, you obviously feel unsafe. So its got to be about safety.'

Queer older adults and queer workers serving seniors told us they experienced 'a barometer of safety' across their communities, with some spaces, places and services offering safer, welcoming environments, others providing more hostile environments, and others presenting continual risks of physical violence. They explained that safety has many dimensions. It means freedom from physical violence, from unwelcoming, 'chilly' environments, and from discrimination in services, public spaces and employment. It means freedom to express sexuality and gender identity without fear that this will affect service access, quality or employment conditions and opportunities. Further, Black, Indigenous, racialised, trans and disabled queer folks must all experience this safety. Safety means accessible washrooms that are safe for all genders. It means being acknowledged and included in public debates, physical environments, service delivery considerations and more, both as older persons and as services/care providers. Further, participants raised the need for cultural safety: 'It's about ... your worldview, your cultural background, and your right to exist in this world being affirmed on some level.' Cultural safety requires acknowledgements of power imbalances, and to do so, service/care providers to develop a reflexive component to their practices that can consider structural homophobia, transphobia, racism, colonialism, sexism, ableism and other forms of discrimination (Churchill, 2017).

Participants pointed out that their concerns about safety have been heightened by rising hate crime incidence. Canada has become more dangerous for those from equity seeking groups, including 2SLGBTQI groups. In 2019, there were 265 police reports of hate crimes due to sexual orientation, and steadily rising numbers each year, with 860 reports in 2023. Overall, hate crimes increased from 1,951 reports in 2019 to 4,777 in 2023 (Statistics Canada, 2024). The reports of these crimes add to older queer adults' concerns arising from their lifetime experiences of persecution. Those who entered adulthood in the 1950s, 1960s, and 1970s recall federal government 'security' campaigns that spied on, interrogated, harassed and fired suspected gay and lesbian federal public employees (Kinsman, 2010). They remember vividly when sexual orientation was removed from classification as a psychiatric disorder, and they know that gender dysphoria remains a psychiatric diagnosis, with harmful impact on trans folks (Daley, 2014). During the AIDS crisis of the 1980s and 1990s, they experienced surveillance by the medical community, fear, loss, grief, stigma, discrimination and illness (Tremblay, 2015; Kinsman, 2018). Further, these older adults are likely to have experienced discrimination in employment, health care, housing, their families and social life. Emphasising that lifelong issues with 2SLGBTQI safety affect older people's abilities to even attempt to use services and trust service providers, one queer older adult explained:

> It's difficult for people to imagine what a 70-year-old person had gone through to get to this point in time, and how many of those experiences linger in the way they see the world, and the way in which they see even the police or persons of authority or the government.

Mentioned repeatedly by queer older adults is the fear of having to access gerontological health-care and long-term care services as they age: 'You know the term LTC and if you ask people what does that mean, they say long-term care. But for many LGBTQ people, it is Long Term Closet.' Queer older adults know that long-term care professionals and organisations have refused same-sex couples a shared room, refused to acknowledge or support trans residents' gender identities, and have blocked intimate partners from participating in their loved ones' medical decision-making. They have reasons to worry that their end-of-life wishes will be overlooked if their biological family disagree (Brotman, 2015; Pang, 2019). They question whether they will have access to hormone therapies, privacy of health records and more. They do not trust that they will have even basic physical safety. As one older adult told us, a trans friend 'was having a life and death situation … and was treated so badly, was made fun of at the initial intake at "emerg". When she finally saw a doctor, the doctor was making fun of her'. Further, when long-term care support is delivered at home, queer adults fear they will need to closet even at home. Some participants receiving home care explained that they hide evidence of their queer lives and relationships in their own homes to avoid harassing and discriminatory remarks and treatment from untrained, poorly informed home care workers: 'I don't like to blame the workers, but I've taken down the vulva artwork and hidden the picture of my [deceased] wife and I kissing … When a worker is rough or mean or doesn't show up, I wonder, is it because I'm a dyke?' For trans older adults receiving personal care, such as support for bathing, dressing and toileting, this fear is heightened, as closeting is not possible. 'My body is a give-away. I can't hide it.'

Queer workers across the many services serving seniors echoed older adults' concerns about safety. They told us that their lack of safety on the job means they are prevented from shaping services to be accessible, welcoming and safe for queer older adults. Workers also experienced a barometer of safety, ranging from welcoming, safer, inclusive workplaces to those where managers, clients and co-workers made homophobic and transphobic comments, to those in which workers were subjected to outright harassment, exclusion and violence. One worker told us, 'I got called into my manager's office and she sat me down and said, I don't think it's a good idea for you to talk about your sexuality on the floor.' Some workplaces were so unsafe, queer workers were not out. They masked their sexuality and/or gender identity by dressing 'straight', staying silent in collegial discussions about intimate relationships or families, and hiding their queer lives. As one worker explained, 'I feel a bit closeted, because I don't want to share my orientation. I felt like I wouldn't get hired or they would fire me'. Others who were out at work had experienced violence:

> I was physically assaulted going into the women's washroom 3 years ago. I reported it to my supervisor and the coordinator, and we spoke with human resources and they said to me, 'What do you want us to do?' I said, 'Really? Shouldn't you be proactive and be doing something?'

Queer workers who were Black, Indigenous or otherwise racialised are more likely to report these experiences, and more often, according to Mills and colleagues (2020).

Seeing the strength of this finding, what are promising approaches that can produce safe, dignified, respectful conditions for queer older adults? In the next section, we draw from our environmental scan, interviews and focus group data on safer services to identify indicators. These indicators have been reviewed and refined through sharing drafts and our report (Streeter et al, 2020) with many groups of 2SLGBTQI older adults and workers in Canada, including and well beyond our research participants and partners.

Indicators to advance age-equity that include queer older adults

Before outlining the indicators, it is important to note that our research findings do not recommend or intend only universal age-equitable services that are safe and accessible for all social groups. As one Senior Pride activist put it, 'There is a place for both, integration versus segregation, because there are many ways in which we can be integrated with the rest of society and we're quite happy about that. But there always will be a need to have programs specific to our community.' With that proviso, we lay out six indicators that show potential to advance age equity across cities and communities via the institutions and organisations that support, or should support, older adults, including queer older adults, with reference to both universal and more targeted services.

Evidence that power has been shifted to diverse 2SLGBTQI groups and communities

As was noted by Senior Pride activists, 'if we are not specifically included, then we are explicitly excluded'. Our research surfaced many developments that shifted power to queer groups by including queer older adults as decision-makers and sharing resources with queer groups. Safer institutions, organisations and services have invited queer community members to help them identify opportunities for change. They have asked queer community members to participate regularly in advice and governance structures. They have sought out Senior Pride groups and similar community activists to help them improve services. They have hired queer activists to help train staff and implement improvement projects. Practices that shifted power were often modest but significant, including offering meeting space on a continuous basis at low or no cost to queer community groups, and engaging queer community members as volunteers and providing them with resources to meet community needs.

Evidence of 2SLGBTQI meaningful representation in policy and practice decision-making

Moving toward age equity requires governments and other funders to meaningfully involve queer older adults and queer organisations at tables where services are regulated, funded and organised. In some municipalities, provincial governments, high-level agencies, charitable and advocacy organisations, queer older adults were highly involved and indicated they were able to contribute meaningfully. These contributions were resulting in important changes that support age equity for queer older adults. As one research participant noted about two organisations that took up this direction, 'Agencies like Elder Abuse Prevention Ontario and the Advocacy Centre for the Elderly are wonderful supports for us and our cause.'

> We found that some municipalities and agencies were working to ensure 'its not just straight people informing ... policy and so on, it is LGBTQ folks as well. And that is certainly obvious on the Toronto [Seniors Strategy Accountability] Table and also the Toronto Council on Aging. Very, very open.'

We found meaningful queer representation at a seniors' housing complex and in some long-term care services in Halifax, and at a policy roundtable and seniors' centre in Ottawa. However, across government and the services regulators and funders who oversee the wide range of services for older adults, very few had yet to specifically include queer older adults in their governance structures and advisory groups, even in cases where there were diversity and inclusion frameworks in place.

We also heard some disappointment about the lack of action from national 2SLGBTQI organisations on older adult issues: 'I've been disappointed over the years that they haven't taken more of a leadership role around seniors ...

because I think it is a national thing ... And for whatever reason, it hasn't happened.' Thus, while mainstream older adult services need to consider queer safety, access and inclusion, 2SLGBTQI organisations need to do better to meaningfully include and provide resources for older adults and their concerns, setting goals and benchmarks to ensure they make progress.

Evidence of sectoral and organisational change to affirm 2SLGBTQI service users and workers

Our research shows that advancing equity to affirm service users and workers in municipalities, organisations and services takes more than rainbow flags. It requires explicit commitments to safety and accessibility in statements of mission and values. Management teams must consult with employees and service users to identify desired outcomes, and then monitor and report on progress, sharing it publicly. It requires working on 2SLGBTQI representation throughout the organisation. It requires comprehensive anti-discrimination and harassment policies that explicitly identify sexuality and gender identity/expression as protected categories and include reporting processes. It requires shifts to gender-neutral language in verbal and written communications and signage. Our research revealed that more equitable institutions and organisations had removed barriers that prevented the involvement of chosen families to favour biological ones. They admitted mistakes on queer issues, both past and present, and explained how they will make concrete improvements. They installed gender-neutral washrooms and redesigned entries, hallways and other areas to ensure good lighting and clear sight lines that supported safety for service users and workers.

Some leading organisations have gone even further to include advancing equity as an aspect of leadership evaluations, to consider whether and how decision-makers and managers are promoting safety and accessibility. Some public sector unions and their employers have embedded anti-discrimination and harassment policies in collective agreements. Some organisations have established explicit teams to advance 2SLGBTQI safety throughout, providing them with a budget, access to senior decision-makers and formal accountability to 2SLGBTQI constituencies on their action plans and progress (Kortes-Miller, 2018).

Organisational change can also mean the development of 2SLGBTQI older adult-specific services within mainstream organisations. Examples from our research include a long-term care home unit, library book clubs, a telephone-based virtual discussion group, a weekly gathering, an outreach program that includes friendly visiting and telephone check-ins and a call-in radio show. There were also burgeoning initiatives 'working on housing for specifically gay, lesbian, and trans'. We encountered inter-generational programs allowing isolated queer older adults opportunities to mentor younger generations in an exchange of mutual support. A younger volunteer with a befriending program for queer older adults told us, 'It helps me too. I work from home and don't get out much.' Another program was a long-term care home visiting program for queer residents that brought young queer-identified people in as visitors. As one participant told us about his friend, 'Whoever wanted visitors could sign up! So, he has all these young people coming to visit him now, from our community.'

Ensure 2SLGBTQI representation and employment equity in the workforce

Over and over, we learned that queer workers' presence and visibility have been critical to creating change within organisations and for service users' experience of safety and accessibility. As one library worker told us, 'I do see having a familiar face makes a big difference for people. They are more comfortable checking out queer material. They are like, "Oh, I am here to pick up my boyfriend's stuff, I have his card" ... I am not going to be weird about it.'

Our participants emphasised that the relationship between staff and service users is key, with both groups benefiting from solidarities among them. One older adult described close relationships that had developed at the local senior's centre:

> well certainly we all feel safe here ... the transgender woman who is ... the manager of the program, it has helped her. She has mentioned many times it has really helped her to come out more, we have helped her, and she has helped us as well. She ... can identify with all of our struggles, coming out of the closet and just sharing how it is in terms of transition, and the loneliness and depression, but also being part of a group, so that you feel more resilient.

Queer workers' experiences on the job at services serving older adults operate as an indicator of these services' age-friendliness for queer older adults. Some told us about work environments imbued with heteronormativity. In these environments, both queer older adults and workers described being afraid, stressed and hyper-vigilant. In other organisations, queer workers told us of their activities to make their services more queer-friendly, often on top of their other job responsibilities and usually unpaid. It is critical that 2SLGBTQI workers, whether paid or volunteer, are acknowledged for their equity work and supported by their colleagues and organisations. Too often, we heard from workers who felt tokenised, overworked, burnt out and discouraged due to their identity. We heard from queer workers who had been given, or took, responsibility for making services safer for queer older adults without acknowledgement in their job descriptions or working time allotments. As one worker explained, 'It puts extra pressure on us ... because if someone comes in and they have HIV or something, they go well oh [name] is the gay guy, we will get him to do this, we will get him to do that, because these are his people.' At the same time, workers explained that sometimes they have been discouraged from doing this work and told they are 'too visible'. These tensions reduce safety and accessibility for both workers and service users.

Ensuring representation and employment equity requires continual attention. Even safer, accessible organisations and services can become complacent. As one worker told us, 'I think because we are so focused on being queer-friendly we forget that it is not particularly trans-friendly.' Like other indicators, this goal needs to be considered and updated regularly, including both hiring practices and supportive, healthy working conditions. One worker explained with pride that their organisation had done well on representational hiring, and believed these workers' contributions were improving service delivery. However, here were new concerns about supporting these colleagues effectively.

> My department is looking at representation ... because we do have ... one non-binary person and a trans-identified person in ... our work unit. So that's pretty great ... I think that's a big deal. We need to also not burn them out, and as a work unit, keep showing up for them.

Ensure evidence-informed training throughout organisations to promote 2SLGBTQI safety and accessibility

Institutions and organisations identified for their superior access and safety had a common trait: consistent high-quality training. All members of Boards, directors, managers, staff, volunteers and, where appropriate, service users, including 2SLGBTQI-identified folks, should have appropriate, evidence-informed training to promote 2SLGBTQI safety and accessibility and reduce and eliminate homophobia and transphobia (Kortes-Miller, 2018; Holman, 2020). This training supports 2SLGBTQI service users by promoting understanding and skills that enhance safety, access and inclusion. It also supports 2SLGBTQI workers by cultivating allies so that these workers are not alone in advancing equity or tokenised on committees and teams. It can also help to prevent overwork and continual assignment to equity-related tasks.

The absence of this training in many professional schools is startling, including medicine, nursing, social work and library science (Obedin-Maliver, 2011; Mulé, 2015; Hillock, 2017; Kellett, 2017; Siegel, 2020; Bain, 2022). Our environmental scan found that many organisations relied on insufficient training of questionable quality and on low-cost training from under-funded queer community groups and organisations. Changes are happening, both within professional bodies and across some municipalities and services. Our research participants told us about home care agencies, long-term care homes, and other health-care, recreation, transportation and social services that had made gender and sexual diversity training mandatory. At the same time, in some Canadian provinces, homophobic and transphobic governments and policies are shutting down these initiatives. Sussman et al (2018) have shown that ongoing training, advancing through levels of increasing difficulty and complexity, is more effective than one-time-only training, and our participants who provided, or have participated in, this training concurred. Further, in-person training that includes trainers who are 2SLGBTQI-identified older people was described as having higher impact and more engagement than on-line modalities. As one participant told us about their municipal services, 'They have LGBTQ ambassador training ... I love that program but I feel they could go ... further with it ... the city has gone to "click" training, right? And its all tied to money, right?' At the same time, our participants criticised those services that relied on volunteer-led training. As one respondent who has 10 years of experience in offering this training made clear,

> [A training program] needs the infrastructure to have professional trainers, research based, evidence-based materials to work from that kind of structure, that kind of predictability, that kind of stability, that kind of independence that comes from that and that kind of objectivity. So that it's a professionally offered service that's not dependent on how many volunteers we can rustle up.

Make 2SLGBTQI affirmation visible in signs, symbols and celebrations

Many services and businesses have been accused of 'rainbow-washing' (Nowack, 2019), deploying signs and symbols to indicate queer safety and accessibility without taking the more difficult steps to change conditions for queer service users and staff. While also expressing concerns about potentially misleading signage, our participants maintained, 'You can't say enough about visibility. Yeah. Because it's really easy to become invisible.'

We heard many examples of ways that organisations and services affirmed queer lives in their signs and symbols. One older adult told us, '[At the hospital], they have a button during Pride Week, "Pride, its good for your health." And they all wear it ... that means so much.' In libraries across one city, a worker told us: 'the full-time staff wear a pronoun pin, which I think is very cool ... for me, growing up queer ... seeing anything that was even slightly gay, it was like, Oh hi!' Celebrations, both large and small, were also mentioned, One older adult told us, 'There was a man who was 70 and he had been in the closet all his life, and at [the long-term care home], he came out. They had announced it and they had a big party for him, and they had such a wonderful celebration!'

We learned that city efforts to display rainbow symbols in public art, by painting crosswalks, and other formats, offered a sense of belonging. As one older adult told us, 'I know these symbols irk the haters, but haters are there, anyway. These symbols feel like the city recognises we need support, that it is on our side, even in a modest way. It gives me hope.'

Gender-neutral, private, enclosed toilets in well-lit areas were an important service mentioned by many research participants that also signaled safer, accessible physical environments. As one worker told us, 'Our senior's centre was the first building in the city to install gender neutral washrooms. You wouldn't think it would be US, would you? But it made a big difference. It was a strong sign of what we were trying to do.'

Queering age-friendly: next steps

This analysis began with observations about the underlying normative assumptions within age-friendly-related policy and practice frameworks, to point out that 2SLGBTQI lives and those of other marginalised and oppressed groups often get left aside or ignored. Next, we drew on our research with queer older adults and queer workers in Canadian services that serve older adults, to identify their key concern for safety. Drawing from our research with them and a national environmental scan to identify promising queer-friendly services for older people, we described six indicators that can help build more age-equitable futures for 2SLGBTQI communities at multiple levels of scale. The indicators are: shifts of power to diverse 2SLGBTQI groups; 2SLGBTQI meaningful representation in policy and practice decision-making; sectoral and organisational change to affirm 2SLGBTQI service users and workers; 2SLGBTQI representation and employment equity in the workforce; evidence-informed training throughout organisations to promote 2SLGBTQI safety and accessibility; and 2SLGBTQI affirmation visible in signs, symbols and celebrations. The actions required by these indicators work together, so one or two is a beginning, but insufficient to promote conditions of safety and access that promote dignity and respect.

This research work is not over. These indicators emerged from research and activism in cities in Canada where legal protections for 2SLGBTQI people were in place. As we continue our research in high-income countries internationally, we have questions about whether and how these indicators will relate to the conditions facing queer workers and older adults living in other jurisdictions, and what age-equity indicators may emerge from their perspectives, given rising intolerance in some jurisdictions, new protections, and continually shifting politics. Resisting and confronting discriminatory right-wing politics that sideline, disparage, and render unsafe any group of 2SLGBTQI people is challenging, necessary and urgent work if dreams for an inclusive age-friendliness that advance age equity are to be pursued and realised.

Notes

1. Language is always dynamic and changing. We use 2SLGBTQI in this volume and in this chapter following the example of our research partner, Egale, the leading national advocacy organisation in Canada for the population groups that are often clustered under the term, 'queer' at this moment in time. This acronym is in keeping with current recognitions in Canada and articulated by one of our study participants: 'I think Two-Spirit should be at the beginning of the acronym, to acknowledge that Two-Spirit Indigenous people were the first sexual and gender minority people in North America, and also to demonstrate solidarity with them in this period of truth and reconciliation in Canada' (older adult).
2. Canada's protections are rooted in the Canadian Human Rights Act (1985), amended in 1996 and 2017 to specifically include the right to equality, equal opportunity, fair treatment and an environment free of discrimination on the basis of sex, sexual orientation, gender identity or expression. Judicial interpretations of the Canadian Charter of Rights and Freedoms have confirmed these rights (see Eberts, 1999).
3. This project is a sub-study of our broader SSHRC Partnership, Age-Friendly Communities-in-Communities: International Promising Practices, that aims to identify promising practices that promote age equity for disadvantaged, oppressed and marginalised older adults.
4. Our partners are Egale and the Canadian Union of Public Employees.
5. Senior Pride is a term used in Canada that refers to older lesbian, gay, queer, bi-sexual, trans, two-spirited and inter-sexed people who are advocating and doing activism on issues affecting the queer community and its diverse members.
6. See the following examples: *Ottawa Older Adult Plan 2020–2022*, https://documents.ottawa.ca/sites/default/files/OAP%202020-2022%20Action%20Plan%20FINAL.pdf

    Toronto Senior's Strategy 2.0 (2018) https://www.toronto.ca/wp-content/uploads/2019/02/93cd-cot-seniors-strategy2.pdf

    Shift: Nova Scotia's Action Plan for an Aging Population (2017) https://novascotia.ca/shift/shift-action-plan.pdf

    The Age-friendly Action Plan: A safe, inclusive, and engaging city for seniors (2013–2015), Vancouver https://vancouver.ca/people-programs/age-friendly-action-plan.aspx.

    Melbourne: A Great Place to Age (2020–24) https://mvga-prod-files.s3.ap-southeast-4.amazonaws.com/public/2024-05/melbourne-great-place-age.pdf

    Tāmaki Makaurau tauawhi kaumātua (Age-friendly Auckland Action Plan) https://www.aucklandcouncil.govt.nz/plans-projects-policies-reports-bylaws/our-plans-strategies/topic-based-plans-strategies/community-social-development-plans/Documents/age-friendly-tamaki-makaurau-framework.pdf*Et ældrevenligt københavn* (2020) Copenhagen https://www.kk.dk/sites/default/files/2022-03/Rapport%20fra%20hovedprojekt%202020.pdf
7. The first study was rapid team ethnographic site study research completed in Toronto, Ottawa and Halifax, Canada (see Chapter 1). The second study was a national environmental scan, interviews and focus groups to explore and identify promising practices in public services for 2SLGBTQI older adults and workers, conducted by our research team in partnership with the Canadian Union of Public Employees and Egale. https://cupe.ca/report-making-public-services-better-lgbtq2-workers-and-seniors.

References

Armstrong, P. and Braedley, S. (2023) *Care Homes in a Turbulent Era: Do They Have a Future?*, Edward Elgar Publishing Limited.

Brotman, S., Ferrer, I., Sussman, T., Ryan, B. and Richard, B. (2015) Access and equity in the design and delivery of health and social care to LGBTQ older adults: a Canadian perspective, in D.C. Kimmel, T. Rose and S. David (eds) *Lives of LGBT Older Adults*, American Psychological Association, pp 111–40.

Buffel, T. and Phillipson, C. (2018) A manifesto for the age-friendly movement: developing a new urban agenda, *Journal of Aging & Social Policy*, 30(2): 173–92.

Churchill, M.M., Parent-Bergeron, M., Smylie, J., Ward, C., Fridkin, A., Smylie, D. et al (2017) *Evidence Brief: Wise Practices for Indigenous-Specific Cultural Safety Training Programs*, Well Living House Action Research Centre for Indigenous Infant, Child and Family Health and Wellbeing, Centre for Research on Inner City Health, St. Michael's Hospital [online], Available from: https://www.nccih.ca/634/Evidence_Brief__Wise_Practices_for_Indigenous-Specific_Cultural_Safety_Training.nccih?id=1092

Daley, A. and Mulé, N.J. (2014) LGBTQs and the DSM-5: a critical queer response, *Journal of Homosexuality*, 61(9): 1288–312.

Debney, K.O. (2021) *The Stories We Tell: Making Sense of Gender, Transition, and the Centrality of Relationships*, Masters thesis, Carleton University.

Eberts, M. (1999) The Charter and equality rights: the Vriend case, *Canada Watch*, 7(4–5): DOI: 10.25071/j2repq24

Freeman, E. (2010) *Time Binds: Queer Temporalities, Queer Histories*, Duke University Press.

Government of Canada (1985) *Canadian Human Rights Act*, R.S.C., 1985, c. H-6 [online], Available from: https://laws-lois.justice.gc.ca/eng/acts/h-6/

Holman, E.G., Landry-Meyer, L. and Fish, J.N. (2020) Creating supportive environments for LGBT older adults: an efficacy evaluation of staff training in a senior living facility, *Journal of Gerontological Social Work*, 63(5): 464–77.

Kinsman, G. (2018) AIDS activism: remembering resistance versus socially organized forgetting, in M. Smith and M. Jackson (eds) *Seeing Red*, University of Toronto Press, pp 311–33.

Kinsman, G. and Gentile, P. (2010) *The Canadian War on Queers: National Security as Sexual Regulation*, University of British Columbia Press.

Kortes-Miller, K., Wilson, K. and Stinchcombe, A. (2018) Care and LGBT aging in Canada: a focus group study on the educational gaps among care workers, *Clinical Gerontologist*, 42(2): 192–7.

Menec, V.H., Means, R., Keating, N., Parkhurst, G. and Eales, J. (2011) Conceptualizing age-friendly communities, *Canadian Journal on Aging*, 30(3): 479–93.

Mills, S., Owens, B., Guta, A., Lewis, N. and Oswin, N. (2020) *Work, Inclusion and 2SLGBTQ+ People in Sudbury and Windsor*, McMaster University [online], Available from: https://macsphere.mcmaster.ca/bitstream/11375/28174/1/work-and-inclusion_for-posting-and-distribution.pdf

Nowack, V. and Donahue, J.J. (2020) Outcomes associated with employee and organisational LGBT value discrepancies. *Psychology and Sexuality*, 11(1–2): 32–44.

Obedin-Maliver, J., Goldsmith, E.S., Stewart, L., White, W., Tran, E., Brenman, S., Wells, M., Fetterman, D.M., Garcia, G. and Lunn, M.R. (2011) Lesbian, gay, bisexual, and transgender-related content in undergraduate medical education, *JAMA : The Journal of the American Medical Association*, 306(9): 971–977.

OECD (2020) *Over the Rainbow? The Road to LGBTQI Inclusion*, OECD Publishing [online], Available from: https://doi.org/10.1787/8d2fd1a8-en

Pang, C., Gutman, G. and de Vries, B. (2019) Later life care planning and concerns of transgender older adults in Canada, *International Journal of Aging & Human Development*, 89(1): 39–56.

Sandberg, L.J. and Marshall, B.L. (2017) Queering aging futures, *Societies*, 7(3): 21.

Statistics Canada (2024) Police-reported hate crime, by type of motivation, selected regions and Canada (selected police services), Table: 35-10-0066-01 [online], Available from: https://www150.statcan.gc.ca/t1/tbl1/en/tv.action?pid=3510006601

Streeter, C., Braedley, S., Jansen, I. and Krajcik, M. (2020) *It's Got to Be About Safety: Public Services That Work for LGBTQ2+ Older Adults and LGBTQ2+ Workers in Canada*, Canadian Union of Public Employees and Egale.

Sussman, T., Brotman, S., MacIntosh, H., Chamberland, L., MacDonnell, J., Daley, A., Dumas, J. and Churchill, M. (2018) Supporting lesbian, gay, bisexual, and transgender inclusivity in long-term care homes: a Canadian perspective, *Canadian Journal on Aging*, 37(2): 121–132.

Tremblay, M. (2015) *Queer Mobilizations: Social Movement Activism and Canadian Public Policy*, University of British Columbia Press.

Wilson, K., Stinchcombe, A. and Regalado, S.M. (2021) LGBTQ+ aging research in Canada: a 30-year scoping review of the literature, *Geriatrics (Basel)*, 6(2): 60.

World Health Organization (2007) *Global Age-Friendly Cities: A Guide*, World Health Organization.

World Health Organization (2015) *Measuring the Age-Friendliness of Cities: A Guide to Using Core Indicators*, World Health Organization.

World Health Organization (2023) *National Programmes for Age-Friendly Cities and Communities: A Guide*, World Health Organization.

8

Super-invisibility: 'older' care workers in home care and residential long-term care

Tamara Daly, Sara Charlesworth and Frode F. Jacobsen

Introduction

Conditions in long-term care (LTC) are a societal indicator of equity, revealing how nation states promote conditions for participation, dignity and respect for us all, as we age (Armstrong et al, 2012). Importantly, LTC working conditions – including residential and home care settings – are considered unacceptable, with negative impacts on the quality of the care and the health and welfare of care workers (Charlesworth et al, 2024; WHO, 2024).

LTC is largely 'care for women by women', given most care workers and most care recipients are women (Armstrong et al, 2023b). Ironically, it is frequently care for older women by older women, while the ageing of the care workforce is largely unacknowledged and unaddressed in policy and practice. While there is a renewed focus on recruiting workers to LTC, especially since the pandemic, there is insufficient attention to what is required to retain existing members of the LTC workforce, in part because the ageing of the LTC workforce is super-invisible. This super-invisibility happens in a context in which the invisibility of care work has already been well-established.

Invisibility is a feature of care work, done mostly in private, behind closed doors, and by women who are poorly paid, and often vulnerable in other ways, owing to low levels of education or migrant status. Among those who are 'critical' to the care economy (Armstrong et al, 2023a), care workers in the LTC sector are nonetheless 'underpaid, unpaid, unseen, and unheard' (Armstrong et al, 2009; Baines et al, 2016), and part of a 'global undervaluing of health and care work' (WHO, 2024). This under-valuing is undergirded by the pervasive challenge to continually assert that home care *and* residential care are important parts of age-friendly frameworks, and health systems more broadly, providing types of care especially needed by some who live longer than 85 years.

There is, without doubt, a whiff of failure attached to residential care – amplified by COVID – and one that prefigures that families, governments and systems have cared too little and residents have failed to maintain their independence. Care workers are often unmentioned and invisible within policies and frameworks addressing older people's needs. This extends to Age-Friendly Frameworks, which centre the older people as care and service recipients but hide the working and retirement needs of those who perform the work. For instance, 'community supports and health services' are the Age-friendly domain (WHO, 2007)[1] for home care and residential LTC. The WHO (nd), notes: 'Accessible and affordable community and health services are crucial in keeping seniors healthy, independent and active. This involves an appropriate supply of aged care services conveniently located close to where older people live and trained health and social workers to provide these services.'

Like the broader Age-Friendly framework, the desired outcome for Age-Friendly policies and programs is the health of older people who can get care and services to support their own health, independence and activity. The guide indicates that the health-care and social services workers who do the 'services' should be trained, in good supply, work in close geographic proximity to older adults, and most importantly, be accessible and affordable. The Age-Friendly framework does not consider care workers, their conditions of work, or outcomes such as health, safety, level of pay or access to robust benefits. Importantly, working conditions affect the retirement possibilities and outcomes for older care workers, most whom are women.

Care work invisibility is not a recent phenomenon. Efforts have been made to counter it, with decades of well-documented studies about care and its conditions, particularly as gendered work. The 'gendered assumptions' about care work (Armstrong and Laxer, 2006) continue to show up in policies and practices that reproduce the gender order (Connell, 2021), undervalue care work, and enforce the 'relations of ruling' (Smith, 2002) of unequal pay, under-staffing, lack of recognition of skills and profit-taking, even in the social democratic countries (Ågotnes et al, 2020). This ordering reifies women as naturally possessing feminine 'care skills', with paid social reproductive care ignoring the workforce skills of care. Specifically, the undervaluing of care work, both paid and unpaid, follows in settings where the regulations are highly prescriptive, such as Canada, where the work is deemed low skill, holds little decision-making authority and is assumed to require little effort, to need less education and remains lowly in the health-care hierarchy (Daly et al, 2016).

This invisibility is amplified for home care workers, where the gendered 'architecture' or spatial location of home care is outside an institutional setting. In Australia, this invisibility is both reflected in weaker labour protections for home care work compared to residential aged care work

(Charlesworth, 2012) exemplified during COVID, when home care workers received limited or no access to the temporary retention bonuses and paid pandemic leave available to residential aged care workers (Charlesworth and Low, 2020).

Across OECD nations and beyond, COVID-19 highlighted and heightened the largely unaddressed issues of LTC understaffing, work overload and higher than acceptable rates of illness, injury and violence facing care workers that are far worse when compared with other workers inside or outside health care (OECD, 2023c). Whether the lessons of COVID will be a catalyst for change remains uncertain. What we know is that the high demand for care, accompanied by a normalised, pervasive under-valuing of care work, contributes to poor working conditions. The plight of paid care workers may be caught up in a collective desire to look away, and a 'gender order' which devalues care, at a time and place when heightened visibility is needed most.

Most direct care workers across LTC are 'care assistants' or nurses, as outlined in Chapter 5. This around the clock work includes a wide range of nursing care as well as personal support for bodily needs, such as getting up and going back to bed, moving, dining, grooming, using the toilet, needed assistance with medicines, wound care and all types of personal support. An important consideration is that a high proportion of paid carers are older women. As Chapter 5 shows, among nurses working in LTC in Australia in 2023, an estimated 16.4 per cent in residential aged care and 25.6 per cent in home care in the home care packages program are 55 years and older. This proportion compares with about 18.8 per cent of Canadian nurses who are aged 55 and older across all care settings, and 31 per cent of Norwegian nurses working for municipal institutional and home care settings and for a variety of client groups. Among care assistants in Australian aged care, it is estimated that 16 per cent in residential aged care and 32.5 per cent in aged home care are 55 and older. Twenty-two per cent of Canadian 'assisting occupations' across all institutional settings, and 31 per cent of workers providing care in home settings – across all age groups – are aged 55 and older. Increasingly, it is 'care for older women by older women', which requires urgent attention in policies and practices that range from the global to the local, including in age-friendly frameworks.

Given these figures, how do *older* care workers, who care for older people, fare? To answer this question, we reviewed a variety of policy documents and publicly available datasets. We argue that the poor conditions within which care work for older adults is performed produce worse health, safety and financial security outcomes for older care workers, a group of care workers who are among the least visible. Further, the overarching invisibility of care workers' working and retirement conditions – in policy, planning and practice – positions older care workers as 'super-invisible'.

In what follows, we outline four 'invisibility traps' that render older care workers super-invisible. First, precarious work, from poor pay and job insecurity, leaves too little income for retirement, leading to *pension precarity* that makes older workers, and, in particular, older women, vulnerable in their own older age and subject to working too long for too little. Second, *work overload*, signaled by weak retention or too early retirement, pushes people out of jobs before they would otherwise stop working and into positions of income precarity. Third, *unacceptable health and safety protections* produce sickness, injury and disability. Finally, *weak, unclear, and hidden data that are specific to the LTC sector*, particularly, about the 'age', 'race' and site of care make workforce analysis and planning impossible and contribute to poor care provision.

We analyse these invisibility traps comparatively, drawing on statistical sources from international sources in Australia, Canada and Norway as our evidence base. Given how COVID highlighted and heightened the poor conditions in LTC care, and examples of advances since 2021, we hold out hope for the promise of change. To conclude, we propose how unions, groups of older people acting in solidarity, and age-friendly plans could provide an important, effective and protective bulwark against the particular precarity associated with ageing as a paid care worker, and against wider societal inequities associated with gender and ageing. We illustrate the potential in considering age equity and care work together, by offering options that build on this analysis: to pursue skills recognition; to promote social unionism strategies that put older adults, their families and care workers in solidarity; and to develop 'age-equity bargaining' to focus on important equity issues like health and safety, retention, improving working conditions and financial security for retirement.

Invisibility traps for older LTC workers

Following welfare state regime theory (Esping-Andersen, 1999), and given polarisations in terms of market provision, Australia and Canada are among the liberal welfare regimes with 'residual' welfare states, and little labour market regulation. Norway in contrast, has a social democratic welfare regime with 'medium regulation' of its labour market, and favours universalism for its welfare state programs (Esping-Andersen, 1999, see Chapter 3 of this volume).

Despite these regime differences, care work invisibility is a feature of all three jurisdictions to varying degrees. The policy and practice variations among the three countries provide an opportunity to consider future possibilities. This section traces evidence of the super-invisibility of older care workers across the four invisibility traps, drawing examples from Australia, Canada and Norway.

Invisibility trap 1: Precarious work leads to pension precarity

Precarious work, an important aspect of working conditions, results from employment that is casual or part-time and produces income insecurity. Pension precarity is the cumulative disadvantage that accrues from precarious work and follows one into a 'precarious retirement' (Polivka and Luo, 2020). We briefly review overall pension conditions across our three countries, then address the specific impacts of job insecurity within care work to understand pension precarity in later life. An example from Australia is presented.

Income from pensions and state benefits are more robust in Norway than in Australia and Canada. As Figure 8.1 shows, most retired Norwegians (57.8 per cent) have a higher proportion of their income coming from public transfers than Canadians (37.6 per cent) and Australians (32.8 per cent). The OECD average is ~57.3 per cent.

There is a greater emphasis on private pensions in Canada than the other two countries. In Canada, private capital (including private personal pensions) comprises an average of 41.4 per cent of income for those 65+, but just 10 per cent of income among older Norwegians and 16.3 per cent for older Australians. Private occupational transfers (in the form of pensions, severance, death grants) comprise 14.2 per cent and 24.8 per cent of income for those 65+ in Norway and Australia respectively, exceeding the OECD average of 7.3 per cent. Canada reports no income of this type.

There are greater public protections for Norwegians over age 65, while older Canadians and Australians both hold greater private, individual responsibility for their income in older age accomplished by working for pay and wealth generation through savings. Among the three countries, Australians have the lowest levels of public sources of funds in retirement. Further, Australians are producing ~67.2 per cent of their own income after 65, from the combination of working, saving and employer pension schemes (Figure 8.1). Canadians, like Australians, personally generate on average 62.4 per cent of income through continued work and savings. Norwegians are more aligned with OECD averages, with less than half – an average of 42.2 per cent – of retirement income coming from personal resources rather than public pensions. The implication of weaker public transfers after retirement means that being in insecure employment, especially in Canada and Australia, has significant income security consequences in later life.

Among the three countries, low income in older age is a more pervasive condition in Australia and Canada, measured as the percentage of those aged 65 and older with incomes less than 50 per cent of the 'median equivalised household disposable income' (Table 8.1). The proportion exceeds one quarter of Australian women aged 65+, and almost a third of women and men aged 75 and older, while 14.6 per cent of women in Canada aged 65+ live with income below the median. The poverty rate in those over 65 is

Figure 8.1: Income sources aged 65+, 2020 or latest available year, as a percentage of income

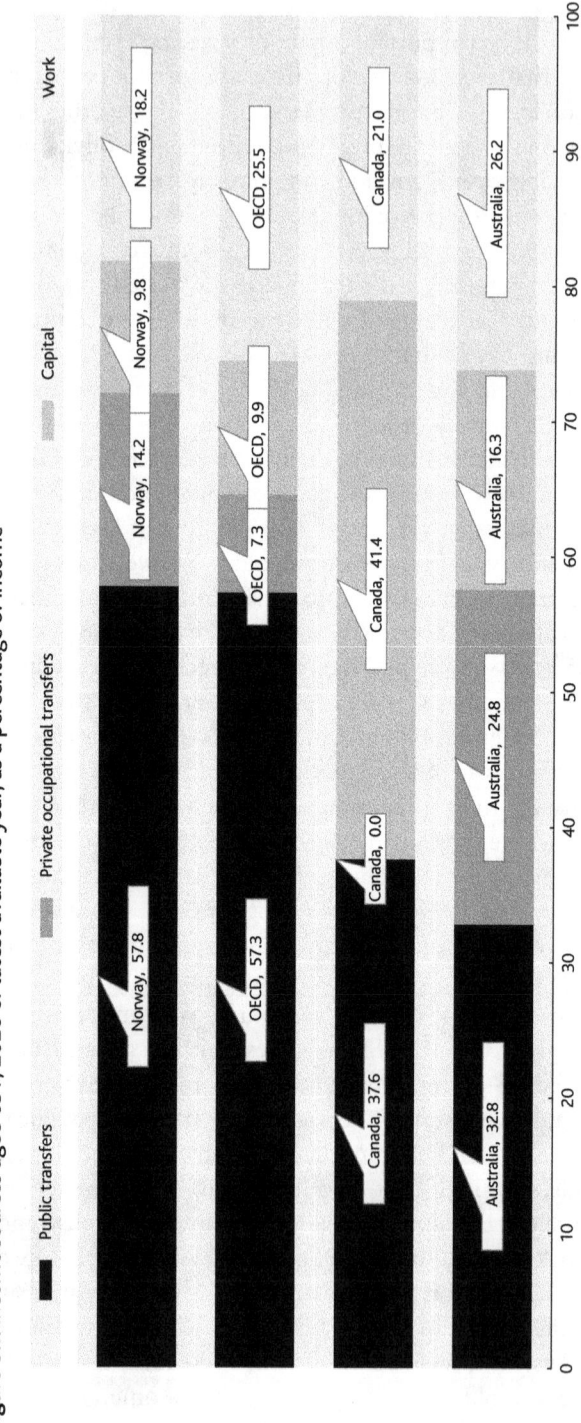

Table 8.1: Income below the median rates, 65+, by gender, 2020 or latest year

	Older people (aged 65+)					Total population (%)
	All (%)	By age		By gender		
		Age 66–75 (%)	Aged 75+ (%)	Men (%)	Women (%)	
Australia	22.6	19.7	27.0	18.2	26.6	12.6
Canada	12.1	11.0	13.9	9.2	14.6	8.6
Norway	3.8	2.7	5.4	2.3	5.1	7.9

Source: Analysis of OECD (2023a)

high in Australia (22.6), while Canada (11.7) and Norway (4.1) are below the OECD (2024) average (14.9).

Canadians retire earlier, but Norwegians and Australians live longer. The normal pensionable age in Canada is 65, while in Australia and in Norway there is a mandatory retirement age of 67 years. Both Australians' and Norwegians' average life expectancy is 2 years longer than Canadians. According to the International Labour Organization (2024), Australia also has the fewest people without any form of pension or old age security coverage, with only 76.5 per cent of women covered (Table 8.2). Both Canada and Norway have universal public pensions, designed to cover almost all previously employed or self-employed persons. The Canadian pension is widely regarded as insufficient, particularly for women, and racialised and Indigenous seniors. It is supplemented by Old Age Security and a Guaranteed Income Supplement for low-income seniors, and by privately held pensions and savings (Block et al, 2021).

The age profile of the overall workforce is an important indicator of how long people remain working. A higher overall proportion of the workforce is 55 and older in Canada (21.4 per cent) and Norway (21.5 per cent) than in Australia (19.2 per cent). For those 65+, more males than females remain in the workforce in all three countries (Figure 8.2).

International Labour Organization statistics, in combination with the national datasets analysed in Chapter 5, show that, overall, there are more female care workers aged 55 and over who remain on the job in Norway compared to its overall female workforce of the same age (Table 8.3).[2] Although Australian data about the 'age' of the care workforce has some reliability challenges, the comparative breakdown available suggests that there are more nurses and care assistants aged 55 and over working in home care than working in institutions, and more women working in care work than other industries, overall. Canada does not have disaggregated age data for nurses in LTC or home care. However, for all Canadian home care workers, which include PSWs along with others, there is a much higher proportion

Table 8.2: Pension conditions, by country, years as specified

Conditions		Australia	Canada	Norway
Pension age, 2024 (yrs)	Years	67	65	67
Average life expectancy, 2022 (yrs)		83	81	83
Average retirement age (yrs)	Males	59.4[3]	64.2[4]	65[5]
	Females	54.7	64.5	66
Total population covered by pension[6] (%)	Total	74.4		
	Male	71.9	100	100
	Female	76.5		
Employed and covered in the event of a work injury[7] (%)	Total	79.9		
	Male	75.8	83.6	Unreported
	Female	84.5		

Source: Analysis of Australian Bureau of Statistics (2024); ILOStat (2024); Norwegian Labour and Welfare Administration (NAV) (2024); Statistics Canada (2024)

aged 55 and older than those working in institutions, such as LTC homes. Table 8.3 shows that in Australia and Canada, home care workers – who require less education, are paid less, and include high proportions of racialised and new migrant workers – have more women working who are aged 55 and above.

The Norwegian proportion of older municipally employed nurses is higher than Canadian and Australian nurses, possibly due to better working conditions. Despite this, ill-health and physically demanding work are the main reasons Norwegian nurses retire ahead of the mandatory pension age of 67. In Norway, a growing share of older care workers remain on the job until retirement, with recent data showing that only one-quarter of 50-year-old RNs are expected to retire prior to turning 62 years old, compared to one fifth of care workers who have less education, according to FaFo (Midtsundstad and Nielsen, 2021), a labour organisation. Among the care workers surveyed, FaFo found that only 7 per cent reported that inadequate working conditions influenced their decision to leave. Overall, there has been a notable decline in early retirements, but Norwegian RNs are more likely to take this route than care workers, who hold less formal education. Hazardous and arduous work designations available to nurses in Norway, but not to care workers, as we outline later, may have some effect on nurses' early retirements.

Given that most LTC services are substantially funded by government transfers in all three countries, insufficient funding tends to shape precarious work conditions that lead to pension precarity. In this way, income insecurity for retiring care workers can be traced to insecure work, poor pay, and poor

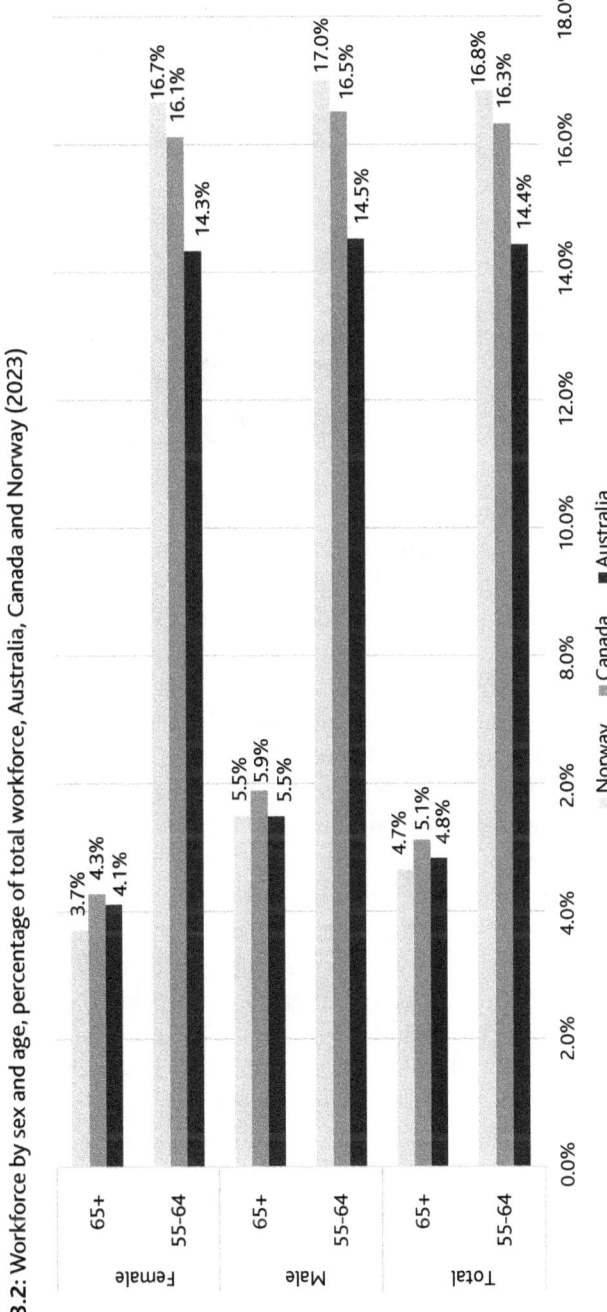

Figure 8.2: Workforce by sex and age, percentage of total workforce, Australia, Canada and Norway (2023)

Table 8.3: Workers aged 55+ as percentage of all workers, by category, most recent data available

Category	Aged 55+	Australia	Canada	Norway
	Total in workforce	19.2%	21.4%	21.5%
Nurses	Institutions	16.4% (**)	18.8% (*) (****)	31% (***)
	Home care	25.6%		
Assisting occupations	Institutions	16.0% (**)	22.2% (****)	Unreported
	Home care	32.5%	31%	

Note: (*) includes nurses + allied health professionals and working across health sites; (**) includes only residential aged care sites; (***) includes municipal workers across institutional and home care sites; (****) includes all health-care sites.
Source: Analysis of Helsedirektoratet (2021); Statistics Canada (2023); Aged Care Provider Workforce Survey, AIHW (2024); ILOStat (2024); unknown responses excluded

work benefits earlier in life, among other conditions (Crystal and Shea, 1990; Crystal et al, 2017; Grenier et al, 2020). Income insecurity is also associated with part-time work that involves too few hours (WHO, 2024).

The extent and impact of part-time work contracts on care workers is highlighted by an Australian example, showing that these contracts often lead to precarity in retirement, particularly when there is not enough of a public pension safety net. While most direct care staff in residential aged care (RAC) and the main home care packages program (HCPP) were in permanent positions (58 per cent), most of those permanent positions were only for part-time hours (85 per cent). Moreover, nearly one-third (28 per cent) were not in permanent positions, but were employed in casual/fixed term contracts. Importantly, another 14 per cent were 'agency staff', not directly employed by the provider, or self-employed contractors, unprotected by Australian minimum labour standards. As we highlight further on, working conditions that include high rates of illness, injury and violence are heightened without labour standards, like sick leave. Of note, between 2020 and 2023, the proportion of part-time nursing positions declined in RAC and HCPP – for RAC nurses from 68 per cent to 56 per cent and HCPP nurses from 51 per cent to 42 per cent. For personal care workers (PCW) part-time positions in HCPP declined from 75 per cent to 64 per cent. The proportion of permanent part-time nursing positions in HCPP increased from 18 per cent to 22 per cent, but the proportion of permanent part-time PCW positions decreased from 51 per cent to 37 per cent (AIHW, 2024). Further, in HCPP, the proportion of permanent full-time positions for PCWs increased marginally from 3 per cent to 6 per cent between 2020 and 2023, while the proportion of casual and fixed-term positions in HCPP ballooned from 3 per cent to 22 per cent for nursing and from 8 per cent to 40 per cent for PCWs. Consequently, while the proportional increase in full-time positions is positive, the shift to casual and fixed term work is not.

Pension precarity remains a condition of retirement for older care workers in Australia, even in 2025. The average retirement age is 55 for Australian women, with many retiring early due to poor job quality and care responsibilities (Welsh et al, 2018). Older workers, including those in aged care, are more likely to be in 'non-standard' employment, which includes part-time, casual, agency and self-employment. Together with low wages and limited, often shifting, assigned work hours, many workers retire with inadequate levels of retirement savings. The Health Employees Superannuation Trust Australia (HESTA) is the main 'superannuation' pension fund, the pension fund that aged care employers and workers contribute to for care workers' retirement savings. Most members, and particularly women, retire with low superannuation balances. For example, in 2015–16, women members aged 55–64 had a median balance of AUD $96,000; this compares to estimates that a dignified retirement balance requires AUD $545,000 for a single person (HESTA, 2020: 16). Furthermore, HESTA reported that, due to work stoppages and financial pressures they experienced during COVID, its aged care members were more likely to access their pensions funds earlier, when compared to members in other health and community services sectors. Approximately one quarter of HESTA's members who work in aged care – more than 45,000 workers – withdrew money from their pension, resulting in substantial decreases to their already low superannuation savings (HESTA, 2021).

As this example from Australia shows, income insecurity due to non-standard work contracts can lead to low pension retirement balances. These low balances were further affected by income insecurity experienced during COVID for care workers, and their pension balances declined even further below what is estimated to be needed to prevent pension insecurity in Australia. In summary, older care workers, in particular older women, who mostly care for older women, are more vulnerable in their own older age due to pension precarity, compromising their income security in later life.

Invisibility trap 2: Retention is not working

LTC has a retention problem. A substantial proportion of new care workers leave the job before they have worked for a year (14.5 per cent in Australia, 8.7 per cent in Norway, compared to an OECD average of 15.3 per cent). These proportions exceed the average for other health-care positions (10.9 per cent) and all employees (13.1 per cent) (de Tavernier et al, 2023). LTC working conditions are heavy and understaffing is rife, especially in

Canada and increasingly in Australia, while conditions are considered better in Norway. When care workers leave, the workload for experienced and older workers increases, as new workers are trained by experienced workers. Further, the payoff of decreased and more shared workload for the training time invested never arrives when new workers do not last even a single year on the job. We now compare the conditions across all three countries.

Prior to the COVID pandemic there was an already recognised shortage of Personal Support Workers (PSW) in Canada. Demand for PSWs has since surged, given a larger population of older adults and added redirection, delegation and downloading of nursing tasks to lower paid health-care workers (CIHI, 2023); however, turnover is significant. Between 2022 and 2023, the number of vacancies in Canadian health-care jobs doubled over 2019–20 and quadrupled over 2015–16. Over one quarter of vacancies (25.7 per cent; 30,800 positions) are for personal support workers, the highest among health-care workers.

In Ontario, Canada's most populous province, more than 100,000 people work in LTC homes. More than half are PSWs (58 per cent), and one-quarter are RNs (25 per cent). Most positions are part-time, with only some RNs (40 per cent) and RPNs (63 per cent) working full-time (Government of Ontario, 2020). National data are unreported, but an Ontario government-funded study reports that despite training more than 8,000 students every year to become a PSW, ~40 per cent of PSWs leave in the first year, and 25 per cent of PSWs with 2 or more years of experience leave LTC every year. Turnover is highest among PSWs in part-time and casual positions, most of whom are in their entry level year (Government of Ontario, 2020). Health Force Ontario, a government report, indicated that half of PSWs stay in LTC for less than 5 years, with 43 per cent leaving the sector, as a direct result of working short-staffed and experiencing burnout (Government of Ontario, 2020). The challenges may be too little supervisor support and insufficient time to do social care, which have been shown to increase the likelihood of wanting to leave care work (Virdo and Daly, 2019). When government and employers pay too little attention to the factors that improve retention, they push people out of jobs who would otherwise stay working.

One way to increase workforce capacity and retention of current staff – including migrant workers – would be to offer more hours to current permanent part-time employees rather than the current norm of creating limited hour, part-time contracts. The most recent Australian data on that question is from the 2016 National Aged Care Workforce Census and Survey (NACWCS): Australian aged care workers want more hours of work, as Mavromaras and colleagues report (2017), with the fewer hours worked, the more likely workers were to want more hours of work. Almost a third of all Australian direct care staff in RAC and 40 per cent of direct care staff in home care wanted more hours of work. Hours-related underemployment was even higher for personal care workers and home care workers, with an analysis of the 2016 NACWCS data suggesting that this was the case for 34 per cent for Australian born PCWs and 50 per cent of non-English speaking background PCWs. Under-employment was even higher for home care workers: 44 per cent among Australian born workers and 56 per cent among those with a non-English speaking background (Charlesworth and Isherwood, 2020). A recent 'Aged Care Work Value Case', described in more detail in the chapter's final section, is a legal case that relied on approaches to retain existing part-time workers with better hours and wages (Fair Work Commission, 2022; Charlesworth et al, 2024: 47). In contrast, the Australian government's dominant focus tends to be recruitment, with LTC providers demanding more migrant workers with special visas.

The working conditions in Norwegian residential LTC are considered better than the two other countries, given higher staff-to-resident ratios (Harrington et al, 2012; Harrington and Jacobsen, 2019). While insufficient staffing and a heavy workload for workers in LTC remains a concern in Norway, the working life of Norwegian LTC workers is less precarious than in many other European and North American countries due to: relatively high staffing levels (Harrington et al, 2012; Harrington and Jacobsen, 2019); comparatively reasonable wages (Eurofund, 2021); a comprehensive system of regulations securing job safety; and high job security even when sick. With a high proportion of women in the labour force, there is a relatively comprehensive level of social benefits. Nonetheless, Knutsen and colleagues (2024) have noted that absenteeism in LTC is 7.7 per cent, almost twice the national workforce average (4.3 per cent), a fact which has been linked to demanding psychosocial working conditions.

Constant turnover will not improve working conditions, and continually focusing on recruitment rather than retention is a flawed plan. Comparative OECD data (Table 8.4) confirms that Canada has the lowest share of LTC workers as a per cent of total employment, a share that has not increased since 2011, meaning that the number of LTC workers for every 100 people aged 65 and older in Canada is about half the number in Australia and one-quarter the number in Norway. The demand for LTC is expected only to increase with time, but Canada's poor average performance does not bode well for access to well-resourced care to meet the future need for care and the ageing of its population, all which impacts women, who are most likely to do unpaid and paid care and be those in receipt of care. Overall, LTC workers comprise 1.9 per cent of total employment in OECD (2023b; 2023c) countries, with demand expected to rise in the coming decade given the 'ageing impact on future demand for LTC workers' category, noted in Table 8.4. Needs are expected to be at least 0.6 per cent more workers as a proportion of the total workforce for all of the countries discussed.

Table 8.4: Comparative attributes of LTC, Australia, Canada and Norway

Factors	Years and units	Australia	Canada	Norway	OECD average
Share of LTC workers – % total employment	2011 (%)	2.0	1.2	3.9	1.7
	2021 (%)	2.3	1.2	4.1	1.9
Share of LTC workers who are part-time	2020 (*) /2021 (%)	92.1 (*)	57.2	29.5	36.6
LTC workers/100 population, aged 65+	2011 (rate)	7.1	4.1	13.2	5.9
	2020 (**) /2021 (rate)	7.3 (**)	3.8	12.0	5.7
'Ageing' impact on future demand for LTC workers	2023–33 (rate)	0.54	0.40	1.07	0.41
Given demand, total projected LTC employment as % of total employment	Projected 2033 (%)	3.1	1.7	5.5	2.5

Source: Analysis of OECD (2023b, 2023c)

Given the growing LTC needs, many OECD countries, including Canada and Australia, are experiencing difficulties, and the high rates of turnover and poor retention must be addressed. Both recruitment and retention represent significant challenges, exacerbated by the difficulties of the pandemic and longstanding issues with challenging working conditions including low pay, understaffing, gendered under-valuing and risky work environments. Younger workers, and younger women specifically, seem unwilling to stick around for the poor pay and poor conditions, adding stresses and strains to the existing, ageing workforce who may lack the ability to change careers later in life, and lending urgency to the need to focus on age equity in union bargaining, as we discuss later.

Invisibility trap 3: Unacceptably low health and safety protections

How are the health and safety of older workers protected given the pandemic experience? There have been unacceptably low health and safety protections across LTC settings, which produce sickness, injury and disability, particularly for older workers. This lack of protection contributed to how the initial pandemic outbreak affected LTC workers, particularly older workers, and highlights their poor working conditions. Among our countries, Canada is an important exemplar because its largest city, Toronto, Ontario, was a site in the initial global SARS outbreak in 2003, with 375 people contracting the virus, and 44 – including seven health-care workers – dying. The Ontario government 'SARS Commission' studied what worked and importantly what went wrong, especially as there was a second wave (Campbell, 2006).

The Commission made numerous recommendations, among them infection prevention and control, monitoring and adequate supply of properly fitted personal protective equipment (PPE), but most importantly, the need for work safety experts, the application of a common-sense precautionary principle related to infection, and a safety culture. Despite the excellent recommendations generated, lessons went unheeded. A mere 17 years after SARS, in other words still within the working lives of many, the infection and death rates in Ontario's LTC sector from the global pandemic were among the world's worst, and Toronto, its largest city, was hit very hard.

The case of COVID-19 in LTC in Toronto is important. It reveals infectious disease as a significant health and safety hazard, given the lack of personal protective equipment (PPE) available, the hazardous and arduous work required to care, and the disproportionately poor outcomes faced by older workers. COVID affected all older adults the most, with higher rates of serious illness and death, and more deaths in places with a higher concentration of people aged 60+ (WHO, 2020). What this meant for those working with older adults, and in particular, those who were also older workers, is underexplored. By July 2020, 48 per cent of Ontario LTC homes had declared an outbreak (Government of Ontario, 2020), with 43 per cent of the provinces' total deaths reported from nursing home residents (CIHI, 2021). By March 2021, just over a year into the pandemic, there were 14,984 cases of COVID among LTC residents across the province's 15 million people.[8] Dozens of LTC homes lacked PPE, especially in Toronto, and particularly in private for-profit facilities, where the surges in cases and deaths were highest (Casey, 2020).

Largely overlooked by the media and broader public was the high rate of exposure and death faced by the frontline care workers in residential LTC. Here we report data from residential LTC; data about home care as a work setting were not reported. By end of July 2020, there were 5,893 resident and 2,558 long-term care worker cases reported (Public Health Ontario, 2020). By the end of April 2021, almost 4,000 residents and 11 staff had died (OLTCC, 2021). Our analysis of Workplace Safety and Insurance Board Ontario (WSIB, 2024) subclass N2 'nursing and residential care facilities' data, which includes but is not exclusively residential LTC, there were 16 to 19 LTC staff deaths due to COVID-19, as of December 2024. There were also an unspecified number of traumatic deaths (<5). From January 2020 to December 2024, the leading 'injury' in LTC was COVID-19 (33 per cent), with 55–59 year olds most affected; the highest absolute number of claims were reported by 50–59 year olds. From 2020 to 2024, there were 32,598 'occupational diseases claims' listed from LTC workers, with COVID-19 accounting for 27,699 (85 per cent) of their claims.

'Assisting occupations in support of health services', or PSWs, were 13 per cent of the claims and 5 per cent of the cost of all workplace injuries from 2020–24, and that is across all workplaces, for the whole province, and mostly among those 50–54 years old. Nurse supervisors and RNs accounted for another 3 per cent of both the cost and number of workplace injuries, mostly from those aged 50–54 years old. Childcare and home support workers, in comparison, comprised 1 per cent of the cost and 3 per cent of all workplace injury claims across the province.

Injury is also rife across health care, but especially in 'nursing and residential care facilities', with the following Ontario WSIB injury claims the most reported in LTC from 2020–24: COVID-19 (62 per cent), strains and sprains (18 per cent), infectious and parasitic diseases (4 per cent), bruises and contusions (3 per cent), traumatic injuries (2 per cent), and concussion (2 per cent). All were claimed most by those aged 50–59, except concussion (which most affected 20–24 year olds). Fractures were just 1 per cent, but it was the largest claim made by those aged 60–64 year olds in LTC, accounting for 389 claims, and an average of 61 days lost per claim. Clearly, LTC workers as a group, and those 50+ report the highest rates of illness and disease and receive too few preventive workplace supports.

What is most shocking is the lack of learning from the earlier SARS Commission. Toronto should have had the best, not the worst outcomes. Most of the COVID containment efforts went towards protecting hospital capacity, and patients sick with COVID were discharged into LTC. However, LTC was ill-prepared for infection prevention and control, given: a lack of staff training; insufficient and inappropriate PPE; ill-suited physical environments; under-staffing; and about one-third of the workforce held positions at more than one facility. There has been little study of the on-going disability and trauma that care workers experienced. What is clear is that Ontario's 'nursing and residential care' sector remains a challenging workplace given the lack of health and safety protections, and there are reasons to believe that this is similar across the country.

While LTC in Australia was also the sector in the country most affected by COVID and a significant site of worker health and safety challenges, its COVID outcomes are a study in contrasts with Canada. There were 28 resident deaths in aged care facilities during the height of COVID, representing more than half (54.9 per cent) of total deaths in the state of New South Wales and over a quarter (26.9 per cent) of total deaths from COVID across Australia by June 2020 (Quigley, 2022). From March 2020 to July 2021, there were 2,060 resident cases, 992 resident deaths and 2,261 residential aged care worker cases. By July 2021, the Australian death rate was 3.7/1,000 residential aged care beds. From July 2021 to January 2022, 13,998 resident cases and 671 resident deaths and 16,773 residential aged care worker cases were recorded (ADHAC, 2024). Canada experienced more than 22 times the number of deaths in care homes compared with Australia (ADHAC, 2024). Like Australia, rates in Norway were worse in LTC, but did not approach the challenges faced by Canadian workers, especially older care workers.

While COVID rates were lower in Australia and Norway, LTC workers were more affected than other workers. COVID was not only a risk for residents of LTC but a significant workplace health and safety issue for older care workers, amplifying existing workplace health and safety issues. It also revealed the ways in which the older care workers are super-invisible. In many ways, both policy makers and employers completely ignored the age of the health-care workforce during the pandemic and its aftermath, despite working to prevent a disease that mostly affected older adults. Furthermore, with high rates of injury in the care workforce, and especially infectious and musculoskeletal types, there has been surprisingly little attention paid to its prevention. The most common health and safety hazards reported in aged care happen when lifting and assisting residents, pushing and pulling equipment, slips, trips and falls, and work-related stress, bullying and harassment (Worksafe Victoria, nd). LTC is dangerous work, but it is much worse for older workers. How COVID affected the families of workers, especially older family members, is also under-explored.

Returning to our earlier point about pension rates and coverage, some countries allow some workers to take an early pension from national pension schemes when working in 'hazardous and arduous jobs' (OECD, 2023a: 108). The overarching list of jobs includes predominantly male jobs (airline pilots, electricians, marine workers, miners, train drivers, bus drivers, firefighters, police and military), mixed gender jobs (journalists), and a few predominantly female jobs (ballet dancers, teachers and nurses). The OECD groups countries into four categories, with group one countries recognising many of the aforementioned jobs as early pension eligible. Norway is part of group one, with airline pilots, marine workers, firefighters, police and military jobs considered to be employed in hazardous and arduous work, but so are ballet dancers, and importantly, nurses are included. Canada classifies firefighting, police and military alone as hazardous and arduous jobs – all predominantly masculine fields – while Australia classes no jobs as either. Australia allows early pension-taking in mandatory individual superannuation pension schemes, but as we have shown, this has been detrimental to care workers, especially women.

The heavy workloads in care work, particularly in the context of under-staffing, should be ample evidence of 'arduousness', as seems to be the case in Norway. On-going workplace injury and illness claims, the highest of all workplaces, as is the case in Canada and Australia, should be sufficient proof of the work hazards. With added evidence about the impacts of infectious disease from COVID, especially for workers 50 and older and particularly in Canada, the arduousness and hazards of care work seems incontrovertible. Yet, while the hazardous and arduous features of the work are well supported by evidence, the overarching context of pension security is important to consider. With Norway's robust public pension funding, enabling early pension may be one way to address the needs of older care workers who must retire early for illness or disability reasons. This would be risky for care workers in the same position who live in Australia or Canada, where care workers are more commodified: workplace protections are fewer, individual savings are such an important part of the income after 65, and the rate of those living below median income who are aged 65 and older, especially for Australian women, is so high.

Invisibility trap 4: Data gaps

How are older workers represented in datasets? As Chapter 5 lays out, national labour market datasets do a poor job of counting the care workforce. Weak, unclear and hidden datasets make a proper workforce analysis nearly impossible, which prohibits planning and independent checking of this overly feminised and increasingly racialised workforce. Each of our countries has key challenges with how it 'counts' care workers, particularly when we need to best understand who works where, for whom, with what labour protections, and who cares for whom, by sex, age or immigrant status. We found challenges with data strength, data clarity, and public availability. In all three countries, data are weak, subject to bias due to data collection challenges (Australia), double-counting (Australia) unknown responses (Australia and Canada) or professional privileging of nurses, with more reported about them than those in assisting occupations (Canada and Norway across all datasets and Australia in its population census). Those who work as private companions, paid directly by older adults and family to provide care, are absent entirely (Daly and Armstrong, 2016).

All these issues raise questions, making planning to meet the needs of older adults, and the health and safety considerations, particularly challenging. Data are 'noisy' when definitional boundaries are too broad, making the data unclear, or making it difficult to parse out who works primarily in care for older adults, by including everyone in receipt of care in the calculations. Noise can also occur due to the conflation of categories of workers who share little more than time in education or the fact that they work in private homes (such as lumping together doulas and personal support workers, in Canada), or due to a lack of disaggregation, such as by location of work or by position (Canada and Norway). We found that data about nurses in Canadian residential care was available, but noisy data about home care workers made it impossible to discern how many nurses are doing that work. Noisiness also occurs when it is impossible to triangulate between different government sources, as is the case with all three countries when comparing the labour force and national census datasets, or when reporting is only about selective groups, such as Norway's municipal workers, for example, or nurses, or when data are of such poor quality that data reporting agencies must seek workarounds, such as Canada does with personal support workers. Finally, a key source of invisibility is when data are not publicly available and shared in ways that make it possible to manipulate and analyse them. Although the data are subject to weaknesses and noise, Australia has a national LTC funding program for 'Aged Care', and as a result, it publicly reports on the workers funded by it in ways that are somewhat clearer than Canada and Norway. Complicating and hindering workforce assessment of the LTC workforce for Canada are its mix of federal/provincial/municipal LTC funding, municipal/non-profit/for-profit LTC delivery, and under-funding. Norway's nationally funded and mostly municipally delivered LTC programs also reveal data gaps related to funding structures, leaving the difference unclear between who is working for the municipal LTC services compared with those working for other employers. Furthermore, data are made available only by sporadic reports released without a reliable schedule, and in forms that don't allow disaggregated analysis.

We need clear, strong *and* publicly available workforce data, and data that show the sex, age and race composition of the care work force, which are lacking in the countries studied. Without accurate knowledge about the composition of the care workforce, we reproduce conditions of invisibility for care workers.

Importantly, poor quality datasets hide the ageing of the workforce and make older care workers super-invisible. This invisibility hinders the advancement of age-friendliness, particularly as it hampers the ability of those responsible for policy and planning. For example, cities implementing age-friendly strategies can push for better working conditions, smarter regulations, and include strategic decisions that protect the retention of older care workers and improve their access to good incomes that avoid pension precarity and enable older people to get better care.

Where to from here? Age-inclusive bargaining to address age equity

In this chapter we have highlighted the 'invisibility traps', that apply across paid care work, but are especially pernicious in some countries, and for older care workers. This section posits one way forward that involves workers including age equity in their bargaining strategies and collectively resisting inequitable and invisibilising conditions through their unions to 'make the case' for better pay. We draw from the example of Australian care workers to discuss this possibility.

Skills and pay

In Australia, an historic legal case on the valuing of skills used by care workers in aged care, the 'Aged Care Work Value Case', started with applications to the Fair Work Commission (FWC) by three major aged care unions in 2020–21. The Australian Nursing and Midwives Federation (ANMF), the Health Services Union (HSU) and United Workers Union (UWU) applied for a 25 per cent 'work value' increase in the minimum wages for registered nurses, other nursing-qualified employees, personal care employees, ancillary residential aged care employees and home care employees. In November 2022, the Australian Fair Work (2022) Commission Full Bench decision accepted the grounds for improving pay for direct care workers in the sector, awarding them an interim 15 per cent increase. It accepted the expert evidence: work in feminised industries, including care work, has been historically undervalued, and the reason for that undervaluation is likely gender based. The 15 per cent pay increase came into effect in June 2023. In its final decision (March 2024), the FWC provided further wage increases for care workers, as well as new classification definitions and structures under the three awards. It extended the minimum award rates of pay for direct care workers beyond the 15 per cent interim increase. To provide a framework for the increases, the Expert Panel set a benchmark payrate of AU$1,223.90 per week for Certificate III-qualified Home Care Workers, Personal Care Workers and Assistants in Nursing, and then constructed a new, uniform classification structure from that benchmark rate. The new rates for direct care workers represented a total wage increase of between 22 and 28 per cent, depending on the classification and job role. Unlike the direct care workers, 'indirect' or ancillary aged care workers, who had not been awarded an interim wage increase in 2022, were awarded a smaller increase of between 3 per cent and 7 per cent, because the FWC determined that their work was not of equivalent value to direct care workers. It did, however, acknowledge that there have been some changes in 'work value' for some indirect care workers, such as laundry workers, cleaners and food services assistants, related to infection prevention and control, dementia care, aged care quality standards, and other training requirements. The FWC decided that the second tranche of wage increases would be paid in two phases: 50 per cent from 1 January 2025 and the remaining 50 per cent from October 2025. However, while it was argued that wage increases for aged care workers would help increase both the retention and recruitment in the sector, this argument was not a major focus of the FWC decision. Further, while the unions pointed to the skills and physical demands of aged care work in this case, the older age profile of workers was not a major feature of the unions' arguments for wage increases.

Unlike Australia, in Canada there is not a national standard for PSW training, and little work is being done to recognise or value the skills of care work with pay or a career ladder. If you start as a PSW in Canada, you could retire at that same level and job title 35 years later. In Canada, there is not even a consistent training standard or one that recognises the skills earned on the job. For instance, some provinces have a mandated curriculum for PSWs – including British Columbia (BC), Alberta, Ontario, Quebec, New Brunswick and Nova Scotia – while other provinces and territories, such as Manitoba, Saskatchewan, Newfoundland, Prince Edward Island (PEI), Nunavut, Yukon and Northwest Territories, do not require any formalised training. Further, as 'unregulated' workers, who are not considered health professionals, there is a wide mix of rules about this work. BC, Alberta, Nova Scotia and the territories – with Ontario soon to follow – require all those doing this work in any setting funded by the public system to hold educational credentials that outline competencies and delimit their roles and responsibilities. In PEI, New Brunswick and Ontario, workers require a certificate, but there remain discrepancies in legislation covering regulated health professions and nursing acts, which requires redress by policymakers.

As of 2023 in Norway, 77.1 per cent of LTC workers have at least 2 years of formal health education (Statistics Norway, 2024). There are also national training standards for registered nurses and for licensed vocational/practical nurses. As for the 25–30 per cent of the LTC staff without a recognised health educational background, some local facility or organisationally based formal initiatives provide on-site training, but like in Canada, there is still a lack of national measures.

The Australian example is promising because care workers earned the right to have their skills and experience on the job recognised with higher pay, which can contribute not only to income security during their working years, but high retirement income as well. These rewards were hard won; the Australian unions fought to have care workers skills recognised. There are opportunities for unions to do more to improve the working conditions, including health and safety, and to improve retention. This next section discusses how unions across our countries can and do make visible the conditions of work for care workers and advance their rights while also finding ways to align in solidarity with groups of older adults needing care.

'Age-equitable' bargaining

A feature of Australian union bargaining, particularly in the public sector, is 'equality bargaining' (Williamson and Baird, 2014); however, there has been far less explicit attention paid to 'age-equitable bargaining' in ways that would produce greater equity for everyone. One of the national minimum labour standards in Australia includes a right to request flexible work after 12 months service with the employer. This right has now been extended to employees aged 55 years or older, those with a disability, those experiencing domestic violence, and those with caring responsibilities. However, arguably the inclusion of older workers was due more to the pressure of carers' advocacy groups than to pressure from the unions, which have focused on extending the general scope and enforcement of this labour standard, and the rights and protections of employees who access it.

Solidarity with those receiving care by those providing it has been advanced in Canada, such as the Hospital Employees Union's (HEU) 'Care Can't Wait' and the Canadian Union of Public Employees of Ontario 'Time to Care' campaigns, both forms of social unionism. In Canada, the example of HEU also shows how unions and sectoral bargaining can prevent privatisation and create more job stability in ways that also make better care possible (Longhurst et al, 2020). Likewise, Norwegian unions have been a formidable force in fighting LTC privatisation, unlike in the other Social Democratic countries (Ågotnes et al, 2020; Jacobsen and Ågotnes, 2020).

Unions can also advocate for governments to pay greater attention to unequal gender conditions within pensions. They can take up the facts about female lower incomes after age 65 and weaker public pensions for both Canadian and Australian workers. Pushing to make LTC settings safe places to work is especially important for older workers, who are the ones with the highest claims for infections, illness and injuries. Union efforts to include age-equity and give urgent attention to the needs of older care workers will have ripple effects on the conditions for all care workers.

Concluding thoughts: Making older care workers super-*visible*

Care workers are paid poorly and overworked. They are mostly women and are increasingly racialised and migrants. They are subject to work overload. Importantly, as we note in Chapter 5, older workers comprise a significant proportion of this workforce, but the conditions that would improve their own working and retirement conditions are largely unaddressed as an outcome of the ways that care work is rendered less visible within policies and practices.

In this chapter, we show that the needs of older care workers in LTC must be recognised at the system level. Immediate issues in the sector that are particularly problematic for older care workers include: a lack of proper protections for illness and infectious disease; the continuation of labour practices that enable precarious working conditions, leading to pension precarity in older age; and government's focus on recruitment strategies that mask or completely overshadow retention strategies. Better data collection and public reporting about socio-demographic characteristics of care workers and their working conditions is required to enable workforce planning to support the sector moving forward and to recognise challenges.

To make the needs of older care workers in LTC super-visible, the sector must, immediately and at a minimum, recognise the increased risks of infectious disease for older workers, not only during pandemics, but with common infectious diseases that affect older people, including older workers. Not having proper personal protective gear is inexcusable. Systems must also increase care workers' low pay by valuing the vital contribution of care work and fixing the pension precarity traps to avoid low income for retired older care workers. Retention is critical, and it is best addressed with a focus on fixing work overload so that new recruits want to stay, and older workers are relieved of what we call the 'train-then-churn' cycle of training new recruits who then leave within the first year or two. This cycle currently infects LTC in many jurisdictions and makes more and harder work for older workers. In addition, converting non-standard jobs into standard employment, making more full-time positions and granting more hours to those in part-time permanent positions are critical strategies to protect against future pension precarity and low income of women in older age. Furthermore, LTC systems must attend to the appalling rates of illness and injury to decrease the likelihood that workers will leave employment early. One path is to address the tremendous understaffing that puts strain on care workers, particularly older workers. The Norwegian model of classifying nursing as hazardous and arduous work subject to early retirement could be extended to care assistants there, but this will not protect care workers in Australia and Canada, who must cover a greater proportion of their pension funds individually.

As the Australia work value case shows, unions, groups of older adults, and even age-friendly planners have a vital role to play in advocating for and achieving better conditions for aged care workers. One important place to start is for unions to push governments to recognise the important skills gained on the job and to reward those skills through certification, pay and a career ladder. Better pay will help immediately, and in future help prevent pension precarity.

The last piece to consider is how overarching policy frameworks, like age-friendly policies, can visibilise and recognise the work of care in their framing, and older workers in particular, in how they advance 'affordable' and 'accessible' health and community care services. It is important that good quality outcomes for seniors are not produced on the backs of workers, who themselves are older and whose concerns are often ignored.

Notes

[1] Recently this domain has been recast as 'community and health care' and an interconnected domain of urban life.
[2] We used a variety of country level datasets to describe the care workforce that are 55 and older, as we outline in Chapter 5 and summarize in Table 9.3, noting that each dataset has specific limitations.
[3] Year 2022–23, Australian Bureau of Statistics (2024) Retirement and Retirement Intentions, Australia 2022–23 financial year, https://www.abs.gov.au/statistics/labour/employment-and-unemployment/retirement-and-retirement-intentions-australia/latest-release#:~:text=Of%20the%20130%2C000%20people%20who,the%20average%20was%2063.2%20years.

4   Year: 2023, Statistics Canada (2024) Table 14-10-0060-01: Retirement age by class of worker, annual. DOI: 10.25318/1410006001-eng
5   Norwegian Labour and Welfare Administration (NAV) (June 2024), Alderspensjon 'Retirement Pension', https://www.nav.no/no/nav-og-samfunn/statistikk/pensjon-statistikk/alderspensjon
6   Year: 2022, ILOStat, https://ilostat.ilo.org
7   ILOStat, https://ilostat.ilo.org; reporting year 2021; Australia, 2022.
8   Home care client cases were aggregated among other community acquired cases.

References

ADHAC (Australian Department of Health and Aged Care) (2024) COVID-19 outbreaks in Australian residential aged care facilities National snapshot 11 [online], Available from: https://www.health.gov.au/sites/default/files/2024-07/covid-19-outbreaks-in-australian-residential-aged-care-facilities-12-july-2024_0.docx

Ågotnes, G., Jacobsen, F.F. and Szebehely, M. (2020) The growth of the for-profit nursing home sector in Norway and Sweden: driving forces and resistance, in P. Armstrong and H. Armstrong (eds) *The Privatization of Care*, Routledge, pp 38–50.

AIHW (Australian Institute of Health and Welfare) (2024) *2023 Aged Care Provider Workforce Survey Summary Report: August 2024* [online], Available from: https://www.gen-agedcaredata.gov.au/resources/reports-and-publications/2024/august/2023-aged-care-provider-workforce-survey-summary-report

Armstrong, P. and Armstrong, H. (2009) Precarious employment in the health-care sector, in L.F. Vosko, M. MacDonald and I. Campbell (eds) *Gender and the Contours of Precarious Employment*, Routledge, pp 270–84.

Armstrong, P. and Laxer, K. (2006) Precarious work, privatization, and the health-care industry: the case of ancillary workers, in L.F. Vosko (ed) *Precarious Employment: Understanding Labour Market Insecurity in Canada*, McGill-Queen's University Press.

Armstrong, P., Armstrong, H. and Daly, T. (2012) The thin blue line: long-term care as an indicator of equity in welfare states, *Canadian Woman Studies*, 29(3): 49–60.

Armstrong, P., Choiniere, J., Harrington, C. and Szebehely, M. (2023a) What's critical to care?, in P. Armstrong and S. Braedley (eds) *Care Homes in a Turbulent Era*, Edward Elgar Publishing Limited, pp 34–49.

Armstrong, P., Jacobsen, F.F., Lanoix, M. and Szebehely, M. (2023b) The crisis in the nursing home labour force: where is the political will?, in P. Armstrong and S. Braedley (eds) *Care Homes in a Turbulent Era*, Edward Elgar Publishing, pp 50–66.

Baines, D., Charlesworth, S. and Daly, T. (2016) Underpaid, unpaid, unseen, unheard, and unhappy? Care work in the context of constraint, *Journal of Industrial Relations*, 58(4): 449–54.

Block, S., Galabuzi, G.E. and King, H. (2021) *Colour-Coded Retirement*, Canadian Centre for Policy Alternatives [online], Available from: https://www.policyalternatives.ca/wp-content/uploads/attachments/Colour%20coded%20retirement.pdf

Campbell, A. (2006) The SARS Commission, Volumes 1–5 [online], Available from: https://www.archives.gov.on.ca/en/e_records/sars/report/index.html

Casey, L. (2020) Long-term care homes suffered due to efforts to help hospitals, inquiry hears, *CBC News* 10 October [online], Available from: https://www.cbc.ca/news/canada/toronto/covid-ont-ltc-commission-1.5759753

Charlesworth, S. (2012) Decent working conditions for care workers? The intersections of employment regulation, the funding market and gender norms, *Australian Journal of Labour Law*, 25(2): 107–27.

Charlesworth, S. and Isherwood, L. (2020) Migrant aged-care workers in Australia: do they have poorer-quality jobs than their locally born counterparts?, *Ageing and Society*, 41(12): 2702–22.

Charlesworth, S. and Low, L. (2020) *The Long-Term Care COVID-19 Situation in Australia*, International Long-Term Care Policy Network [online], Available from: https://ltccovid.org/wp-content/uploads/2020/10/Australia-LTC-COVID19-situation-12-October-2020-1-2.pdf

Charlesworth, S., Cunningham, I. and Daly, T. (2024) *Decent Work and Quality Long-Term Care Systems*, Independent report commissioned by Public Services International [online], Available from: https://publicservices.international/resources/digital-publication/decent-work-and-quality-long-term-care-systems?id=14383&lang=en

CIHI (Canadian Institute for Health Information) (2021) *The impact of COVID-19 on long-term care in Canada Focus on the first 6 months* [online], Available from: https://www.cihi.ca/sites/default/files/document/impact-covid-19-long-term-care-canada-first-6-months-report-en.pdf

CIHI (Canadian Institute for Health Information) (2023) *Recommendations for Advancing Pan-Canadian Data Capture for Personal Support Workers* [online], Available from: https://www.cihi.ca/sites/default/files/document/recommendations-advancing-pan-canadian-data-capture-psws-report-en.pdf

Connell, R. (2021) *Gender: In World Perspective* (4th edn), Polity Press.

Crystal, S. and Shea, D. (1990) Cumulative advantage, cumulative disadvantage, and inequality among elderly people, *The Gerontologist*, 30(4): 437–43.

Crystal, S., Shea, D.G. and Reyes, A.M. (2017) Cumulative advantage, cumulative disadvantage, and evolving patterns of late-life inequality, *The Gerontologist*, 57(5): 910–20.

Daly, T. and Armstrong, P. (2016) Liminal and invisible long-term care labour: precarity in the face of austerity, *Journal of Industrial Relations*, 58(4): 473–90.

Daly, T., Struthers, J., Müller, B., Taylor, D., Goldmann, M., Doupe, M. et al (2016) Prescriptive or interpretive regulation at the frontlines of care work in the 'three worlds' of Canada, Germany and Norway, *Labour/Le Travail*, 77(77): 37–71.

de Tavernier, W., Boulhol, H., Cazes, S. and Garnero, A. (2023) Work environment and collective bargaining in long-term care, in *Beyond Applause? Improving Working Conditions in Long-Term Care*. OECD.

Esping-Andersen, G. (1999) *Social Foundations of Postindustrial Economies*, Oxford University Press.

EUROFUND (2021) *Living conditions and quality of life: wages in long-term care and other social services 21% below average* [online], Available from: https://www.eurofound.europa.eu/en/resources/article/2021/wages-long-term-care-and-other-social-services-21-below-average

Fair Work Commission (2022) *Aged Care Work Value Case: Summary of Decision* [online], Available from: https://www.fwc.gov.au/documents/sites/work-value-aged-care/decisions-statements/2022fwcfb200-summary.pdf

Government of Ontario (2020) *Long-Term Care Staffing Study*, Ministry of Long-Term Care [online], Available from: https://files.ontario.ca/mltc-long-term-care-staffing-study-en-2020-07-31.pdf

Grenier, A., Phillipson, C. and Settersten, R.A. (2020) Precarity and ageing: new perspectives for social gerontology, in A. Grenier, C. Phillipson and R.A. Settersten (eds) *Precarity and Ageing: Understanding Insecurity and Risk in Later Life*, Policy Press, pp 1–16.

Harrington, C. and Jacobsen, F.F. (2019) Nurse staffing in nursing homes in industrialised countries, in P. Armstrong and H. Armstrong (eds) *The Privatization of Care: The Case of Nursing Homes*, Routledge.

Harrington, C., Choiniere, J., Goldmann, M., Jacobsen, F., Lloyd, L., McGregor, M., Stamatopoulos, V. and Szebehely, M. (2012) Nursing home staffing standards and staffing levels in six countries, *Journal of Nursing Scholarship*, 44(1): 88–98.

Helsedirektoratet [Norwegian Health Directorate] (2021) *Personell og Kompetanse i den Kommunale Helse- og Omsorgstjenesten (Personnel and Expertise in the Municipal Health and Care Service)* [online], Available from: https://www-helsedirektoratet-no.translate.goog/rapporter/personell-og-kompetanse-i-den-kommunale-helse-og-omsorgstjenesten?_x_tr_sl=no&_x_tr_tl=en&_x_tr_hl=en-US&_x_tr_pto=wapp

HESTA (2020) *Treasury Retirement Income Review submission* [online], Available from: https://treasury.gov.au/sites/default/files/2020-02/hesta030220.pdf

HESTA (2021) *State of the Sector: Aged Care Workforce insights* [online], Available from: https://www.hesta.com.au/agedcarereport21

ILO (International Labour Organization) (2024) ILOSTAT [online], Available from: https://ilostat.ilo.org

Jacobsen, F.F. and Ågotnes, G. (2020) Towards accountable for-profits in nursing home services?, in P. Armstrong and H. Armstrong (eds) *The Privatization of Care: The Case of Nursing Homes*, Routledge.

Knutsen, R.H., Nielsen, M.B., Lunde, L.K., Skare, Ø. and Johannessen, H.A. (2024) Impact of psychosocial work factors on risk of medically certified sick leave due to common mental disorders: a nationwide prospective cohort study of Norwegian home care workers, *BMC Public Health*, 24(1): 773.

Longhurst, A., Ponder, S. and McGregor, M. (2020) Labor restructuring and nursing home privatization in British Columbia, Canada, in P. Armstrong and H. Armstrong (eds) *The Privatization of Care: The Case of Nursing Homes*, Routledge.

Mavromaras, K., Knight, G., Isherwood, L., Crettenden, A., Flavel, J., Karmel, T. et al (2017) *The Aged Care Workforce 2016*, Department of Health.

Midtsundstad, T. and Nielsen, R. (2021) *Det erfarne blicket Seniorer I plei- og omsorgssektoren* (The experienced perspective Seniors in the care sector), FAFO [online], Available from: https://lengrearbeidsliv.no/kunnskap/forskning-og-utvikling/det-erfarne-blikket/

OECD (2023a) *Pensions at a Glance 2023: OECD and G20 Indicators*, OECD.

OECD (2023b) *Health at a Glance 2023: OECD Indicators*, OECD.

OECD (2023c) *Beyond Applause? Improving Working Conditions in Long-Term Care*, OECD [online], Available from: https://doi.org/10.1787/27d33ab3-en.

OECD (2024) *Income Distribution Database* [online], Available from: http://www.oecd.org/social/income-distribution-database.htm

OLTCC (Ontario Long-term Care Commission) (2021) Long-term care COVID-19 Commission: Final Report [online], Available from: https://files.ontario.ca/mltc-ltcc-final-report-en-2021-04-30.pdf

Polivka, L. and Luo, B. (2020) From precarious employment to precarious retirement: Neoliberal health and long-term care in the United States, in A. Grenier, C. Phillipson and R.A. Settersten Jr (eds) *Precarity and Ageing*, Policy Press, pp 191–214.

Public Health Ontario (2020) *COVID-19 in Ontario: July 2020* [online], Available from: https://www.publichealthontario.ca/en/Data-and-Analysis/Infectious-Disease/COVID-19-Data-Surveillance/Archives/Daily-Epi-Summary

Quigley, A., Stone, H., Nguyen, P.Y., Chughtai, A.A. and MacIntyre, C.R. (2022) COVID-19 outbreaks in aged-care facilities in Australia, *Influenza and Other Respiratory Viruses*, 16(3): 429–37.

Smith, D.E. (2002) *Texts, Facts, and Femininity: Exploring the Relations of Ruling*, Routledge.

Statistics Canada (StatsCan) (2023) *Class of Worker Including Job Permanency by Occupation Minor Group, Labour Force Status, Age and Gender: Canada, Provinces and Territories and Census Divisions* [online], Available from: https://www150.statcan.gc.ca/t1/tbl1/en/tv.action?pid=9810059101

Statistics Canada (StatsCan) (2024) *Retirement Age by Class of Worker, Annual* [online], Available from: https://www150.statcan.gc.ca/t1/tbl1/en/tv.action?pid=1410006001

Virdo, G. and Daly, T. (2019) How do supervisor support and social care matter in long-term care? Correlates of turnover contemplation among long-term care facility workers, *International Journal of Care and Caring*, 3(3): 413–24.

Welsh, J., Strazdins, L., Charlesworth, S., Kulik, C.T. and D'Este, C. (2018) Losing the workers who need employment the most: how health and job quality affect involuntary retirement, *Labour & Industry: A Journal of the Social and Economic Relations of Work*, 28(4): 261–78.

WHO (World Health Organization) (2007) *Global Age-Friendly Cities: A Guide* [online], Available from: https://iris.who.int/bitstream/handle/10665/43755/9789241547307_eng.pdf?sequence=1&isAllowed=y

WHO (World Health Organization) (2020) *COVID and the Decade of Healthy Ageing* [online], Available from: https://cdn.who.int/media/docs/default-source/decade-of-healthy-ageing/decade-connection-series---covid-19-en_c49604e5-7d8f-4ae8-9c16-563a576c3103.pdf?sfvrsn=d3f887b0_7&download=true

WHO (World Health Organization) (2024) *Fair Share for Health and Care: Gender and the Undervaluation of Health and Care Work*, World Health Organization.

WHO (World Health Organization) (nd) *Community and Health Care* [online], Available from: https://extranet.who.int/agefriendlyworld/age-friendly-practices/community-and-health/

Williamson, S. and Baird, M. (2014) Gender equality bargaining: developing theory and practice, *Journal of Industrial Relations*, 56(2): 155–69.

Worksafe Victoria (nd) *Injury Hotspots: Aged Care* [online], Available from: https://www.worksafe.vic.gov.au/injury-hotspots-aged-care

WSIB (Workplace Safety and Insurance Board) (2024) *Health and Safety Statistics* [online], Available from: https://www.wsib.ca/en

9

Resistance, resilience and relationship: Indigenous older adults and ageing in the Canadian city

Lauren Brooks-Cleator and Sean Hillier

Introduction

What is age equity for Indigenous older adults living in cities in Canada? We address this question at a time when Indigenous peoples around the world are increasingly living in urban areas, including 69 per cent of North American Indigenous People, 33.6 per cent of European and Central Asian Indigenous People and 27.2 per cent of Asian and Pacific Indigenous people, as just a few examples (Tzay, 2021). The Indigenous older adult population in Canada is both increasingly urban and diverse in terms of nation, age, ability, education, income and sexuality. In our research, we have discovered that Indigenous older adults' experiences of ageing in a city are defined simultaneously by exclusions and inclusions shaped by ongoing settler colonialism that permeates Canadian society, as well as by their Indigeneity, their relationships and their resiliency. Throughout this chapter, we highlight the significance of culture, agency, equity and connection in reimagining age-friendly communities for Indigenous older adults. To begin, we discuss the literature related to Canadian Indigenous older adults' health, issues with the reliability of statistics about Indigenous older adults and the impacts of settler colonialism on Indigenous Peoples in Canada. Next, we share stories and experiences of Indigenous older adults living in Toronto and Ottawa to illustrate the impacts of settler colonialism alongside the relationship between Indigeneity and ageing in a Canadian city. We discuss the complexities of this relationship and how it creates both inclusion and exclusion within so-called 'age-friendly' communities. We conclude with our effort to reimagine ageing for Indigenous older adults, highlighting knowledge gaps that remain about Indigenous older adults' experiences of ageing in the city.

Indigenous populations in Canada are the youngest and fastest growing sub-group of the Canadian population and are also highly diverse in terms of varied languages, cultures and histories (Statistics Canada, 2022). This group is comprised of 634 different sovereign First Nations ('Indian' status and non-status), the Métis Peoples (registered and non-registered), and Inuit across the circumpolar north. Indigenous Peoples represent 5 per cent of Canada's total population (Statistics Canada, 2022). This non-homogeneous group can be found in densely populated urban centres, on reserves, including isolated fly-in reserves and in small remote communities as far north as the Arctic Circle. Indigenous communities are comprised of distinct nations with diverse cultures, languages, traditions and histories. In 2021, 801,045 Indigenous Peoples (44.3 per cent of the total Indigenous population) lived in a large urban centre of at least 100,000 people (Statistics Canada, 2022).

When compared to the non-Indigenous population in Canada, the Indigenous population is relatively young. This demographic is the result of genocidal policies and practices, with residential schools as a prime example, that have decimated the Canadian Indigenous population through disease, abuse and neglect, and meant that many Indigenous Peoples did not live to old age (Truth & Reconciliation Commission of Canada, 2015). However, between 2016 and 2021, the proportion of Indigenous Peoples aged 65 years and older grew from 7.3 per cent to 9.5 per cent (Statistics Canada, 2022) and is expected to continue to grow.

Due to ongoing racism and policies that discriminate against Indigenous Peoples, Indigenous older adults face many more health and social inequities in comparison to non-Indigenous older adults (O'Donnell et al, 2017). In 2011, more than half of the Indigenous older adult population in Canada were living in an urban community (O'Donnell et al, 2017), a fact that challenges dominant assumptions that Indigenous Peoples live primarily on reserve or in rural and/or remote communities (Andersen, 2013; Maddison, 2013).

Now, more than ever, it is important to understand Indigenous older adults' experiences of ageing in a city. How does settler colonialism, understood as the process of replacing the Indigenous Peoples of a land with foreign settlers (Lefevre, 2015), affect Indigenous older adults living in an urban context? In Canada, just a few researchers have sought to explore the ageing experiences of Indigenous older adults living in cities (the few exceptions include Baskin and Davey, 2015; Ginn and Kulig, 2015; Brooks-Cleator et al, 2019). A key focus of this chapter is to ensure appropriate voice is given to Indigenous ageing adults in the context of the impact that colonisation has on Indigenous Peoples' health today.

While this chapter attends to the experiences of Indigenous older adults living in *Canadian* cities, it is worth noting that Indigenous older adults living in cities in other settler colonial nations (including Australia, New Zealand and the United States) face similar impacts resulting from colonialism, such as loss of culture, experiences with poverty and racism, disconnection from families, poor health outcomes and lower life expectancies – all of which influence their ability to age equitably. Importantly, however, the specific mechanisms through which these impacts occur are shaped by the unique political, historical and socio-economic contexts of each country, and thus result in diverse experiences of ageing between Indigenous older adults globally. This chapter describes the unique context of Canada and the manifestations of settler colonialism through Canadian policies and practices.

Background

Data considerations with Indigenous older adult population size

There are two important considerations when discussing statistics related to Indigenous older adults: 1) who counts as older, and 2) who gets counted and who does not. First, given Indigenous peoples' younger populations and their experiences of social and health inequities, researchers have argued that who counts as an Indigenous older adult should be those 55 years of age and over, rather than 65 years and over (Wilson et al, 2010; Beatty and Weber-Beeds, 2012; Statistics Canada, 2018). Indigenous older adults themselves have called for this change (Brooks-Cleator et al, 2019).

Second, as argued by Smylie and Firestone (2015), the quality of statistics for Indigenous populations in Canada, particularly when it comes to identifying inequities between Indigenous and non-Indigenous Peoples in health determinants, health status and access to health care, is poor. They point out that most data collection 'significantly undersample[s] urban [Indigenous] people who are homeless, highly mobile, have lower levels of educational achievement in written English or French, or who do not want to participate in the census for personal or political reasons' (77). They argue for 'the need for meaningful Indigenous leadership and participation in the governance and management of Indigenous health data' (68).

Indigenous older adults' health: the problem of statistics

Indigenous older adults experience high rates of poor health and medical morbidities (Anstey et al, 2011; Habjan et al, 2012). These medical morbidities include respiratory diseases, hypertension and diabetes (Mckercher et al, 2014). In addition, Indigenous older adults as a group are affected by their overall lower socio-economic status (Browne et al, 2014). These factors compound to yield substantially lower life expectancies for Indigenous Peoples compared to the general population (Tjepkema et al, 2019). These health gaps result in the shortest life expectancy rates of any one identifiable group within Canada and the Western world. In 2017, the projected life expectancy of an average Canadian was 79 years of age for men and 83 years for women. However, this falls dramatically to 73–74 years for men of Métis and First Nations descent and 78–80 years for women.

Even more dramatic is that of 64 years for Inuit men and 73 years for Inuit women (Statistics Canada, 2015).

Kelm (1999) argues that health statistics like the ones mentioned contribute to a harmful societal perception that Indigenous bodies are naturally and inevitably diseased, 'broken' and disabled. Furthermore, she asserts that the ways in which Indigenous bodies have been socially and historically constructed through statistical representations have been central to settler colonialism (Kelm, 1999). Therefore, it would be problematic to only assess statistics to understand the ageing experiences of Indigenous older adults, which not only fail to show the mechanisms through which negative health outcomes for Indigenous older adults occur (including traumas and settler colonialism) but also ignore the strength and resilience of Indigenous older adults. This chapter attends to these mechanisms and Indigenous older adults' resilience, to consider not only how Indigenous lives are understood and counted, but how Indigenous Peoples and communities prevail and resist their circumstances.

Settler colonialism's impact on Indigenous Peoples' health

Prior to colonisation in the 17th century, Indigenous Peoples had their own traditional practices that guided their living, healing and ageing (Hillier and Al-Shammaa, 2020). Contemporary health disparities faced by Indigenous Peoples in Canada have been directly linked to centuries of colonial policies that have resulted in cultural genocide. While colonialism is defined as the domination of individuals or groups over the territory and behaviour of other individuals or groups, historically, in Canada, colonialism has taken a form where the dominant relationship between the colonisers and the colonised is the extermination of the latter (Horvath, 1972). Further, Canada's settler colonial nation-state is based on white supremacy and heteropatriarchy (Arvin et al, 2013). As others have argued, settler colonialism involves the interactions of colonialism, racism, gender, class, sexuality and desire, capitalism and ableism (Snelgrove et al, 2014). Racism is a multi-layered phenomenon that must be investigated through a structurally layered approach to understand its true impact on Indigenous Peoples' health and experiences of ageing (Juutilainen, 2014). Colonialism is at the heart of power structures within Canadian bureaucracy, which in turn has sought to suppress Canada's Indigenous Peoples since first contact (Reading and Wien, 2009). In combination, colonial policies, attitudinal and systemic racism and socio-economic disparities present significant barriers to creating a healthy environment for Indigenous Peoples in Canada (Smylie et al, 2006).

The impact of settler colonial structural, deliberate practices to remove and kill Indigenous Peoples' language and culture is still felt. The reserve system, residential 'industrial' schooling, the '60s scoop',[1] over-incarceration of

Indigenous men and women, missing and murdered Indigenous women and girls and the continued over-apprehension of Indigenous children by the state, who are then placed in foster care, are just some of the factors that cause the continuation of poor health among Indigenous Peoples, due to their systematic removal from connections with their cultures, families and communities. Health disparities between Indigenous and non-Indigenous older adult populations are undoubtedly attributable to this ongoing history of trauma.

Settler colonialism, as a political and social structure, shapes the conditions for Indigenous older adults living in urban communities by limiting the spaces, experiences, and traditions to which they have access. In our research, Indigenous older adults in Ottawa and Toronto spoke of many ways in which their lives are impacted by colonial policies, including that they are living in a city, far away from their traditional connections to kinship, community and land.

Older adults often speak about a loss of agency, autonomy and voice as they get older and that they are viewed as frail and unable to make decisions for themselves. Similarly, Indigenous Peoples in Canada as a group have been left without a voice due to colonisation that suppresses not only their voices but also their Indigeneity. Indigenous voices and knowledges have historically been suppressed and forgotten. According to Wilson (2003), non-Indigenous Peoples became experts on Indigenous Peoples and these experts (including anthropologists, physicians, psychologists and professors) felt qualified to pass on their learning about Indigenous Peoples. This left Indigenous Peoples without a voice, with others only speaking of them and occasionally for them, thereby making the Indigenous voice unnecessary or even impossible to be heard (Wilson, 2003). Therefore, in our work, we amplify the voices of Indigenous older adults, providing their direct words and experiences of ageing in cities using data from site studies conducted in 2018 in Toronto and 2019 in Ottawa, conducted as part of the 'Imagining Age-Friendly Communities within Communities' project (see Chapter 1 for more details).

Settler colonialism and ageing

Settler colonialism remains central in the lives of Indigenous Peoples in Canada, impacting virtually all aspects of day-to-day being. This all-encompassing reality not only has implications for the health of all Indigenous Peoples, but it impacts the process and reality of ageing for Indigenous older adults through direct and indirect policies and systems. This includes the use of the arbitrary age of 65 years and older to determine access to some services, as this rule excludes many Indigenous Peoples younger than 65 years who have experienced accelerated ageing due to the compounded effects of lifetimes of trauma resulting from colonisation. For Indigenous older adults who participated in our research in Ottawa and Toronto, experiences of settler colonialism were reflected in loss of culture, experiences with poverty and racism, disconnection from families and forced migration away from traditional home communities and territory.

The stories recounted here were shared in interviews with Indigenous older adults whom we met through Indigenous community centres in the respective cities. These older adults use a variety of terminology to describe their Indigeneity, including using the names of Indigenous nations, specific communities or groups. Many call themselves 'Natives' in the interviews included here.

Loss of culture

Indigenous older adults face significant barriers in accessing traditional knowledge, practices and culture when they move into urban areas. The violence, displacement and loss of culture experienced by Indigenous Peoples in Canada can be directly linked to a history of traumatic policies, which sought to destroy the 'Indian' in Canada (Truth & Reconciliation Commission of Canada, 2015). As one Indigenous older adult in Ottawa highlighted in sharing her story:

> So basically mine is very simple. I get very emotional but what happens is that I was born in the city and we were not allowed to say we were Native in any respect. We were not allowed to have anything to do with our culture. For my grandfather, it was a gift he was giving us because of the prejudice. Being French in this country you were only good to sweep the streets. If you added you were Indigenous, you were not even good enough to sweep the streets because this was an Anglo city, an Anglo country.

An Indigenous older adult in Toronto told us that while growing up, she was never allowed to practice her culture:

> Oh, no, nothing. Oh, there was nothing taught. We weren't allowed to talk about it and I had wondered when people are guiding me on that kind of subject. We weren't allowed to talk about it. We weren't allowed to smudge. We weren't allowed to speak our language. And to me that was just normal life for me, but it hurts the people that were raised with that and they were subjected to don't speak, don't dress, don't smudge, you know. It's just an all-over bad thing.

However, for some Indigenous older adults, coming to the city meant being able to connect with their culture. This participant told us about experiencing her culture through programming initiatives that brought Indigenous older adults and other Indigenous community members together: 'I didn't grow up with the Native music at all. I didn't even know about it. I didn't know how it sounded or anything. But since I moved here (Toronto), oh, it's amazing. Oh, I just love it' (Indigenous older adult, Toronto).

Poverty and disability

Poverty is one of the key determinants of Indigenous Peoples' poor health and well-being and of Indigenous older adults' experiences of ageing. Through the processes of colonisation, children were systematically removed from their families and communities, cultural practices and speaking of traditional languages were forbidden, and a legacy of poverty and silence began. The development of contemporary 'unhealthy lifestyle choices' is rooted in structural factors such as poverty that are a main driving force of poor health in this community (Majumdar et al, 2010). Older adults in both Toronto and Ottawa spoke of the impacts of poverty, including on their overall well-being. An Indigenous older adult in Toronto told us:

> I've seen in the Native community that I have yet to find a person over 55, and I think that's very young. I don't see a person over 55 who's not disabled. I see in other ethnic groups, that's not the case. A lot of that comes from poverty, and it'll be interesting to see in the next few generations, 'cause I mean, they'll be directly out of the effects of, you know, getting beaten up and all this sort of stuff, residential school nonsense. You know, foster homes are just hell on wheels. You get people developing stress components and even though they may be able to psychologically get above it, the stress is still there because it's cellular or impacts cellularly for one's entire life. This leads to a lot of the disabilities that Native people have, far too early, such as inflammatory ones. And it's the inflammatory ones take you out a lot sooner. If we didn't have people's distress for such prolonged periods of time in infancy, toddlerhood, childhood, we'd probably have healthier old people.

Poverty and its related outcomes, as a direct consequence of colonisation, have worked toward damaging the Indigenous body to a point where it struggles to remain resilient or oppose deeply engrained colonial forces. Significantly, the history of colonial abuse has had a particular impact on Indigenous women, with a high percentage of women living in poverty and disconnected from their family and communities (Varcoe and Dick, 2008).

Racism

Health disparities are manifested in a long history of experiences of oppression, systematic racism and discrimination, all of which can be linked directly to a lack of access to resources, such as education, employment, social services or control over Indigenous land and governance (Frohlich et al, 2006). Indigenous older adults in Toronto and Ottawa discussed racism and other forms of discrimination that they experienced both within the health-care system specifically, but also across their cities. Overall, Indigenous older adults told us that there was a lack of cultural competency when it came to addressing the needs of Indigenous Peoples. An Indigenous staff member in Toronto stated:

> I found that there was this whole thing when I would take clients into the hospital, they were treated as like a second-class citizen because they are native. There is racism in the hospitals, it is what it is, right? So I just put a big X on that hospital and tried to navigate everybody into a different hospital. One that's a little bit more friendly, we're not going there, they're not cool, we're going to go here. Unfortunately, it is the reality.

Relatedly, an Indigenous older adult in Toronto talked about the difficulty of getting a general practitioner (GP) to take her as a patient:

> Unfortunately, I've lost all my doctors. So, I have been without a GP [general practice doctor] for 9 years. I consistently try to get a GP but they don't want people like me because, as one doctor told me, 'I couldn't make any money from working with you'. So, I've stuck to trying to get onto a hospital. The odd time when I've had to show up in emergency, you know, like, going into coma, because my diabetes is off, I've been shocked at how nasty people unnecessarily are, even though I'll have a little note there that explains conditions they have to be careful of. They're not. You're very much discounted in many ways by the vast majority of people.

An Indigenous older adult in Ottawa told us their experiences of racism were so consistent and significant that they simply don't talk about being Indigenous in the hope of avoiding discrimination: 'And that's why many don't want to say nothing or acknowledge they're native because of the racism.'

(Dis)connection

Culturally, Indigenous Peoples across Canada perceive older adult care as a social responsibility of the family and community (Browne et al, 2014; Bell et al, 2015); however, Indigenous families face systemic financial and emotional barriers to providing this care. Consequently, ageing family members are sometimes left out, with no family to look after them and inadequate older adult care services in their community (Habjan et al, 2012). Significantly, this results in a disconnection and dislocation of Indigenous older adults from their families, communities and from younger people. However, Indigenous older adults value their family's role in providing primary or secondary support (Bell et al, 2015). For an Indigenous older adult in Toronto, the lack of family meant the perception of being less healthy:

> You know them, they know you, and that's what I miss. People who know me. My family's all gone. I had great kids. Great partner. But, they're gone. And, you know, my friends are gone. So, I basically live alone, because there's nobody I know who knows me. I think I would be a lot healthier if ... there are people who know me.

An Indigenous older adult in Ottawa discussed the traumas he went through and the impact it had on his family, but he maintains a desire to be close with them:

> I don't know, but all the time they were kids, I drank a lot, like, quite a bit. So the trust level, I guess, is not there. I just hope someday it will happen, but things are a little tipsy. If I go to Manitoba, I could probably talk to my other sons, I think they'll talk to me. It's just, I haven't seen them for 35 years, I guess.

An important factor related to connection that older adults in both Toronto and Ottawa discussed was the promising practice of attending programs that provided them with an opportunity to interact and engage with children. Indigenous older adults have a desire to teach their children and grandchildren about their ancestry, ultimately feeling responsible for culture preservation (Hillier and Al-Shammaa, 2020). Kinship was not understood just as blood family ties, but as the responsibility of older Indigenous adults to impart their wisdom to younger people, no matter their family connection. One Indigenous older adult in Ottawa illustrated this point when he told us: 'Bring in babies, bring children and babies and let them teach. Curiosity, seniors have curiosity just as much as children but getting the children, to have them around would be one of the biggest things [to improve the program].' Older adults in both Toronto and Ottawa discussed the importance of interacting with, and passing on their knowledge to, the younger generations, as a rewarding and important aspect of ageing.

Forced migration

Beyond migration for employment in earlier life, Indigenous older adults are often forced to leave their communities to access better care in cities as on-reserve services are often inadequate (Coombes et al, 2018), despite growing older adult populations who face many chronic health conditions (Habjan et al, 2012). Accordingly, many Indigenous older adults must leave their communities to access adequate care programs and services (Habjan et al, 2012; Browne et al, 2014; Bell et al, 2015). This forced migration is a modern-day form of colonisation (Hillier and Al-Shammaa, 2020). Yet, Indigenous older adults attach great importance to their home communities; a connection to the land is a determinant of their well-being (Coombes et al, 2018). An Indigenous services staff member in Toronto stated:

> They seem to come to Toronto to get it [health care] done, that their reserves up north when people do come down, the health care system is much worse in the smaller community, sometimes they just have a nursing station, so they don't get the proper care that they need or tests or anything like that. They just don't have the equipment or the funds to provide the equipment. And then to come down here alone, and then to figure out what is going on, to learn all that alone without any support or anyone coming down with you, because no one could pay for their partner to be there.

The result is a disconnection imposed onto Indigenous Peoples who are forced to relocate to access health care, engendering intense loneliness, isolation, alienation and negative mental and physical health outcomes (Allan and Smylie, 2015).

Relationships and ageing

While settler colonialism as a political and social structure shapes the ageing experiences of Indigenous older adults living in cities, these experiences are also shaped by relationships. For Indigenous older adults living in Toronto and Ottawa, these relationships include those to their home in the city, those with other Indigenous older adults, and those with workers in the health and social services sectors.

Relationship to home in the city

Indigenous older adults living in both Toronto and Ottawa identified that their relationship and connection to their home in the city was a significant part of their ageing experience. This was regardless of whether they lived alone or with others, in a building run by a health or social services organisation, or with other Indigenous older adults. Our participants described a feeling of home underpinned by conditions that included stable housing, being comfortable, feeling safe and being connected to other residents. When asked what it meant to have a home, one Indigenous older adult in Ottawa shared: 'It means everything. I've never had this kind of stability before, and it's very comfortable.' For this individual, stable housing gave her a sense of home. Another participant in our Toronto study identified safety and feeling comfortable as part of her feeling of home in the city: 'I feel very comfortable here. Comfortable, protected. It's like I feel like this is where I should be. People call this my forever home. It's a seniors' building, I can see that ... I feel more balanced here. Like I've got everything I need.' Being connected to others and less lonely also contributed to her feelings of home. When asked about her living situation, another Toronto participant told us, 'this is the kind of living situation that I've dreamed of, that I'd imagined me living in, with a lot of people around. Because the 8 years that I spent living in an apartment, there was a lot of lonely times and here you can't really feel lonely.'

Across our interviews, participants' stories reveal the relationship to home as a significant part of Indigenous older adults' ageing experience in a city, including more than the physical space of a house, but also the meaning given to this space and the comfort, safety and relationships that come from it.

Relationships with other indigenous older adults

Relationships with other Indigenous older adults also positively contribute to experiences of ageing in the city. These relationships are typically reciprocal in that Indigenous older adults rely on others for support while also offering support to their peers and friends. For example, one Indigenous older adult explained how he supports other Indigenous older adults in Ottawa, particularly those who are homeless: '[I'm] just going out to the communities and ensuring that everyone is okay, and walking down the streets of Ottawa, downtown mainly, and telling people that we give them a little bit of country food and tell them that there may be feasts [at the organisation].' In a conversation with one of our research team members, a participant in Toronto shared that her friendships with other Indigenous older adults in her building had turned into relationships similar to that of a family: 'I hope I'm around for a little bit longer because in my family I'm the only one left. They all passed away ... so my friends – we just got closer.' For Indigenous older adults who do not have many family members around, who are disconnected from their families, or who no longer live in their home communities, friendships with and support from other Indigenous older adults contribute to making ageing in the city a positive experience.

Urban Indigenous populations are diverse, particularly in Toronto and Ottawa, yet community is often built across this diversity, based on shared experiences related to their Indigeneity that takes many forms. For example, as one Indigenous older adult in Toronto explained, being around other

Indigenous older adults who experienced intergenerational trauma from residential schools made her better understand her own family's experience and realise that she was not alone in dealing with it:

> I didn't know this until a couple of years ago, but my sister guided me that they [my parents] were actually in residential school so they were actually survivors of being there and I said, 'Seriously?' And she said, 'Doesn't that make sense now?' And I'm like yeah, okay. And there are a lot of people in this building, I am finding out that they were actual survivors of residential schools. And plus there's a program. I haven't gone yet, but transgenerational survivors. It's for those generations after the people have survived it, the residential schools, and they're speaking up about it. There are repercussions. You think sometimes in your life you're the only one struggling with a certain subject, but then you're hearing others and it really did affect them, really pretty badly.

Shared cultural experiences also help some Indigenous older adults feel more comfortable with acknowledging and connecting to their culture in the city, as another participant explained: 'I mean now that I'm living here in a native seniors' building, I am far more comfortable displaying native stuff, smudging. Like all that kind of stuff. And we have such a common ground going on all living here and we have common stuff. It's amazing.'

In addition to shared cultural experiences, Indigenous older adults feel more connected to each other through their shared experiences of their home communities. For example, despite that residents in a housing complex came from different communities in northern Ontario, a research participant in Toronto found that residents' shared experiences of life in a certain geographic region established her sense of community in the city: 'Mostly why we get along so good is that we all come from around the same place, so we're all 100 miles apart. And we didn't know each other before now, before I moved here, but it didn't matter. We became friends right away.' We noted another group of Indigenous older adults who told us they sit together every day at lunch, saying they were all from the same geographical area in the north. This shared experience helped to create a sense of unity among the group. Although living in diverse age-friendly cities, Indigenous older adults' experiences of gaining were enhanced by relationships with other Indigenous Peoples in the city, built on shared experiences tied to their Indigeneity.

Relationships with health and social care workers

Relationships with other Indigenous people contribute positively to Indigenous older adults' lives, but so too do their relationships with workers in health and social services organisations, including both Indigenous-specific and non-Indigenous-specific services, as we learned from both Indigenous older adults and workers in these services. As one Indigenous older adult in Toronto shared about one service: 'the girls are really good there, that work in the seniors' department, they're very helpful. Anything you need filled in or anything, instead of having to wait and wait, then you just go over there and they'll help you with anything.' Another participant in Ottawa told us she knew that the workers at an Indigenous centre would always support them: 'I just know that they take care of us ... they still do their best to take care of us.' Workers' perspectives also highlighted the importance of their connections to the older adults they served. In a discussion with two workers at an Indigenous organisation in Toronto, one explained that, 'at the end of the day, they are our Elders', seconded by the other, 'Yeah, they're our Elders and I respect them.' A worker from a non-Indigenous specific organisation in Ottawa shared that, 'I always think that I want to treat the clients that are ageing like my own grandparents when they were alive.'

Concluding thoughts

For Indigenous older adults, ageing in a city is a complex negotiation of Indigeneity, culture and relationships. It is also influenced by settler colonialism, including their resistance to it and resiliency in the face of it. Given this complex negotiation, how might we imagine ageing equitably when it comes to Indigenous older adults living in cities, keeping in mind their stories and experiences?

Indigenous older adults living in Toronto and Ottawa told us that their ageing should not be solely defined by poor health outcomes and low socio-economic status that many statistical representations depict and reinforce (Chandler and Dunlop, 2015), as we discussed earlier in the chapter. To promote perspectives that imagine health and well-being for older Indigenous adults, notions of the Indigenous body as broken, poor and helpless must be overcome (Kelm, 1999; Chandler and Dunlop, 2015). To imagine age equity for Indigenous Peoples in the city or elsewhere, we can begin by acknowledging and supporting older adults' relationships tied to their Indigeneity through relationships to home, to other Indigenous older adults, to other Indigenous Peoples in the city, and to the staff at the organisations and services that they need and use. However, we must also attend to and confront the relations and actions of the settler colonial state that continuously erode and destroy Indigenous lives and health by removing Indigenous Peoples from their lands, culture, language and families.

At its root, settler colonialism is the exclusion and erasure of Indigenous Peoples from settler society (Veracini, 2010). Our research participants' experiences depict some of the many ways in which Indigenous older adults face exclusion stemming from settler colonialism while living in a city. At the policies and systems level, an arbitrary age of 65 years and older restricts access to services, excluding many Indigenous Peoples under 65 years old who are experiencing accelerated ageing due to the compounding effects of a lifetime of abuse and trauma related to colonialisation. Additionally, through colonial systems, including residential 'industrial' schooling, the '60s scoop', over-incarceration of Indigenous men and women, missing and murdered Indigenous women and girls and forced migration from home communities, many Indigenous older adults faced, and continue to face, exclusion from knowing their culture, their families and their home communities. Further, they are excluded from accessing services, by choice or by force, based on the racism and discrimination they receive from some service providers in the city (Monchalin et al, 2020).

At the same time as they face these forms of exclusion, Indigenous older adults are fostering inclusion through their relationship-building. Inclusion through relationships is not just about relationships with other people, it also includes connections with place, one's own culture and to organisations. Even though they may be disconnected from their home communities and/or their families, whether by choice or by force, the experiences and stories of Indigenous older adults living in cities illustrate how they have made 'family' among their friends and workers at the organisations where they feel safe and included. While many Indigenous older adults have experienced loss of culture due to colonisation, through shared experiences with other Indigenous Peoples in the city, some are rediscovering their Indigenous culture, sharing it, and celebrating it. Furthermore, finding a sense of home in a city and having a relationship to these places is a form of resistance to colonial policy and discourses that suggest Indigeneity cannot exist within urban environments (Maddison, 2013). Consequently, for Indigenous older adults living in a city, these relationships are ways that they resist settler colonialism by fostering inclusion, building community and being resilient.

Reimagining Indigenous ageing in the city to be equitable, healthy and meaningful moves us away from a 'broken' stereotype of Indigenous older adults to one that is based on resilience and strength and is empowering to Indigenous older adults. It means giving voice and agency to Indigenous older adults, who have been the leaders and knowledge holders for our communities for thousands of years. Reimagining ageing includes establishing equitable conditions for ageing, at the levels of systems, policy and practice, grounded in Indigenous older adults' knowledge and self-identified needs. Alongside this, reimagining ageing involves critically examining how existing systems, policies and practices reinforce settler colonialism, resulting in inequitable conditions for ageing (Brooks-Cleator et al, 2019). It includes identifying promising practices for programming that accounts for the historical traumas and loss of culture, language and tradition Indigenous older adults have faced. This should be the responsibility of both Indigenous-specific *and* non-Indigenous-specific organisations to provide opportunities for people to reconnect with what has been taken away and erased and foster relationships tied to place, culture, people and organisations. Identifying and developing these promising practices is only possible through the creation of strong partnerships and relationships between Indigenous older adults and the service organisations, local governments, health-care professionals and Indigenous organisations/governments, which seek to support them.

Importantly, there is much that we do not know related to Indigenous older adults and ageing in the city. We know little about what promising practices exist, particularly within and between countries, and are just beginning to work with Indigenous older adults and organisations to identify and contextualise them. Further, we know that there are certain groups of Indigenous older adults whose voices remain excluded from conversations on ageing, including Indigenous older adults living with HIV, living in long-term care facilities, who are homeless, who are incarcerated, who are two-spirit and who have lost all connections to their culture and families and may not know their Indigenous identity. We must not forget all those who did not live to become an older adult due to settler-colonial policies and practices aimed at erasing Indigenous Peoples from Canada.

We are just beginning to understand what equitable, healthy, meaningful ageing means for Indigenous older adults living in cities. As this population continues to grow, these voices and perspectives need to be part of reimagining age-friendly communities.

Note

[1] The '60s scoop' in this context relates to a period from the 1940s to the 1970s in which thousands of Indigenous children were apprehended by the state. Issues surrounding the continued apprehension of Indigenous children in what is known as the 'millennium scoop' is an on-going issue.

References

Allan, B. and Smylie, J. (2015) First Peoples, Second Class Treatment: The Role of Racism in the Health and Well-being of Indigenous Peoples in Canada [online], Available from: https://www.wellesleyinstitute.com/wp-content/uploads/2015/02/Summary-First-Peoples-Second-Class-Treatment-Final.pdf

Andersen, C. (2013) Urban Aboriginality as a distinctive identity, in twelve parts, in P.D. Howard and E.P. Peters (eds) *Indigenous in the City: Contemporary Identities and Cultural Innovation*, University of British Columbia Press, pp 46–68.

Anstey, K.J., Kiely, K.M., Booth, H., Birrell, C.L., Butterworth, P., Byles, J., et al (2011) Indigenous Australians are under-represented in longitudinal ageing studies, *Australian and New Zealand Journal of Public Health*, 35(4): 331–6.

Arvin, M., Tuck, E. and Morrill, A. (2013) Decolonizing feminism: challenging connections between settler colonialism and heteropatriarchy, *Feminist Formations*, 25(1): 8–34.

Baskin, C. and Davey, C.J. (2015) Grannies, elders, and friends: aging Aboriginal women in Toronto, *Journal of Gerontological Social Work*, 58(1): 46–65.

Beatty, B. and Weber-Beeds, A. (2012) Mitho-pimatisiwin for the elderly: the strength of a shared caregiving approach in Aboriginal health, in D. Newhouse, K. FitzMaurice, T. McGuire-Adams and D. Jetté (eds) *Wellbeing in the Urban Aboriginal Community: Fostering Biimaadiziwin*, Thompson Educational Publishing, pp 113–29.

Bell, D., Lindeman, M.A. and Reid, J.B. (2015) The (mis)matching of resources and assessed need in remote Aboriginal community aged care, *Australasian Journal on Ageing*, 34(3): 171–6.

Brooks-Cleator, L.A., Giles, A.R. and Flaherty, M. (2019) Community-level factors that contribute to First Nations and Inuit older adults feeling supported to age well in a Canadian city, *Journal of Aging Studies*, 48: 50–9.

Browne, C.V., Mokuau, N., Ka'opua, L.S., Kim, B.J., Higuchi, P. and Braun, K.L. (2014) Listening to the voices of Native Hawaiian elders and Ohana caregivers: Discussions on aging, health, and care preferences, *Journal of Cross-Cultural Gerontology*, 29(2): 131–51.

Chandler, M.J. and Dunlop, W.L. (2015) Cultural wounds demand cultural medicines, in M. Greenwood, S. de Leeuw, N.M. Lindsay and C. Reading (eds) *Determinants of Indigenous Peoples' Health in Canada*, Canadian Scholars' Press, pp 78–89.

Coombes, J., Lukaszyk, C., Sherrington, C., Keay, L., Tiedemann, A., Moore, R. et al (2018) First Nation Elders' perspectives on healthy ageing in NSW, Australia, *Australian and New Zealand Journal of Public Health*, 42(4): 361–4.

Frohlich, K.L., Ross, N. and Richmond, C. (2006) Health disparities in Canada today: some evidence and a theoretical framework, *Health Policy*, 79(2): 132–43.

Ginn, C.S. and Kulig, J.C. (2015) Participatory action research with a group of urban First Nations grandmothers: decreasing inequities through health promotion, *International Indigenous Policy Journal*, 6(1): 4.

Habjan, S., Prince, H. and Kelley, M.L. (2012) Caregiving for elders in First Nations communities: social system perspective on barriers and challenges, *Canadian Journal on Aging*, 31(2): 209–22.

Hillier, S. and Al-Shammaa, H. (2020) Indigenous Peoples' experiences with aging, *Canadian Journal of Disability Studies*, 9(4): 146–79.

Horvath, R.J. (1972) A definition of colonialism, *Current Anthropology*, 13(1): 45–57.

Juutilainen, S.A., Miller, R., Heikkilä, L. and Rautio, A. (2014) Structural racism and Indigenous health: what Indigenous perspectives of residential school and boarding school tell us? A case study of Canada and Finland, *International Indigenous Policy Journal*, 5(3): 3.

Kelm, M.E. (1999) *Colonizing Bodies: Aboriginal Health and Healing in British Columbia, 1900–50*, University of British Columbia Press.

Lefevre, T.A. (2015) Settler colonialism, in *Oxford Research Encyclopedia of Politics*, Oxford University Press.

Maddison, S. (2013) Indigenous identity, 'authenticity' and the structural violence of settler colonialism, *Identities: Global Studies in Culture and Power*, 20(3): 288–303.

Majumdar, B., Guenter, D. and Browne, G. (2010) HIV prevention in an Aboriginal community in Canada, *Journal of the Association of Nurses in AIDS Care*, 21(5): 449–54.

McKercher, C., Chan, H.W., Clayton, P.A., McDonald, S. and Jose, M.D. (2014) Dialysis outcomes of elderly Indigenous and non-Indigenous Australians, *Nephrology*, 19(10): 610–16.

Monchalin, R., Smylie, J. and Nowgesic, E. (2020) 'I guess I shouldn't come back here': racism and discrimination as a barrier to accessing health and social services for urban Métis women in Toronto, Canada, *Journal of Racial and Ethnic Health Disparities*, 7(2): 251–61.

O'Donnell, V., Wendt, M. and National Association of Friendship Centres (2017) Aboriginal Seniors in Population Centres in Canada [online], Available from: https://www150.statcan.gc.ca/n1/pub/89-653-x/89-653-x2017013-eng.htm

Reading, C.L. and Wien, F. (2009) *Health Inequalities and the Social Determinants of Aboriginal Peoples' Health*, National Collaborating Centre for Aboriginal Health.

Smylie, J. and Firestone, M. (2015) Back to the basics: identifying and addressing underlying challenges in achieving high quality and relevant health statistics for Indigenous populations in Canada, *Statistical Journal of the IAOS*, 31(1): 67–87.

Smylie, J., Williams, L. and Cooper, N. (2006) Culture-based literacy and Aboriginal health, *Canadian Journal of Public Health*, 97(Suppl 2): S22–7.

Snelgrove, C., Kaur Dhamoon, R. and Corntassel, J. (2014) Unsettling settler colonialism: the discourse and politics of settlers, and solidarity with Indigenous nations, *Decolonization: Indigeneity, Education & Society*, 3(2): 1–32.

Statistics Canada (2015) *Life Expectancy* [online], Available from: https://www150.statcan.gc.ca/n1/pub/89-645-x/2010001/life-expectancy-esperance-vie-eng.htm

Statistics Canada (2018) Social Isolation of Seniors: A Focus on Indigenous Seniors in Canada [online], Available from: https://www.canada.ca/en/employment-social-development/corporate/seniors-forum-federal-provincial-territorial/social-isolation-indigenous.html

Statistics Canada (2022) *Indigenous Population Continues to Grow and is Much Younger Than the Non-Indigenous Population, Although the Pace of Growth Has Slowed* [online], Available from: https://www150.statcan.gc.ca/n1/daily-quotidien/220921/dq220921a-eng.htm

Tjepkema, M., Bushnik, T. and Bougie, E. (2019) Life expectancy of First Nations, Métis, and Inuit household populations in Canada, *Health Reports*, 30(12): 1–10.

Truth and Reconciliation Commission of Canada (2015) *Canada's Residential Schools: The Final Report of the Truth and Reconciliation Commission of Canada* (Vol. 1), McGill-Queen's University Press.

Tzay, J.F.C. (2021) *Report of the Special Rapporteur on the Rights of Indigenous Peoples*, United Nations General Assembly, seventy-sixth session, Item 75(b), 21 July [online], Available from: https://un.arizona.edu/sites/default/files/2022-02/UNSRIP_Report_to_GA_on_IPs_in_Urban_Areas.pdf

Varcoe, C. and Dick, S. (2008) The intersecting risks of violence and HIV for rural Aboriginal women in a neo-colonial Canadian context, *International Journal of Indigenous Health*, 4(1): 42–52.

Veracini, L. (2010) *Settler Colonialism: A Theoretical Overview*, Palgrave Macmillan UK.

Wilson, K., Rosenberg, M.W., Abonyi, S. and Lovelace, R. (2010) Aging and health: an examination of differences between older Aboriginal and non-Aboriginal people, *Canadian Journal on Aging*, 29(3): 369–82.

Wilson, S. (2003) Progressing toward an Indigenous research paradigm in Canada and Australia, *Canadian Journal of Native Education*, 27(2): 161–78.

10

Triple jeopardy: addressing age equity for older immigrant women

Susan Braedley, Karine Côté-Boucher and Renate Ysseldyk

Introduction

In the contemporary politics of high-income welfare states, the perceived triple threats of immigration 'floods', ageing population 'tsunamis' and worries about government spending levels position older immigrants as a triple threat (Braedley et al, 2021). Immigrants have been portrayed as net drains on national social welfare, unfairly depleting the resources accumulated by native-born people (Ugelvik, 2013; Grady and Grubel, 2015; Barrass and Shields, 2017; Burgoon and Rooduijn, 2021), despite cross-national research that shows that 'immigrant exclusion [from social welfare programs] does not have a significant fiscal effect and therefore should not be defended on the grounds of its fiscal implications' (Rigzin and Kaushal, 2022: 122). At the same time, immigration has been touted as an answer to problems associated with rapid socio-demographic ageing. Some jurisdictions have increased labour migration to address both labour shortages and 'dependency ratios', understood as the ratio between those who are not in paid employment (children, retirees and people with complex disabilities), and the population in paid employment whose taxes pay for public services. To work as a solution to rising welfare costs, labour must be extracted from newcomers while keeping welfare costs for these populations low.

The result of these political currents is that older immigrant women tend to be perceived as drains on welfare states, as this population tends to have low lifetime earnings. Immigrant women who emigrated earlier in life are considered more likely than men to draw on public health care, old age security programs, social housing and other resources. Those who arrive in later life are viewed as poor candidates for integration, unlikely to learn official languages and incapable of contributing substantially to the formal economy through paid labour, investment or consumption.

The Canadian context is instructive. Between 2015 and 2024, the Canadian federal government advanced an ambitious immigration program to accept 500,000 immigrants per year, aimed to address socio-demographic ageing and related welfare spending concerns, to fill labour shortages and stimulate economic productivity and innovation (Gabriel, 2024). Canadian immigration policy has been considered as a model internationally for so-called managed migration (Roy and Cheatham, 2024). This chapter draws on research from three empirical studies in Ottawa, Canada to consider the experiences of older immigrant women in this context, using a feminist bordering theory approach that integrates feminist political economy together with critical bordering theory (Braedley et al, 2021). We argue that older women make substantial contributions to immigrant-receiving countries through their social reproductive labour in the care economy, including both paid and unpaid labour. We point out that every immigrant has a mother, somewhere in the world. Further, older immigrant women typically work in the informal care economy of their receiving country, doing low-waged and unpaid housework, childcare and other care work. This labour is essential work in their receiving country and deserves recognition. Whether newly arrived or a long-term resident, older immigrant women contribute to their families' social reproduction in later life, enabling their children's labour force participation and caring for their grandchildren, their children's homes and their communities. Yet, their conditions of life are not secure. Our data reveals that these women experience a triple jeopardy of insecurities related to their gendered, immigrant, older social location, including insecurities in the material conditions of daily life, barriers to social connection and a lack of support for their community-building.

Why does this matter? We argue that advancing age equity requires attending to inequities among women related to their age, race, class and immigration status and to their gendered multiple relationships to the care economy. In what follows, we briefly describe the three studies that have led us to these conclusions, then provide a description of the older immigrant women population in Canada and their involvement in the care economy. Next, we draw from our research to show how together, these women's gendered care work, immigrant status, age, racialisation, language and a triple jeopardy of insecurities shape their lives, producing inequities that age-equity movements, policies and practice must consider.

The studies

This chapter draws on data from and about immigrant older women[1] in three related research studies conducted over an 8-year period. Study 1, conducted in 2016–17, was community-based research developed with graduate students and a non-profit agency in Ottawa working with independent ethnocultural senior's groups.² We conducted research on caregiving among the members of the Nepalese, Chinese, Indian, Vietnamese, Polish and Sri Lankan seniors' groups, with a total of 34 women participating.

Study 2,³ conducted in 2019–24, examined the impact of immigration and social welfare policies that shape relationships between working age immigrants to Canada and their parents. We drew from this project's policy documents, academic and grey literature reviews, interviews and focus groups conducted in the Ottawa-Gatineau region with so-called 'zero-generation' migrant older adults and with immigrants who have, or are trying to, sponsor their parents to come Canada, including older immigrants to Canada from India, Pakistan, Thailand, China, Vietnam, Cambodia, Sri Lanka, Kenya, Congo and Iran, and with key informants from services for immigrants and older adults. Here we include analysis of interviews with 24 older immigrant women and four key informants.

Study 3⁴ is an international comparative study that aims to identify promising practices that can advance age equity in cities, with a focus on how these conditions affect older people from subordinated and oppressed groups and the care workers on whom they depend. This chapter draws on this projects' policy and practice reviews, focus groups, and observational research conducted in 2019 with older immigrants in Ottawa, Canada from China, India, Italy, Portugal and Arabic speaking countries. We drew on participant contributions from 45 older immigrant women and seven key informants.

The research participants varied in terms of income and class, age, ability, migration histories, countries of origin, status, education and employment. For the participants for whom we have socio-demographic data, over 90 per cent came from low- and middle-income households, with a very few from high income households. Those for whom we do not have detailed data were either participants in seniors' services that served mainly low- and moderate-income older adults, or those we encountered while observing community groups. Interviews and focus groups were conducted in many languages, with translation into English provided by paid community people, by qualified graduate students and through transcript translation services. Interviews were conducted by teams composed of Canadian researchers who identify as white, South Asian, Asian and Indigenous, including faculty, graduate students and a research associate. At least three researchers were immigrants to Canada.

Initially, each project's data were analysed separately by the teams involved. The first author, involved in all three projects and noting considerable congruence across the project findings, reviewed them for continuities, tensions and differences, and developed this analysis. The second author was involved in the second and third project, the third author was involved in the first and third project.

Older immigrant women in Canada: a focus on care labour

Immigrants make up fully 30 per cent of Canadian permanent residents over 65, and 21 per cent of the total population (Employment and Social Development Canada, 2018). Those from India and China form the largest immigrant populations, including among older adults. Older immigrant women in Canada have arrived via numerous migration pathways at widely varying points in the life course. Some entered as children with their families, most arrived as young adults and a smaller group arrived as older adults, some as refugees, some as temporary but long-stay visa holders and some as sponsored parents and grandparents. Older immigrant women in Canada may be permanent residents and/or citizens or have temporary migration status. Length of stay in Canada varies widely, from those who emigrated in youth to those who emigrated only weeks ago.

Those older women who came to Canada through labour, family and refugee programs and have permanent residency can access all welfare state services. Those who emigrated through parent and grandparent sponsorships can access public health care after a short waiting period but are subject to restrictions that make them ineligible for public income supports and public housing for 20 years, or 10 years in the province of Quebec. Other older adults come to Canada on short or longer-term renewable visas, must pay to access health-care services, and are mostly restricted from other welfare services, including those who spend the rest of their lives in Canada (Côté-Boucher and Braedley, 2025).

These women's contributions begin with the reality that Canada relies on mothers around the world to ensure its labour force. Overall, in 2022 immigrants were responsible for almost 100 per cent of the growth in the labour force and 75 per cent of Canada's population growth (Statistics Canada, 2023). Predictions are that by 2036, half of Canada's children will have at least one parent born outside Canada, with economists seeing this generation as a particularly capable and willing labour force (Billy-Ocheieng and Arif, 2023). But these mothers of Canada's labour force are paying a price. One group of mothers remains outside of Canada, and experiences significant barriers that limit their support to children in Canada (Côté-Boucher and Braedley, 2025). Immigrant women, and especially the two-thirds of immigrant women in Canada who are racialised, are much more likely than native-born women to be employed in the informal/hidden sector; agricultural, service and industrial work that may not be (fully) reported to tax authorities, does not comply with labour standards, and is typically poorly compensated. These women are also over-represented in the low-waged care economy, working in child care, disability services, elder care, housekeeping, sanitation and food preparation (Drolet, 2022). Their lower earnings in paid work mean that a higher percentage of immigrant women aged 65 years and older remain in paid employment than both Canadian-born seniors and immigrant men, because they cannot afford to retire (Morissette and Hou, 2024). Further, whether their now adult children were born in Canada or abroad, most older immigrant women in Canada had limited or no access to paid maternity and parental leave or affordable childcare other than familial care, further reducing their potential lifetime earnings.

Older immigrant women's care contributions do not end with their children's entry to the labour force. Their unpaid caring labour maintains the current labour force, helping to maintain their adult children and raise the next generation through providing domestic work and childcare for their grandchildren. Government survey research showed that 79 per cent of older adults who came to Canada under the parent and grandparent sponsorship program provide childcare, 85 per cent prepare meals, and 69 per cent do housecleaning, gardening, and/or laundry for their sponsoring children and their families (Immigration, Refugees and Citizenship Canada, 2024), as just one example. Our qualitative research substantiates these survey results, showing that older immigrant women, no matter their time and type of entry to Canada, make substantial contributions to care through both paid and unpaid work, as our next section discusses.

Triple jeopardy: the conditions of ageing and caring for immigrant older women

Across our research studies, participants made it clear that immigration was a family project, deeply entwined with their concerns for both finances and care. All participants were part of extended family systems that involved two to five generations, with members of at least two generations in Canada, and often more. Typical of those who emigrate as young adults, one older woman from Italy who arrived in the 1970s indicated:

> I came when I was young, with my new husband. There was no work, no future, in our hometown [in Italy]. When I got work at a factory [in Canada], I sent money to my mother every cheque, for my sisters and brothers. Then some of them came here, and I helped them to come. (Study 3)

A woman who moved from Iran to Canada with her husband and young children in the 1990s indicated, 'We came for our kids – to give them a peaceful life' (Study 2). A woman from Sri Lanka, who was a nanny in Canada for years, explained, 'I came with the caregiver [immigration] program, left my kids behind because that is what you must do. But I always planned to bring them and my mom, to be together, here' (Study 1). Some participants also came as refugees and sponsored their parents to come to Canada through refugee streams. They too worked hard to make settlement a family project.

For those who emigrated at age 55 or older, family was their main motivation. As an older woman from China told us:

> I came to help my daughter and her family, to look after the kids, do the cooking, help in the house. She was going to school and working too, all the time. My husband stayed behind, but then he came, because he likes me to take care of him (laugh). (Study 2)

Further, most participants provided significant unpaid care within their households, extended families, and/or communities. In Study 1, most participants were caring for their frail or ill spouses, and many of those between 55 and 75 were also caring for parents or in-laws. Across our three studies, just under half of the women provided regular care to their children and grandchildren, ranging from daily childcare, housekeeping and/or cooking to occasional childcare and housework, with another small group indicating they had provided this care in the recent past. Some participants were providing care for parents, spouses, children and grandchildren in a round-robin of constant caring. Many participants provided care to friends, neighbours and throughout their communities via volunteer work. This volunteering included formal roles, such as running ethnocultural seniors' groups, and extensive informal helping such as transporting and accompanying other seniors to medical and social appointments, religious services, grocery shopping and errands. Some provided snow removal, gardening and housekeeping, some checked in regularly on those who were housebound, ill or grieving. Another group of participants told us they had provided care in the past, but their own health and functioning meant that they could no longer help and instead needed care from their families and friends.

On the surface, this list of caring activities might look the same as what Canadian-born older women provide to their families and communities. However, our studies show that caregiving within immigrant communities has distinctive dimensions. These women's lives were characterised by insecurities related to their social location as immigrants, as older people, as caring women and, for most of our participants, as racialised people. They were often insecure in their material conditions of daily life, including their income, housing, and for some, their immigration status. Second, they experienced loneliness, social isolation and a lack of support shaped by barriers associated with language, culture, mobility and their caregiving responsibilities. These conditions intertwined, affecting all our participants, but differently depending on their circumstances.

These immigrant women's third insecurity is a contradiction related to an age-equity promising practice. In Ottawa there are a range of culturally based and linguistically specific community groups for immigrant seniors, including groups designed for caregivers. Our studies show that these groups offer older immigrant women opportunities to share resources, support one another, create community and advocate collectively. While this practice did not eradicate the material disadvantages in these women's lives, it did much to address social isolation, loneliness and lack of support, while also providing a platform for advocacy and activism. However, our studies found that the structural conditions maintaining these groups are highly precarious in Ottawa, introducing the third jeopardy into these women's lives.

Jeopardy 1: Material conditions

Immigrant older women are disproportionately affected by the material conditions of ageing for Canadians. Concerns about income were evident throughout our interviews and focus groups. Canadian income security programs mean that overall, only 6.1 per cent of seniors 65 years and older who are residents of Canada were considered to be living in poverty and the overall poverty rate in Ottawa was 7.1 per cent in 2021 (Statistics Canada, 2022). But older women were more likely to live in poverty, as are (new) immigrants, and racialised people. The cost of housing relative to income was mentioned repeatedly as a major constraint that limited research participants' disposable income for food, transportation, health-related expenses such as prescriptions, weather-appropriate coats and footwear, and recreation and leisure. Problems with winter outerwear affordability were noted in Study 2 which were confirmed when we learned that Ottawa charities and thrift stores had distributed their entire stock of winter coats and boots by December in 2023.

Income constraints and care needs were reported as the key factors in determining that nearly half of our participants lived with family, with cultural preference for shared households only occasionally noted. Those who had immigrated recently were most likely to be housed with extended family, usually with their adult children and grandchildren. This sample mirrors 2016 census data showing that almost half of older immigrant women in Canada lived with extended family, while only 4.6 per cent of Canadian-born older women have similar arrangements (Hou and Ngo, 2021). Many of our participants reported that they were happy living with family, but we heard from a significant number who had experienced one or all of three problems. Some women were moved regularly among the homes of multiple family members, with little control over which household they would be living in, when, or for how long. Some participants had experienced deteriorating relationships with their family, including quarrels, and physical and financial abuse. Some described serious overcrowding, with large families sharing small apartments and homes. Many participants told us they had no alternative, due to costs, being needed for childcare, and/or due to stigma within their cultural communities if they moved out. Two participants in Study 2 told us that their children had dropped them at shelters for the homeless after they had been advised that this was the fastest route to move up the long waitlists for public housing, which was the only affordable route to living independently from family.

Another problem with familial co-housing was social isolation and loneliness. A common story was that the family were often gone all day, to school and to work, leaving older women alone to keep house in neighbourhoods full of similarly empty households. One participant told us she felt 'in the way, lonely and unwanted' in her daughter's home in the suburbs when she was no longer needed for childcare. She had recently moved to a non-profit affordable apartment building for Chinese older adults, located close to services and bus routes. 'It changed my life, to get an apartment here. I have friends, I can look after myself, my children don't feel guilty, and we have a good relationship' (Study 3). In this case, living independently removed this older woman's isolation from her peers, and improved her relationship with her children.

Confirming other research, those who lived in market rental housing were concerned about the costs and many indicated they were spending an inordinate percentage of their income on rent (Thurston, 2023). As one participant told us, 'My son helps out to pay my rent, but he has other expenses. I am on the list for social housing – I have been waiting for 3 years. I don't know if I will ever get it' (Study 2).

Participants who had lived in Canada for longer periods tended to either own their homes or live in more affordable rentals. Their insecurities paralleled those of many Canadian-born older adults. Those who owned homes reported worries about the potential impact of rising property taxes, keeping up with maintenance and their personal safety as they aged. Those who rented worried about rising rents, gentrification that includes evictions, personal safety and the condition of their rental properties (August, 2021). Added to these concerns were issues related to their social location, including fears that as they age, they might have to move to housing where they would be isolated due to their language, racialisation, religion or culture. 'My friend, she moved to a nice building, but nobody talks to her. As one participant from the Muslim Pakistani community told us, 'She is too different. They don't understand her' (participant, Study 2).

Transportation was a major barrier for older immigrant women across our projects (see Chapter 13 for more on public transportation and ageing). Many immigrant older women told us they did not drive in the city. Most did not own a car, and many relied on family members and friends to drive them to appointments, activities and shopping. Others relied on public transportation.

Although we asked, only a few used taxi or similar services, due to both costs and worries about safety. Transportation problems influenced their lives in many ways. Despite two free days weekly for seniors, participants reported that Ottawa's public transportation was a challenge to use, due to bus infrequency (for example, buses only coming once every hour), the need for multiple transfers, and problems with access (for example, bus stops too far away, unplowed after snowfalls, no benches). These challenges kept many older immigrant women from venturing out. One woman told us, 'I'm very small, so even that big step getting onto the bus is a challenge' (Study 3). One woman told us it took her 1.5 hours each way by bus to go 7 kilometres to her weekly seniors' group at her mosque (Study 2).

Caregivers and women with disabilities complained bitterly about dedicated public transportation for those with disabilities. Typical was one participant's comment: 'It's not very practical. You can only call it at a certain time, 24 hours before and even then it's not reliable' (Study 3). Although our three studies were conducted over an 8-year period, there was little change, including consistent stories about delays of 2 to 3 hours that discouraged participants from attending any optional activities, such as social gatherings or recreational activities.

Transportation costs were also a factor. Commenting on challenges involved in ensuring immigrant older adults could attend linguistically specific groups and services, one key informant shared, 'Most of the people [in the program] are lower income. We do try and find funding to provide transportation for people to come to events when we have them, but you know, there are lots of obstacles.' Organisation staff told us they were often unable to acquire funding for transportation, preventing older adults from attending events and programs.

As has become clear in this section, material conditions related to gender, caring, race, class and immigration shape older immigrant women's incomes, housing and transportation, jeopardising their opportunities for ageing well in Ottawa. But there are other, related jeopardies, as the next sections will show.

Jeopardy 2: Language, loneliness and social isolation

According to Islam and Gilmour (2023) immigrant women are the loneliest group of older adults in Canada, with those who have been in Canada since childhood or working age lonelier than those who emigrated in later life. Our findings shed light on the conditions that shape this loneliness. While policy concerns about older people's social isolation, including among immigrants, has been raised and studied (Employment and Social Development Canada, 2018; Johnson et al, 2019; Salma and Salami, 2020), the connections between social isolation and care needs and care work for older immigrants are not well understood. In our studies, social isolation and loneliness were shaped by issues related to care needs and care work together with language barriers, discrimination and exclusions.

Compared to other older adults in Canada, those whose first language is not English or French are much more likely to live in a multi-generational household, and much less likely to live in other collective living arrangements with peers, like seniors' housing (Hou and Ngo, 2021). In our research, language barriers presented a continual struggle for many of our participants, particularly in accessing services that could support them in ageing well, getting the care they needed, supporting their caregiving and developing community relationships. Those who were fluent in English or French had fewer difficulties and often provided translation for others, but most participants in our studies mentioned language barriers as a continual struggle.

Many women told us about language barriers encountered in health care, home care and other services frequently used by older people. While some were able to find others to translate for them, many women told us about preparing for appointments in advance by learning English terms: 'Before I need to see a doctor, I had to prepare the terminology ... like a student preparing for class. For example, how to say heart, fibrillation. My kids need to go over [this] beforehand' (Study 1). Another participant explained: 'Some words in the hospital I didn't understand, so I had to call my nephew in the United States to translate them for me' (Study 1). Many women complained that a lack of reliable interpretation services in Ottawa's health-care system meant they had to abandon any privacy around their sensitive health concerns, as they had no choice but to rely on family or friends for translation.

Language issues shaped these women's care arrangements in many ways. For example, home care services did not provide much of a break or help for participants who were caregivers or needed home care support themselves. As one Urdu and English-speaking participant, who cares for her frail husband told us:

> I have to do so much translation, it is easier to do the work myself. The workers were never the same. I had to explain over and over, to each new person. And my husband gets very upset by this. It takes me a long time to get him settled after. (Study 2)

In this case, her husband had once spoken English fluently but lost this capacity due to age-related memory loss, a common occurrence for those experiencing dementia (Ellajosyula et al, 2020). Another participant who has disabilities that make dressing and bathing very difficult shared, 'I would rather them not come ... I asked if there was anyone who could speak Cantonese. They said no one.' As another participant told us, language barriers are compounded by situations in which home care workers were not fluent in English and could not communicate easily. In these situations, a shared weak fluency in a common language meant that communication was reduced to drawings or gestures, and workers, typically other immigrant women struggling to settle in Canada, 'might not do the things that we instruct them to do' (Study 1).

A key informant explained that day programs for those with dementia also often excluded immigrant older adults due to language:

> [This older adult] had dementia. He went to one adult day program [at a mainstream organization] ... He didn't speak English at all, never learned English, so he couldn't say, 'I want washroom. I don't feel comfortable. I'm sick' in English and stuff for his own safety. [The staff] called the family caregiver and said, 'Sorry, for his own safety I cannot keep him'. (Study 3)

Across our studies, it was clear that language barriers operated not only as exclusionary barriers to services but meant that caregivers in immigrant communities were taking a larger share of caring work than those without language barriers. As one focus group participant commented after hearing other participants describe their often-unsupported unpaid caring: 'I think in the big spectrum of things ... these caregivers are helping the system ... they're helping to make sure that the care receivers are taking their medication on time, and following instructions, and providing them [with care] in their own language' (Study 1).

Many participants told us they were providing childcare to their grandchildren or had done so in the past. Language barriers were also noted by these carers as an isolating factor, but differently. As one participant told us, 'I look after my grandkids ... even when they were small, they could help me with English. Still, I am afraid when a stranger comes – I don't open [the front door]. I don't know what they say' (Study 3). Another participant told us, 'I take the little ones to their bus stop in the morning. While we wait, the other [adults] talk a lot. To me they say hi, they smile. It is too hard to say more' (Study 3). These participants spend their days with their grandchildren or alone and have little opportunity to improve their skills in official languages, meet with peers or participate in the wider life of the community.

Many immigrant older women told us they made efforts to connect to community groups, faith communities and senior centres. For some, these experiences transformed their lives, offering friendships, a sense of belonging and meaningful activities, as will be described in the next section. But others had experienced a deepening social isolation and loneliness due to experiences of exclusions, discrimination and marginalisation at community centres and senior's groups in Ottawa. As one participant noted about her efforts to get involved at a senior's centre: 'I noticed that [Canadian] seniors have lot of ... activities to do, like bingo, and they are so happy and they play cards ... and compared to that, the South [Asian] cultures ... don't play bingo, cards, but we play other things, but not these activities' (Study 1).

An older woman and caregiver for her frail husband came to Canada from Cambodia in the 1970s. Commenting on her sense of loneliness, she said to one Canadian-born white older researcher, 'Do you have any Asian friends? I live here a long time, I work at a bank, I volunteer. But my friends are Asian. I know a lot of white people, nice but not friendly' (Study 2). Her comment reflected experiences described in many interviews suggesting what Martin Luther King called 'polite racism' (Theoharis, 2021), the excluding, discriminatory practices of white liberals, who, while holding commitments against racism and xenophobia, do not take the steps to fully consider or fight against them, including in their own attitudes and actions. As another South Asian immigrant woman told us about her experiences with white Canadians, 'I'm born under loneliness. I do not like to speak to people because I find it's too much time and for what? I don't find people that I respect. I must respect and people must understand me and we must be in mutual relationships' (Study 2).

Jeopardy 3: The material conditions of ethnocultural groups for older adults

For many immigrant older adults in our studies, no matter their length of time in Canada, culturally based and/or linguistically specific groups offered an antidote to social isolation and loneliness and opportunities to share resources and knowledge, meaningful activities and a sense of belonging. In Ottawa, these promising programs met many of this populations' needs. Our research studies included visiting linguistically specific groups for caregivers of people with dementia, some which also included people with dementia; 'grassroots ethnocultural groups' organised via a community development approach; and various seniors' and other groups at synagogues, churches, community centres and mosques that offered social activities, often including intergenerational activities. While women and men were included in most groups, consistently, women outnumbered men in every group included in our studies.

Our participants told us that these community groups were very important to them, often with the inference that they felt 'other' in mainstream Canadian society. A Polish older woman told us, 'coming here gives you a feeling of belonging' (Study 1). A member of the Chinese older adults' group told us 'we gain courage and strength from telling our own stories' (Study 1). At a group for Punjabi older adults, one participant explained it well, 'Here we can be without feeling outside the world. We are inside, we feel at home' (Study 2).

Across our studies, group leaders and volunteers explained that the groups are very successful, well-attended and popular. In some religious organisations and one senior centre, we met with groups that had stable financial support, dedicated space, help with volunteer recruitment, a small budget for activities and food and help with communications. However, most groups had no stable, reliable funding to run their programs, and any short-term funding was very modest. Most groups found low-cost or free space to meet at libraries, community centres, and health care, settlement, and other social services centres, but described ongoing challenges. Most groups wanted to meet on Wednesdays or Sundays in spaces near transit, so members could travel on the free public transit days for seniors. They wanted to meet regularly in the same spaces and at times convenient for members. Many groups needed larger spaces, as their memberships had grown. These conditions were difficult to achieve.

Throughout the eight years of our research studies, the material conditions for these groups were continually precarious, creating more jeopardy in the lives of immigrant older adults who relied on them. Pandemic lockdowns in 2020 and 2021 meant that most groups stopped meeting with some failing to resume. Other groups stopped and restarted. Some groups jumped successfully online for the short term. All levels of government and many charitable foundations shifted their funding priorities, defunding many of these programs. Fewer immigrant older adult groups had funding in 2024 than in 2017, and of those who had some funding, all but two groups had decreased levels.

Most groups were led by unpaid volunteers who were older adults themselves. We met many dynamic, dedicated community volunteers and, in cases where funding had been found, immigrant women and men hired from their communities coordinated these groups on short-term contracts for low wages. Volunteer burnout was a constant issue. The volunteers were 'working day and night', not only running groups, but often providing direct care to community members, seeking sources of funding, space and other resources, and communicating with often extensive memberships. When we asked volunteers how much time they spent coordinating their group, most concurred: 'Every day ... it's a lot, a time-consuming thing. But then, when you are in it you have to do it' (Study 3). While some volunteers were men, the majority were older immigrant women, and it was these women who also provided most direct support to community members.

Volunteer leaders struggled to resource these groups, applying to local charities and government funds offered on a competitive basis through calls for proposals. Preparing proposals consumed hundreds of hours of volunteer time, and involved many applications, as our volunteer participants told us: 'So we have to give them a number how many seniors, how many volunteers will be working, it's a very extensive [funding] application. That's why I said it takes me about a week to 10 days to do one application' (Study 3).

One community development agency had applied for and received several short-term grants that allowed them to hire a coordinator to support immigrant and racialised communities that wanted to develop seniors' groups. The coordinator told us, 'I started outreaching with the different groups so was able to connect – we have now I think 26 seniors' groups and there's more that want one, right? There's so many more that I haven't connected because we don't have the funding' (Study 3). These small grassroots groups and initiatives were competing for limited government and charitable funding against larger, mainstream organisations with much more capacity to meet funders' requirements for evaluations and financial reporting.

Despite these conditions, these older adult group leaders were strong advocates for their members, sometimes representing their individual, informal organisations and sometimes banding together as a politically active collective. As one key informant told us, 'we were at the funders table – this is a federal funder – and I said, "You need to create a separate stream for immigrant seniors to apply ... The needs are so high, look at our numbers, like look at our volunteer numbers, look at the work they are doing and it's going to cost the government less if you have this stream of funding for [immigrant older adults]"' (Study 3).

In sum, culturally based and linguistically specific group programs for immigrant older adults, including groups for caregivers, were important resources that advanced age equity for the many immigrant women across these studies. These groups helped these women know they were not alone in their precarious conditions affecting their caregiving, family life, income, housing, and transportation. They allowed them to share resources, information and develop advocacy and activist interventions. The groups also seemed to significantly reduce social isolation and loneliness, providing immigrant older women with opportunities for friendships, meaningful activity, a sense of belonging and joy.

Yet, these groups are precarious, jeopardised by the lack of political and financial support and by wide public failures to recognise the barriers experienced by immigrant older adults in mainstream services and society. They rely on extensive unpaid care labour provided by countless immigrant older women and some men who care for their communities through thousands of volunteer hours each year. Without sufficient resources, these groups can quickly fall apart, intensifying age inequities for all those who rely on them.

Advancing age equity: concluding remarks

This chapter began by briefly explaining the politics that situated older immigrant women as economic drains on welfare states. We argue that this characterisation misses entirely women's contributions to receiving countries as mothers and carers in paid and unpaid work, providing a sharp rebuttal to these economic claims. Our analysis demonstrates that Canada's economic reliance on relatively long-standing and high levels of immigration means that its economy relies heavily on the many immigrant older women who have produced and continue to help reproduce generations of workers, from cradle to grave.

Despite this reliance, our empirical studies show that immigrant women's opportunities for ageing well are jeopardised by inequitable and discriminatory conditions related to their paid and unpaid caring, age, gender, immigrant status, racialisation and language. The resulting disadvantages include lower lifetime earnings, loneliness and social isolation. Culturally based and linguistically specific groups, including those for caregivers, offer a refuge from exclusions but also rely on these women to provide significant unpaid caring labour, with uneven, uncertain support from government and charitable funders. Further, some of these conditions could be readily addressed through, for example, longer-term secure funding for older adult community groups, required use of digital and other translation services in public services, public housing initiatives that recognise disadvantages among specific older populations and more.

We conclude with a call for the revaluation of older immigrant women's lives and contributions in receiving countries, but not because we wish to redeem them as 'deserving' of welfare state support: in our view, welfare rights must exceed this kind of narrow categorisation. Rather, we aim toward a conception of age equity that takes up consistently its relationship with equity in the care economy. As a strategy in advancing this direction, our feminist border analysis attends not only to welfare state bordering related to gender, race, class, age and immigration status, but to how these borders shape the relationship between the productive economy and the care economy. As we have demonstrated, this approach surfaces inequities often missed by approaches that centre on identity, race or immigration status alone, both troubling conventional approaches and opening new possibilities.

Notes

[1] Men were also participants in all of these studies, but this data was not included in this analysis, Gender fluid and trans immigrant older adults participated in the 'Imagining Age-Friendly Communities within Communities' study, but had a different range of concerns and did not participate in the immigrant seniors' groups. This absence suggests that these seniors' groups are not safe, accessible or of sufficient interest to these older adults.

[2] This was team-based capstone project in the MSc in Health program at Carleton University, co-supervised by Renate Ysseldyk and Susan Braedley, in collaboration with Sybil Braganza and the Grassroots Ethnocultural Seniors' Network supported by the Social Planning Council of Ottawa. The students involved were: Mehreen Anjum, Natalie Fersht, Hayley Miloff, Laura O'Dell and Claire Pilon-Robertson.

[3] *Bordering Old Age, Bordering Care: Comparing Welfare State Approaches*, P.I. Susan Braedley and Karine Cote-Boucher. Social Sciences and Humanities Research Council 435-2019-0663.

4 Imagining Age-Friendly Communities within Communities: International Promising Practices. Director: Tamara Daly. Social Sciences and Humanities Research Council 895-2018-1013.

References

August, M. (2021) Financialization of housing from cradle to grave: COVID-19, seniors' housing, and multifamily rental housing in Canada, *Studies in Political Economy*, 102(3): 289–308.

Barrass, S. and Shields, J. (2017) Immigration in an age of austerity: morality, the welfare state and the shaping of the ideal migrant, in B. Evans and J. Shields (eds) *Austerity: The Lived Experience*, University of Toronto Press, pp 195–221.

Billy-Ochieng, R. and Arif, A. (2023) *Offspring: How Canadians Born to Newcomers Are Shaping Canada's Future*, TD Economics [online], Available from: https://economics.td.com/domains/economics.td.com/documents/reports/rb/Newcomers_Shaping_Canadas_Future.pdf

Braedley, S. and Luxton, M. (2021) Social reproduction at work, social reproduction as work: a feminist political economy perspective, *Journal of Labor and Society*, 25(4): 559–86.

Braedley, S., Côté-Boucher, K. and Przednowek, A. (2021) Old and dangerous: bordering older migrants' mobilities, rejuvenating the post-welfare state, *Social Politics*, 28(1): 24–46.

Burgoon, B. and Rooduijn, M. (2021) 'Immigrationization' of welfare politics? Anti-immigration and welfare attitudes in context, *West European Politics*, 44(2): 177–203.

Côté-Boucher, K. and Braedley, S. (2025) Bordering social reproduction: the welfare/immigration regimes of Quebec and Ontario in Canada, *Critical Social Policy*, 45(1): 27–48.

Drolet, M. (2022) *Unmasking Differences in Women's Full-Time Employment*, Statistics Canada [online], Available from: https://www150.statcan.gc.ca/n1/en/pub/75-006-x/2022001/article/00009-eng.pdf?st=Z9cyKS2G

Ellajosyula, R., Narayanan, J. and Patterson, K. (2020) Striking loss of second language in bilingual patients with semantic dementia, *Journal of Neurology*, 267(2): 551–60.

Employment and Social Development Canada (2018) *Social Isolation of Seniors: A Focus on New Immigrant and Refugee Seniors*, Government of Canada [online], Available from: https://www.canada.ca/en/employment-social-development/corporate/seniors-forum-federal-provincial-territorial/social-isolation-immigrant-refugee.html

Gabriel, C. (2024) Business as usual? Immigration policy in a tumultuous time, in K. Scott, L. MacDonald and S. Trew (eds) *The Trudeau Record: Promise vs. Performance*, Lorimer Press, pp 291–305.

Grady, P. and Grubel, H. (2015) Immigration and the welfare state revisited: fiscal transfers to immigrants in Canada [online], Available from: https://papers.ssrn.com/sol3/papers.cfm?abstract_id=2612456.

Hou, F. and Ngo, A. (2021) *Differences in Living Arrangements of Older Seniors by Mother Tongue*, Statistics Canada [online], Available from: https://www150.statcan.gc.ca/n1/en/pub/36-28-0001/2021005/article/00003-eng.pdf?st=PphuAyvU

Immigration, Refugees and Citizenship Canada (2024) *Evaluation of the Family Reunification Program*, Government of Canada [online], Available from: https://www.canada.ca/content/dam/ircc/documents/pdf/english/corporate/reports-statistics/evaluations/family-reunification_en.pdf

Islam, M.K. and Gilmour, H. (2023) Immigrant status and loneliness among older Canadians, *Health Reports*, 34(7): 3–18.

Johnson, S., Bacsu, J., McIntosh, T., Jeffery, B. and Novik, N. (2019) Social isolation and loneliness among immigrant and refugee seniors in Canada: a scoping review, *International Journal of Migration, Health and Social Care*, 15(3): 177–90.

Morissette, R. and Hou, F. (2024) *Employment by Choice and Necessity Among Canadian-Born and Immigrant Seniors*, Statistics Canada [online], Available from: https://www150.statcan.gc.ca/n1/pub/36-28-0001/2024004/article/00002-eng.htm

Rigzin, T. and Kaushal, N. (2022) It ain't about the money: a cross-country study of the fiscal implications of immigrant exclusion, in E.A. Koning (ed) *The Exclusion of Immigrants from Welfare Programs*, University of Toronto Press, pp 101–33.

Roy, D. and Cheatham, A. (2024) *Backgrounder: What is Canada's Immigration Policy?*, Council on Foreign Relations [online], Available from: https://www.cfr.org/backgrounder/what-canadas-immigration-policy

Salma, J. and Salami, B. (2020) 'Growing old is not for the weak of heart': social isolation and loneliness in Muslim immigrant older adults in Canada, *Health & Social Care in the Community*, 28(2): 615–23.

Statistics Canada (2022) *Census in Brief: Disaggregated Trends in Poverty from the 2021 Census of Population*, Government of Canada [online], Available from: https://www12.statcan.gc.ca/census-recensement/2021/as-sa/98-200-x/2021009/98-200-x2021009-eng.pdf

Statistics Canada (2023) *Canada's Population Estimates: Record High Population Growth in 2022*, Government of Canada [online], Available from: https://www150.statcan.gc.ca/n1/en/daily-quotidien/230322/dq230322f-eng.pdf?st=GVvRog22

Theoharis, J. (2021) 'The thin veneer of the North's racial self-righteousness': Martin Luther King Jr.'s challenge to Northern racism, *Journal of Civil and Human Rights*, 7(1): 35–70.

Thurston, Z. (2023) *Housing Experiences in Canada: Renters Who Are in Poverty, Seniors and Recent Immigrants, 2021*, Statistics Canada [online], Available from: https://www150.statcan.gc.ca/n1/en/pub/46-28-0001/2021001/article/00025-eng.pdf?st=6w6YGQrl

Ugelvik, T. (2013) Seeing like a welfare state: immigration control, statecraft, and a prison with double vision, in K.F. Aas and M. Bosworth (eds) *The Borders of Punishment: Migration, Citizenship, and Social Exclusion*, Oxford University Press, pp 183–200.

11

'East' meets 'West': trans-national ageing in a space of 'cultural liminality'

Elias Chaccour and Tamara Daly

Introduction

Demographic shifts driven by migration from 'East' to 'West' are diversifying the experience of ageing, with more older adults navigating between inherited and adopted cultural and social systems. Many find themselves in a liminal space, ageing within structures not built for them and relying on care systems and policies that do not fully account for their cultural norms, linguistic needs or transnational ties. These mismatches highlight deeper questions of equity in ageing, particularly how support and care are structured across borders. 'Liminality' derives from the Latin limen, meaning threshold (Sweeney, 2009). It is used in scholarship to describe the 'in-between' experience of those who are neither 'in nor out' and are in an unfamiliar space removed from a familiar social order (Sweeney, 2009). The term has been applied to the liminal position of privately paid companions working in long-term care (Daly et al, 2015; Daly and Armstrong, 2016); the non-standard work performed by tree-planters in Northern Ontario (Sweeney, 2009); the role of midwives in the Middle East (Giladi, 2010); and the gender liminal experiences of those with trans-gender identities (Nanda, 2000; Wilson, 2002). This chapter considers how cultural norms coupled with migrant status construct ageing in a space of 'cultural liminality'. People migrating to a new country can inhabit a long-lasting, even permanent sense of 'in-between-ness' or liminality (Cannella and Huerta, 2019). This in-betweenness, we argue, is felt more acutely by certain groups of migrants, particularly those who migrate later in life and are forced to migrate or move to countries with political, economic, religious, linguistic and cultural environments that differ significantly from their country of origin.

In the context of considering how age equity can be advanced, our focus in this chapter is to consider cultural norms of ageing, the conditions for ageing, and the liminality or in-betweenness experienced by older adults in transnational families living between Lebanon and Canada. We aim to trouble assumptions often made in jurisdictionally based analyses by introducing this concept of liminality and its operations in transnational older adults' lives and experiences.

To do so, we conducted a thorough literature review, supplemented by the first author's insider–outsider perspective as a Lebanese Canadian who immigrated with their parents to Canada from Lebanon. We take up our example in the context of East-to-West migration, experiences of political upheaval, war and occupation, and comparative differences in state supports and family formation. We view cultural norms as the shared values, languages and beliefs of a particular group, often formalised by the state policies, including its inaction, and the practices of individuals, families, the market and the voluntary sector. We highlight what is known about Lebanese older adults' experiences of ageing in North America and Europe, and particularly the interplay between 'Eastern' and 'Western' cultural norms, with a particular focus on how older adults in transnational families negotiate their lives.

Our example

Our example of cultural liminality between 'East' and 'West' is the case of older Lebanese adults living in transnational families that straddle Canada and Lebanon. Many families live transnational lives between Canada and Lebanon, with older adults and/or younger generations dividing their time between these contexts, but this is especially the case for those who are retired (Stasiulis, 2017). Cultural liminality is shaped by many factors. First, the Lebanese diaspora, with communities around the world, exemplifies transnationalism through maintaining connections to Lebanon through remittances, family ties and political involvement (Tabar, 2020). Lebanon's ongoing political strife and sectarian divisions are mirrored within the diaspora, with many Lebanese Canadians actively participating in Lebanese elections, lobbying efforts and political campaigns (Tabar and El-Zakka, 2024). Cultural liminality is an inevitable result of minds and hearts straddling loyalties and worries in Lebanon and the relative political and economic security and safety in Canada. Second, in these countries, the state role in providing care supports for older adults differs dramatically. Canada's state-funded health and social care systems are comparatively robust for older adults, while those in Lebanon are poor compared with other countries, shaping cultural differences between what individuals, families and households must manage and what services are funded through the state in these two contexts. Third, and shaped in part by the different roles of the state, cultural liminality is a product of tensions between Lebanese and Canadian cultural norms around support for older adults, influenced by different patterns of family formation and gender roles. Fourth, ageing itself is perceived differently in these contexts.

Canada and Lebanon also present a socio-demographic contrast. Canada's population is comparatively older: nearly one-fifth of the population of Canada is over 65 (Statistics Canada, 2022), while the proportion of people aged 65+ still living in Lebanon is only 9.5 per cent in 2020 (Central Intelligence Agency, 2024). Further, Canada has ten times the population of Lebanon. Both countries are multicultural and multi-lingual, but in distinctive ways. As a country of immigration, Canada is home to several large migrant communities worldwide: nearly 2 million older adults aged 55+ who identify as visible minorities live in Canada (n = 1,909,635). Important to this example is that almost 100,000 migrant adults in Canada aged 55 and older identify as Arab (Statistics Canada, 2023a). Among all groups of visible minority migrants to Canada older than 55, Arabs are the sixth largest group. Nearly 40 per cent of these Arabs have migrated from Lebanon, with 18,585 older than 65 and 19,855 between 55 and 64 years old. Lebanon is a meeting place of Middle Eastern, Arab and European cultures, resulting in a unique language polyglotism of Arabic, French, English and Armenian (Marcus, 2016). Importantly, Arabic, specifically Lebanese Arabic, is the main language connecting Lebanon to the Arab world (Abou, 1962). Today, the Lebanese-Canadian population totals 210,605 (Statistics Canada, 2023b). It spans a mixed demographic profile: 41.1 per cent are aged 25 to 54, while 23.3 per cent are under 14, indicating steady family growth. An ageing trend is also evident, with 19.8 per cent aged 55 or older, primarily first-generation immigrants from the 1970s and 1980s. With 49.8 per cent of Lebanese Canadians identifying as Christian and 30 per cent as Muslim, religious institutions are crucial in providing social support and maintaining cultural identity in the diaspora (Statistics Canada, 2023b).

The example of older adults within Lebanese transnational families is instructive, but also suggests a research gap, as little is known and much of the available research was conducted over a decade ago. However, their circumstances are potentially important for both policy and practice. Available literature on older migrants demonstrates that while age at arrival is no doubt important, the path to get to Canada makes a difference to health and well-being. Compare, for instance, the circumstances of economic and student migrants who relocate to take a secure job or further education, to refugees who migrate to flee war or other difficult circumstances. Then there are those who are understudied, including the Lebanese migrant population in Canada, who experience forced migration, emigrating to seek safety, economic opportunities and stability while their homeland remains in a state of violent political, economic and social upheaval. Many have close family and friends remaining behind. The effects of these circumstances on settlement, health and well-being needs further study, and this is especially important when considering the needs of older adults.

Thus, given our example of the Lebanese–Canadian transnational community and its older adults, how might immigrant older adults living in Canada move from a space of 'cultural liminality' to one of ethnocultural inclusion and equity that takes their cultural norms and challenges into account? How might immigrant younger generations move from their space of cultural liminality to one of ethnocultural inclusion and equity that acknowledges the importance of their relationships with older generations, whether in distant 'Eastern' homelands or in Canada? Drawing on the extant literature, we outline four dimensions that contribute to producing the experience of cultural liminality for older adults from transnational families living between Lebanon and Canada. Further, we ask, how does this liminality shape their ageing experience?

Cultural liminality 1: Political and economic security

The cultural norms held by older Lebanese migrants in Canada are rooted in Lebanese history, including its political, social and economic systems and more than two decades of war, violence and political instability (Chahine and Chemali, 2009). These circumstances have instilled fear, anxiety and insecurity in Lebanese individuals, shaping their experiences of ageing regardless of their location. Leaving Lebanon because of war and political strife is common (Tabar, 2010). Lebanese people have a long history of settling in the so-called West: North American, European and Australasian countries, including Canada. The result is that many Lebanese individuals and families straddle multiple cultural identities and realities, presenting challenges for older Lebanese adults at home and in the diaspora who navigate between their country of origin, often affected by war and conflict, and new environments that differ significantly.

Lebanese migration to Canada has occurred in multiple waves, driven by conflict, economic opportunities and family reunification. Beginning in the mid-19th century, when Lebanon was under Ottoman rule, the earliest migrants sought opportunities in the Americas through commercial activities (De Bel-Air, 2017). The Lebanese civil war (1975–89) displaced nearly 990,000 people – 40 per cent of the population – prompting Canada to offer humanitarian visas primarily to refugees from economically disadvantaged regions of Lebanon, like North Lebanon (Tabar and El-Zakka, 2024). Many of those who emigrated in this wave were low-skilled workers who gravitated to cities such as Montreal, Ottawa and Toronto. Post-civil war migration patterns shifted toward skilled immigrants. By 2010, over 50 per cent of Lebanese youth were pursuing higher education, one of the highest rates in the Arab world (Tabar, 2020). However, political instability and a weak job market in Lebanon pushed many to seek opportunities abroad. Canada's immigration programs, including refugee resettlement, economic pathways and family sponsorship, helped build a large, interconnected community across Canadian urban centres (De Bel-Air, 2017).

Another factor shaping cultural liminality are the communal and political allegiances in Lebanon that tend to split along largely religious sectarian cleavages. The Lebanese state officially recognises 18 sects, primarily classified as either Muslim and Christian. Lebanese politics is enmeshed with religious group membership as these sects play a central role in society and are the primary social organisations through which political security is preserved (Faour, 2007). Religious group membership is an inherited attribute in Lebanese and Middle Eastern societies. Sectarian identities in this region resemble ethnic identities in the West and exist independently from any broader national identity (Starr, 1978). Like other communal identities, sectarian ones are socially and historically constructed and treated as inheritable social differences, although they can be changed through complex conversion processes, regardless of personal faith or religious belief (Deeb, 2020). In 2022, it was estimated that the Lebanese population was mostly comprised of members of the Sunni and Shia Muslim sects (67.8 per cent), with smaller proportions of Alawites and Ismailis; Christians (~32.4 per cent) are mostly members of the Maronite and Greek Orthodox sects, with smaller numbers of Greek Catholic and other Christians groups; and Druze (~5 per cent) (Central Intelligence Agency, 2024). The Lebanese diaspora reflects the country's religious diversity; while most Lebanese living abroad are Christians, there are also Muslim sects within the diaspora. Following a century of tumultuous nation-state building efforts, Lebanon's civil society organisations and collectives have developed some non-sectarian political and social movements that strive to reconcile deeply divided identities and promote national unity (Vértes et al, 2021). Thus, sectarian identities are continually reproduced and challenged at various social, political and interpersonal levels (Deeb, 2020), including within the diaspora.

Most Lebanese older adults have been profoundly influenced by Lebanon's history and politics, including decades of war, sporadic violence, and political and economic instability. These experiences can instill persistent fear, anxiety and insecurity among Lebanese individuals, regardless of where they now live (Chahine and Chemali, 2009). The experiences of older Lebanese adults in the 'West' tend to be characterised by negotiation and integration of 'Eastern' and 'Western' cultural norms and expectations, creating complex transitional 'borderland' spaces where new and old identities coexist and influence close relationships (McDaniel and Gazso, 2014). The effects are unclear, but studies document that Lebanese people who migrated early in life and are now ageing in the United States (Abu-Bader et al, 2011) and Canada (Chams, 2017; Nasir et al, 2022) can find it difficult to remain socially connected. In addition, life experiences shape individuals' attitudes, values, beliefs and behaviours as they age (Gelfand and Yee, 1992). The expectations, adaptational requirements, and coping mechanisms for old age in the West do not align well with the experiences of older Lebanese migrants, that have included war and occupation in their country of birth. Consequently, experiences of wars, civil strife and occupation can have lasting effects on the life course, shaping resilience, identity and well-being, both positively and negatively, for individuals from politically unstable countries (Abdulrahim and Ajrouch, 2014). However, while pre-immigration cultural identity and goals hold great significance for older adult immigrants, these aspects tend to take a back seat when the immediate demands of adjusting to a new society and ensuring a livelihood take precedence (Gelfand and Yee, 1992). As a result, Lebanese older adult immigrants navigate between values and practices rooted in their Lebanese heritage and the systems and structures of the Western societies they may call home. The interplay of these cultural influences shapes their identity, social relationships and experiences of ageing. The acculturation process requires balancing cultural heritage with the demands of receiving societies, often leading individuals to reconcile potentially conflicting expectations.

Cultural liminality 2: State support for older adults

Lebanon's demographic ageing, described earlier, has not been met by corresponding state-sponsored increases in health and social services (Kronfol et al, 2013). Lebanese older adults in Lebanon are vulnerable, given the absence of a strong welfare safety net. While the state provides some welfare services, they are limited, and Lebanese families often rely on their limited resources to manage health, financial, and social needs (Farhood et al, 1993; Sibai and Beydoun, 1999). Employment and income can be precarious, and social services such as health insurance and pensions are not consistently regulated, reinforcing the importance of family care.

In contrast to Lebanon's weak state system that provides little health care or social care support (Chahine and Chemali, 2009), high-income countries with established welfare systems (Estes, 2020) provide more support to older adults. Canada provides citizens access to health care, old age security and pension programs that can help ensure economic stability and well-being in older age. Despite the availability of these supports in Canada, however, immigrants' interactions with the rules and processes involved in state and health-care bureaucracies can deeply challenge them, leading to feelings of alienation, conflict, language and identity confusion, and a sense of othering. This experience is common among those struggling to reconcile their cultural understandings and customs with those of their new context (Azim, 2015). As Braedley and colleagues (2021) highlight, Canada's immigration policies prioritise young economic migrants while limiting permanent migration options for older family members and bordering their access to social welfare supports, both acting on and reinforcing assumptions that older immigrants pose economic burdens on the welfare system, contributing to this othering effect.

Cultural liminality 3: Family formation and gender roles

In Lebanon, the family functions as the primary social welfare unit, with family responsibility embedded in state policy and cultural values (Salibi, 1971; Khalaila, 2020; Tabar et al, 2020). Without extensive state welfare systems, family networks tend to remain a vital source of social and economic security (Al Wekhian, 2015; Khalaila, 2020). Care for family members, including for older adults, is a family responsibility, organised around gendered divisions of labour as part of the normative order, if not the reality of people's lives and circumstances. Lebanon's demographic profile is relatively 'old' among Arab countries, with the highest percentage of older persons and one in ten people aged 65+ (Khoury and Karam, 2020). To deal with the costs involved in supporting older family members in Lebanon, families compensate for lower earnings through migration, shaping a widespread reliance on strong family networks across borders. Emigrated family members send remittances back 'home' to Lebanese older people and extended family. The lack of a social safety net makes these remittances necessary, making the outmigration of young adults a key determinant of older adults' well-being in Lebanon (Ajrouch et al, 2015; Tabar, 2020).

Family reunification migration, whether on a temporary or permanent basis, is another strategy to bring older adults to family for extended regular stays or to settle permanently. In high-income countries, multigenerational family dwellings and reliance on adult children for support are as common as in Lebanon (Nassar-McMillan et al, 2013); however, changes in family structure are gradually challenging this norm (Yount and Sibai, 2009), and this is very likely the case for those in Canada. This emphasis on familial care aligns with cultural expectations, where responsibility for the well-being of older relatives is a collective family obligation, a norm that continues among Lebanese migrants abroad.

In the Lebanese diaspora, social identity and a sense of responsibility remain closely tied to family affiliation (Aswad, 1997), producing strong links in many families between the well-being of older adults and the quality of family relationships, including the proximity of children and the strength of the bonds (Ajrouch et al, 2015). Consequently, the family is central to Lebanese society, including its diaspora, and serves as the primary unit of support and social connectedness for older adults.

Regarding gender roles, Lebanese families are traditionally extended, patriarchal and cohesive, which enables parents to age in a multigenerational family environment and receive support from their children (Barakat, 1985).

Many older men in Lebanon continue to work late into their life, while most older women do not participate in the formal economy (Ajrouch et al, 2015). Regardless of age, women in Lebanon do most of the social reproductive work, and their principal occupation is housewife (Sibai and Beydoun, 1999). This gendered division of domestic labour and social reproduction encompasses activities, behaviours and relationships vital for the maintenance of daily life and the reproduction of future generations (Luxton and Bezanson, 2006).

But these circumstances are changing somewhat. Lebanon's population is ageing, with those aged 65+ accounting for 7.3 per cent of the population in 2017, 9.5 per cent in 2020, and projected to rise to 21 per cent by 2050 (Abyad, 2021; CIA, 2024). Economic pressures, increased emigration, and the growing participation of women in the workforce have weakened intergenerational support systems (Abdulrahim and Ajrouch, 2014). Additionally, Lebanon has experienced a rise in older adults living independently, reflecting shifts also seen in high-income countries, driven by similar socio-economic and cultural dynamics (Abyad, 2021).

Although Lebanon has seen significant demographic shifts, up-to-date and comprehensive data on older adults and their living arrangements remain limited. In 2013, approximately 12 per cent of adults aged 65+ live alone, with women more likely to live with family than men (Ajrouch et al, 2013). These changes in housing patterns reflect the evolving Lebanese family system in Lebanon and migrant-receiving countries. Economic pressures on younger generations, the emigration of children from Lebanon, and the increased presence of women in the workforce have shifted the availability of a traditional intergenerational support system (Abdulrahim and Ajrouch, 2014). Economic factors, gender dynamics and the influence of 'Western' cultural norms have contributed to the rising trend of Lebanese older adults living alone, reflecting the approach in high-income countries (Sibai et al, 2007).

It is likely that changes to household and family living arrangements are especially common among families that are stretched across the globe. Normatively, Canadian households are composed of the nuclear family, and while women in families carry most responsibilities for domestic work and care while also maintaining paid employment, gender norms have shifted significantly, with men and women sharing to provide economic support and domestic labour for their households. Familial care for older adults is expected, but co-housing is not the norm, and spouses are the main carers. This typical pattern in the 'West' is one perceived to be in sharp contrast to 'Eastern' norms and is an important factor in the experiences of cultural liminality experienced by older adults and their families who negotiate their lives between Lebanon and Canada. Even while the family remains a crucial source of support and connectedness once Lebanese people migrate to the

West (Joseph, 2000), it is common to find older Lebanese adults residing in Lebanon while their children live in multiple, different countries. In other instances, multigenerational families have migrated and continue to live together, with multigenerational family dwellings and reliance on adult children for support remaining common (Nassar-McMillan et al, 2013). This living arrangement can foster a strong sense of connectedness and provide a support network for older adults; however, changes in family structure are gradually challenging this cultural norm (Yount and Sibai, 2009). Economic and social shifts have redefined traditional intergenerational support systems (Abdulrahim and Ajrouch, 2014). Consequently, while the family continues to play a vital role in providing hands-on care (Gibbons et al, 2014), recent generations of ageing parents are less likely to have access to the same level of familial support as in the past, because families now live apart across long distances.

Older Lebanese can live 'between' countries as well. Increasing numbers of older migrants adopt a transnational lifestyle or return to their countries of origin after retirement, exhibiting complex attachments to the multiple places they inhabit (Palladino, 2019). Lebanese grandparents often travel periodically between East and West to care for their grandchildren, maintaining traditional family arrangements and facilitating intergenerational transfer of care while preserving familial connections. The dynamics of intergenerational solidarity could differ between well-established immigrants and recent arrivals, as immigration can disrupt family networks (Abdulrahim and Ajrouch, 2014). A distinct 'transnational family' is thus constituted through these interactions and sustained connections. The acculturation process gradually influences the family relations of Lebanese immigrants over time, leading to changes in beliefs, relationships and everyday life (Abdulrahim and Ajrouch, 2014).

While multigenerational living is the norm in Lebanon itself, where older age is associated with extensive networks and generally more positive perceptions (Antonucci et al, 2015), there is a lack of studies specifically examining the intergenerational living arrangements of Lebanese older adult migrants living in Western countries and arrangements for intergenerational care. The experiences of other groups of migrants suggest this would be a fruitful area of study. For instance, a study on caregiving among Mexican-American women revealed substantial caregiving burdens for both highly acculturated and less acculturated caregivers, with the latter experiencing more stress and lower satisfaction despite fulfilling their family role obligations (Jolicoeur and Madden, 2002).

Cultural liminality 4: Normative views of ageing

As noted, evidence suggests that Lebanese older adults are likely to continue to rely heavily on their families in the West to navigate the challenges of ageing. Further, as a bulwark against persistent ageism in the West, Lebanese culture, characterised by its collectivistic nature, fosters more positive views of ageing and holds older individuals in higher esteem than more individualistic cultures typical of the West (Ibrahim and Bayen, 2019). In traditional Arab and Lebanese cultures, ageing is viewed positively, and older family members are held in high esteem and revered (El-kholy, 1981).

Within the Lebanese context, and in the absence of a robust welfare state and related spending concerns, older adults are not necessarily viewed as a problem to be fixed; the normative assumption is that they are productive and essential members of a well-functioning family structure. In the Lebanese diaspora, older adults can play a vital role in caring for grandchildren and supporting their children's participation in the labour market, thereby reducing the financial burden on their children as they strive to integrate into the Western socio-economic system. Despite a more positive normative orientation to ageing in the East, the views on ageing could change due to the acculturation of Lebanese people in the diaspora. However, there are indications that a positive view of ageing persists and is even reinforced in countries that also have a positive view of ageing. Research by El Bcheraoui and colleagues (2015) suggests that while age is increasingly stigmatised in Lebanon due to economic and social conditions, ageing remains more valued among the African Lebanese diaspora. Further research is required to understand whether there are shifts to how ageing is understood and positioned. In contrast, Western welfare state policies and norms reflect a view that older adults should be independent and procure services not funded by the state from markets or family, failing to recognise the fundamental interdependency that social reproductive work requires (Daly, 2013).

'Western' policy and practice developments have often relied on definitions of successful ageing that involve being satisfied, active, independent, self-sufficient and defying traditional narratives of decline (Katz and Calasanti, 2015). However, as Katz and Calasanti (2015) posit, this is more appealing than illuminating. Culturally, ageism in the West positions older people as a social burden, perpetuating doomsday narratives of demographic shifts and the potential destruction of the welfare state (King and Calasanti, 2006). Considering the experiences of older Lebanese migrants who have settled in Canada highlights the normative bias within 'successful ageing' that fails to consider that being less active, interdependent, reliant and slowing down can be normal, natural processes of ageing that can be celebrated. Further, as ageing is a process that occurs over time, individuals who immigrate at a younger age and adapt successfully to the established labour market and social systems are more likely to align with standards of 'successful ageing' in their receiving countries, due to acculturation. On the other hand, those Eastern immigrants who immigrate to the West as older adults undergo a more challenging integration process and may be less likely to conform to Western social views of ageing.

Cultural liminality: a useful concept for policy and practice

Based on what we know of diasporic ageing and the example of older adults living in transnational families between Lebanon and Canada, it is evident that they navigate a complex set of cultural, social and familial factors that are likely to impact their experiences of ageing. With increasing numbers of people immigrating both temporarily and permanently from Eastern to Western countries at older ages (Treas and Torres-Gil, 2008), research and dialogue are needed to inform constructive interventions and policies that account for immigrants' varied familial dynamics and situations, including how contrasting cultural norms are involved. A notable research gap remains on the experiences of Lebanese older adults who have immigrated to the West, particularly to countries like Canada with large Lebanese-born populations (Treas and Torres-Gil, 2008; Sibai et al, 2012). Additionally, high immigration rates among Lebanese young adults due to political instability and economic uncertainties are changing the nature of support ageing parents can expect from their children (Chaaban, 2009). The knowledge gap extends to the relationship between children living in the West and their parents who remain in Lebanon in conditions of high political conflict, which is especially pressing considering the significant cross-border medical, social and financial challenges for their families in the diaspora related to their care (Sibai et al, 2012).

Differing ideas about ageing inherent to 'Eastern' and 'Western' cultural norms is a key challenge for addressing the in-betweenness of cultural liminality for migrant older adults. Without acknowledging these key differences, even in light of the comparatively robust supports available for health and social care in high-income, migrant-receiving countries, ageing migrants are destined to experience inequality.

There are some emerging practice responses, mostly at the community level. Community-based organisations (CBOs) and cultural groups can assist and promote the well-being of older migrant adults, as Chapter 10 shows. These organisations are positioned to support the ageing population within the Lebanese diaspora by providing a sense of belonging, preserving cultural heritage and addressing unique needs (Wilson et al, 2010). By offering practical, day-to-day support, CBOs could significantly contribute to the well-being of older migrants as these organisations can provide culturally safe, para-professional and referral to professional services, as well as a non-stigmatised space where immigrants may feel more comfortable utilising services (Rusch et al, 2020).

In addition, in the Lebanese diasporic context, the church, the mosque, and the community bakery are the points of reconnections with the past self and culture in Canada. These institutions allow older adult immigrants to experience their past identities and the cultural context that shaped their initial life course, not always easy to access in everyday life. The interplay between family support and community connections lays the groundwork for a broader discussion on the implications of immigration and ageing on the identities of older Lebanese adults in the diaspora. Religious institutions significantly influence the Lebanese community in general and within the diaspora. These organisations are critical in maintaining the sense of cultural and community continuity. While specific research focusing on Lebanese community organisations is limited, studies highlight the fragmented nature of the secular and religious community sectors, reflecting internal divisions in Lebanon. Canada's Lebanese community-based organisation network is highly decentralised and lacks coordination (Asal, 2012), but efforts can be made to establish better coordination and communication among these organisations to optimise their impact on the well-being of the Lebanese diaspora community.

However, there remain many policy and practice issues at other levels in receiving countries. These include those associated with immigration processes and rules that prevent and curtail family reunification, and with policies for settlement services that focus solely on employment support and ignore older adults' needs. Many health care, social welfare and employment standards policies do not consider the possibility of transnational living and caring.

In summary, the experiences of older Lebanese adults in the diaspora reveals the interplay of immigration, ageing and cultural values and norms. This exploration suggests that older Lebanese adults in Canada experience cultural liminality as they navigate the dynamic space between their country of origin and adopted home. Not only do they face the challenges of adapting to a new cultural context while maintaining connections to their country of origin and familial roots, but their very understanding of how ageing is understood, organised and supported is challenged. Straddling multiple cultural identities and expectations presents challenges and tensions for older Lebanese adults that produce a cultural liminal space or an in-betweenness of the past, the present and the future.

Understanding the parameters of cultural liminality can be helpful for rethinking dominant models of migrant ageing and care, which often assume either full independence or direct family caregiving. Policies and services must recognise the transnational realities of migrant ageing, where older adults rely on cross-border family networks, diaspora communities and non-traditional forms of support. Age-equity policies should integrate culturally responsive health care, flexible family reunification pathways, and greater recognition of transnational care relations that stretch across borders and around the globe. Community-based organisations and diaspora networks can help bridge gaps in formal support, ensuring that older migrants are not left navigating ageing in isolation or forced to conform to care models that do not reflect their realities. By embracing cultural liminality, policies and practices can move beyond one-size-fits-all approaches, creating ageing systems that are more inclusive, adaptive and attuned to the complexities of migration, belonging and care across borders.

References

Abdulrahim, S. and Ajrouch, K.J. (2014) Arab Americans and the aging process, in A.M. Nassar-McMillan, K.J. Ajrouch and J.G. Hakim-Larson (eds) *Biopsychosocial Perspectives on Arab Americans*, Springer US, pp 107–25.

Abou, S.L. (1962) *Le Bilinguisme Arabe-Français au Liban: Essai d'Anthropologie Culturelle*, Presses Universitaires de France.

Abu-Bader, S.H., Tirmazi, M.T. and Ross-Sheriff, F. (2011) The impact of acculturation on depression among older Muslim immigrants in the United States, *Journal of Gerontological Social Work*, 54(4): 425–48.

Abyad, A. (2021) Aging in the Middle East and North Africa: demographic and health trends, *International Journal on Aging in Developing Countries*, 6(2): 112–28.

Ajrouch, K.J., Yount, K.M., Sibai, A.M. and Roman, P. (2013) A gendered perspective on well-being in later life: Algeria, Lebanon, and Palestine, in H. Tabatabai and C. Smith (eds) *Aging in the Middle East and North Africa*, Routledge, pp 49–77.

Ajrouch, K.J., Abdulrahim, S. and Antonucci, T.C. (2015) Aging in Lebanon: challenges and opportunities, *The Gerontologist*, 55(4): 511–18.

Al Wekhian, J. (2015) Acculturation process of Arab-Muslim immigrants in the United States, *Asian Culture and History*, 8(1): 89–99.

Antonucci, T.C., Ajrouch, K.J. and Abdulrahim, S. (2015) Social relations in Lebanon: convoys across the life course, *The Gerontologist*, 55(5): 825–35.

Asal, H. (2012) Community sector dynamics and the Lebanese diaspora: internal fragmentation and transnationalism on the web, *Social Science Information*, 51(4): 502–20.

Aswad, B. (1997) Arab American families, in M.K. DeGenova (ed) *Families in Cultural Context: Strengths and Challenges in Diversity*, Mayfield Publishing Company, pp 213–37.

Azim, K.A. (2015) Traveling through liminal space: the autoethnographic account of an immigrant, *International Review of Qualitative Research*, 8(4): 453–62.

Barakat, H. (1985) *Arab Families*, Austin, TX: University of Texas Press.

Braedley, S., Côté-Boucher, K. and Przednowek, A. (2021) Old and dangerous: bordering older migrants' mobilities, rejuvenating the post-welfare state, *Social Politics: International Studies in Gender, State & Society*, 28(1): 24–46.

Cannella, G.S. and Huerta, M.E.S. (2019) Introduction: becomings with hybrid bodies – immigration, public policy, and the in-between, *Cultural Studies, Critical Methodologies*, 19(3): 147–51.

Central Intelligence Agency (2024) Lebanon [online], Available from: https://www.cia.gov/the-world-factbook/countries/lebanon/#people-and-society

Chaaban, J. (2009) Youth and development in the Arab countries: the need for a different approach, *Middle Eastern Studies*, 45(1): 33–55.

Chahine, L.M. and Chemali, Z. (2009) Mental health care in Lebanon: policy, plans and programmes, *Eastern Mediterranean Health Journal*, 15(6): 1596–612.

Chams, N. (2017) Examining and Understanding Social Connectedness and Social Engagement among Muslim Lebanese Canadian Older Adults, Master's thesis, University of Western Ontario, Canada, Electronic Thesis and Dissertation Repository [online], Available from: https://ir.lib.uwo.ca/etd/4844

Daly, T. (2013) Imagining an ethos of care within policies, practices, and philosophy, in S. Braedley and M. Luxton (eds) *Troubling Care: Critical Perspectives on Research and Practices*, Canadian Scholars Press, pp 33–45.

Daly, T. and Armstrong, P. (2016) Liminal and invisible long-term care labour: precarity in the face of austerity, *Journal of Industrial Relations*, 58(4): 473–90.

Daly, T., Armstrong, P. and Lowndes, R. (2015) Liminality in Ontario's long-term care facilities: private companions' care work in the space 'betwixt and between', *Competition & Change*, 19(3): 246–63.

De Bel-Air, F. (2017) *Migration Profile: Lebanon* (Policy Brief No. 2017/12), Migration Policy Centre, Robert Schuman Centre for Advanced Studies, European University Institute, DOI: 10.2870/537304

Deeb, L. (2020) Beyond sectarianism: intermarriage and social difference in Lebanon, *International Journal of Middle East Studies*, 52(2): 215–28.

El Bcheraoui, C., Adib, S. and Chapuis-Lucciani, N. (2015) Perception of agism and self-esteem among Lebanese elders at home and abroad, *Lebanese Medical Journal*, 103(1716): 1–7.

El-Kholy, A.A. (1981) The Arab American family, in C. Mindel, R. Habenstein and R. Wright Jr. (eds) *Ethnic Families in America: Patterns and Variations*, Elsevier, pp 145–62.

Estes, C.L. (2020) The new political economy of aging: introduction and critique, in C.L. Estes (ed) *Aging, Globalization, and Inequality: The New Critical Gerontology*, Routledge, pp 19–36.

Faour, M.A. (2007) Religion, demography, and politics in Lebanon, *Middle Eastern Studies*, 43(6): 909–21.

Farhood, L., Zurayk, H., Chaya, M., Saadeh, F., Meshefedjian, G. and Sidani, T. (1993) The impact of war on the physical and mental health of the family: the Lebanese experience, *Social Science & Medicine*, 36(12): 1555–67.

Gelfand, D. and Yee, B.W.K. (1992) Trends and forces: influence of immigration, migration, and acculturation on the fabric of aging in America, in C.L. Estes (ed) *Aging, Globalization, and Inequality: The New Critical Gerontology*, Routledge, pp 5–14.

Gibbons, S.W., Ross, A. and Bevans, M. (2014) Liminality as a conceptual frame for understanding the family caregiving rite of passage: an integrative review, *Research in Nursing & Health*, 37(5): 423–36.

Giladi, A. (2010) Liminal craft, exceptional law: preliminary notes on midwives in medieval Islamic writings, *International Journal of Middle East Studies*, 42(2): 185–202.

Ibrahim, C.N. and Bayen, U.J. (2019) Attitudes toward aging and older adults in Arab culture: a literature review, *Zeitschrift für Gerontologie und Geriatrie*, 52(Suppl 3): 180–7.

Jolicoeur, P.M. and Madden, T. (2002) The good daughters: acculturation and caregiving among Mexican-American women, *Journal of Aging Studies*, 16(2): 107–20.

Joseph, S. (2000) Civic myths, citizenship, and gender in Lebanon, in S. Joseph (ed) *Gender and Citizenship in the Middle East*, Syracuse University Press, pp 107–36.

Katz, S. and Calasanti, T. (2015) Critical perspectives on successful aging: does it 'appeal more than it illuminates'?, *The Gerontologist*, 55(1): 26–33.

Khalaila, R. (2020) Caregiver burden and compassion fatigue among Arab family caregivers of older relatives, *Journal of Applied Gerontology*, 40(11): 1259–67.

Khoury, R. and Karam, G. (2020) Impact of COVID-19 on mental healthcare of older adults: insights from Lebanon (Middle East), *International Psychogeriatrics*, 32(10): 1177–80.

King, N. and Calasanti, T. (2006) Empowering the old: critical gerontology and anti-aging in a global context, in C.L. Estes (ed) *Aging, Globalization, and Inequality: The New Critical Gerontology*, Routledge, pp 139–57.

Kronfol, N., Sibai, A.M., Troisi, J. and von Kondratowitz, H.-J. (2013) Aging in the Mediterranean, in T. Maltby, G. de Vries and C. Rodrigues (eds) *Fifteen: Aging in Lebanon: Evidence and Challenges*, Policy Press, pp 325–44.

Luxton, M. and Bezanson, K. (2006) *Social Reproduction Feminist Political Economy Challenges Neo-liberalism*, McGill-Queen's University Press.

Marcus, E.J. (2016) The two language problem: Sélim Abou, Lebanon and the ethnolinguistic nation, *British Journal of Middle Eastern Studies*, 43(2): 219–33.

McDaniel, S. and Gazso, A. (2014) Liminality and low-income aging families by choice: meanings of family and support, *Canadian Journal on Aging / La Revue Canadienne du Vieillissement*, 33(4): 400–12.

Nanda, S. (2000) Liminal gender roles in Polynesia, in S. Nanda (ed) *Gender Diversity: Cross-Cultural Variations*, Waveland Press, pp 57–70.

Nasir, N., Hand, C. and Huot, S. (2022) Examining social relationships among older Muslim immigrants living in Canada: a narrative inquiry, *Societies*, 12(3): 74.

Nassar-McMillan, S.C., Ajrouch, K.J. and Hakim-Larson, J. (2013) Biopsychosocial perspectives on Arab Americans: an introduction, in S.C. Nassar-McMillan, K.J. Ajrouch and J.G. Hakim-Larson (eds) *Biopsychosocial Perspectives on Arab Americans*, Springer, pp 1–9.

Palladino, S. (2019) Older migrants reflecting on aging through attachment to and identification with places, *Journal of Aging Studies*, 50: 100788.

Rusch, D., Walden, A.L. and DeCarlo Santiago, C. (2020) A community-based organization model to promote Latinx immigrant mental health through advocacy skills and universal parenting supports, *American Journal of Community Psychology*, 66(3–4): 337–46.

Salibi, K.S. (1971) The Lebanese identity, *Journal of Contemporary History*, 6(1): 76–86.

Sibai, A.M. and Beydoun, M. (1999) Elderly Lebanese women in an aging world, *Al-Raida Medical Journal*, pp 11–21 [online], Available from: https://alraidajournal.lau.edu.lb/images/issue085-page011.pdf

Sibai, A.M., Yount, K.M. and Fletcher, A. (2007) Marital status, intergenerational co-residence and cardiovascular and all-cause mortality among middle-aged and older men and women during wartime in Beirut: gains and liabilities, *Social Science & Medicine*, 64(1): 64–76.

Sibai, A.M., Tohme, R., Yamout, R., Yount, K. and Kronfol, N. (2012) The older persons: from veneration to vulnerability?, in S. Jabbour, R. Giacaman, M. Khawaja and I. Nuwayhid (eds) *Public Health in the Arab World*, Cambridge University Press, pp 264–75.

Starr, P.D. (1978) Ethnic categories and identification in Lebanon, *Journal of Contemporary Ethnography*, 7(1): 111–42.

Stasiulis, D. (2017) Respatializing social citizenship and security among dual citizens in the Lebanese diaspora, in J. Mann (ed) *Citizenship in Transnational Perspective*, Palgrave Macmillan, pp 49–76.

Statistics Canada (2022) In the midst of high job vacancies and historically low unemployment, Canada faces record retirements from an aging labour force: Number of seniors aged 65 and older grows six times faster than children 0–14 [online], Available from: https://www150.statcan.gc.ca/n1/daily-quotidien/220427/dq220427a-eng.htm

Statistics Canada (2023a) Table 98-10-0351-01: Visible minority by gender and age: Canada, provinces and territories [online], Available from: https://www150.statcan.gc.ca/t1/tbl1/en/tv.action?pid=9810035101

Statistics Canada (2023b) Table 98-10-0341-01: Religion by ethnic or cultural origins: Canada, provinces and territories and census metropolitan areas with parts [online], Available from: https://doi.org/10.25318/9810034101-eng

Sweeney, B. (2009) Producing liminal space: gender, age, and class in Northern Ontario's tree planting industry, *Gender, Place and Culture: A Journal of Feminist Geography*, 16(5): 569–86.

Tabar, P. (2010) Lebanon: a country of emigration and immigration, *American University in Cairo* [online], Available from: https://fount.aucegypt.edu/faculty_journal_articles/5056

Tabar, P. (2020) Transnational is not diasporic: a Bourdieusian approach to the study of modern diaspora, *Journal of Sociology*, 56(3): 455–71.

Tabar, P., and El-Zakka, Y. (2024) Lebanese diaspora and the October 17 uprising, *Studies in Ethnicity and Nationalism*, 24(2): 182–96.

Tabar, P., Denison, A. and Alkhomassy, M. (2020) Access to social protection by immigrants, emigrants, and resident nationals in Lebanon, in J.-M. Lafleur and D. Vintila (eds) *Migration and Social Protection in Europe and Beyond (Volume 3)*, Springer, pp 183–98.

Treas, J. and Torres-Gil, F. (2008) Immigration and aging: the nexus of complexity and promise, *Generations*, 32(4): 6–10.

Vértes, S., van der Borgh, C. and Buyse, A. (2021) Negotiating civic space in Lebanon: the potential of non-sectarian movements, *Journal of Civil Society*, 17(3–4): 256–76.

Wilson, M. (2002) I am the prince of pain, for I am a princess in the brain: Liminal transgender identities, narratives and the elimination of ambiguities, *Sexualities*, 5(4): 425–48.

Wilson, M., Lavis, J.N., Travers, R. and Rourke, S.B. (2010) Community-based knowledge transfer and exchange: helping community-based organizations link research to action, *Implementation Science*, 5(1): 33.

Yount, K.M. and Sibai, A.M. (2009) Demography of aging in Arab countries, in P. Uhlenberg (ed) *Aging in the Arab World*, Springer Netherlands, pp 277–315.

12

The promise of dementia-friendly approaches: addressing stigma

Sienna Caspar and Kelsey Berg

Introduction

Ensuring inclusivity for people with dementia supports their quality of life and well-being throughout the dementia trajectory (Hebert and Scales, 2019). Yet, people with dementia are often overlooked in Age-Friendly movements (Craig et al, 2024). This exclusion of people with dementia not only detracts from equity (Rahman and Swaffer, 2018) but also reinforces harmful social norms associated with the stigma of dementia. Stigma can be defined as 'the co-occurrence of labeling, stereotyping, separation, status loss, and discrimination in a context in which power is exercised' (Hatzenbuehler et al, 2013). According to Goffman (2009), stigmatising occurs when social meaning with negative connotations is attached to individuals and behaviours. In short, stigma causes people to be judged by others as 'not normal', to experience 'othering'. Ultimately, it leads to discrimination, stereotyping and rejection (Harris and Caporella, 2014). Unfortunately, stigma has emerged as a particularly damaging aspect of people's experiences with dementia. Following diagnosis, people with dementia often report experiences of stigma and, in some cases, lose friends and social networks (Bamford et al, 2014). The most common emotions associated with the stigma of dementia are humiliation, shame and disgust (Werner, 2008).

Dementias are more commonly experienced by older adults; thus, those with dementia often experience the effects of stigma of dementia *in addition to* ageism – the wider discrimination against people due to their older age. Ageism is one of most common forms of stigmatisation, but it is not commonly addressed in socially progressive movements against discrimination (Drury et al, 2016).

Within the Age-Friendly movement (WHO, 2007), research and activism to reduce stigma is lacking (Keefe and Kostiuk, 2019). Stigma inextricably intertwines with social marginalisation. Those who experience dementia together with ageing live with greater vulnerability to discrimination, compounded by intersecting factors such as gender identity, sexual orientation, socio-economic status, ethnicity or disability (Hasselgren et al,

2019; Livingston, 2020). The combination of stigma and discrimination can lead to human rights violations against people with dementia, such as coercive or forced treatment, and disregard for an individual's legal capacity to make decisions (WHO, 2021). Significantly, the indifference to, or violations of, the rights of a person can result in serious health consequences (WHO, 2021).

Stigma also often leads to segregation and segregation can, in turn, reinforce stigma. We have the propensity to want autonomy for ourselves, but safety for the ones we love (Gawande, 2014). Often, when we deem loved ones, such as those with dementia, to be vulnerable, our desire to ensure their safety intensifies and tends to take precedence over everything else, including honouring their rights to experience the dignity of risk and autonomy. The focus on safety provides at least some of the justification for the segregation of people with dementia in secured 'special-care units' within long-term care homes and, more recently, in 'dementia villages' within communities. While segregated living areas and community programs (such as adult day programs that require a diagnosis of dementia for participation) can and do help to address many of the needs of people with dementia, the act of segregation most certainly contributes to the stigma of having a dementia diagnosis (Calkins, 2018). Segregation further decreases opportunities for people with dementia to create and sustain friendships with people without dementia and to feel seen, heard and valued within their communities. This is significant because, as Turner and Morken (2016: 10) write, '[w]ithout ensuring that people with dementia feel understood, valued and accepted ... other efforts are worth little'. Thus, we must seek to find a balance between our desire to ensure the safety and security of people with dementia while honouring their calls to be active, vital and valued members of our communities.

How can this aim be accomplished? In this chapter, we explore how dementia-friendly frameworks go beyond mere 'friendliness' towards ageing people and call attention to a community's capacity to empower and celebrate the capabilities of people with dementia. We focus on inclusive and integrated systems of support that recognise people with dementia as equals, honouring their experiences and capabilities, and enabling them to live with meaning and purpose in societies. The dementia-friendly movement challenges us to view people with dementia – who now number 50 million worldwide – as having the same vitality and value as any of us. It asks us to recognise stigma explicitly as a barrier to those with dementia who deserve to live fully and engage with the wider community.

Age- and dementia-friendly communities

The Age-Friendly movement proports that, rather than segregating older adults to address their specific needs, communities must become accessible and inclusive for older adults. This approach focuses on broad structural change rather than segregating older people who experience frailty and disability, confronting the reality that most communities are not consistently or systematically inclusive. Existing social inequities – based on gender, race, sexuality, gender identity, socio-economic status and the stigmas that perpetuate these constructs – can exacerbate any hardships that may arise from the ageing process (Hasselgren et al, 2019).

Older adults from groups that experience social inequities are at heightened risk for dementia (Livingston et al, 2020). For example, dementia is known to disproportionally affect women, those with low educational attainment, and those who work in unskilled or low-skilled occupations (Livingston et al, 2020). It is important to note that other identified risk factors for dementia (such as lack of physical activity, depression, stress, poor social networks, obesity and smoking, as noted by Livingston et al, 2020) are related to socio-economic status; thus, those who experience barriers to educational attainment and skilled occupations are likely at increased risk of dementia (Hasselgren et al, 2019).

But for people with dementia, it is not enough for a community to identify as 'age-friendly'. The dementia-friendly movement seeks to change the way we think about living with dementia, not only in terms of physical environments, dementia services and health, but in the language we use to describe living with dementia and through improvements in social support (Alzheimer's Disease International, 2021).

Those who advocate for dementia-friendly communities have two primary objectives: to reduce stigma and promote awareness, and to empower people with dementia to make decisions about their own lives. Members of dementia-friendly communities are therefore encouraged to make adaptations to the physical and social aspects of an environment to ensure that people with dementia experience continuity of life and well-being (Davis et al, 2009). Further, places or groups of people that profess to be 'dementia-friendly' should emphasise inclusion, support and empowerment of people with dementia (Alzheimer's Disease International, 2012; Shannon et al, 2019). The underlying premise of the dementia-friendly movement is that access to community services and resources, from grocery stores to community centres, faith communities and bus systems, should not disappear for people with dementia, nor should recognition for their contributions. Accordingly, community-based dementia-friendly organisations frequently advocate for dementia awareness and often provide dementia education for the public (Hebert and Scales, 2019). Contemporary dementia-friendly initiatives tend to promote integration with the broader community as a core concept (Smith et al, 2016). Although these initiatives still set apart people with dementia as a distinct community, acceptance and cohesion between the dementia community and the community at large is central to these initiatives (Smith et al, 2016).

The movement towards broader societal infrastructure to accommodate the needs of people affected by dementia, along with other members of distinct communities within cities, marks a shift beyond a singular focus on safety to a more holistic perspective of the spectrum of human needs and capacities. Dementia advocates have been central in this shift. According to activist and academic Kate Swaffer, inclusivity entails greater accountability than 'friendliness' (Kadane, 2018). The notion of 'nothing about me without me', a cornerstone of patient-centred care principles, implies reciprocal relationships with shared decision-making power (Quinlan, 2018). We cannot create such catalytic relationships or develop truly dementia-friendly communities without positive acceptance of people with dementia, and dispelling 'unjust negative societal perceptions of dementia' (Hebert and Scales, 2019).

As ageing and dementia have risen as priorities for policy makers, service providers, and other community leaders (Turner and Cannon, 2018; Shannon et al, 2019), interest is growing in how age- and dementia-friendly frameworks interact with and complement each other. International organisations, such as Dementia Friendly America (2019) and Dementia Australia, have outlined how the pursuit of age-friendliness intersects with efforts to advance dementia-friendliness in communities, from villages to towns, to cities or counties. Generally, age- and dementia-friendly frameworks align in their values of autonomy and inclusion for either older adults or people with dementia. Both also require broad engagement with multiple civic sectors. For example, a WHO age-friendly city requires assessment and accommodations for older adults in outdoor spaces and buildings. Dementia Friendly America's participants commit to political action in transportation, housing and public spaces, emergency planning and first response (Turner and Morken, 2016). While the comprehensive cadre of actions might differ slightly based on the objective (age friendly or dementia friendly), the overlap in areas of engagement and in target populations lead to a strong impetus to coordinate efforts.

While the WHO's age-friendly domains address respect and social inclusion of older adults, an express call to address stigma around ageing and dementia is not explicit. Alternatively, dementia-friendly communities inherently and overtly seek to address the stigma of dementia by envisioning a future where all members of the community empower, value and celebrate people with dementia (Alzheimer's Disease International, 2016). The following section discusses how the added impact of stigma makes it necessary to take the concept of 'age-friendly' a step further if we are going to have wide social inclusion for those with dementia.

Stigma and dementia

Research demonstrates that experiencing stigma harms the psychological well-being of persons with dementia because it adds to their feelings of social isolation, depression, abandonment and 'otherness' (Snyder, 2000; Harris,

2012). The stigma of dementia also reduces socialisation and care-seeking behavior, which reduces quality of life (Evans, 2018). Sadly, substantial evidence shows that the stigma of dementia exists worldwide (Moniz-Cook and Manthorpe, 2009; Prince et al, 2011). Thus, despite significant efforts made to increase public awareness about Alzheimer disease and related dementias, the associated stigma is persistent and pervasive.

In response, the *World Alzheimer's 2012 Report* was solely devoted to the issue of stigma (Alzheimer's Disease International, 2012). The report presented findings from survey and qualitative data collected from more than 2,500 people with dementia and family members from more than 54 countries. The report gave ten recommendations: educate the public; reduce isolation of people with dementia; give people with dementia a voice; recognise the rights of people with dementia in their local communities; support and educate informal and paid caregivers; improve the quality of care at home and in care homes; improve dementia training of primary health-care physicians; call on governments to create national Alzheimer Disease plans; and increase research into how to address stigma (Alzheimer's Disease International, 2012). These recommendations are based on the best interests of people living with dementia and their care partners.

It is both noteworthy and problematic that improved education is listed three times. The tendency to emphasise education as a means of producing changes in people's perceptions and behaviours associated with stigma is prevalent in the literature (Thornicroft et al, 2016). This emphasis remains despite research demonstrating that education is not necessarily the most effective way to produce this change (Thornicroft et al, 2016). Furthermore, a review of the literature confirms that the experience of stigma associated with dementia remains a serious and significant problem, despite significant efforts to alter its prevalence (Alzheimer's Disease International, 2012; Bamford et al, 2014).

Friendships as a central feature of dementia-friendly communities

Contact theory makes a simple claim: if we can get more people without dementia to interact with and create friendships with people affected by it (whether as community members, project partners, neighbours or in a host of other contexts), the incidence of stigma related to dementia will decrease (Harris and Caporella, 2014). It would be easy to discount this idea as idealistic or simplistic; however, a growing body of evidence demonstrates that intergroup contact that enables and supports the development of personal relationships between majority and minority group members is more effective in reducing stigma, discrimination and prejudice than interventions that focus on education (Griffiths et al, 2014; Thornicroft et al, 2016). Additionally and promisingly, research shows that extended, high quality intergroup contact that enables the creation of friendships can effectively reduce ageism (Harris and Caporella, 2014; Drury et al, 2016; Caspar et al, 2019). Thus, it is reasonable to assert that creating spaces and places for the creation of friendships between people with and without dementia may provide a promising practice for those wanting to address and reduce the stigma of dementia.

An example can be found in the advent of intergenerational living arrangements in which university students are invited to live in subsidised seniors' housing rent-free in exchange for spending time each week with their older neighbours. These models emerged in Scandinavian countries in the late 1960s and have become increasingly popular in Europe and North America (Vestbro, 1992; Scanlon and Arrigoitia, 2015). They were driven by a combination of factors, including the need to combat loneliness and create a sense of community in older people's living environments; the rising costs of post-secondary education; and the lack of affordable and quality housing (Ahn et al, 2018; Quinio and Burgess, 2018). The models vary, but central to each is the requirement of social interaction between the older and younger residents. A review of the published articles on these models indicates that the students engage with the older residents in many ways, such as screening movies, gardening, preparing and eating meals together, performing recitals, leading art classes specifically for residents with dementia, teaching residents new skills such as how to use e-mail and social media and teaching residents to play piano (Jansen, 2015; Hansman, 2015; Cummings, 2017). But both older and student residents also just 'hang out', which, according to these residents, can be even more valuable (Jansen, 2015). A universal outcome of these living arrangements seems to be that inter-generational friendships form organically, and ageism diminishes (Jansen, 2015; Hansman, 2015; Cummings, 2017).

Recent studies have demonstrated that simply finding ways to bring people with and without dementia together in support of the same goal can be good for all involved. This is especially true when people are brought together in music-based programs designed to encourage creative expression. For many, such programs are particularly well-suited to create positive, joyful experiences and promote social connections. These programs have been used to reach across the barriers of age, race, gender, disabilities and other dividing social constructs and, by doing so, assist in community building (Hays and Minichiello, 2005; Camic et al, 2013; McDermott, et al, 2014; Unadkat et al, 2017). One such example comes from Harris and Caporella (2014), who conducted a study to determine whether singing in a choir composed of undergraduate college students and people with early-stage dementia and their family members could lay the foundations for a dementia-friendly community on a college campus. Results from this study found that, because of the social connections with the students, members of the choir with dementia felt included, welcomed, valued and respected (Harris and Caporella, 2014). Tamburri and colleagues (2019) conducted a similar study of a program involving high-school-aged adolescents who joined together with people with dementia and their family care partners to form an intergenerational choir. These researchers demonstrated that creating a supportive community environment, which adds meaning the lives of people with dementia and fosters development of meaningful relationships, resulted in significant declines in depressive symptoms of the choir members with dementia (Tamburri et al, 2019).

Other studies have explored the outcomes of intergroup contact between group members from even wider age ranges. For example, Caspar and colleagues (2019) brought together school-age volunteers and long-term care home residents to participate in activities lasting approximately 60 minutes each once a week for the duration of a school year. Residents and youth volunteers engaged in six different types of activities that could be grouped into three focus areas – socialisation (including talking and visiting with students), creativity (such as crafts) and cognitive stimulation (for example, puzzles). Participation in this intergenerational program resulted in positive engagement of both the residents and the youth, as well as significant decreases in the youth volunteers' ageist perceptions of older adults. Significantly, Caspar and colleagues (2019) found that the type of activity was not an influential factor in achieving these positive outcomes; rather, ensuring the activities were meaningful to the residents and that they fostered shared growth and relationship building between the residents and youth volunteers seemed to be most important.

We believe that it is possible to envision a world where contact, and the friendships that can be formed because of that contact, reduces stigma and enables the cultivation of age- and dementia-friendly communities. The tenets of contact theory highlight the importance of people from different groups (such as people with dementia and people without dementia) becoming personally acquainted with one another such that intergroup friendships can be developed and hopefully sustained. The essential message of contact theory can be summed as follows: when you have close relationships with members of another group, it is much harder to embrace or harbour negative stereotypes about them, or to look the other way when they are mistreated. Relationships, and the strong, long-lasting emotions they can elicit, will almost always influence beliefs and behaviours more than information about how people we deem as 'others' are treated.

Can 'age-friendly' cities and communities exist without opportunities to create friendship across intersections of age and ability? We argue that they cannot, and that creating opportunities for friendships between people with dementia and those without should be foundational to any age- or dementia-friendly initiative.

In conclusion, we assert that the WHO Age-Friendly Network, a nexus for age-friendly practices, can benefit from the dementia-friendly movement's intrinsic emphasis on stigma reduction and improved age equity. Within anti-stigma initiatives, inter-group contact is one promising approach for reducing discrimination due to ageism and the stigma of dementia. Initiatives that aim to promote positive social interactions and friendships among people at all stages of life and levels of ability will contribute to the development of communities that are truly age-friendly. Adopting attitudes of cohesion and inclusion, rather than segregation in the face of diverse needs, will result in more friendly and equitable communities for all.

References

Ahn, J., Tusinski, O. and Treger, C. (2018) *Living Closer: The Many Faces of Cohousing*. Studio Weave in collaboration with RIBA [online], Available from: https://www.housinglin.org.uk/_assets/Resources/Housing/OtherOrganisation/LivingCloser_StudioWeave.pdf

Alzheimer's Disease International (2012) World Alzheimer Report 2012: Overcoming the Stigma of Dementia [online], Available from: https://www.alz.co.uk/research/world-report-2012

Alzheimer's Disease International (2016) Dementia Friendly Communities – Key Principles and Global Developments [online], Available from: https://www.alz.co.uk/news/dementia-friendly-communities-key-principles-and-global-developments

Alzheimer's Disease International (2021) Dementia Friendly Communities [online], Available from: https://www.alzint.org/what-we-do/policy/dementia-friendly-communities/

Bamford, S., Holley-Moore, G. and Watson, J. (2014) *New Perspectives and Approaches to Understanding Dementia and Stigma*, ILC-UK.

Calkins, M.P. (2018) From research to application: supportive and therapeutic environments for people living with dementia, *The Gerontologist*, 58(suppl_1): S114–28.

Camic, P.M., Williams, C.M. and Meeten, F. (2013) Does a 'singing together group' improve the quality of life of people with dementia and their carers? A pilot evaluation study, *Dementia*, 12(2): 157–76.

Caspar, S., Davis, E., McNeill, D.M.J. and Kellett, P. (2019) Intergenerational programs: breaking down ageist barriers and improving youth experiences, *Therapeutic Recreation Journal*, 53(2): 149–64.

Craig, S., Halloran, P.O., Mitchell, G., Stark, P. and Brown Wilson, C. (2024) Dementia friendly communities (DFCs) to improve quality of life for people with dementia: a realist review, *BMC Geriatrics*, 24: Article 776.

Cummings, M. (2017) Edmonton seniors residence Invites University of Alberta students to live among the elderly, *Edmonton Journal*, 17 October [online], Available from: https://edmontonjournal.com/news/local-news/edmonton-seniors-residence-invites-university-of-alberta-students-to-live-among-the-elderly

Davis, S., Byers, S., Nay, R. and Koch, S. (2009) Guiding design of dementia-friendly environments in residential care settings: considering the living experiences, *Dementia*, 8(2): 185–203.

Dementia Friendly America (2019) What is DFA? [online], Available from: https://dfamerica.org/.

Drury, L., Hutchison, P. and Abrams, D. (2016) Direct and extended intergenerational contact and young people's attitudes towards older adults, *British Journal of Social Psychology*, 55(3): 522–43.

Evans, S.C. (2018) Ageism and dementia, in L. Ayalon and C. Tesch-Römer (eds) *Contemporary Perspectives on Ageism*, Springer, pp 263–75.

Gawande, A. (2014) *Being Mortal: Medicine and What Matters in the End*, Metropolitan Books.

Goffman, E. (2009) *Stigma: Notes on the Management of Spoiled Identity*, Simon and Schuster.

Griffiths, K.M., Carron-Arthur, B., Parsons, A. and Reid, R. (2014) Effectiveness of programs for reducing the stigma associated with mental disorders: a meta-analysis of randomized controlled trials, *World Psychiatry*, 13(2): 161–75.

Hansman, H. (2015) College students are living rent free in Cleveland retirement home, *Smithsonian Magazine* [online], Available from: https://www.smithsonianmag.com/innovation/college-students-are-living-rent-free-in-cleveland-retirement-home-180956930/

Harris, P.B. (2012) Maintaining friendships in early-stage dementia: factors to consider, *Dementia*, 11(3): 305–14.

Harris, P.B. and Caporella, C.A. (2014) An intergenerational choir formed to lessen Alzheimer's disease stigma in college students and decrease the social isolation of people with Alzheimer's disease and their family members: a pilot study, *American Journal of Alzheimer's Disease and Other Dementias*, 29(3): 270–81.

Hasselgren, C., Ekbrand, H., Fässberg, M. M., Zettergren, A., Zetterberg, H., Blennow, K., Skoog, I. and Halleröd, B. (2019) APOE ε4 and the long arm of social inequity: estimated effects of socio-economic status and sex on the timing of dementia onset, *Ageing and Society*, 39(9): 1951–1975.

Hatzenbuehler, M.L., Phelan, J.C. and Link, B.G. (2013) Stigma as a fundamental cause of population health inequalities, *American Journal of Public Health*, 103(5): 813–21.

Hays, T. and Minichiello, V. (2005) The contribution of music to quality of life in older people: an Australian qualitative study, *Ageing and Society*, 25(2): 261–78.

Hebert, C.A. and Scales, K. (2019) Dementia-friendly initiatives: a state of the science review, *Dementia*, 18(5): 1858–95.

Jansen, T. (2015) The nursing home that's also a dorm, *CityLab* [online], Available from: https://www.citylab.com/equity/2015/10/the-nursing-home-thats-also-a-dorm/408424/

Kadane, L. (2018) Nothing about us without us, *Dementia Connections* 11 September [online], Available from: https://www.dementiaconnections.ca

Keefe, B. and Kostiuk, R. (2019) Strengthening age-friendly communities through capacity building to address behavioral health concerns, *Innovation in Aging*, 3(Supplement_1): S311.

Livingston, G., Huntley, J., Sommerlad, A., Ames, D., Ballard, C.G., Banerjee, S. et al (2020) Dementia prevention, intervention, and care: 2020 report of the Lancet Commission, *The Lancet*, 396(10248): 413–46.

McDermott, O., Orrell, M. and Ridder, H.M. (2014) The importance of music for people with dementia: the perspectives of people with dementia, family carers, staff and music therapists, *Aging & Mental Health*, 18(6): 706–16.

Moniz-Cook, E. and Manthorpe, J. (2009) Personalising psychosocial interventions to individual needs and context, in E. Moniz-Cook and J. Manthorpe (eds) *Early Psychosocial Interventions in Dementia*, Jessica Kingsley Publishers, pp 45–66.

Prince, M., Bryce, R. and Ferri, C. (2011) *World Alzheimer Report 2011: The Benefits of Early Diagnosis and Intervention*, Alzheimer's Disease International.

Quinio, V. and Burgess, G. (2018) Is co-living a housing solution for vulnerable older people?, *ResearchGate* [online], Available from: https://www.researchgate.net/publication/331993482_Is_co-living_a_housing_solution_for_vulnerable_older_people_Literature_review

Quinlan, C. (2018) Nothing about me without me – 20 years later, *Science37* 25 April [online], Available from: https://www.science37.com/blog/nothing-about-me-without-me-progress-in-participatory-healthcare/

Rahman, S. and Swaffer, K. (2018) Assets-based approaches and dementia-friendly communities, *Dementia*, 17(2): 131–7.

Scanlon, K. and Arrigoitia, M.F. (2015) Development of new cohousing: lessons from a London scheme for the over-50s, *Urban Research & Practice*, 8(1): 106–21.

Shannon, K., Bail, K. and Neville, S. (2019) Dementia-friendly community initiatives: an integrative review, *Journal of Clinical Nursing*, 28(11–12): 2035–45.

Smith, K., Gee, S., Sharrock, T. and Croucher, M. (2016) Developing a dementia-friendly Christchurch: perspectives of people with dementia, *Australasian Journal on Ageing*, 35(3): 188–92.

Snyder, L. (2000) *Speaking Our Minds: Personal Reflections from Individuals with Alzheimer's*, Times Books.

Tamburri, N., Trites, M., Sheets, D., Smith, A. and MacDonald, S. (2019) The promise of intergenerational choir for improving psychosocial and cognitive health for those with dementia: the Voices in Motion project, *The Arbutus Review*, 10(1): 66–82.

Thornicroft, G., Mehta, N., Clement, S., Evans-Lacko, S., Doherty, M., Rose, D. et al (2016) Evidence for effective interventions to reduce mental-health-related stigma and discrimination, *The Lancet*, 387(10023): 1123–32.

Turner, N. and Cannon, S. (2018) Aligning age-friendly and dementia-friendly communities in the UK, *Working with Older People*, 22(1): 9–19.

Turner, N. and Morken, L. (2016) Better together: a comparative analysis of age-friendly and dementia-friendly communities, *AARP* [online], Available from: https://www.aarp.org/livable-communities/network-age-friendly-communities/info-2016/dementia-friendly-communities.html

Unadkat, S., Camic, P.M. and Vella-Burrows, T. (2017) Understanding the experience of group singing for couples where one partner has a diagnosis of dementia, *The Gerontologist*, 57(3): 469–478.

Vestbro, D.U. (1992) From central kitchen to community cooperation: development of collective housing in Sweden, *Open House International*, 17(2): 30–8.

Werner, P. and Heinik, J. (2008) Stigma by association and Alzheimer's disease, *Aging & Mental Health*, 12(1): 92–9.

World Health Organization (2007) *Global Age-Friendly Cities: A Guide*, World Health Organization [online], Available from: https://iris.who.int/handle/10665/43755.

World Health Organization (2021) *Towards a Dementia-Inclusive Society: WHO Toolkit for Dementia-Friendly Initiatives (DFIs)*, World Health Organization [online], Available from: https://www.who.int/publications/i/item/9789240031531

13

Addressing social barriers to age-equitable public transportation: don't miss the bus!

Madeline McCoy, Susan Braedley and Renate Ysseldyk

Introduction

Access to suitable transportation has been identified by the World Health Organization (WHO) Age-Friendly Community movement as one key dimension of advancing age equity. Age-Friendly Communities aim to ensure accessible, affordable transportation services that allow older adults to engage with their communities and participate in activities that create and maintain meaningful social connections, thereby reducing social isolation and improving health and well-being (Emlet and Moceri, 2012). The Age-Friendly Communities Guide (WHO, 2007) encourages cities and communities to reduce barriers of all kinds for older adults, but also tends toward a 'one-size-fits-all' approach that does not consider how social location, including gender, culture and the needs of diverse older adults, may affect people's experiences (Menec et al, 2011; Moulaert and Garon, 2016; Syed et al, 2017). In this chapter, we contribute to policy and practice discussions that advance age equity through public transportation by exploring the relationships between older adults' differential access to public transportation and their social exclusion and social isolation. We ask, what physical and social barriers do some older adults experience in accessing transportation and what promising practices might address those barriers?

We address these questions through an analysis of findings from a 2019 study that explored promising practices to advance age equity within services and environments in Ottawa, Ontario. Ottawa's public transportation system is an interesting case. In Canada, municipalities have primary responsibility for organising, funding and operating public transportation, with provincial and federal governments providing some funding but also withdrawing or restricting funding at times, creating challenges for municipalities that have little power to tax and have been characterised as 'creatures of the provinces' (Good, 2021). Almost all public transportation in Canada relies on fares for a significant portion of its revenue, while also aiming to provide accessible transportation to those living with low incomes. In the context of these constraints, we explored whether and how older adults were included and accommodated in the everyday operations of the public transportation system. Our research shows that low-income older adults, those with mobility challenges, and those with language barriers often experience problems with finding and using transportation, and further, that gender was a significant intersecting factor. It also identifies promising practices that advance age equity for these groups, despite the system's constraints. Further, our research traces connections between transportation that promotes physical access to the city/community and older adults' social inclusion.

Unlike many other studies, we included service providers' perspectives in our research, to better understand possibilities and constraints that shape the logistics of age-equitable transportation from the perspectives of bus drivers and transportation services managers. Understanding these connections is vital to ensure that policymakers and transportation access advocates do not 'miss the bus' in advancing age equity (Scharlach, 2012; Syed et al, 2017).

Transportation, social exclusion and social isolation

We root this analysis in the social determinants of health (SDoH) and, in line with the WHO's (2007) age-friendly initiative, perceive transportation as a factor in older adults' social participation and inclusion. This approach makes connections between people's relative social and economic (dis)advantage and their differential health status (Marmot, 1999; Braveman and Gottlieb, 2014; Raphael, 2016). Social inclusion is a SDoH. Social exclusion occurs when political, social and economic conditions prevent people from participating and contributing to social and cultural activities available to others in a society (Warburton et al, 2013; Serrat et al, 2018). Social isolation is closely related to social exclusion, and results from lack of contact with others or a lack of participation and social activity (Saito et al, 2012). Social exclusion and social isolation can result in fewer meaningful relationships and opportunities for participating in society, which in turn negatively affects quality of life, health and well-being (Zavaleta et al, 2017; Chen et al, 2022). While poor health may limit or prevent social activity and cause social exclusion and/or social isolation, social exclusion and social isolation can contribute to declines in physical and mental health for older adults (Nicholson, 2012; Van Regenmortel et al, 2016; Sacker et al, 2017; Macleod et al, 2019; Seifert et al, 2021). Further, social exclusion is associated with high stress levels that, in turn, are a factor in many other adverse health conditions (Pfundmair et al, 2015; Beekman et al, 2016; Wang et al, 2017).

When people have limited access to transportation, they are at risk of social exclusion (Engels and Liu, 2011; Walsh et al, 2017; Serrat et al, 2018; Fields et al, 2019). Older adults are over-represented among those who either cannot afford a vehicle or are unable to operate one, and public transportation is particularly vital to them (Turcotte, 2012; Council of Canadian Academies, 2017). Access to public transportation not only enables older adults to grocery shop, visit the doctor, and get to other needed services but also allows them to access social networks, including religious communities, sport and recreation, family and cultural activities, and community events (Council of Canadian Academies, 2017; Lamanna et al, 2019). Accessible transportation, including well-designed public transportation, can significantly reduce social exclusion and isolation for older adults, especially those who experience language and other social barriers, mobility limitations and declining cognitive abilities (CanAge, 2020; see a discussion of dementia-friendliness in Chapter 12).

The term 'transport disadvantage' refers to problems with transportation, including personal vehicles and public transportation, that limit or prevent participation in socio-economic or political life; in other words, the inability to access transportation for any number of reasons (Currie et al, 2010; Shay et al, 2016; Xiao et al, 2018). The overarching term does not differentiate the nuanced reasons why barriers to transportation exist for many groups of people. Transport disadvantage is generally used to describe barriers to transportation that result from transit system design (Engels and Liu, 2011; Shergold and Parkhurst, 2012; Serrat et al, 2018; Lamanna et al, 2019). However, factors such as gender, racialisation, language, health, ability, age and income (among others), also influence access to transportation (Shay et al, 2016; Xiao et al, 2018).

Age is a significant factor shaping the incidence of transport disadvantage, including access to public transit. It is often assumed that transportation problems are experienced similarly by all age groups, and all will benefit from policies that address what are seen as universal transportation issues (Bittner et al, 2011; Council of Canadian Academies, 2017). However, for many older people there is a perfect storm of factors involved in transport disadvantage that operate in combination, including physical disability, cognitive decline, economic disadvantage, residence location and discrimination based on age, gender, race, immigration, sexuality and gender identity. Like other users, older adults experience barriers to transportation access due to route changes, timing and unreliable buses or trains, as well as inaccessible buses, stations and stops (Bryanton et al, 2010; Bittner et al, 2011; Broome et al, 2011; Broome et al, 2013; Curl et al, 2014; Levasseur et al, 2015; Ravensbergen et al, 2021). But they also confront these barriers as people who are more likely to live alone, to have cognitive and physical disabilities and/or health issues that require regular medical attention, to have low incomes, and to have experienced lifetimes of sexism, racism, homophobia and other experiences of discrimination and exclusion.

For the most part, transportation policy and research have responded to older adults' transport disadvantage by focusing on how built environments, designs and logistical issues affect access for older adults, emphasising physical disability as a barrier (Lucas, 2012; Gharebaghi et al, 2018; Toohey et al, 2018). This emphasis has led to improvements such as benches and shelters at bus stops, and lifts and designated seating on buses (Council of Canadian Academies, 2017). However, our research showed that older adults experience many other barriers related to intersections of gender, age, income, language and disability. Nonetheless, we also found some promising ways these barriers are being addressed by both public transportation systems and services for older adults.

Older adults' transport disadvantage in Ottawa: the study

> [My] daughter had left and I was alone ... I had a panic attack and it was about groceries. How was I going to go grocery shopping? Because I have to get grocery shopping. I would need to bring my walker, and you can't really shop with a walker.

This research participant's comment is representative of many older adults' perspectives on negotiating their mobility around the city in Ottawa. This woman had a fixed low income and lived too far from grocery stores to walk in her condition. Her daughter, who had been driving her to shops, had moved out of the city. The public bus service in her suburban neighbourhood was scheduled primarily for commuters, with services mostly in the early mornings and late afternoons, making it difficult or impossible to get to shops and back again during the day. This is transportation disadvantage.

Our research revealed many contours of older adults' transport disadvantage and its effects, including variations due to older adults' social locations. Drawing from our team's rapid ethnography data set collected in 2019 (see Chapter 1 of this volume for more details on method), we analysed interview transcripts with 36 seniors' service providers,[1] including volunteers, program coordinators, community care workers, committee members, nurses and social workers, as well as policymakers and seniors' council members. We also analysed interview transcripts with 17 older adults and data sets from two focus groups – one each with service providers and older adults. Further, we examined fieldnotes from our team members' rapid ethnographic research on major bus routes that included informal discussions with 30 older adult riders and interviews with three bus operators. Finally, the first author conducted interviews with six managers from OC Transpo, the municipal public transportation services.

The data set included respondents' use and knowledge of Ottawa's public transportation services and a wide range of other transportation. OC Transpo's public transportation system includes an extensive public bus service, a light rail transit line, and a personal pick-up transportation system of vans and small buses, called Para Transpo, that serves people who cannot use conventional public transit due to disability, illness or cognitive impairment (OC Transpo, 2020). 'Seniors', defined as people aged 65 or older, are offered reduced fares on all these public transportation services. Free transit on buses and trains is available for older adults on Wednesdays and shortly after our study was completed in 2019, free Sunday transit was added for seniors.

There are other low-cost transportation options for older adults, including privately owned, non-profit buses and vans run by seniors' centres and services that take older adults to grocery stores, medical appointments, seniors' day programs or community centres. These services charge modest fees or include transportation services in the membership fees for a seniors' centre or day program. We learned that many older adults drive independently or rely on lifts from family, friends and service staff.

Many older adults drive their own cars in Ottawa, and those who can afford taxis and commercial ride sharing often do so. Older adult drivers were commonly healthy and mobile. Many older adult drivers told us that they enjoyed the independence of having their own vehicle. These drivers also indicated that they used public transportation, often on a regular basis, and did not experience many barriers to using it. They chose whether to drive, use public transit, walk, or otherwise get around the city using the mode of transportation that best suited their needs on any given day. Most indicated that they often provided rides to other older adults.

Non-drivers told us a different story. They experienced many barriers to public transportation, while also having no option to drive. Many respondents told us they had to stop driving because of physical mobility issues that also prevented them from walking several blocks to a bus stop or transit station and standing to wait for public transit. They described feeling isolated and dependent. Some non-drivers told us they preferred to use public transit to travel to activities, programs and other locations because it allowed them more independence and self-reliance than when friends or family gave them a lift. A service provider told us, '[another] challenge that we are facing, and we haven't yet found a solution, is that the people, seniors, are immobile. They cannot drive, they don't get a ride to come. They want to come but then they have limitations, right?'

Non-drivers in our study were more likely to be women, a finding supported by other research (for example, City of Ottawa, 2011; Kim, 2011; Choi et al, 2012). Women tend to live longer than men and live alone in later life (Zarulli et al, 2018; Baum et al, 2021). They are also less likely to own a car and/or have a drivers' licence (Kim, 2011; Choi et al, 2012). While many women respondents reported using public transit, others preferred to ride with a friend, a volunteer or a family member. Our data indicated that although women may be at elevated risk for the negative outcomes associated with transport disadvantage, some older women build and maintain social relationships that help to mitigate this risk.

Many research participants told us about problems with public transit. Reliable, timely, convenient service was a concern for older adults who attended regular social, health-related and recreational activities, and for the service providers who offered them. For example, one busy seniors' centre had a bus stop directly outside its door, but the bus route was about to be replaced with a light rail transit line. This train would stop '300 meters away' from the seniors' centre. As one staff member told us, it 'does not sound far, but it is significant for some of our members who walk, use a cane, a walker'. In another case, a Francophone seniors' centre was located on a bus route, but buses were scheduled only in the early morning and late afternoon to meet the needs of commuters working in the business district. These timings were too far apart and too inconvenient for the many seniors who frequented the centre or wanted to do so.

Older adults often discussed walking around the city, too. They told us about tripping and falling on sidewalks in poor condition, and a lack of sidewalks and convenient, safe street crossings leading to bus stops and stations in some locations. They reported that there were too few bus shelters, or shelters that were ill-equipped for all weather conditions in this city with snowy, cold winters and hot, humid summers. One older adult noted his own efforts to check bus stops, to see if 'there's enough shade, and enough benches' for older people to feel 'adequately protected'.

In Ottawa, many older adults reported that winter was a barrier to transportation. Snowy, icy sidewalks and roadways make it easy to slip and fall, and being older makes falling more likely due to common age-related health issues that affect balance and flexibility. Further, falls are a serious health risk in later life. As noted in other research (Ravensbergen et al, 2021), public transit inaccessibility in winter can lead to seasonal social isolation for older adults, as older adults in our study confirmed: 'A lot of people just didn't go out this winter [because] they just couldn't.'

In our study, older adults who experienced higher levels of transport disadvantage tended to be from equity-seeking groups. For example, both Francophone and immigrant older adults reported transport disadvantage shaped by language. For those not fluent in English, public transportation was only convenient if they did not require information or direction. Although Ottawa is officially a bilingual city with all public services advertised as available in English or French, older adults and services staff told us that they could not expect service in French on the city's public transportation. Service providers told us many stories of having to arrange services for older adults, due to communication barriers:

> For [the older adults who speak Mandarin and have mobility issues], we have Para Transpo in Ottawa, but you have to call in English to request all those rides, right, which they can't really do … [The older adults] are afraid of calling [Para Transpo] because they know there is nobody [who] can speak Mandarin there.

Immigrant older adults with limited knowledge of English or French told us they have trouble accessing information about available transportation services. Likewise, bus operators in our study confirmed that they found it especially challenging to answer questions when older adults spoke languages other than English or French. Pamphlets and 'ride guides' handed out at stations were available only in English and French. However, and promisingly, we learned about one Ottawa Transit staff person who used a cell phone translation app to assist those who did not speak English or French, but more can be done.

Another group of older adults who experienced transportation disadvantage were those with disabilities and frailties. Although city buses have cooperative seating rules that designate convenient seats for older people, people with disabilities, and parents with small children, other passengers did not consistently abide by these rules. As one respondent described, '[People] don't even get up from the seats that are reserved for people who are handicapped – those with physical disabilities – they don't stand up and let you in.'

Older adults had many complaints about Para Transpo, the public transportation service for those with mobility and health issues who are unable to use public buses. Offered at low cost, it requires eligible users to reserve their transportation at least 24 hours in advance, offering door-to-door service with a driver who will provide support. Wheelchairs, walkers and guide dogs are all accommodated. However, our respondents reported problems with booking pick-ups and drop-offs over the phone and very inconsistent, unreliable pick-up and drop-off times. Some respondents told us they no longer trusted this service and had stopped using it altogether. Compounding their physical disabilities, these respondents experience social disadvantage, exacerbated by transport disadvantage.

Low income was also a continual issue shaping transport disadvantage. Bryanton and colleagues (2010) noted that some older adults will choose 'needs', such as grocery shopping, and sacrifice 'wants', such as social activities, if their transportation options do not allow them to fulfill both. This finding was confirmed in our study. Low-income older adults told us that they tried to arrange their appointments and shopping on Wednesdays to take advantage of Ottawa's free transit day for seniors, but this was difficult. Seniors' services staff told us that demand for recreational, health care and other services peaked on Wednesdays, creating both organisational challenges and social divisions between those with higher income and more transportation possibilities who could participate any day, and low-income folks who wanted programming on Wednesdays. While there are discounted fares for seniors on other days, low-income older adults told us they worked hard to stretch their dollars and chose free days over discounted fares. Broome and colleagues (2013) reported that older adults' satisfaction with transportation services could be attributed to fare prices; our results extend these findings to suggest that many older adults would be blocked from regular public transit use without reduced fares.

In this section, we have described older adults' transport disadvantage as shaped by language issues, weather, low income, and physical disabilities and frailty, issues that affect many other groups, but that intersect in the lives and circumstances of diverse older adults. For our respondents, these factors often affected their lives in combination, shaping social exclusion and social isolation. Older adults were not only inconvenienced or stressed by these issues. They were trapped at home, sometimes lacking nutrition because they could not get groceries, missing medical attention because they could not get to appointments and sacrificing social interactions and opportunities to contribute to the community because they could not gather. Women were disproportionately affected by low income, language barriers and disability, no doubt due to women's longer life spans, lower lifetime wages and responsibilities for unpaid work in the home that can prevent immigrant women from developing fluency in English or French (see Chapter 10 for more on the conditions for older immigrant women), suggesting some of the ways that gender may specifically shape transport disadvantage.

Moving along: what makes for age-equitable public transit?

Given these findings, we were interested to learn whether and how Ottawa had incorporated age-friendliness into its public transit system, to address barriers confronting older adults and associated with low income, disability, gender and language. It was not surprising that 'Free Days for Seniors' was touted as an age-friendly practice by the Mayor of Ottawa, and similar claims were made by OC Transpo managers who participated in our study. While free transit days were appreciated by respondents, it also created problems for older adults and bus operators due to high demand. They confirmed that: 'there just isn't enough room; people are going to work, so there's a lot, there's more people on the bus, people have walkers, [there] are parents with strollers'.

Wednesdays were busy on Ottawa buses, as our team members discovered when we rode all Ottawa's major bus routes on several Wednesdays. We observed that older adults had trouble getting a seat on the bus on those days and were often left standing, sometimes teetering precariously as buses stopped and started. Cooperative seating areas, shared among those with disabilities and those with small children, were sites of frequent conflict about who needed the seats most. Many older adults expected priority when they were visibly struggling to stand on the bus, due to their disabilities or balance issues.

Waits at bus stops were longer on Wednesdays than on other days. Operators told us that slowdowns resulted because many older adults have mobility issues. Operators had to lower the mechanical steps more often and sometimes needed to leave their seats to offer physical assistance to older passengers. They told us they spent more time talking with older riders, too, who had questions and concerns. One operator mentioned that there is a trade-off between giving older adults the time they need to be seated and the time pressure operators experience on Wednesdays. He indicated he could not always wait for older adults to be seated before pulling into traffic. In contrast, another operator told us he took extra time to ensure older adults were seated before advancing because he did not want to be liable if they got injured from falling. He said that he took these precautions both for the customer and to avoid the required paperwork after an injury on the bus. However, all operators agreed that time delays were an inevitable consequence of the large number of older travellers on Wednesdays and that there were no additional buses running to accommodate this increased ridership.

Time schedules are a metric used to assess a bus operator's skill and effectiveness, so increased delays added pressure to operators' working days. Two bus operators discussed situations in which they could not accommodate a person in a wheelchair on the bus, due to the crowdedness of no-charge days. The bus operators stressed that they felt troubled by having to leave these people behind, especially in winter, but that their buses could not accommodate the number and combination of strollers, wheelchairs and assistive devices that tended to peak on Wednesdays. They told us that in cases when they left a passenger at a bus stop, they called the dispatcher to tell them they left a person behind. This was done both to inform the customer service department so they could clarify the circumstances to the customer if they phoned with a complaint, and to inform the next bus that there was a person waiting in a wheelchair, or to dispatch another bus.

This free transit day was well used by older adults. Transit-riding older adults told us that the free day was crucial to their lives, including maintaining social connections and participating in activities. While some mentioned they used the free bus service to save a little money, others revealed that free days were their only means of accessible, affordable transportation. In contrast, some transportation managers questioned whether the free days and seniors' discounts were a sustainable policy direction, given socio-demographic ageing and municipal budget pressures:

> More people are going to be able to qualify for these really, really discounted rates and that might be a financial – call it a burden right now,

but that might be a financial challenge that the city will slowly or quickly see over the next 5 or 10 years given, like given the no-charge days, plus the 62 or 63 per cent monthly pass discount. (Manager, OC Transpo)

The proposed second weekly free day for older adults on Sundays was not considered an age-friendly approach to public transit by any of our study's older adults or seniors' service provider participants, due to the choice of day. They argued for either free transit on another weekday when health care and other services were open, or a pass that would allow older adults a limited number of free trips each week to be taken at any time, or a free transit policy every day.

Beyond the free days for seniors, we noted other promising practices, especially for those with mobility issues. Physical accessibility is a requirement on all OC Transpo buses, trains and Para Transpo vans. In our observations, bus operators were working hard to facilitate older adults' use of OC Transpo services. Many older adults told us about bus operators who accommodated their mobility needs with kindness and respect. While we did not investigate bus operator training or hear about it from managers, we learned that bus operators' age-friendly approach was appreciated and trusted.

The Para Transpo service was also identified by many respondents as a promising practice, offering assistance with accessible public transportation. Many older adults told us they were 'grateful for the service'. Although older adults and seniors' service providers stated that there were many problems with Para Transpo service, they recognised the importance of having this service as an accessible option for transportation and argued for improvements rather than a different kind of service.

Travel training programs for passengers, designed and administered by OC Transpo in collaboration with service providers, had also been established and showed promise, as other analyses have found in other cities (Bittner et al, 2011). These programs trained older adults, newcomers and people with disabilities to use the public transportation system independently. These programs were organised so that older adults who spoke the same languages could support each other, with older adults helping other older adults to navigate the system. Outreach staff from OC Transpo were joined by interpreters for select sessions. Further, older adults who were participants in the travel training program and understood English and/or French helped older adults who experience language barriers and could not sufficiently understand the travel-training instructors.

Moving along: filling the gaps with community-based transportation

Given the barriers older adults experienced with public transit, some seniors' service providers in Ottawa developed alternative transportation programs as part of their ongoing organisational commitments to engage and listen to diversely located older adults. When older adults' experiences were heard by seniors' service providers, promising practices developed to reduce transportation inequities, directly addressing social disadvantage. This practice of relationship-building and community consultation was built into the everyday and every year practices of many but not all seniors' service organisations included in our study and was a promising practice itself.

These kinds of consultations resulted in, for example, a pilot project that transported older adults with dementia and other disabilities to a seniors' day program at a cultural centre. Many larger organisations provided transportation vouchers to low-income adults to cover the cost of a taxi ride to older adults' social activities. Several services offered 'grocery' buses and vans that transported groups of older adults to shop for food with support from volunteers. These programs included, for example, grocery trips for Chinese older adults with round-trip grocery shopping at stores offering culturally appropriate foods, with assistance from Mandarin speaking volunteers. These half-day outings were filled with laughter, chatter and sharing of 'good deals'. Volunteers retrieved food from high grocery shelves and carried shopping bags into the homes of participants. Some senior centres' transport programs also included possibilities for transport to medical appointments and events. Based on their close relationships with the communities they served, these organisations used their limited funding to prioritise culturally and linguistically appropriate transportation services, filling gaps in public transit services.

Our research participants did not mention any promising practices that explicitly addressed gender equity. We noted that of the participants included in this study, transportation managers were primarily (younger) men, while seniors' service providers and older adults were most often women. This gender imbalance shaped a policy and practice environment in which mostly men transportation managers were making decisions about transportation services for mostly women older adults. Meanwhile, the seniors' service providers, who were also mostly women, planned transportation services to fill gaps in public transportation for older adults. Gender inequities were addressed in part via measures for low-income, disabled and non-Anglophone older adults, who were mostly women. We conclude that women's and men's differential transport disadvantage needs closer attention by both researchers and transportation services.

Across our data sources, older adults, seniors' service providers and bus operators tended to discuss similar barriers, challenges and problems with transportation for older adults. In contrast, transportation managers' remarks focused on broad, systematic issues that had potential to affect older adults. However, their perspectives did not reflect how barriers were experienced by specific groups. Interviews with managers, when taken as a group, showed managers as unable to articulate or reflect on the impact of their transportation decisions for older adults, even when asked directly. This finding is relevant to policy development; the process of social exclusion is situated within social norms and practices, economic and political structures, and governance and decision-making frameworks, and can be addressed (Lucas, 2012).

Moving toward age-equitable public transportation

Unlike most transportation research, this project used a multi-perspective approach that included the perspectives and experiences of four groups: older adults, seniors' service providers, bus operators and transportation managers. However, its limitations include our small sample size of transportation providers (bus operators in particular); thus, generalisations to the entire transportation field in Ottawa (and elsewhere) should be made cautiously. Second, data collection was conducted in June 2019, before the COVID-19 pandemic complicated the lives of older adults (and everyone) and significantly altered transportation services and use. Nonetheless, in the post-pandemic return to 'normal', many of the challenges we've noted here continue.

Indeed, the findings from our Ottawa study reveal that many problems prevent specific groups of older adults from accessing transportation: those who are living with mobility challenges, language barriers, low income and/ or are women. Promising practices have helped to advance age-equitable transportation, but barriers remain. Public transportation management could do more to engage with the perspectives of older adults, especially those who experience transportation disadvantage, and seniors' services providers.

Further, research to advance age-friendly transportation in practice tends to address problems of physical accessibility without considering social inclusion (Scharlach, 2012; Syed et al, 2017). This tendency gets built into transportation policy as it is translated into practice using the Age-Friendly Community framework (City of Ottawa, 2013; City of Ottawa, 2015), which, while acknowledging intersections between physical and social factors, tends to focus on alleviating physical barriers. In contrast, when older adults are listened to and understood, promising practices emerge to reduce problems related to social access.

Note
[1] While we refer to older adults throughout this chapter, we refer to seniors' services because that is how these services are named and designated in the Ottawa jurisdiction at the time of writing.

References

Baum, F., Musolino, C., Gesesew, H.A. and Popay, J. (2021) New perspectives on why women live longer than men: an exploration of power, gender, social determinants, and capitals, *International Journal of Environmental Research and Public Health*, 18(2): 661.

Beekman, J.B., Stock, M.L. and Marcus, T. (2016) Need to belong, not rejection sensitivity, moderates cortisol response, self-reported stress, and negative affect following social exclusion, *Journal of Social Psychology*, 156(2): 131–8.

Bittner, J., Fuchs, P., Baird, T. and Smith, A. (2011) *Addressing Elderly Mobility Issues in Wisconsin*, Wisconsin Department of Transportation [online], Available from: https://wisconsindot.gov/documents2/research/WisDOT-Policy-Research-0092-10-19-final-report.pdf.

Braveman, P. and Gottlieb, L. (2014) The social determinants of health: it's time to consider the causes of the causes, *Public Health Reports*, 129(1_suppl2): 19–31.

Broome, K., Worrall, L.E., Fleming, J.M. and Boldy, D.P. (2011) Identifying age-friendly behaviors for bus driver age-awareness training, *Canadian Journal of Occupational Therapy*, 78(2): 118–26.

Broome, K., Worrall, L.E., Fleming, J.M. and Boldy, D.P. (2013) Evaluation of age-friendly guidelines for public buses, *Transportation Research Part A: Policy and Practice*, 53: 68–80.

Bryanton, O., Weeks, L.E. and Lees, J.M. (2010) Supporting older women in the transition to driving cessation, *Activities, Adaptation & Aging*, 34(3): 181–95.

CanAge (2020) *VOICES of Canada's Seniors: A Roadmap to an Age-Inclusive Canada*, CanAge [online], Available from: https://www.canage.ca/advocacy/policy-book/

Chen, E., Wood, D. and Ysseldyk, R. (2022) Online social networking and mental health among older adults: a scoping review, *Canadian Journal on Aging*, 41(1): 26–39.

Choi, M., Mezuk, B., Lohman, M.C., Edwards, J.D. and Rebok, G.W. (2012) Gender and racial disparities in driving cessation among older adults, *Journal of Aging and Health*, 24(8): 1364–79.

City of Ottawa (2011) *A Portrait of Ottawa Older Adults: Demographic and Socio-Economic Characteristics*, City of Ottawa [online], Available from: https://app06.ottawa.ca/calendar/ottawa/citycouncil/cpsc/2011/08-18/07%20-%20Document%203%20-%20Demographic%20and%20Socio-Economic%20Characteristics%20EN.pdf [Accessed 30 April 2024].

City of Ottawa (2013) *Transportation Master Plan*, City of Ottawa [online], Available from: https://documents.ottawa.ca/sites/documents/files/documents/tmp_en.pdf

City of Ottawa (2015) *Older Adult Plan*, City of Ottawa [online], Available from: https://documents.ottawa.ca/en/files/city-ottawa-older-adult-plan-2015-2018

Council of Canadian Academies (2017) *Older Canadians on the Move: The Expert Panel on the Transportation Needs of an Aging Population*, Council of Canadian Academies [online], Available from: https://cca-reports.ca/wp-content/uploads/2018/08/transportaging_fullreport_en.pdf

Curl, A.L., Stowe, J.D., Cooney, T.M. and Proulx, C.M. (2014) Giving up the keys: how driving cessation affects engagement in later life, *The Gerontologist*, 54(3): 423–33.

Currie, G., Richardson, T., Smyth, P., Vella-Brodrick, D., Hine, J., Lucas, K. et al (2010) Investigating links between transport disadvantage, social exclusion, and well-being in Melbourne – Updated results, *Research in Transportation Economics*, 29(1): 287–95.

Engels, B. and Liu, G.-J. (2011) Social exclusion, location, and transport disadvantage amongst non-driving seniors in a Melbourne municipality, Australia, *Journal of Transport Geography*, 19(4): 984–96.

Fields, N., Cronley, C., Mattingly, S.P., Murphy, E.R. and Miller, V.J. (2019) 'You are really at their mercy': examining the relationship between transportation disadvantage and social exclusion among older adults through the use of innovative technology, *Transportation Research Record*, 2673(7): 12–24.

Gharebaghi, A., Mostafavi, M.A., Chavoshi, S.H., Edwards, G. and Fougeyrollas, P. (2018) The role of social factors in the accessibility of urban areas for people with motor disabilities, *ISPRS International Journal of Geo-Information*, 7(4): 131.

Good, K.R. (2021) *Reconsidering the Constitutional Status of Municipalities: From Creatures of the Provinces to Provincial Constitutionalism*, Centre of Excellence on the Canadian Federation [online], Available from: https://centre.irpp.org/research-studies/reconsidering-the-constitutional-status-of-municipalities-from-creatures-of-the-provinces-to-provincial-constitutionalism/.

Kim, S. (2011) Assessing mobility in an aging society: personal and built environment factors associated with older people's subjective transportation deficiency in the US, *Transportation Research Part F: Traffic Psychology and Behaviour*, 14(5): 422–9.

Lamanna, M., Klinger, C.A., Liu, A. and Mirza, R.M. (2019) The association between public transportation and social isolation in older adults: a scoping review of the literature, *Canadian Journal on Aging*, 39(3): 393–405.

Levasseur, M., Généreux, M., Bruneau, J.F., Vanasse, A., Chabot, É., Beaulac, C. et al (2015) Importance of proximity to resources, social support, transportation and neighborhood security for mobility and social participation in older adults: results from a scoping study, *BMC Public Health*, 15(1): 503.

Lucas, K. (2012) Transport and social exclusion: where are we now?, *Transport Policy*, 20: 105–13.

MacLeod, C.A., Ross, A., Sacker, A., Netuveli, G. and Windle, G. (2019) Re-thinking social exclusion in later life: a case for a new framework for measurement, *Ageing and Society*, 39(1): 74–111.

Marmot, M. (1999) The solid facts: the social determinants of health, *Health Promotion Journal of Australia*, 9(2): 133–9.

Menec, V.H., Means, R., Keating, N., Parkhurst, G. and Eales, J. (2011) Conceptualizing age-friendly communities, *Canadian Journal on Aging*, 30(3): 479–93.

Moulaert, T. and Garon, S. (eds) (2016) *Age-Friendly Cities and Communities in International Comparison: Political Lessons, Scientific Avenues, and Democratic Issues*, Springer.

Nicholson, N.R. (2012) A review of social isolation: an important but underassessed condition in older adults, *Journal of Primary Prevention*, 33(2–3): 137–152.

OC Transpo (2020) *Service Types*, OC Transpo [online], Available from: https://www.octranspo.com/en/our-services/bus-o-train-network/service-types/

Pfundmair, M., Aydin, N., Du, H., Yeung, S., Frey, D. and Graupmann, V. (2015) Exclude me if you can: cultural effects on the outcomes of social exclusion, *Journal of Cross-Cultural Psychology*, 46(4): 579–96.

Raphael, D. (ed) (2016) *Social Determinants of Health: Canadian Perspectives* (3rd edn), Canadian Scholars Press.

Ravensbergen, L., Newbold, K.B., Ganann, R. and Sinding, C. (2021) 'Mobility work': older adults' experiences using public transportation', *Journal of Transport Geography*, 97: 103221.

Sacker, A., Ross, A., MacLeod, C.A., Netuveli, G. and Windle, G. (2017) Health and social exclusion in older age: evidence from Understanding Society, the UK household longitudinal study, *Journal of Epidemiology and Community Health*, 71(7): 681–90.

Saito, M., Kondo, N., Kondo, K., Ojima, T. and Hirai, H. (2012) Gender differences on the impacts of social exclusion on mortality among older Japanese: AGES cohort study, *Social Science & Medicine*, 75(5): 940–5.

Scharlach, A. (2012) Creating aging-friendly communities in the United States, *Ageing International*, 37(1): 25–38.

Seifert, N., Seddig, D. and Eckhard, J. (2021) Does social isolation affect physical and mental health? A test of the social causation hypothesis using dynamic panel models with fixed effects, *Aging & Mental Health*, 26(7): 1353–67.

Serrat, R., Warburton, J., Petriwskyj, A. and Villar, F. (2018) Political participation and social exclusion in later life: what politically active seniors can teach us about barriers to inclusion and retention, *International Journal of Ageing and Later Life*, 12(2): 53–88.

Shay, E., Combs, T.S., Findley, D., Kolosna, C., Madeley, M. and Salvesen, D. (2016) Identifying transportation disadvantage: mixed-methods analysis combining GIS mapping with qualitative data, *Transport Policy*, 48: 129–38.

Shergold, I. and Parkhurst, G. (2012) Transport-related social exclusion amongst older people in rural Southwest England and Wales, *Journal of Rural Studies*, 28(4): 412–21.

Syed, M.A., McDonald, L., Smirle, C., Lau, K., Mirza, R.M. and Hitzig, S.L. (2017) Social isolation in Chinese older adults: scoping review for age-friendly community planning, *Canadian Journal on Aging*, 36(2): 223–45.

Toohey, A., Kristjansson, E., Baxter, D., Enns, A., Menec, V., Sheets, D. et al (2018) A tale of eight cities: housing and transportation, *2018 Canadian Association on Gerontology Conference*, Vancouver, BC.

Turcotte, M. (2012) *Profile of Seniors' Transportation Habits*, Statistics Canada, Canadian Social Trends, Catalogue no 11-008-X, no 93 [online], Available from: https://www150.statcan.gc.ca/n1/en/pub/11-008-x/2012001/article/11619-eng.pdf?st=Bf9fvAxZ

Van Regenmortel, S., De Donder, L., Dury, S., Smetcoren, A.-S., De Witte, N. and Verté, D. (2016) Social exclusion in later life: a systematic review of the literature, *Journal of Population Ageing*, 9(4): 315–44.

Walsh, K., Scharf, T. and Keating, N. (2017) Social exclusion of older persons: a scoping review and conceptual framework, *European Journal of Ageing*, 14(1): 81–98.

Wang, H., Braun, C. and Enck, P. (2017) How the brain reacts to social stress (exclusion) – a scoping review, *Neuroscience and Biobehavioral Reviews*, 80: 80–8.

Warburton, J., Ng, S.H. and Shardlow, S.M. (2013) Social inclusion in an ageing world: introduction to the special issue, *Ageing and Society*, 33(1): 1–15.

World Health Organization (2007) *Global Age-Friendly Cities: A Guide*, World Health Organization [online], Available from: https://iris.who.int/handle/10665/43755.

Xiao, R., Wang, G. and Wang, M. (2018) Transportation disadvantage and neighborhood sociodemographics: a composite indicator approach to examining social inequalities, *Social Indicators Research*, 137(1): 29–43.

Zarulli, V., Jones, J.A.B., Oksuzyan, A., Lindahl-Jacobsen, R., Christensen, K. and Vaupel, J.W. (2018) Women live longer than men even during severe famines and epidemics, *Proceedings of the National Academy of Sciences of the United States of America*, 115(4): E832–40.

Zavaleta, D., Samuel, K. and Mills, C.T. (2017) Measures of social isolation, *Social Indicators Research*, 131(1): 367–391.

14

Your days are numbered: active ageing, wearable technologies and surveillance capitalism

Albert Banerjee, Jacqueline Choiniere and Martha MacDonald

Introduction

The age-friendly cities movement is built upon the concept of active ageing. An age-friendly city, according to the World Health Organization (2007: 1), 'encourages active ageing by optimising opportunities for health, participation and security'. However, while the WHO age-friendly cities program calls for adaptations of urban structures and services to promote accessibility and inclusiveness for older adults, and in spite of long-standing recognition that individuals' contexts (including economic status, gender and ethnicity) are critical to health (Commission on the Social Determinants of Health, 2008), the concept of active ageing is often taken up in ways that place the primary onus on the individual. Individual actions (such as exercise and diet) tend to be viewed as the path to attaining good health, and individual, measurable indicators (such as blood test results, blood pressure readings and heart rate) are considered key representations of good health.

Utilising a feminist political economy lens, we argue that this reductive narrative is reflective of neo-liberal ideologies that have advocated for the retreat of the welfare state and the concomitant responsibilisation of individuals. We discuss how these assumptions play into the neo-liberal emphasis on market-based solutions, thus serving the interests of for-profit corporations that design and sell products promising to assist individuals in achieving and maintaining their health. Our analysis, while focusing predominantly on the Canadian context, represents patterns found in other high-income countries. It also surfaces the implications of the recent shift to surveillance capitalism, with a growing number of corporations collecting personal data, intending to use it to encourage behaviour which, in turn, commercially benefits the corporation (Zuboff, 2019a:18). Moreover, surveillance capitalism is reimagining the city as a smart city and, in these efforts, explicitly draws on narratives of age-friendliness to sell a largely hidden agenda.

In this chapter, we take the example of Fitbit: a smart, wearable technology touted as helping individuals become and remain active. Wearable devices like fitness trackers, smartwatches and health monitors have evolved from fitness gadgets to tools for health management (S&S Insider, 2024). The global wearable technology market – dominated by brands such as Fitbit, Garmin, Samsung and Apple – is currently valued at US$63 billion. It is expected to triple to nearly US$200 billion over the next decade, as usage becomes even more common. We draw on an autoethnographic account of 'Fit-bitting' to highlight the tensions inherent in its use. It is fun, certainly. And it is helpful. It gathers data that can assist users to track their progress and spur their motivation.

Foucault (1984: 343) notes that 'not that everything is bad, but that everything is dangerous, which is not exactly the same as bad. If everything is dangerous, then we always have something to do'. The Fitbit is not bad but it may be dangerous. There is work to do to uncover and think through these dangers, as we begin to do in this chapter. These data can also be used in problematic ways, foreshadowed by Google's purchase of Fitbit, its repositioning as a health-care company, and its relationships with the insurance industry and smart cities.

Setting the context: the roots of active ageing

> In practice ... the term 'active ageing' often serves merely as a convenient label for a wide range of contrasting policy discourses and initiatives concerning ageing and demographic change ... [T]his lack of clarity about precisely what active ageing consists of is a serious barrier to its widespread adoption as a policy strategy. (Walker, 2016: 47)

Though the concept of active ageing is of relatively recent origin, its roots stretch back to the 1950s and 1960s. Active ageing is one of a network of related terms – including successful ageing, productive ageing, positive ageing, effective ageing, healthy ageing – that are held to signify a paradigmatic shift in thinking. Together they brought about the new gerontology at the turn of the 21st century, which held a much more optimistic vision of ageing and its possibilities (Bülow and Söderqvist, 2014). The new gerontology was a counterpoint to disengagement perspectives that had characterised the field. Disengagement theory understood growing old as a form of withdrawal, with the disengagement being mutual. As people aged, they withdrew from society and society withdrew from them.

Against this passive representation of ageing, there emerged a suite of theories that drew attention to the possibilities of activity during old age and its importance in maintaining health, meaning and social engagement. Within North America, John Rowe and Robert Kahn (1987, 1997) proffered the most influential formulation of this perspective through their research on what came to be known as 'successful ageing'. In their work, Rowe and Kahn observed that there was considerable heterogeneity in so-called normal ageing, and that gerontology had up until this point focused on pathology. Instead, they argued that there were people who experienced little or no loss in physiological functioning and the new gerontology should be focusing on and learning from these people.

Importantly, Rowe and Kahn (1987) believed that the effects of ageing could be mitigated through research and lifestyle modifications. They offered a highly optimistic view of the ageing process in which decline, disability and disease might be avoided. This optimism is palpable in the tone of the abstract of their first article (1987: 143) in the journal *Science*:

> Research in aging has emphasized average age-related losses and neglected the substantial heterogeneity of older persons. The effects of the aging process itself have been exaggerated, and the modifying effects of diet, exercise, personal habits, and psychosocial factors underestimated. Within the category of normal aging, a distinction can be made between usual aging, in which extrinsic factors heighten the effects of aging alone, and successful aging, in which extrinsic factors play a neutral or positive role. Research on the risks associated with usual aging and strategies to modify them should help elucidate how a transition from usual to successful aging can be facilitated.

Successful ageing was a clarion call for researchers to identify the risks associated with usual ageing and develop strategies to modify them. In the neo-liberal political context of the 1980s, this position was welcomed by those fearful of the potential costs of an unhealthy ageing population and the claims they might make for government support (Bülow and Söderqvist, 2014). Inherent in the new paradigm, and in line with neo-liberalism's celebration of the entrepreneurial subject, was that much of the effort to improve one's chances of success could be undertaken by the individual, who would be empowered by the research produced by the new gerontology. As Rowe and Kahn write:

> Our concept of success connotes more than a happy outcome; it implies achievement rather than mere good luck ... To succeed in something requires more than falling into it; it means having desired it, planned it, worked for it. All these factors are critical to our view of aging, which, even in this era of human genetics, we regard as largely under the control of the individual. In short, successful aging is dependent on individual choices and behaviors. It can be attained through individual choice and effort. (Quoted in Calasanti and King, 2017: 37)

Thus, the paradigm was a happy one. It offered a seductive solution to the ageing 'crisis' that lined up well with the neo-liberal ideology of less government and privatised responsibility. Indeed, it gave scientific credence to this rhetoric.

Current formulations of active ageing

While successful ageing inspired researchers and policymakers in North America, one of the concept's major weaknesses lay in the way the notion of success necessarily brought with it judgments about failure and unsuccessful ageing (Foster and Walker, 2015). In partial response to the limits of successful ageing, the concept of active ageing emerged, spearheaded by the World Health Organization. Active ageing maintained the same optimistic orientation as successful ageing but sought to add an ecological and social dimension to the focus on the individual (Walker, 2016). It was also intended to move beyond health concerns, through the addition of goals of participation, security and quality of life. However, as Walker (2016) observes, its application has been uneven, with its uptake more common in Europe than North America where successful ageing continues to be favoured by many academics.

What's more, the critiques that dogged successful ageing similarly plague the use of active ageing. These criticisms, according to Moulaert et al (2016), fall into three main camps. The first is a failure to include decline. The second is a lack of conceptual clarity such that active ageing continues to be conflated or reduced to healthy ageing, and activity is reduced to exercise. And finally, as with successful ageing, active ageing can be co-opted to serve the neo-liberal economic agenda by either placing the responsibility for decline (and avoiding decline) on individuals or taking on a productivist understanding of activity as economic participation (working longer and typically for less remuneration).

The 'fluidity' of the concept of active ageing and its optimistic terrain can thus be captured and drawn upon in marketing technologies for individuals to keep active and hopefully healthy. We examine this uptake through the use of the Fitbit, which is currently among the most popular wearable monitoring technologies and foreshadows a neo-liberal vision of an age-friendly city. Fitbits and other fitness trackers (such as Garmin, Apple Watch, Oura rings, Whoop bands) promote and reflect the model of active ageing, with its emphasis on individual responsibility (and blame). The individual is enticed by the hopeful plasticity of the body. It is part of the increasing role of measurement in the neo-liberal health system and highlights the role of technology in quantifying and monitoring behaviour.

But what counts in the metrics used? Furthermore, what happens to the individual's data once collected? The individual willingly contributes to data collection that potentially can be used against them or in ways they may not countenance. According to Zuboff (2019b), by 2015 fitness tracking devices were being used by 29.5 million American adults, reflecting their popularity. As of 2023, more than 320 million wearable fitness devices were sold worldwide (SNS, 2024). Health insurance corporations constitute one industry that is very interested in the data from these devices, an indication of the importance placed on an individual's fitness activity and its relationship to health-care costs. While the Fitbit began as a device marketed primarily to a younger demographic, it has increasingly been promoted to a broader cross-section of the population, including older adults, reflecting an acceptance of these devices as health promotive.

Neo-liberalism and surveillance capitalism

It is important to consider the Fitbit within the context of other technologies relying on individual, measurable indicators that are currently used as a means of attaining and maintaining good health (for example, Oura, Garmin, Whoop, Apple Watch). We trouble the idea that these technologies are simply about empowering individuals to be more active. Instead, we argue there are other concerning implications, not the least of which is how these technologies are part of a broader neo-liberal approach to health and care. Throughout the health-care system and beyond, we are witnessing an increased use in web-based data repositories that facilitate the storage of, and access to, information regarding an individual's health, such as blood tests, x-rays and scan results, medications, and more. In this way, wearable technologies play an integral role in the growth of surveillance capitalism.

While generally targeting all adults, there are specific initiatives encouraging older adults to utilise these repositories to store and thus ensure ready access to their health data. Further, the use of these repositories is expanding. Health-care agencies routinely distribute confidential passwords to patients, encouraging them to access their own test results instead of contacting health-care personnel for them. An example is the service offered to members by the Canadian Association of Retired Persons (CARP, nd), through CARP HEALTH 360, which is promoted as a repository for members' health-data, to ensure that they and their health-care providers have immediate access to test results, treatments, and prescriptions. The website assures that 'CARP 360 remembers so you don't have to (and) … When the specialist asks about test results … you can access them on your phone right away … Your health record speaks for you when you cannot' (Canadian Association of Retired Persons, nd).

The use of technology to monitor and manage individuals, including those who are ageing, has been likened by Zuboff to capitalism concealing itself within the Trojan horse of technology (2019a: 11–12). First, there is the reductive nature of the types of data or information that are monitored and collected. This focus is not only evident in fitness tracking devices, but as Zuboff (2019a) argues, includes the collection of extensive personal data on our everyday lives.

Zuboff (2019a, b) argues that technologies, including fitness trackers such as Fitbit, intensify the reach of market-based principles into everyday lives. They monitor, collect and store copious amounts of information on our living habits, preferences, and interests, reflecting a new surveillance capitalism era in which private experiences are translated into commodities that are then marketed back to us. As she states: '[these technologies] become a means to profits in new behavioral futures markets ... users are the human natural source of free raw material that feeds a new kind of manufacturing process ... the products are calculations that predict what individuals and groups will do now, soon and later' (Zuboff, 2019a: 13).

Zuboff's analysis takes in a broad cross-section of data-gathering technologies, including but not limited to Google searches, smartphones, and Amazon's worker monitoring systems. What is particularly important is not the specific data that they collect but the ways these data sets can be mined, networked and analysed to provide information that one never sought to disclose. For example, the retail company, Target, was able to identify, and market to, pregnant women before they had disclosed their pregnancy, a case that captured the public's attention and shows what is possible based only on an analysis of shopping behaviour (Duhigg, 2012). According to Zuboff, a crucial element of surveillance capital is that the networking and analyses of data occur in the shadows, hidden from consumers and citizens. They may be used in a myriad of ways, many yet to be imagined. A key to the success of these technologies is their ability to predict behaviour and then sell these predictions for a variety of purposes, most noteworthy (and perhaps most benign) for the purpose of targeted advertising. As Zuboff observes in the following passage:

> Just as industrial capitalism was driven to the continuous intensification of the means of production, so surveillance capitalists are now locked in a cycle of continuous intensification of the means of behavioral modification, [that] aims to produce behavior that reliably, definitively, and certainly leads to predicted commercial results for surveillance customers. (Zuboff, 2019a: 18)

These developments hint at the future of ageing and age-friendly cities in which individuals' active behavior is monitored and inserted into complex predictive algorithms, with a variety of potentials that magnify with the number of devices linked (such as Fitbits, smart fridges, credit card charges, smart thermostats and Google searches). This is a development that takes up age-friendly notions of activity, participation and security but skews them in ways that are difficult to anticipate, while further discounting the social and ecological contributors to ageing well. At the same time, it celebrates technology, 'innovation' and an optimistic future under our individual control, while creating new markets for data analysis that remain mostly hidden and unregulated. This tendency to neglect social and environmental factors while promoting the utopian potential of individual agency is perhaps understandable, given the history of active ageing and the new gerontology from which it emerged. What's more, these technologies can also be both useful and fun, further disguising the ends they may be put to. We turn to our case study of the Fitbit next.

A Fitbit user case study: notes from an autoethnography

As a Fitbit user for 2 years, I (Martha) have experienced the seduction of the approach to fitness and ageing it embodies. I am the perfect candidate: a senior who has tried to follow healthy eating and regular exercise her whole adult life and now hopes there will be a payoff as I age. What I've pursued for pleasure and general well-being for many years becomes more of a duty to oneself, one's family, and, indeed, society. I want to be that 'poster child' for successful ageing and I willingly rise to the challenge. I am also white, educated and financially secure, which fits the demographic for such devices. My Fitbit, which was a present from my son, seems at first to be a logical extension of the efforts I already make to stay fit. I believe I can improve my health as I age, buying into the models of successful ageing discussed earlier.

My competitive instincts kick in. I want to do well on Fitbit metrics. It can monitor so much (sleep, exercise, steps, heart rate, food intake, weight). I also like the sense of community with my family as we challenge each other.

The Fitbit is all about setting goals and tracking your progress. I can see how well I am doing compared to my own goals and past performance and compared to benchmarks for my age and gender. Of course I want to outdo those benchmarks, though I have no idea where the data and models for the benchmarks come from. It is quite addictive. You can see how you are doing on several aspects throughout the day. You get reminded when you need to move more, and you get banners and kudos when you meet goals throughout the day. You can see if your numbers are up or down on a weekly basis. It tells you when you have had a good night's sleep, and very quickly I find I'm relying on these data. When asked by my spouse in the morning how I slept, I say 'I don't know, I haven't checked my Fitbit yet'. The device shows time spent in various sleep stages and time awake. There is also a summary score where the quality of sleep is reduced to one number. If one purchases a Fitbit Premium subscription this number (and others, apparently) will be explained. For now, it remains a mystery, and the sleep number is driving me crazy. Good judgment and knowing my own body begin to take a backseat to Fitbit's analysis. While the age/sex benchmarks for such things as heart rate and sleep are somewhat mystifying, happily I do relatively well so I usually don't question them, except for the sleep number!

Various challenges are available that one can invite friends and family to join. These include a 'workweek hustle' (Monday to Friday) that I engage in with family. The language and the imagery reflect healthy, active, working age, middle-class people. It's fun at first. I usually beat my husband and daughter, so I know I am doing something right. And I get constant cheers from Fitbit. One day I noticed my son had no steps before noon. What was going on? Did he skip work?

Soon nagging questions arise about the vision of fitness and health embedded in the device. How are they defining fitness? What is being measured? What is being missed? The fundamental unit of 'steps' remains elusive – playing the piano gives steps but riding a bicycle 40 km does not (though it includes going up flights of stairs). Yoga also is not step-worthy. My daughter told me she performs poorly on our weekly family challenges because Fitbit does not give her steps when she is pushing a stroller (presumably the same limitation would apply to pushing a wheelchair). Quantity (poorly measured) and not quality, seems to matter. The emotional and social aspects of being active are missed.

Fitbit: a health-care company?

Given Martha's experience and questions, what do we know about Fitbit? It is a public US company started in 2007 and purchased by Google in 2021. A quick internet search, including the company's own website, shows their increasing focus on the role fitness trackers can play in the health-care industry. In 2016 the company changed their mission and branding from a 'consumer electronics' company to a 'digital health-care' company, according to the CEO (Stevenson, 2016).

In view of this shift, it is important to explore what type of health-care company it is and how this fits with other trends in approaches to health care and ageing. An early step has been to partner with insurance companies. In 2018, Blue Cross Blue Shield partnered with them and now includes Fitbit in its Blue365 program to track fitness (Blue Cross Blue Shield, 2018). While the user can be rewarded with lower premiums and various perks, it raises questions about what other uses are being made of the data. Through the Fitbit 'Health Solutions' initiative, the company partners with employers to change employee health behaviours. According to their website, the 'Fitbit Care' enterprise health platform 'motivates members to own their own health across the care continuum … We create a deeply personal health experience' (Fitbit Care Wellness Program, nd). The platform includes tracking by employees and 'reporting tools' for employers. This raises a lot of red flags.

Fitbit is now marketing itself to health systems as a way to monitor patients 24/7 (Fitbit Remote Care Monitoring, nd). They are also partnering with health researchers to facilitate data collection. Researchers can incorporate Fitbits in their studies and pay for the use of a Fitbit platform to access and analyse the data collected by participants' Fitbits (Fitbit Clinical Trial Research Enablement, nd). These uses make it even more important to question the underlying approach to health manifested in these devices. Are the right things being measured? Who 'fails' based on these analytics in terms of factors such as gender, race, class and age? Are those who 'succeed' necessarily healthy, happy or engaged?

As Fitbit increasingly labels itself a 'health-care' company, we need to know more about the reliability of what they are promising and selling. For example, what research evidence is there for long-term impacts of the use of tracking devices on diet or weight? Organizations focused on eating disorders have raised the alarm over the potential of the devices to harm the recovery of people already obsessed with counting, and to contribute to a rise in eating disorders (see for example, Australian Centre for Eating Disorders, 2017). Research has shown an impact on eating disorder symptomatology from fitness trackers, along with other apps that track calorie intake (Simpson and Mazzeo, 2017). Psychologists are finding evidence that the devices can take away the pleasure of being active, undermining intrinsic motivation (Etkin, 2016).

While the Fitbit is characterised as having a potential role in measuring and managing ageing, what is really known about the ageing body? Katz and Marshall (2018) note three areas where networked devices such as Fitbit are being promoted: providing information relevant to treatment decisions, assessing care needs and supporting 'ageing in place'. However, they identify concerns with these uses. In particular, the focus on the instrumental aspects of healthy living misses the cultural and social embeddedness of the activities being monitored. Furthermore, they argue the use of Fitbits for the older demographic will likely focus more on external monitoring and risk management rather than the current focus of self-improvement, as marketed to a younger demographic.

Meanwhile, it seems that individuals will continue to use Fitbits and other tracking devices as part of their private efforts to age 'successfully'. It is notable that the use of this technology skews towards middle- to upper-class individuals: those who can afford the cost of the technology and have time to engage in and monitor measurable exercise. As the social determinants of health emphasises, generally these individuals are healthier, compared to poor and working-class individuals. In the following sections, we explore further the implications inherent in the approach to health and ageing Fitbit represents and how it may contribute to problematic imaginings of age-friendly cities.

Implications

Neo-liberal monitoring

Fitbits are but one type of monitoring device and, as discussed, there are layers of monitoring in this networked interface between the device and the user, family and friends, employers, insurance companies and health-care providers. The individual may simply want to self-monitor, but the current and potential uses of the data go far beyond this aim, raising issues of privacy and consent. Fitbit has faced court challenges about their privacy terms (suggesting it is not very private), as records have been used in criminal cases to show where a person was and what they were doing at the time of the (alleged!) crime.

As noted earlier, Fitbit partners with health systems, employers and researchers to monitor behavior. Like other forms of measurement in the health system, monitoring readily turns into surveillance. There are many potential institutional users of the data, including employers, insurance companies and health-care providers (who can monitor both patients and workers). In Canada, a Privy Council report (Beeby, 2019) explored the possibility of using the devices to monitor public sector workers and thus reduce insurance premiums, which has not been implemented to date. The police can use this data for evidence of one's activities and whereabouts. There is also potential for surveillance by those closer to home, as Martha discovered when she deduced her son had skipped work. He, in turn, can keep an eye on his ageing mother from a distance.

We agree with others that while self-monitoring (weighing scales, food diaries and blood pressure readings are examples) has occurred for some time, technologies like Fitbit have different implications, as data are networked rather than remaining under the individual's control. Data that are automatically shared across a network raise serious privacy concerns. Klauser and Albrechtslund (2014: 275) argue that '(t)he introduction of ever "smarter" and increasingly networked self-tracking technologies and practices has opened new questions relating to surveillance, privacy, ethics and the self'. Indeed, the uncritical promotion of these technologies as the path to better health, an approach Lupton (2013) has labeled as a 'techno-utopian perspective' ignores many unanswered questions about these technologies, including questions such as, what is or is not tracked? How are the data classified? How are the data utilised? Klauser and Albrechtslund (2014: 274) reiterate the tensions apparent in our Fitbit user's story, making the point that 'classification processes are often invisible'. When it comes to the

Fitbit, what constitutes a step (and what does not), as well as the inability to consider other relevant contexts when these measurable steps are captured, underline the limitations. We see similar shortcomings when it comes to the repositories of health-related data where what gets labelled 'normal' or 'abnormal' in test results fails to consider the person's context.

It is easy to understand how individuals are enticed into self-tracking, given the promises of better health and reduced medicalisation, especially as they age. Yet, as others have argued, this self-tracking can be understood as opening the door to surveillance, which is arguably a more ominous type of control than traditional medicalisation. There are very real implications when insurance companies have access to our health data. As Katz and Marshall (2018: 64) have argued, it can bind individuals 'to specific sets of numbers, standards, and profiles linked to a tyranny of healthy activities and lifestyle expectations'. In other words, these technologies, in relying on a de-contextualised 'normal', set the stage for potentially serious, negative implications when it comes to insurance companies or health-care providers having access to only part of the picture. It also opens the door to ever greater levels of market manipulation.

Narrowed meaning of health

As our Fitbit case study indicates, certain activities are simply not captured – such as yoga. This limitation is shared with other neo-liberal-informed tracking initiatives – such as the RAI-MDS data systems used in nursing homes internationally. In the latter example, only indicators that can be measured are measured. As argued elsewhere, 'what counts is what can be counted' (Armstrong et al, 2016: 349). While important, RAI-MDS does not necessarily capture the aspects of care most valued by nursing home residents just as the Fitbit does not necessarily capture activities most enjoyed by, or even more healthful for, wearers. Indeed, as noted earlier, many activities that contribute to fitness fall into the 'can't be counted' category.

How we understand health changes dramatically when confined by the popularity of narrow, measurable indicators and the attendant assumptions that they convey the 'truth' of health status. Governing or control from a distance is facilitated, including creating opportunities for greater market incursion, as has been shown in research elsewhere in health care (Armstrong et al, 2016, 2019). Consequently, understandings of the connection between health and the broader social and economic contexts are left aside. There is little room to consider the shortcomings of these indicators, including important issues such as joy or happiness. The data become synonymous with health status and, as such, the responsibility of the state to improve access to social determinants of health in promoting healthier residents is weakened.

The focus on measurable indicators, represented by the Fitbit, reflects a conceptual shift in how the body is viewed. As Katz and Marshall (2018: 63) argue, the notion of the functional ageing body has replaced a focus on normality, accompanied by expanding technologies that enable 'self-care and forms of knowing as [older adults] strive to meet neo-liberal mandates of activity, enablement and independence'. This is possible given the rise of the notion of the infinitely malleable body, which Katz and Marshall describe as 'endowing the human body with an expansive plasticity ... allowing the body to be visualised and modified at micro levels of functioning' (2018: 63). The expectation is that you can and should be healing yourself – suggesting it is your fault if you don't – even as your body ages. Stated another way, individuals are encouraged towards self-monitoring and self-care with digital engagement as the path to accomplish it (Lupton, 2013). The answers to our health problems lie within – not external to our bodies.

Responsibilisation

Responsibilisation is understood as the shifting of responsibility from the state to individuals, who are 'empowered' to meet their own needs (Dwyer, 2000: 62). Neo-liberal assumptions contribute to this shift, by encouraging a productive self-reliance, 'unbeholden to society' (Mason, 2016: 73). Yet instead of reflecting greater egalitarianism, responsibilisation 'replaces top-down regulation with a network of self-regulated individuals in horizontal relationships – [meaning that] – both empowerment and responsibilisation constitute techniques of state power' (Mason, 2016: 73). It becomes a more insidious type of control, deepened by the shifting of responsibility/accountability away from the state for ensuring the conditions for a healthy life (such as a living wage, safe working conditions, reasonable shelter/housing and other public health considerations).

We are concerned that these technologies may advance responsibilisation and the attendant 'biomedical thrall', which Aberdeen and Bye (2011) argue is the preoccupation behind individual indicators, generally divorced from gender, class, ethnicity and other social determinants of health. Reflecting these neo-liberal and biomedical perspectives, ageing becomes a 'problem' that must be managed primarily by individuals and their families (Aberdeen and Bye, 2011: 10).

Tracking by insurance companies and employers also serves to further responsibilise the employee or the customer/client, since the onus is on the individual and not on the state or employer to take account of the contexts in which the individual lives and works. Counter to what Fitbit promotes, while individuals may 'own their health', they are not necessarily in a position to engage with or change the factors leading to either better or declining health, especially as they age.

Synergies between age-friendly cities and surveillance capitalism

While the Fitbit technology raises concerns about monitoring and continues to reproduce narrow understandings of health that undervalue the role of social determinants, research on surveillance capitalism prompts us to ask how the data produced by Fitbits are, or will be, networked with other data. The economic value of the data generated by Fitbits amplifies when it is linked to other data, of which Fitbit's parent company Google holds an ever-increasing amount. This is also where we return to the concept of the age-friendly city, because age-friendly cities are increasingly being imagined as 'smart cities' (Rocha et al, 2019). Smart cities are cities that use a range of sensors and data management tools to collect and analyse data, producing and interlinking data as the creation of a vast resource that is then mined for a variety of purposes, such as to produce targeted advertisements, to assess the use and effectiveness of services, to identify crimes or potential health events, and to keep populations in line. Many more uses will undoubtably be imagined.

A Canadian example is Waterfront Toronto's attempt to create a smart community in the Quayside neighbourhood. Waterfront Toronto partnered with Sidewalk Labs, owned by Google's parent company, Alphabet, to pilot the development of a smart community. The publicly stated goal of the pilot, as Sidewalk Lab's website indicates, was auspicious and benevolent (Sidewalk Labs, nd). 'The Sidewalk Toronto project aimed to advance a new model of inclusive urban development along Toronto's eastern waterfront, striving for the highest levels of sustainability, economic opportunity, housing affordability, and new mobility.' However, the project raised many concerns among the public (Project for Public Spaces, 2018), including questions about who would own the data and its analyses, whether for-profit companies were the best partners for community building, as well as the usual privacy concerns. Ann Cavoukian, the former Information and Privacy Commissioner of Ontario, was hired by Sidewalk Labs to help embed privacy into the design of the pilot. However, she ultimately resigned in protest over privacy concerns (CBC, 2020). The project was terminated, putatively because of the economic uncertainty caused by the pandemic.

One of the dangers we draw attention to is the way age-friendly narratives are being used to promote the development of smart cities. For instance, consider the following vision from Sonja Pedell, Director of the Future Self and Design Living Lab at Swinburne University of Technology in Australia and Ann Borda, Professor at the Centre for Digital Transformation of Health at the University of Melbourne. They ask us to imagine the following:

> Growing numbers of active ageing seniors are 'connected' every day using mobile phones to interact with smart city services. Many have wearable devices like smart watches that help monitor and manage their

health and physical activity. These personal devices can also be used to better connect older adults to public data about urban environments. For example, imagine an age-friendly smart city 'layer' linked to a smart watch, to highlight facilities such as public toilets, water fountains and shaded rest stops along exercise routes. (Pedell and Borda, 2021)

There is obvious promise in this strategy. As with the Fitbit, it is useful. The authors' recommendation to involve seniors in the co-design of the 'digital layer' is also promising. Pedell and Borda (2021) suggest: 'We need to start asking senior citizens questions like "How would you like to access this data?" and "What would you like the digital layer to tell you?" Their goals and needs must drive the information provided.' But this is not the only layer that gets created in the production of smart cities and co-design is not the same thing as co-ownership. Age-friendly narratives are useful, however, and may help pave the way for the Trojan horse of surveillance capitalism to market itself to a skeptical public, by marshalling discourses of healthy and active ageing and capitalising on fears of isolation and ageing. The shadow layer of surveillance becomes less visible.

Further, there are plenty of corporations willing to invest in these technologies. Sidewalk Labs' commitment to Waterfront Toronto was in the order of CAD$50 million (Project for Public Spaces, 2018). This can be understood as an investment to add 'friendly' layers to surveillance capitalism.

Conclusion

Devices such as Fitbit embody the emphasis on self-improvement (and, by corollary, self-blame) in the active ageing concept. In our discussion, we trouble the idea that these technologies are simply about empowerment. Instead, we argue there are other, concerning implications, not the least of which is how these technologies fit into a broader neo-liberal approach to health and to care. As others have noted (Katz and Calasanti, 2015), we are concerned by the failure of both successful and active ageing concepts to take broader social, economic, and political forces into account. The social determinants of health, long recognised as key to the promotion and maintenance of health (WHO, 1986; Commission on Social Determinants of Health, 2008), are at best undermined, if not completely ignored in these concepts.

We also move beyond concerns about neo-liberalism and monitoring to suggest that such wearable technology, and the age-friendly 'brand' if you will, may also serve as a Trojan horse by which surveillance capitalism enters our communities. To return to the quote by Foucault, it's not that these technologies are bad, but they are dangerous. We are arguing that it is important to pay attention to the synergies between wearable technologies, age-friendly discourses, and the incursion of surveillance capitalism. There may be fun and utility in knowing our numbers and being able to count our steps, but this near-addictive gamification of health also feeds into a growing apparatus that is collecting and analysing data, the extent of which, and the purposes to which they are put, remain firmly hidden. They are, and may be further manipulated to support profit extraction, and could be annexed by governments for their own purposes. With a rise in authoritarianism, we may well be cautious about creating a surveillance net under the guise of health and age-friendliness that later, we may be caught in. Less ominously, we conclude by suggesting we ask how people could benefit from a future where we can expect the 'internet of things' to create synergies between mobile devices, sensors, the internet and analytic software powered by rapidly growing developments in artificial intelligence. What type of ownership laws, privacy protections and transparency requirements are necessary to ensure that the social, political and ecological understandings of health that ground age-friendly cities are realised rather than subverted?

References

Aberdeen, L. and Bye, L.A. (2011) Challenges for Australian sociology: critical ageing research – ageing well?, *Journal of Sociology*, 49(1): 3–21.

ACFED (Australian Centre for Eating Disorders) (2017) *Trackorexia – A New Way to Judge Yourself*, Australian Centre for Eating Disorders.

Armstrong, H., Daly, T.J. and Choiniere, J.A. (2016) Policies and practices: the case of RAI-MDS in Canadian long-term care homes, *Journal of Canadian Studies*, 50(2): 348–67.

Armstrong, P., Armstrong, H., Daly, T. and Choiniere, J. (2019) Caring for seniors the neo-liberal way, in M.P. Thomas, L.F. Vosko, C. Fanelli and O. Lyubchenko (eds) *Change and Continuity: Canadian Political Economy in the New Millennium*, McGill-Queen's University Press, pp 229–44.

Beeby, D. (2019) Federal agency looking at fitness trackers for public sector workers, *CBC News* [online], Available from: https://www.cbc.ca/news/politics/fitbit-trackers-fitness-wearable-premiums-health-insurance-rewards-points-1.5046724

Blue Cross Blue Shield (2018) Blue Cross Blue Shield Association partners with Fitbit to deliver special offer on Fitbit devices to over 60 million members, Press release [online], Available from: https://www.bcbs.com/press-releases/blue-cross-blue-shield-association-partners-fitbit-deliver-special-offer-fitbit

Bülow, M.H. and Söderqvist, T. (2014) Successful ageing: a historical overview and critical analysis of a successful concept, *Journal of Aging Studies*, 31: 139–49.

Calasanti, T. and King, N. (2017) Successful aging, ageism, and the maintenance of age and gender relations, in S. Lamb (ed) *Successful Aging as a Contemporary Obsession: Global Perspectives*, Rutgers University Press, pp 27–40.

CARP (Canadian Association of Retired Persons) (nd) *CARP 360*, CARP [online], Available from: https://www.carp.ca/health360-home/

CBC (2020) I resigned in protest from Sidewalk Labs' 'Smart City' project over privacy concerns, *Canadian Broadcasting Corporation (CBC)*, YouTube video [online], Available from: https://www.youtube.com/watch?v=1t12UqYl5SA

Commission on Social Determinants of Health and World Health Organization (2008) *Closing the Gap in a Generation: Health Equity Through Action on the Social Determinants of Health: Commission on Social Determinants of Health Final Report*, World Health Organization.

Duhigg, C. (2012) How companies learn your secrets, *The New York Times* [online], Available from: https://www.nytimes.com/2012/02/19/magazine/shopping-habits.html?pagewanted=1&_r=1&hp

Dwyer, P. (2000) *Welfare Rights and Responsibilities: Contesting Social Citizenship*, Polity Press.

Etkin, J. (2016) The hidden cost of personal quantification, *The Journal of Consumer Research*, 42(6): 967–84.

Fitbit Care Wellness Program (nd) *Fitbit Health Solutions*, Fitbit [online], Available from: https://healthsolutions.fitbit.com/wellness/

Fitbit Clinical Trial Research Enablement (nd) *Fitbit Health Solutions*, Fitbit [online], Available from: https://healthsolutions.fitbit.com/researchers/

Fitbit Remote Care Monitoring (nd) *Fitbit Health Solutions*, Fitbit [online], Available from: https://healthsolutions.fitbit.com/healthsystems/

Foster, L. and Walker, A. (2015) Active and successful aging: a European policy perspective, *The Gerontologist*, 55(1): 83–90.

Foucault, M. (1984) On the genealogy of ethics: an overview of a work in progress, in P. Rabinow (ed) *The Foucault Reader*, Pantheon Books, pp 340–72.

Katz, S. and Calasanti, T. (2015) Critical perspectives on successful aging: does it 'appeal more than it illuminates'?, *The Gerontologist*, 55(1): 26–33.

Katz, S. and Marshall, B.L. (2018) Tracked and fit: FitBits, brain games, and the quantified aging body, *Journal of Aging Studies*, 45: 63–8.

Klauser, F.R. and Albrechtslund, A. (2014) From self-tracking to smart urban infrastructures: towards an interdisciplinary research agenda on Big Data, *Surveillance & Society*, 12(2): 273–86.

Lupton, D. (2013) The digitally engaged patient: self-monitoring and self-care in the digital health era, *Social Theory & Health*, 11(3): 256–70.

Mason, K. (2016) Responsible bodies: self-care and state power in the U.S. Women, Infants, and Children Program, *Social Politics*, 23(1): 70–93.

Moulaert, T., Boudiny, K. and Paris, M. (2016) Active and healthy aging: blended models and common challenges in supporting age-friendly cities, in T. Moulaert and S. Garon (eds) *Ageing-Friendly Cities and Communities in International Comparison*, Springer International, pp 277–303.

Pedell, S. and Borda, A. (2021) This is how we create the age-friendly smart city, *The Conversation* [online], Available from: https://theconversation.com/this-is-how-we-create-the-age-friendly-smart-city-152973.

Project for Public Spaces (2018) If we had $50 million: 5 big ideas for Sidewalk Toronto's first year, *Project for Public Spaces* [online], Available from: https://www.pps.org/article/if-we-had-fifty-million-dollars-5-big-ideas-for-sidewalk-torontos-first-year

Rocha, N., Dias, A., Santinha, G., Rodrigues, M., Queirós, A. and Rodrigues, C. (2019) A systematic review of smart cities' applications to support active ageing, *Procedia Computer Science*, 160: 306–13.

Rowe, J.W. and Kahn, R.L. (1987) Human aging: usual and successful, *Science*, 10(237): 143–149.

Rowe, J.W. and Kahn, R.L. (1997) Successful aging, *The Gerontologist*, 37(4): 433–40.

S&S Insider (2024) Wearable Technology Market Size, Share & Segmentation by Product (Wrist-Wear, Eyewear & Headwear, Footwear, Neckwear), by Application, by Industry, by Region and Global Forecast 2024–2032 [online], Available from: https://www.snsinsider.com/reports/wearable-technology-market-1265

Sidewalk Labs (nd) *Sidewalk Toronto*, Sidewalk Labs [online], Available from: https://www.sidewalklabs.com/toronto

Simpson, C.C. and Mazzeo, S.E. (2017) Calorie counting and fitness tracking technology: associations with eating disorder symptomatology, *Eating Behaviors: An International Journal*, 26: 89–92.

Stevenson, A. (2016) Fitbit CEO reveals he's transforming the mission and purpose of the company, *CNBC* [online], Available from: https://www.cnbc.com/2016/10/06/fitbit-ceo-reveals-hes-transforming-the-mission-and-purpose-of-the-company.html

Walker, A. (2016) Population ageing from a global and theoretical perspective: European lessons on active ageing, in T. Moulaert and S. Garon (eds) *Age-Friendly Cities and Communities in International Comparison*, Springer, pp 47–64.

World Health Organization (1986) *The Ottawa Charter for Health Promotion*, World Health Organization [online], Available from: http://www.who.int/healthpromotion/conferences/previous/ottawa/en/

World Health Organization (2007) *Global Age-Friendly Cities: A Guide*, World Health Organization.

Zuboff, S. (2019a) Surveillance capitalism and the challenge of collective action, *New Labor Forum*, 28(1): 10–29.

Zuboff, S. (2019b) *The Age of Surveillance Capitalism: The Fight for a Human Future at the New Frontier of Power*, Public Affairs.

15

The longevity divide in a globalised climate – a forward conclusion

Tamara Daly

Introduction

There are numerically and proportionally more older people living across advanced capitalist states than the past, and more people are living longer and healthier. These demographics have been hailed as a longevity dividend. Stable jobs and access to health and pensions have produced the longevity dividend for this generation of long-living retirees and older adults, combined with advances in biomedicine, pharmaceuticals, devices, retirement savings programs and other trappings of a middle-class life that followed some older adults into retirement. Meanwhile, more and more older people are facing a growing tide of precarity, insecurity and inequity. For the 'bottom', life is punctuated with stretches of little or no supports, precarious work, food, housing and income insecurities, illness without access to medicines, migration and disability. Consequently, while stable pension and retirement prospects have benefitted some, not everyone can retire, or even retire securely.

Amidst the statistical slight-of-hand of dependency pyramids and life expectancy charts favoured by planners and actuaries, these 'longevity dividend'[1] data hide the varying social, political and economic locations from which older people in advanced capitalist countries navigate increasingly individualised, and inequitable, paths through older age. People grow older as modestly reliant, more heavily reliant or precluded from access to battle-worn welfare state supports, and amidst growing income inequality. Some are needing, and reaching for, ageing supports at younger ages. For instance, in Vancouver, service providers working with people who use drugs and substances consider 45 as the age when their client population needs ageing support services (Baines et al, 2025).

I call this divide among older populations the 'longevity divide', marking those who will live longer, healthier and wealthier by cashing in their 'longevity dividend', from those who will not. The latter group live and die under a 'longevity penalty': the result of a cumulative disadvantage that accrues interest over their lives, ballooning their individual costs, and robbing them of time. Climate change, among other issues, reveals the longevity divide.

This volume is part of the *Ageing in a Global Context* series, with goals to (1) transform debates in a 'fast-moving field' by rethinking key questions about ageing; (2) advance interdisciplinary connections for gerontology; and (3) articulate how globalisation and its related processes, which have eroded nation state boundaries, impact ageing, particularly as nation states remain the foundation to analyses of ageing (Hyde and Higgs, 2016; Philipson et al, 2020). Previous chapters in this volume have addressed the first two goals. This last chapter is a conclusion that looks forward – a forward conclusion – pointing beyond the confines of the collective work in this volume to address the third goal. The chapter raises more questions than it answers, but in ways that highlight how the task of exploring globalisation and ageing is incomplete.

The life course is, as Phillipson (2006a) argues, destabilised. Most scholars have located destabilisation *within* the nation state in advanced capitalist countries, in declining welfare state programs, which previously provided stability in older age (Phillipson, 2015). Many have cited increased individual responsibility, market-based solutions, and precarity owing to attacks on the welfare state (Grenier et al, 2020).

In the context of climate change and growing political and economic instability around the world, this chapter argues that limiting the analysis of longevity and the conditions of old age to the nation state fails to account sufficiently for the impacts of economic globalisation and the struggle between economic freedoms and political rights and freedoms. Further, the assumption that a nation state is merely eroded by globalisation and its consequences, including climate change, ignores how the nation state has simultaneously weathered the ascendancy of economic freedoms over political ones, and where resistance can be deployed. With broad brush strokes and in a preliminary way, gesturing forward, this chapter traces the historical ways that welfare states have been constructed through political struggle, then contorted, squeezed and pulled apart by domestic actors favouring economic freedoms. Meanwhile, international actors have pierced, deconstructed and splintered the nation state in their aims to advance their own economic freedoms. These tensions, emerging from globalisation, affect the nation state as the container within which people live their everyday lives and struggle for rights. 'Polycrises', like climate change, that increasingly span nation state borders (Lawrence et al, 2024), amplify the pressures on nation states. In turn, these pressures affect the who and what of getting older.

Economic globalisation, and the processes it sets in motion, matter for ageing. In a world in which economic freedoms are less regulated and political freedoms are diminished, the nation state has also shifted seismically from the development of new technologies that are staking out new markets extending beyond the reach of nation states. Nation states are hiving off zones to accelerate free trade, destabilise labour and erode other political rights and freedoms. Alt-right rhetoric is dividing us in ways that make it harder to address crises like climate change. Growing division, rather than solidarity, are features. How we think about the problem of ageing in future, then, must consider the fate of the nation state, and the ways in which the latest processes of economic globalisation are bolstered by the spread of economic freedoms and the contraction of political ones, globally. New forms of solidarity, resistance and political struggle will define how the problem of ageing is sorted.

The tension between economic and political freedoms sets the stage. In what follows, I first trace, broadly and in brief, this history over three phases. Then, I show that since 2006, there have been seismic shifts favouring economic freedoms and the politics of division. Finally, I provide an exemplar of agency, activism and solidarity, to highlight the global space for political struggle. The 'Swiss Grannies' used a global court to hold their own politicians to account for not addressing sufficiently the impacts of global climate change on their own health, forcing the hand of politicians to act on behalf of everyone. Their example presents one way forward.

Setting the stage: tensions between economic and political freedoms

The history of globalisation is complex, with variable impacts around the world. However, setting the stage for this discussion, there have been some historic turning points affecting the contemporary politics of ageing in advanced capitalist states.

Post-First World War, Keynesianism and welfare state programs

A cornerstone project of the 1930s advanced capitalist welfare state was solving the problem of inequality that resulted from laissez-faire economic freedoms, including addressing the abject poverty and poor health-care access affecting many older adults. The struggle for and advancement of political rights and freedoms emerged as democracy advanced, following the First World War, a pandemic and a stock market crash. As Piketty (2022: 127) noted, 'the state escaped from the dominant classes ... as a result of universal suffrage, parliamentary and representative democracy, the electoral process, and frequent changes of power among different parties, the whole spurned on by an independent press, and the labour union movement'. Struggles for political freedoms resulted in historic redistribution in the USA New Deal politics, as one example, premised on Keynesian economics and risk-sharing through state programs.

In the decades following the Second World War, political struggles in Global North democracies resulted in fundamental political economy shifts that produced greater economic equality. Despite the signing of the General Agreement on Tariffs and Trade in 1947 – aimed at reducing trade barriers and promoting international trade – by the early 1950s, growing political freedoms exercised democratically in advanced capitalist countries produced various types of welfare states (Esping-Andersen, 1990). State-led social and health-care policies tethered the economic freedoms of the advantaged members of society to the heel of democratic, political freedoms. This was also supported by controls on the movement of wealth, in that it was not easy to move wealth internationally. This was a time when sending money across borders still involved trunks stuffed with gold bars. Piketty (2022: 155) argues that the resulting Keynesian welfare economics were a 'systemic transformation of capitalism', associated with 'logics that are decentralised and self-managing, ecological and multicultural … more emancipatory and egalitarian than the present'.

This transformation included a variety of state-led old age security, public pension, health-care and employment protections, funded from taxation and oriented to share risk and enable the partial or complete 'decommodification' of citizens. Programs relied on inter-generational solidarity, since, in many nations, pensions and health care were paid out of current accounts, and not initially limited by contributory benefits, as with the Old Age Security pension, in Canada. Furthermore, during this period, 'age' was institutionalised by state pension and retirement rules (Estes, 1979). Programs slowly stabilised the experience of ageing and addressed the problem of abject poverty in older life. This was especially important for women, who outlived men, did more unpaid social reproductive work, experienced income gaps and pay gaps when in paid work, and lower income later in life (Estes, 2006).

Advancing neo-liberalism

By the late 1970s, the Keynesian approach to solving problems via welfare programs and shared risk was woven deeply into these nations' social fabric. Thus, those who aimed to assert capital interests needed a shift in approach involving a 'third order change' across policy instruments, instrument settings, and goal hierarchy (Hall, 1993: 277). The shift to neo-liberalism involved all three, with those wanting economic freedoms competing more effectively against political freedoms involving claims for equality.

Neo-liberalism espouses economic freedom to enable cross-border flows of capital, goods and services, freedom from regulation, including for environmental protections, while also restricting the movement and/ or rights of labour. Credited to the 1940s and 1950s thinking of Frederik

Hayek and other ordoliberal Mont Pellerin Society members, including Milton Friedman, it was taken up seriously after Keynesian approaches were trounced, especially following the economic shocks of the 1970s. Through the open window of opportunity, neo-liberalism was yanked from academic theory into the political mainstream by Pinochet in Chile, followed by Thatcher in the UK and Reagan in the US (Piketty, 2022). Neo-liberal policies and practices spread elsewhere quickly but unevenly (Hall, 1993).

Despite the shift, in the initial days of neo-liberalism there remained a political détente across many advanced capitalist countries between increasing economic freedoms and democratic and political rights to equality. For the middle class, the assurances provided by welfare state policies secured their strong political backing and a willingness to share in socialised risk so that the bottom 50 per cent could access support, even when not at the level of substantive equality. Progressive taxation was the basis of their compromise (Piketty and Goldhammer, 2014).

However, throughout the 1980s, attacks on welfare state policies that increased equality intensified, focused on whether welfare state programs constituted rights or benefits, and with growing critiques about cost and coverage. The political strategy was typically an attempt at breaking solidarity among the middle- and lower-income socio-economic classes by assigning blame and labelling those using social assistance as 'welfare bums', free riders or in the case of older people, as being too costly. These neo-liberal attacks were coupled with policies that reduced taxation, increased individual responsibility, valorised work and productivity, returned care work to the family and away from collective state responsibility and turned public goods and services into potential markets for capitalism, even in areas of proven market failure, like health care.

There was on-going political resistance to the result of unfettered economic unleashing. Those supportive of the democratic project to increase equality produced significant scholarly analyses about welfare state programs, included analyses of popular, effective programs important to many groups of older people who were living longer due to greater income security and advances in biomedicine. Neo-liberal politics diminished the power of political actors within nation states owing in part to the inability to control capital flight.

Repeatedly, scholars showed that neo-liberal approaches diminished the robustness of welfare state policies and programs. A flurry of research activity produced analyses of unemployment insurance and old-age assistance (Heclo, 1974), ageing, life course and welfare states (Guillemard, 1983; Leisering and Leibfried, 1999; Mayer, 2009) the welfare state and retirement (Kohli et al, 1991; Guillemard and Rein, 1993), pension policy (Myles, 1984), ageing and labour markets (Myles and Quandagno, 1991), gendered welfare states and ageing policy (Estes, 1979; O'Connor et al, 1999). The study of how advanced capitalist societies were addressing ageing through welfare state programs, directed by nation states, formed the core of social gerontology into the early 2000s (Dannefer, 2003).

Scholars took up analyses of the variations among welfare states' founding struggles and the advance of neo-liberalism, identifying 'three worlds' of welfare (Esping-Andersen, 1990), varieties of capitalism from varying configurations of the state, business firms, and labour (examples are Hall and Soskice, 2001; Slobodian and Plewhe, 2022) and critiques of the gendered division of labour in paid work and in family relations from the unpaid social reproductive work done in households in the maintenance of everyday life (such as Orloff, 1993).

Despite differences among welfare states, scholarly analyses showed that consistently, where neo-liberal approaches were adopted, there were also political efforts aimed to minimise the size of the state (which were seldom successful) and to alter its role to emphasising its responsibility to create competitive conditions for market players to flourish (which were usually successful) (Skogstad, 2000). Meanwhile, many responsibilities for social welfare and care were individualised in gendered ways. In some contexts, state services were transferred to non-profit organisations, though less so in the social democratic countries. For some programs, like health care and pensions, state support persisted, albeit often with new exclusions, reduced benefits, and new, individualised responsibilities attached. Where neo-liberal tendencies were most deeply rooted, the state role became increasingly residual. Social democratic countries were the slowest to succumb to neo-liberal promises, and actively resisted in various areas (Szebehely and Meagher, 2017). The neo-liberal project advanced through repeated attacks on the quality and coverage of welfare programs throughout the 1980s. Yet, despite the resulting erosions of democratic governance and equality, Fukuyama (1992) argued that capitalist democracy was the end of history and would spread globally. Similarly, Fennell and colleagues (1988) predicted that modern western ageing models that relied on strong protections for ageing populations underwritten by the state, would spread globally. Both arguments failed time's test. If anything, capitalist democracy and welfare state durability, including in supporting older age, have become rarer over time, as the next sections will highlight.

Economic globalisation

In the late 1980s and early 1990s, the rising wave of spreading neo-liberalism ushered in greater economic freedoms through processes of globalisation under the auspices of states that aimed to remain 'competitive' in attracting and retaining global capital. Increasingly, democracy was identified as *the* obstacle to gaining greater economic freedom; strategies to ratchet down political freedoms were key neo-liberal goals. These ideas, credited to Hayek and other ordoliberals (Slobodian, 2023), continued to gain traction, setting the stage for the next phase of globalisation: amplifying economic freedoms with international trade agreements.

The signing of the Canada U.S. Free Trade Agreement (1989) and the Maastricht Treaty (1992) remain emblematic of what was to come: the liberalisation of cross-border trade in goods, and, importantly, free trade in capital flows and services as well, facilitated by advances in information and communication technologies. This liberalisation was underscored by policies that promoted increased mobility of in-demand, low skilled workers, while imposing significant limits on most other migrating people. It also involved cross-border patent protections for intellectual property. Importantly, these international agreements tied the hands of domestic politicians, sinking the political project of redistribution while advancing the goals of the 'competitive' state.

Two important domestic policy consequences resulted from the signing of international trade agreements: first, the range of policy and agenda setting tools deployed by nation state actors was limited by an emerging global competitive logic underscored by information and communication technology; and second, the state shifted operations to attract capital investment by preparing its work force and economy to offer the needed required skills and technologies (Skogstad, 2000). Nation state actors worked to enact domestic policies protective of private property, and preventative of redistribution, limiting taxation and liberalising cross-border capital flows, while impeding domestic policies that favoured people over profits (Piketty, 2022; Slobodian, 2023). By the end of that 'greedy decade', policymakers had increased economic freedom by supporting deregulation and advancing the 'competitive state' (Skogstad, 2000). The age of globalisation had arrived.

Economic globalisation processes emanate from multiple sources. They emerge from neo-liberal policy practiced within nation states, facilitating freely moving capital, goods and services and placing restrictions on labour rights, protections and mobilities, all mediated by information and communication technologies (Harvey, 2007). They are encoded in trade agreements and legal/regulatory mechanisms signed by nation states and governed by global financial bodies, like the World Trade Organization, that police the behaviour of national political and economic actors in their pursuit of market exchange. Private property, such as land and intellectual property, are protected (Harvey, 2007).

Cross-border trade agreements proliferated alongside the overarching global architecture supported by the World Trade Organization and International Monetary Fund. The agreements acted as 'conditioning frameworks' by channelling future options towards certain policies over others, effectively functioning as institutional mechanisms to promote and consolidate neo-liberal reforms in nation states, and sub-nationally (Grinspun and Kreklewich, 1994).

These agreements were well-situated to challenge domestic political freedoms. The anti-democratic terms of international trade agreements granted corporations the legal status of individuals able to make claims against foreign nations to compensate for profit loss, while denying those same rights to domestic firms or citizens. These agreements also protected intellectual property rights across borders. These new legal protections unleashed corporations globally.

Strange (1997) argued that understanding changes to markets is key to understanding globalisation, given that changes to the structure of production can concentrate power outside of the territorial jurisdiction of a single nation state and re-locate that power within transnational corporations. This shift can subjugate and assimilate state actors' abilities to set national level agendas, favouring instead those policies supportive of the logic of competition and profit-taking. During this period, global multi-national corporations created global value chains – from resource extraction, supply and manufacturing, to sales, service, delivery and finance – to develop their products. Corporations in the services fields also grew, notably in finance and insurance, but also in long-term care, with markets newly opened to export the market approach to care to other countries. As an example, the globalisation of long-term care markets, enshrined in trade agreements, increased marketisation and commercialisation of the sector throughout this period, with significant negative consequences for quality of care for older people and quality of working conditions.

Value chains bind global corporations economically and politically across multiple jurisdictions, so that shifts reverberate across time and place. This reverberation produces a contradictory tendency within globalisation: a race to the bottom to produce value with the lowest cost inputs where regulations are lightest and wages are lowest, and, simultaneously, a chase to the top, to break open new markets, to capitalise on market share, and/or to appeal to consumer preferences. In some instances, globally branded corporations have found that gaining market share was advanced by achieving labour, environmental, and other standards in their value chain that are higher than domestic laws would otherwise require.

Thus, globalisation has created winners and losers. Winners include the 'global cities' that became centres of finance, such as London, whose traders can move money across borders at lightning speed. These financial cross-border dynamics have been enabled by leaps in information and communication technology networks (Sassen, 2001). These networks enabled money-making based on the speed of data transmission, underscoring time/space compression (Harvey, 2007). Losers include those places that can no longer compete, with huge costs for political leaders unable to sell their locales and maintain productive employment. Cities across advanced capitalist countries have been outcompeted by countries and territories with different economies, including offshore territories and zones, a trend addressed in the next section.

Though some have argued that globalisation is over-theorised and illusory, studying its policy consequences makes it possible to fix it 'to the ground,' and report on actions or inactions to address problems (Skogstad, 2000). This fixing can surface gains and losses in economic and political freedoms, but only if the scope of analysis is widened and calibrated across borders. Thus, critical studies of ageing may miss the mark if they assess only the tangible impacts for older people *within* nation states but ignore impacts *between* and *across* borders. Analysts assuming an autonomous state that can independently regulate the market and provide welfare to the citizenry are ignoring the ways in which processes of globalisation shape and constrain domestic policy choices and their impacts on ageing.

Perhaps due to the 'cultural turn' in gerontology (Twigg and Martin, 2015), it was not until the early 2000s that processes of globalisation were even identified as an 'influential force in the construction of old age' (Phillipson, 2006a: 201; Phillipson, 2006b). Prior to that, and with an assumption of an autonomous nation-state, political economy of ageing studies had showed how 'age' was socially constructed by nation state level labour market and welfare state policies, producing economic and material dependency and socio-economic inequities of class, gender and race/ethnicity in older age (Estes and Phillipson, 2002; Phillipson, 2005; Estes, 2006; Walker, 2006). Adding the study of globalisation to their analysis, it was argued, would add perspective, guide theory and direct attention to the influence of global actors and institutions over domestic public policy for older age. Further, it would highlight the subsequent capacity of domestic actors to independently enact social and economic policies, to address, manage and regulate population ageing (Vincent et al, 2006; Marshall 2011; Phillipson, 2013; Baars et al, 2016).

Consequently, nation state policy, it was argued, was newly confronted by the challenge of population ageing and impacted by global institutions pressing down on states, resulting in shifts to the 'meaningful boundary' once held by the welfare state in sustaining the lives of older people (Phillipson, 2006a). Further, globalisation's impact on ageing was considered a 'destabilising force', disrupting the conventional meaning of 'growing old' and interrupting the life course, given changes to labour markets such as eliminating jobs for life, shifting to defined benefit pension plans and individualising the need to fund retirement (Phillipson, 2006a).

Subsequent scholarly contributions have advanced Beck's notion of 'risk' (1992), to argue that there is increasing insecurity and precarity in old age in the context of increasing longevity and rapidly changing cultural, economic and social circumstances (Phillipson, 2015; Grenier et al, 2020). Grenier and colleagues (2020) argued that retrenching welfare state social programs, by individualising responsibility for social and health care to individuals and families, was affecting the level of risk and precarity experienced by older adults. Other recent writing situates risk within a global context, taking up, for instance, the case of retirees moving from wealthier northern and western countries to ones in the south and east (Ripetti and Calasanti, 2025); the role of international remittances from children in determining either security or vulnerability in older age (Bastia and Calsina, 2025); the global-to-local interactions of ageing in place (Peace, 2023); older people's experiences of health and social care with austerity (Simmonds, 2021); and age-friendly communities (Buffel et al, 2019). Most 'global' analyses preserve the autonomy of the nation state (Hyde and Higgs, 2016). In contrast, Hyde and Higgs (2016) considered globalisation and ageing spatially and temporally to assess whether there was convergence in ageing approaches and outcomes across countries. They found no convergence in the time-space of later life and perhaps too quickly concluded that the processes of globalisation had a very weak effect on later life conditions.

Despite Hyde and Higgs (2016) dismissal, the weight of studies outside and within gerontology suggest that economic globalisation has had an important and enduring impact on the conditions for getting older that merits further investigation. Furthermore, given the speed of technological, economic and political changes to freedoms that have occurred in the past two decades and continue at an accelerated pace today, it is important to consider whether we have entered a new phase of globalisation against which new conditions for ageing must be assessed. The next section turns to recent history.

New phase: divide and conquer

Just as scholars were documenting the impacts of economic globalisation for older people, the world shifted seismically, with the creation of new market frontiers, new zones and new divisive politics, as this section outlines.

New market frontiers

International finance was arguably the first sector to benefit from economic globalisation, with financial centres across the globe networked by information and communication technologies, making money by splitting the seconds it took to trade. Then came the Apple iPhone, released in 2007, an event that may have signalled the beginning of the new order of economic globalisation. While the making, sales and servicing of Apple iPhone hardware is the epitome of the earlier phase of economic globalisation just described (involving the assembly of parts and a supply chain spread over multiple zones) the new market frontiers created by software apps have shepherded us to the next, current phase, and the one with which we must now grapple.

Awareness of this shift surfaced when Zuboff (2019) broke the 'fourth wall', and revealed to the world the powerful 'surveillance capitalism' markets that big tech had created and exploited with smartphones, tablets and watch apps. This new market frontier first turned us, its users, into the product. We populate corporate databases with our actions and behaviours, while their collecting, analysing and harnessing of these data gives these platforms the power to encourage users to adopt new behaviours and alter course (see Chapter 14 for more on this point). Next, when COVID closed the world, and shrunk individual lives, privacy within households was pierced by ZOOM, Discord, and other livestreaming technologies. That we collectively entered a whole new stage of global capitalism became even clearer on 30 November 2022, when ChatGPT released its research preview to the world, upending our ideas about where ideas come from. Not long afterward, the Nobel laureate in physics and pioneer of artificial neural networks, Dr Geoffrey Hinton, became a household name, both as godfather of AI, and its doomsayer. His predictions, it seems, are that we are placing ever more blind faith in the power of machines to power decisions. To highlight that it is global and state-funded corporations and their cadre of engineers fuelling this 'decisional' market space is obvious. To raise the problematic that the energy requirements to power the machines of AI to supposedly solve the world's problems actually tax to the limit the planet's sustainable environmental capacities dabbles in grand irony. To say that the space is unregulated by any one group or state is an understatement. Yet, most, if not all, of our decisions about life and older age requires the full realisation of what it means to be human, to grow, to love, to share and to age.

Getting in the zone

While there are pro-democracy adherents of neo-liberalism, the goals of economic globalisation are also associated with those who believe in restricted democracy and autocracy. In the late 1990s, these ideas begun fuelling real-world experiments in economic freedom that include elements of extra-territoriality that seriously limited peoples' political rights and freedoms. Among places cordoned off as zones of hyper-economic activity are post-colonial Hong Kong, and zones in China, India, Vietnam and in the city-state of Singapore. The growing number of extra-territorial, hyper-capitalist free trade zones demonstrate further how the pursuit and realisation of market radical's goals amplifies inequities. Over the course of the next two decades, the boundary of the nation state, as a container, has changed, with extra-territorial zones hived off within and offshore to nation states. This changes the 'rules', even within national state borders. Slobodian (2023, e-book chapter 1) explains:

> The world is pockmarked, perforated, tattered and jagged, ripped up and pinpricked. Inside the containers of nations are unusual legal spaces, anomalous territories, and peculiar jurisdictions. There are city-states, havens, enclaves, free ports, high-tech parks, duty-free districts, and innovation hubs. The world of nations is riddled with zones – and they define the politics of the present in ways we are only starting to understand.

This zone proliferation accompanies the increasing spread and ascendancy of ideological movements representing minarchist (minimal state) and anarcho-capitalist (no state) projects that privilege economic freedoms completely over, or in lieu of, political democratic rights-based ones (Slobodian, 2023).

These experiments also demonstrate how unchallenged economic freedoms flourish in places with authoritarian politics, significantly reduced political freedoms, low levels of taxation, small populations of citizens with few dependencies on the state and large populations of segregated groups of migrant labourers cordoned apart in dormitory living spaces and holding limited labour and human rights. These experiments also elevate governance of disputes to global institutions, many of which are dedicated to economic freedom (Slobodian, 2023). What this proliferation of zones also makes clear is that economic freedoms are advancing while political freedoms are either diminished or completely restricted, and most particularly for groups of migrant labour. These zones are stark reminders of a world of economic freedoms untethered to people, lacking the political rights and freedoms that have been fought for, with wins dating back a century.

By shape-shifting nation states and creating extra-territorial free-trade zones, market radicals have found a way to enjoy economic freedom untethered by the bothersome demands for political rights and freedoms made in the democracies. Migrant workers, willing to labour under such limited conditions, leave behind older family members reliant on their earnings while caring for their grandchildren, the left-behind children of migrant workers, in exchange.

These zones of low wage labour offer few protections while creating the low-cost products that sustain the purchasing power of the middle classes in many advanced capitalist nations, the same middle-class whose own incomes are absorbed by taxes to support welfare state programs for everyone, to scramble to make up for the losses due to capital flight and corporations that are clever at offshoring gains so as to hold onto the risk-shared supports. For everyone, and not just those ageing, changes to labour standards, health care and pensions are key, because a precarious work life leads to a precarious older life (see Chapter 8 for more). The ways in which these zones compete with nation states in places that have higher standards and higher taxation, including how these zones are governed in terms of labour and the environment, raise serious questions for advancing ageing with equity and care, domestically and globally.

Weakening solidarity, spreading divisions

Regressive taxation – approaches to taxation that do little to redistribute income and increase socio-economic inequality – has become more common in advanced nation states, and is weakening solidarity across populations, while spreading divisions. This taxation approach ends up with under-funded systems, like pensions and health care, that had been hard won through political struggles and, in other eras, have been funded securely with progressive taxation (Piketty, 2022). Furthermore, new opportunities for hiding wealth have developed in some tax systems, allowing the wealthy to evade taxation, although globally, some states retain robust tax laws that keep such loopholes closed. As the Panama and Paradise Papers' release revealed, wealthy citizens and corporations often secure their monies from taxes in extra-territorial, offshore or special economic zones. This is 'a secretive parallel economy' (Acosta, 2023), which supports capital flight and creates economic freedom for individuals and market players who can buy whatever services they need on the global market (Piketty, 2022). New wealth-hiding strategies, like 'buy, borrow, die', which involves borrowing against stocks to fund tax free consumption, further fuel income inequality (Karma, 2025) and tax evasion. In nation states where wealth hiding has accelerated (and morphed over time), middle classes either bear increasing responsibility to fund the collective risks of ill-health, old age security and unemployment, or these programs are eroded and completely individualised or some combination of both.

Ideas are also important in weakening solidarity and spreading divisions The minarchist and anarcho-capitalist projects, are further supported by the politics of 'diagonalist thinking' and 'diagonal movements'. These politics are arced alt-right, though claiming to defy left and right conventions. They join together the strangest bedfellows, such as anarchist, spiritualists, anti-vaccine wellness folks and libertarians (Callison and Slobodian, 2021; Klein, 2023). For these 'ungovernables', 'freedom is defined in the negative, reduced to individual license and shorn of any sense of mutual responsibility or solidarity' (Callison and Slobodian, 2021). A 'freedom'-focused anti-state rhetoric unites the anti-vaccine, anti-mask, anti-climate ideas, that sees all power as conspiracy. The tactics, rampant on social media, and spilled over into real-world politics, include: dismiss the message, distort the facts, distrust the source, distract the audience and express dismay.

The challenge coming from these politics of diagonalism is that they amplify individualised responsibility in the name of freedom and weaken solidarity in ways that turn citizens on one another. They turn our gaze from the collective problems that we need to struggle to solve and leave ample space for economic freedoms to unleash. Diagonalist thinking, blaming and anti-solidarity are clear tactics, too, in the anti-climate change rhetoric. Diagonalist thinking blames older people for making poor decisions and taking more than their fair generational share of social welfare, distracting from the realities of increasing income inequality and growing economic freedoms that overtake political freedoms.

In the space of five short years (2020–25), information has been upended by disinformation powered by social media platforms; individual behaviour has been altered by algorithms; and AI and neural networks have been enabled to decide, all in ways which are secret, unknowable, unregulated, uncontrolled, and undemocratic to the core. The growing number of groups expressing anarcho-capitalist and diagonalist politics across the world is a concerning trend, fueling anti-solidarity and inequality.

This depressing assessment is lightened, however, by resistance coming from perhaps unexpected groups. Using the tactics of political struggle and solidarity, older people are leading resistance efforts, showing that such movements can be effective counterweights against inequality (Pillemer et al, 2017).

Fighting back: climate change and Swiss Grannies

On 28 January 2025, atomic scientists moved the doomsday clock 89 seconds to midnight, its closest since the clock was created in 1947. Among the main indicators for this foreshortening is the acceleration in climate change. As scientists noted:

> sea-level rise and global surface temperature, surpassed previous records. The global greenhouse gas emissions that drive climate change continued to rise. Extreme weather and other climate change-influenced events – floods, tropical cyclones, heat waves, drought, and wildfires – affected every continent. (Mecklin, 2025)

Extreme weather exacerbates ill-health. While many people grow older in good health, there are others for whom the toll of cumulative disadvantage, loneliness and poor health are the norm. Ample evidence points out that poor health is exacerbated by climate change, and doubly so for those who are ageing and in poor health.

How does climate change affect older people? Older people, and particularly those who have led lives of cumulative disadvantage, are more likely to have cardiovascular and respiratory health conditions. Older people are more vulnerable to heat and cold stresses, because over time we lose our ability to thermoregulate (Filiberto et al, 2009; Ebi et al, 2022). *The Lancet* reported that the oldest and youngest members of society, have been made most vulnerable:

> Because of the rapidly increasing temperatures, vulnerable populations (adults older than 65 years, and children younger than one year of age) were exposed to 3.7 billion more heatwave days in 2021 than annually in 1986–2005 ... and heat-related deaths increased by 68% between 2000–04 and 2017–21 ... a death toll that was significantly exacerbated by the confluence of the COVID-19 pandemic. (Romanello et al, 2022)

Air pollution is an everyday reality for more than 90 per cent of the planet (WHO, 2016). Extreme weather events carry risks of distress, anxiety, mortality, food-borne pathogens and dehydration that put social and health systems under strain. Further, when people are socially isolated, extreme weather events include the risk of being forgotten. Older people may require assistance to leave and may be hesitant if pets are not also cared for. Finally, immune systems change as we age, and our capacity to fend off severe infections lessens. Vector-borne diseases associated with climate change, including those like Zika, West Nile and Lyme disease, pose greater challenges for vulnerable people.

But lest we be tempted to believe that older and younger people are rendered vulnerable by their bodies alone, we need to be reminded of the socio-cultural factors that have contributed to elevating the threat of climate inaction for older people, among others. As Robert Keller (2015) explained, it was isolation and poverty that shaped the incomparably high death rate among older people in the Paris heatwave of 2003. Older people who died disproportionately were mostly living in isolation and poverty in 'chambres de bonne', single room dwellings located in attics directly beneath the tin roofs of larger buildings, and in a previous era, the abode of domestic workers. These accommodations are located in inner parts of Paris, in rooms usually separated from the main building by doors and service stairs, without elevators. Sometimes only cold water is available, and some lack running water. Paris had been unaccustomed to this type of heat, and chambres de bonne, as well as most other apartments in Paris, are rarely fitted with air conditioning. Further, in these particular rooms, cross-ventilation is impossible given there is normally only one window or skylight. Keller describes these conditions as structural violence. While the living conditions vary, structural violence in the form of poverty and isolation experienced by older adults has combined with record-breaking heat to injure and kill isolated and poor older adults in many cities, including across Canada. We should be further troubled by the fact that this case of deadly outcomes from isolation and poverty has been repeated elsewhere.

Climate change is a tipping point; it is one of the polycrisis problems that takes us to the limit. Facing a longevity divide – the delta between those who can enjoy a longevity dividend from those who pay a longevity penalty – there are older people who are poor, isolated and disproportionately impacted by climate change, bearing the biggest cost, an early death. The deaths during weather emergencies experienced by isolated older people living in poverty have shed needed light on a divide that separates people based on their incapacity to afford to weather storms owing to individual or group accumulation of social and economic disadvantages. The divide is clearly evident in these types of early deaths from climate change. Meanwhile, diagonalist use of 'deny' and 'distract' re-framings purport that climate change is either a non-problem or that any 'divide' is a product of inter-generational competition for resources, and one that draws heavily on inter-generational tropes. In reality, climate change is fuelled by the processes of economic globalisation and unfettered economic freedoms that continue to shape the conditions for inequity over peoples' lifetime.

As with other points of inflection, what comes next is a matter of political struggle. Drawing attention to the impacts of climate change on those who are older, and the activism older adults do to address climate change that spans the diagonalist social media onslaught of generational 'blame' not only recasts 'ageing' and 'climate change' as non-competing problems, but it demonstrates a path towards age equity that is based around issue-based coalitions and cross-identity solidarity, addressing age and inequity, and linking people in shared ideas and goals.

The example of the Swiss Grannies is exemplary. In the midst of on-going political mudslinging and handwringing across countries around the world, history was made on 9 April 2024. With fists raised high and surprised but jubilant faces, *KlimaSeniorinnen* group (Swiss Senior Women for Climate Protection), or 'Swiss Grannies' as they have been referred to, departed the court, having won a landmark victory in the first ever climate case against their own Swiss government at the European Court of Human Rights Grand Chamber (2024). The applicants were more than 2,000 women aged 60 and older. The court ruled in their favour, finding that the Swiss government had put the women at increased risk of dying during heat waves because the state had not adequately put into effect domestic policies to fight climate change. The court found that their government had failed to limit greenhouse gas emissions with a carbon budget and meet its 'positive obligation' to implement measures to achieve previously set targets. Importantly, using Articles 2, 8 and 13 of the Human Rights Convention, the case sets a legally binding precedent for suing governments for their inaction on climate change, but not for reparations, but to make governments act responsively. Using human rights as the basis of claim is a win for all age groups.

In making their claim, the group was bolstered by the global science. The *Lancet Countdown on Health and Climate Change* (Romanello et al, 2022), cited previously, was among the scientific reports submitted by the applicants. The applicants' lawyers also argued persuasively that heatwaves strain and dehydrate the body, impair and aggravate heart and lung, kidney functions, exacerbate mental illness and stress, and ultimately lead to more emergency department visits and untimely deaths. The case noted that older adults, women and persons with chronic diseases were 'at the highest risk of temperature related morbidity and mortality ... Overall, women aged above 75 ... were at greater risk of premature loss of life, severe impairment of life and of family and private life, owing to climate change-induced excessive heat than the general population' (European Court of Human Rights, 2024). Older women also happen to experience greater poverty and increased isolation later in life.

The triumph of the *KlimaSeniorinnen* group reminds us of several key truths. We are in a warming world, affected by the accelerating activities of economic globalisation. Even as the world keeps trying to look away, fires, atmospheric rivers, devastating floods and glacial melting have continued unabated. On Monday 28 February 2024, a little over a month before this decision, the Intergovernmental Panel on Climate Change Working Group II issued its sixth – and what has been called its bleakest – warning about global warming to date. António Guterres was quoted as saying 'I have seen many scientific reports in my time, but nothing like this. [It is] an atlas of human suffering and a damning indictment of failed climate leadership' (Harvey, 2022).

Where politicians have tried, not tried or failed to implement climate change agendas, the courts remain an important place to struggle and make demands of state and markets to defend the commons and to reframe solidarity for the next phase of economic globalisation. Furthermore, drawing attention to the activism of older generations shines light on the important democratic and political capacities we have, as well as the role older generations can play to push for social change.

A forward conclusion: Why the new processes of economic globalisation matter for ageing

The explorations, investigations and analyses undertaken throughout the chapter, volume, and series overall, hold implications for how we question, research, contextualise, boundary, assume, scale, collect, track and analyse data, and what inter-disciplinary approaches we use to study ageing.

This concluding chapter addresses the impact of economic globalisation on the nation state and ageing, arguing that unaddressed economic freedoms create and exacerbate inequity, including in older age. Neo-liberal policies advanced economic freedoms and whittled down gains from political struggles for health, pension and labour standards in advanced capitalist countries. The basis for a secure older age was built from political struggles that built solidarity to collectively fund its costs. Neo-liberal policies that enhanced economic freedoms and ratcheted down on political freedoms diminished the post-war welfare consensus and solidarities of many kinds, including across the life course. Increasing social welfare individualisation and attacks on the welfare state have made it easier to sow the seeds of division.

We are at another historical inflection point. The processes of globalisation, in the form of surveillance capitalism and AI supported by global information and communication technologies' thirst for energy and market power in ways that tax the planet's capacities and fuel some types of consumption. Meanwhile, the proliferation of free trade zones creates places for capital to hide their wealth from taxes and political demands to redistribute in shrines devoted to a thriving of inequity across the globe. The spread of market radical, authoritarian and diagonalist political ideas have seismically shifted the terrain for political struggle with distracting, divisive politics spread using social media to fracture solidarity with *ad hominem* attacks. Diagonalism may be the new politics of division, fuelled by a figuring of us and them, but who are the 'them' in an online world amplified by algorithms and non-human 'bots'? The vitriol directed at older people as a group has escalated real-world ageism and even a generationalism, targeting 'baby boomers' broadly, and erasing cross-generational locations of gender, class, race, disability and others, and the political struggles that produce greater equality overall.

One key irony is that the ageing of the older population is often likened to a tsunami; in reality, growing numbers of older people themselves are the ones facing a perfect storm. In a world of economic and political elites engaged in their Faustian bargain, backing and bolstering economic freedoms, wrestling with political ones, ratcheting down hard-won rights to welfare, ignoring labour standards and increasing income inequality, who gets to age and the conditions for ageing are changing rapidly. Piketty (2022: 174) notes: '[t]he current economic system, based on the uncontrolled circulation of capital, goods and services, without social or environmental objectives, is akin to neocolonialism that benefits the wealthiest'.

Climate change threatens us all, and new solidarity movements are required to fight back. The longevity dividend enjoyed by some hides the longevity penalty paid by groups of people who are 'younger' old people, care workers, migrants, racialised, Indigenous, poorer and more. A more individualised, destabilised and longevity divided path through ageing is the result. Climate change exacerbates all kinds of inequities.

As this chapter has also discussed, collective action and building solidarity remain important and relevant. Resistance can take many forms, from bringing awareness, marshalling evidence, to seeking legal remedy, among other actions. Older adults' activism and agency is visible on many fronts, including others who are fighting climate and environmental degradation. Examples in the US range from Fire Drill Fridays by Jane Fonda to the work of older conservationists, like Dr. Jane Goodall, who have spent lives researching habitat decline, to those performing everyday acts of resistance.

The example of the Swiss Grannies who took their country to court for not protecting their human rights to health is particularly noteworthy. It is a model of political struggle that stands counter to many of the threats that increased economic freedoms enable, including income inequality, resource depletion, climate change and unstable work lives. The Swiss Grannies built inter-generational solidarity and pushed back on ageist tropes. They held politicians to account for competitive state decisions by using a global court and human rights protections to stand up for the lives of people in their nation.

On the steps that April 2024 day in Strasbourg, the same Greta Thunberg that had earlier denounced older generations, blaming them for climate change, was there to witness the first ever climate case victory in the European Court of Human Rights. These older women won their historic case, with implications for everyone, by arguing that their age and gender made them particularly vulnerable to climate change. These women showed that the way to fight was not through division. The way to victory was through mobilising a sense of shared risk and solidarity.

We are left with the overarching question of how can we increase the likelihood that more people will enjoy a longevity dividend and not pay the longevity penalty? We must continue to struggle to answer this and other related questions, raised in this chapter. How do we foster solidarity and inclusion across generations? How can we foster sufficient taxation to enable meaningful redistribution and shared risk, while attending to differences in needs? How can we improve conditions to create decent work for care workers while also improving the quality of and access to care? How can we select out advances from AI that will serve humanity and the planet, while we also protect our humanness in an algorithmic, big data, large language models, AI world? Given the impacts of climate change, how can we harness the collective agency of older adults and foster resistance? These and other questions raised by the reality of a longevity divide are important to consider.

Note
[1] The 'longevity dividend' represents the health and economic gains expected to accrue to individuals and societies resulting from successful efforts to slow the biological processes of ageing (Olshansky, 2022).

References

Acosta, C.M. (2023) Where are the key Panama Papers figures, seven years later?, *ICIJ – The International Consortium of Investigative Journalists* [online], Available from: https://www.icij.org/investigations/panama-papers/where-are-they-now-2023/

Baars, J., Dannefer, D., Phillipson, C. and Walker, A. (2016) *Aging, Globalization and Inequality: The New Critical Gerontology*, Routledge.

Baines, D., Braedley, S., Daly, T., Hillier, S. and Cabahug, F. (2025) Low-barrier harm reduction and housing for older people in Vancouver's opiate crisis: meeting people where they are, *Critical and Radical Social Work*, 13(1): 41–56.

Bastia, T. and Calsina, C. (2025) *Diverse Transnational Care: Ageing and Migration in Bolivia*, Bristol University Press.

Beck, U. (1992) *Risk Society: Towards a New Modernity*, Sage.

Buffel, T., Handler, S. and Phillipson, C. (2019) *Age-Friendly Cities and Communities: A Global Perspective*, Policy Press.

Callison, W. and Slobodian, Q. (2021) Coronapolitics from the Reichstag to the Capitol, *Boston Review* [online], Available from: https://www.bostonreview.net/articles/quinn-slobodian-toxic-politics-coronakspeticism/

Dannefer, D. (2003) Toward a global geography of the life course, in J.T. Mortimer and M.J. Shanahan (eds) *Handbook of the Life Course*, Kluwer Academic Publishers, pp 647–59.

Ebi, K.L. (2022) Managing climate change risks is imperative for human health: climate change in 2021, *Nature Reviews Nephrology*, 18: 74–5.

ECtHR (European Court of Human Rights) (2024) *Verein KlimaSeniorinnen Schweiz and Others v. Switzerland*, Application no. 53600/20. Judgment of 9 April 2024 [online], Available from: https://hudoc.echr.coe.int/eng?i=002-14304

Esping-Andersen, G. (1990) *The Three Worlds of Welfare Capitalism*, Princeton University Press.

Estes, C.L. (1979) *The Aging Enterprise*, Jossey-Bass.

Estes, C.L. (2006) Critical feminist perspectives, aging, and social policy, in J. Baars, D. Dannefer, C. Phillipson and A. Walker (eds) *Aging, Globalization, and Inequality: The New Critical Gerontology*, Baywood, pp 81–101.

Estes, C.L. and Phillipson, C. (2002) The globalization of capital, the welfare state, and old age policy, *International Journal of Health Services*, 32: 279–97.

European Union (1992) *Treaty of Maastricht on European Union* [online], Available from: https://eur-lex.europa.eu/EN/legal-content/summary/treaty-of-maastricht-on-european-union.html

Fennell, G., Phillipson, C. and Evers, H. (1988) *The Sociology of Old Age*, Open University Press.

Filiberto, D., Wethington, E., Pillemer, K., Wells, N., Wysocki, M. and Parise, J.T. (2009) Older people and climate change: vulnerability and health effects, *Generations*, 33: 19–25.

Fukuyama, F. (1992) *The End of History and the Last Man* (New edn), New York, NY: Free Press.

Government of Canada (1989) The Canada U.S. Free Trade Agreement [online], Available from: https://www.international.gc.ca/trade-commerce/assets/pdfs/agreements-accords/cusfta-e.pdf

Grenier, A., Phillipson, C. and Settersten, R.A. (2020) *Precarity and Ageing: Understanding Insecurity and Risk in Later Life*, Policy Press.

Grinspun, R. and Kreklewich, R. (1994) Consolidating neo-liberal reforms: 'free trade' as a conditioning framework, *Studies in Political Economy*, 43(1): 33–61.

Guillemard, A.-M. (1983) *Old Age and the Welfare State*, Sage.

Guillemard, A.-M. and Rein, M. (1993) Comparative patterns of retirement: recent trends in developed societies, *Annual Review of Sociology*, 19: 469–503.

Hall, P.A. (1993) Policy paradigms, social learning, and the state: the case of economic policymaking in Britain, *Comparative Politics*, 25(3): 275–96.

Hall, P.A. and Soskice, D. (eds) (2001) *Varieties of Capitalism: The Institutional Foundations of Comparative Advantage*, Oxford University Press.

Harvey, D. (2007) *A Brief History of Neoliberalism*, Oxford University Press.

Harvey, F. (2022) Q&A: has the IPCC's bleak warning of climate breakdown been heard?, *The Guardian* [online], Available from: https://www.theguardian.com/environment/2022/mar/05/qa-has-the-ipccs-bleak-warning-of-climate-breakdown-been-heard

Heclo, H. (1974) *Modern Social Politics in Britain and Sweden: From Relief to Income Maintenance*, New Haven: Yale University Press.

Hyde, M. and Higgs, P. (2016) *Ageing and Globalisation*, Bristol: Policy Press.

Karma, R. (2025) Buy, borrow, die, *The Atlantic* 17 March [online], Available from: https://www.theatlantic.com/ideas/archive/2025/03/tax-loophole-buy-borrow-die/682031/

Keller, R.C. (2015) *Fatal Isolation: The Devastating Paris Heat Wave of 2003*, University of Chicago Press.

Klein, N. (2023) *Doppelganger: A Trip into the Mirror World*, Farrar, Straus and Giroux.

Kohli, M., Rein, M., Guillemard, A.-M. and van Gunsteren, H. (1991) *Time for Retirement: Comparative Studies of Early Exit from the Labor Force*, Cambridge University Press.

Lawrence, M., Homer-Dixon, T., Janzwood, S., Rockstöm, J., Renn, O. and Donges, J.F. (2024) Global polycrisis: the causal mechanisms of crisis entanglement, *Global Sustainability*, 7.

Leisering, L. and Leibfried, S. (1999) *Time and Poverty in Western Welfare States*, Cambridge University Press.

Marshall, V. (2011) Global aging and families: some policy concerns about the global aging perspective, in M. Silverstein (ed) *From Generation to Generation: Continuity and Discontinuity in Aging Families*, Johns Hopkins University Press.

Mecklin, J. (2025) Closer Than Ever: It Is Now 89 Seconds to Midnight – 2025 Doomsday Clock Statement [online], Available from: https://thebulletin.org/doomsday-clock/2025-statement/

Myles, J.F. (1984) *Old Age in the Welfare State: The Political Economy of Public Pensions*, Little, Brown.

Myles, J.F. and Quadagno, J. (1991) *States, Labor Markets, and the Future of Old-Age Policy*, Temple University Press.

O'Connor, J.S., Orloff, A.S. and Shaver, S. (1999) *States, Markets, Families: Gender, Liberalism, and Social Policy in Australia, Canada, Great Britain, and the United States*, Cambridge University Press.

Orloff, A.S. (1993) Gender and the social rights of citizenship: the comparative analysis of state policies and gender relations, *American Sociological Review*, 58(3): 303–28.

Peace, S. (2023) *The Environments of Ageing: Space, Place and Materiality*, Policy Press.

Phillipson, C. (2005) The political economy of old age, in M.L. Johnson (ed) *The Cambridge Handbook of Age and Ageing*, Cambridge University Press, pp 502–9.

Phillipson, C. (2006a) Ageing and globalization, in J.A. Vincent, M. Downs and C. Phillipson (eds) *Globalization and the Future of Old Age*, SAGE Publications.

Phillipson, C. (2006b) Aging and globalization: issues for critical gerontology and political economy, in J. Baars, D. Dannefer, C. Phillipson and A. Walker (eds) *Aging and Globalization: Issues for Critical Gerontology and Political Economy*, Routledge, pp 43–58.

Phillipson, C. (2013) *Ageing*, Polity Press.

Phillipson, C. (2015) The political economy of longevity: developing new forms of solidarity for later life, *Sociological Quarterly*, 56(1): 80–100.

Phillipson, C., Calasanti, T. and Scharf, T. (2020) Series editors' preface, in A. Grenier, C. Phillipson and R.A. Settersten (eds) *Precarity and Ageing: Understanding Insecurity and Risk in Later Life*, University of Chicago Press.

Piketty, T. (2022) *A Brief History of Equality*, Harvard University Press.

Piketty, T. and Goldhammer, A. (2014) *Capital in the Twenty-First Century*, Harvard University Press.

Pillemer, K. and Filiberto, D. (2017) Mobilizing older people to address climate change, *Public Policy and Aging Report*, 27: 18–21.

Ripetti, M. and Calasanti, T. (2025) *Retirement Migration and Precarity in Later Life*, Policy Press.

Romanello, M., Di Napoli, C., Drummond, P., Green, C., Kennard, H., Lampard, P. et al (2022) The 2022 report of the 'Lancet' Countdown on health and climate change: health at the mercy of fossil fuels, *The Lancet*, 400: 1619–1654.

Sassen, S. (2001) *The Global City: New York, London, Tokyo* (2nd edn), Princeton University Press.

Simmonds, B. (2021) *Ageing and the Crisis in Health and Social Care: Global and National Perspectives*, Policy Press.

Skogstad, G. (2000) Globalization and public policy: situating Canadian analyses, *Canadian Journal of Political Science*, 33(4): 805–28.

Slobodian, Q. (2023) *Crack-Up Capitalism: Market Radicals and the Dream of a World Without Democracy*, Metropolitan Books.

Slobodian, Q. and Plehwe, D. (2022) *Market Civilization: Neoliberals East and South*, Zone Books.

Strange, S. (1997) *Casino Capitalism*, Manchester University Press.

Szebehely, M. and Meagher, G. (2017) Nordic eldercare – weak universalism becoming weaker?, *Journal of European Social Policy*, 28: 294–308.

Twigg, J. and Martin, W. (2015) The challenge of cultural gerontology, *The Gerontologist*, 55(3): 353–9.

Vincent, J.A., Downs, M. and Phillipson, C. (2006) *The Futures of Old Age*, SAGE Publications.

Walker, A. 2006. Reexamining the political economy of aging: understanding the structure/agency tension, in J. Baars, D Dannefer, C. Phillipson and A. Walker (eds) *Aging, Globalization and Inequality*, Abingdon: Routledge.

WHO (World Health Organization) (2016) Ambient Air Pollution: A Global Assessment of Exposure and Burden of Disease [online], Available from: https://iris.who.int/bitstream/handle/10665/250141/9789241511353-eng.pdf

Zuboff, S. (2019) *The Age of Surveillance Capitalism: The Fight for the Future at the New Frontier of Power*, Profile Books.

Index

References to figures appear in *italic* type; those in **bold** type refer to tables. References to endnotes show both the page number and the note number (128n1).

2SLGBTQI 59, 60–1, 128n1
  queering age-friendliness 114–17
    indicators 121–7
    next steps 127–8
    research outline 117–18
    safety 118–21, 125–6
  see also transgender persons
2SLGBTQI representation 122–3, 124–5
2SLGBTQI rights 113–14

A

access 23, 57, 120, 164, 200, 214, 223–6
active ageing 54, 239, 240–3, 252
age, long-term care (LTC) workforce 75–6, 81, 86–9, 90, 133
age-equitable bargaining 151–2
age equity 24–5
age-friendliness 37–8, 41–5
  equality and equity 45–8
  queering age-friendliness 114–17
    indicators 121–7
    next steps 127–8
    research outline 117–18
    safety 118–21, 125–6
age-friendly cities 19–25, 42, 101–3, 215, 239, 251–2
Age-Friendly Cities and Communities movement 17, 24, 25, 223
  Canada 53, 115
  and dementia 212–13, 219
  Norway 38, 45
Age-Friendly Communities Guide (WHO) 223
age equity 24–5, 63–4, 114, 121–8, 149–52, 190–1
age-friendly policies 19–21, 53–4, 101–3, 230
  Norway 41–5, 47–8
  queer 114–17, 127–8
Age Friendly Cities and Communities 17, 22, 132, 213–14, 223
age inclusion 21–4
Aged Care Provider Workforce Survey (ACPWS), Australia 73–4, 76
ageing 4–5, 205
  and globalisation 264–5, 272–4
  Lebanese views of 203–5
  and relationships 168–71
  and settler colonialism 163–8
  see also active ageing; healthy ageing; successful ageing
ageing identity 96–7
ageing in place 40
ageing statistics 53
  see also health data collection; health statistics; health surveys
ageism 97, 204
agency staff 140
Ågotnes, G. 38, 39, 40, 44, 48, 85, 132, 152
air pollution 270
anti-oppressive practice 96, 98
Apple iPhone 265–6
Armstrong, P. 4, 63, 80, 81, 96, 114, 131, 132, 148, 195, 249
artificial intelligence (AI) 266, 269
Austin, C.D. 21
Australia
  long-term care (LTC) workforce
    age-equitable bargaining 151–2
    characteristics **89**, *139*
    data gaps 73–7, 148–9
    health and safety protections 146–8
    home care workers 132–3
    pension precarity 135–41
    retention 141–4
    skills and pay 149–50, 151
    para-professional care work 71–2
    welfare regime 134

B

Baines, D. 3, 4, 68, 101, 256
Banerjee, A. 3
Barrett, G. and McGoldrick, C. 21
Beck, U. 264
Bell, S. and Menec, V. 23
Berg, K. 10
Biggs, S. and Carr, A. 23
Black Lives Matter (BLM) 104
Blix, B.H. 39, 41, 48
Braedley, S. 96, 114, 177, 178, 180, 200
Brooks-Cleator, L.A. 25, 160, 161, 172
Bryanton, O. 229
Buffel, T. 21, 24, 26
bus service 228, 229, 230–2

C

Canada
  2SLGBTQI rights 113–14

demographics 197
health data collection 53, 62–3
health surveys 56–7, 60–2
immigrants 178, 180, 197
Indigenous older adults 159–73
  health statistics 161–2
  impact of settler colonialism 162–3, 163–8, 171–2
  population size 161
  relationships 168–71, 172
Indigenous populations 159–60
long-term care (LTC) workforce 133
  age-equitable bargaining 151–2
  characteristics **89**, *139*
  data gaps 77–82, 148–9
  health and safety protections 144–6, 147–8
  home care workers 137–8
  pension precarity 135–41
  retention 142–4
  skills and pay 150–1
Lebanese Canadians 196–8
  cultural liminality 205–7
  family formation and gender roles 201–3
  normative views on ageing 203–5
  political and economic insecurity 198–200
  state support 200–1
older immigrant women 180–1, 190–1
  ethnocultural groups 188–90
  immigration as family project 181–2
  language, loneliness and social isolation 185–8
  material conditions 183–5
  research studies 178–9
para-professional care work 71–2
public transportation 223–4
  age-equitable 230–2, 234
  community-based 232–4
  Ottawa case study 226–30
  social exclusion, social isolation and 224–6
queering age-friendliness 114–17
  indicators 121–7
  next steps 127–8
  research outline 117–18
  safety 118–21, 125–6
smart cities 251–2
welfare regime 134
Canada U.S. Free Trade Agreement 1989 262
Canadian Association of Retired Persons (CARP) 243
Canadian Community Health Survey 61
Canadian Institute for Health Information (CIHI) 77, 78, 79

Canadian Longitudinal Study of Aging (CLSA) 62, 62–3
capital flight 268
capitalism *see* surveillance capitalism
capitalist societies 260–1
care assistants 69, 71–88, 133, 137
care labour 3, 181, 182, 187
  see also family care
care networks 24
care work 2–3, 68
  paid 69, 89, 90, 133, 149
  unpaid 90, 182, 190
  see also long-term care (LTC); older adult care
care workers 2
  Indigenous older adults' relationships with 170–1
  older 133–41, 147–8, 149
  queer workers 120–1, 123, 124–5
  see also home care workers; long-term care (LTC) workforce
care workforce characteristics **89**, 132–3, 137–8, *139*, **140**
carers 2
Caspar, S. 218
Center for an Age-friendly Norway 43
Chaccour, E. 10
Charlesworth, S. 3, 69, 76, 131, 133, 143
ChatGPT 266
childcare 187, 203, 204
Choiniere, J. 84, 85
choirs 217–18
chrononormativity 116
cities 5
  see also age-friendly cities; Age-Friendly Cities and Communities movement; global cities; intergenerational cities; smart cities
citizenship rights 24
class 102, 166, 247, 256, 260, 264, 267, 268
climate change 257, 269–72, 273
College of Licensed Practical Nurses of Alberta (CLPNA) 79
colonialism 160–1, 162–8, 171–3
Combahee River Collective 95
communities within communities 5
community-based organisations (CBOs) 205
community-based transportation 232–4
community consultation 233
community groups 187–8
  ethnocultural 188–90
compassionate ageism 97
contact theory 216, 218
Coordination Reform, Norway 40
Côté-Boucher, K. 180
counter-storytelling 101–2
Courtney-Pratt, H. 21
COVID-19 pandemic 104, 133, 145–7, 266

Index

Crenshaw, K. 95
Criado Perez, C. 68, 89
critical reflexivity 102
cultural liminality 195
  Lebanese Canadians 196–8, 205–7
    family formation and gender roles 201–3
    normative views on ageing 203–5
    political and economic insecurity 198–200
    state support 200–1
cultural safety 119
culture 60, 61
  loss of 164–5
cumulative advantages
cumulative disadvantages

D

Dalmer, N.K. 24
Daly, T. 3, 69, 71, 79, 85, 91, 132, 142, 195, 204
data analyses 244
data clarity 72–3
data collection *see* health data collection; surveillance capitalism
data gaps, long-term care (LTC) workforce 68, 69–70, 71–91
  Australia 73–7, 148–9
  Canada 77–82, 148–9
  Norway 82–8, 148–9
data regimes 70, 73–88
data strength 71–2
Debney, O. 117
Decade of Healthy Ageing 2020–2030 report (WHO) 54–5
dementia 20–1, 23, 187, 212, 213, 214, 215–16
Dementia Australia 215
dementia care 1
Dementia Friendly America 215
dementia-friendly communities 213–15
  friendships as central feature of 216–19
democracy 261
demographics 1, 197, 201, 202
  see also ageing statistics
dependency ratios 177
diagonalism 268–9, 271, 273
diaspora
  Lebanese 196–207
disability 165, 185, 229
disadvantaged groups 1–2
  see also marginalised groups
disconnection 166–7
discrimination 212–13
disengagement theory 240
disinformation 269
diversity 20–1, 24, 37, 45–8
doomsday clock 269
drug use 256

E

eating disorders 247
economic freedom 257, 259–60, 261–2, 266–7, 268–9, 271, 272–3
economic globalisation 261–5
  and ageing 272–4
  new phase of 265–9
economic insecurity 198–200
  see also material conditions; poverty
economic rights 273
El Bcheraoui, C. 204
employment 38–9
equality and equity 45–8
equity *see* age equity; gender equity; health equity
Esping-Andersen, G. 45
ethnic minorities 25
ethnicity 46–7, 60, 61, 82
ethnocultural groups 188–90
euthanasia 1
extreme weather events 269–70

F

Fair Work Commission, Australia 150
familial co-housing 183–4
  see also intergenerational living arrangements; multigenerational living arrangements
families, transnational 196, 203
family care 24, 40, 166–7, 181, 182, 187, 201, 202–3
family formation 201–3
family reunification migration 201
Fazzi, L. 103–4
feminist political economy (FPE) 3, 11, 96, 98, 117, 178, 239
Fennell, G. 261
Ferguson, H. 102
Fitbit 240, 242, 246–8, 251, 252
  implications 248–50
  user case study 245–6
  see also surveillance capitalism
Fook, J. and Gardner, F. 102
forced migration 167–8, 197
Foucault, M. 240
Fraser, N. 101
free trade zones 266–8, 273
Freeman, E. 116
Friedman, M. 260
friendships 216–19
Fukuyama, F. 261

G

gay 118, 119, 125
gender 25, 59, 60–1, 132, 152
  see also women
gender bias 89

gender data gap 68
gender identity *see* 2SLGBTQI
gender inequity 233
gender roles 201–3
gendered ageism 97
General Agreement on Tariffs and Trade 1947 259
General Social Survey, Canada 62
generationalism 273
global cities 263
global value chains 263
globalisation 257–8, 272–4
  history of 258–65
  new phase of 265–9
Goffman, E. 212
Greenfield, E.A. 25
Grenier, A. 265
Gudowsky, N. 23
Guterres, A. 272

H

Harris, P.B. and Caporella, C.A. 217
hate crime 119
Hayek, F. 259–60, 261
health and safety protections 144–8, 152–3
health care 1, 46–7, 186
health care system 166
health data collection 53, 55, 62–3
  and age equity 63–4
  wearable technology 243–4, 248–50, 251–2
  see also health statistics; health surveys
Health Employees Superannuation Trust Australia (HESTA) 141
health equity 27, 55
health inequity 54
health, narrowed meaning of 249–50
health outcomes 162–3
Health Services Access Survey, Canada 57
health statistics 161–2
  see also ageing statistics
health surveys 55–8
  age equity 63–4
  data collection practices 62–3
  gender and culture 58–62
healthy ageing 17, 54
heat waves 270
heteronormativity 124
hidden data 73
higher education 198
Hillier, S. 162, 167, 168
Hinton, G. 266
Holocaust survivors 102–3
home 168–9
home care 40
Home Care Packages Program (HCPP), Australia 74, 75
home care workers 132–3, 137–8
  language barriers 186–7

homelessness 1, 169
Hospital Employees Union (HEU), Canada 152
Hospital Morbidity Database, Canada 57
housing 1, 100, 183–4, 270
  see also intergenerational living arrangements; multigenerational living arrangements
Hyde, M. and Higgs, P. 265

I

identity
  ageing 96–7
  individual-based analyses of 97–8
  intersectional analyses of 98–9, 105
    conceptual tools 101–3
    critical skills 103–4
    field note examples 99–101
  see also sectarian identities
Imagining Age-friendly Communities within Communities 3–5
immigrants 177, 229
  Canada 178, 180, 197 (*see also* Lebanese Canadians; older immigrant women)
  see also migrant workers; migration
inclusion *see* age inclusion; social inclusion
inclusivity 215
income constraints 183
  see also poverty
Indigeneity 10, 24, 60, 61–2, 159, 163–4, 169–70
Indigenous older adults 159–73
  health statistics 161–2
  impact of settler colonialism 162–3, 163–8, 171–2
  population size 161
  relationships 168–71, 172
Indigenous peoples 25, 61, 62–3, 99–100, 159–60
individual-based identity analyses 97–8
individual responsibility 43, 44
inequality 38
injury 146, 147
intergenerational activities 188, 218
intergenerational choir 218
intergenerational cities 23
intergenerational competition 271
  see also generationalism
intergenerational equality 45
intergenerational living arrangements 203, 217
  see also familial co-housing; multigenerational living arrangements
intergenerational programs 123–4, 218
intergenerational relations 23
intergenerational solidarity 259, 274
intergenerational support systems 202
  see also family care

Index

intergenerational trauma 170
Intergovernmental Panel on Climate Change 272
international finance 265
international health surveys 57–8
International Monetary Fund 262
international trade agreements 262–3
intersectional analyses 98–9, 105
  conceptual tools 101–3
  critical skills 103–4
  field note examples 99–101
intersectional literature 95–7
intersectionality 94, 98
invisibility, long-term care (LTC) workforce 131–2
  invisibility traps 134–49
  health and safety protections 144–8
  pension precarity 135–41
  retention 141–4
  ways to address 149–53
Islam, M.K. and Gilmour, H. 185
isolation 270

J

Jacobsen, F.F. 42, 85
Joy, M. 25

K

Katz, S. and Calasanti, T. 204
Katz, S. and Marshall, B. 247, 249, 250
Keller, R. 270
Kelm, M.E. 162
Keynesianism 258–9
King, M.L. 188
Klauser, F.R. and Albrechtslund, A. 248
KlimaSeniorinnen 271–2, 274
Knutsen, R.H. 143

L

Labour Force Survey, Canada 57, 61–2
labour migration 177
  see also migrant workers
Lancet 270
Lancet Countdown on Health and Climate Change 272
language 128n1, 164, 165, 185–8, 228, 232
language barriers 186–7
Laxer, K. 80, 81, 132
Lebanese Canadians 196–8
  cultural liminality 205–7
  family formation and gender roles 201–3
  normative views on ageing 203–5
  political and economic insecurity 198–200
  state support 200–1
Lebanese civil war 198

Lebanon
  demographics 197, 201, 202
  family networks 201
  welfare system 200–1
Lehning, A.J. 21, 25
lesbian 118
Levasseur, M. 23
Levine-Rasky, C. 98
life expectancy 53, 137, 161–2
Lightman, N. and Baay, C. 82
liminality 195
London 263
loneliness 184, 185–6, 187–8
long-term care (LTC) 120
long-term care (LTC) workforce
  age-equitable bargaining 151–2
  health and safety protections 144–8
  invisibility 131–2, 134–49
  ways to address 149–53
  pension precarity 135–41
  retention 141–4
  skills and pay 149–51
  workforce characteristics **89**, 132–3, 137–8, *139*, **140**
  workforce data gaps 68, 69–70, 71–91
    Australia 73–7, 148–9
    Canada 77–82, 148–9
    Norway 82–8, 148–9
longevity divide 2, 256–7, 271
longevity dividend 256, 273, 274n1
longevity penalty 256–7
low income 229–30
  see also poverty
Lupton, D. 248

M

Maastricht Treaty 262
MacDonald, M. 11
marginalised groups 1–2, 25, 63
  see also minority groups
material conditions
  ethnocultural groups 188–90
  older immigrant women 183–5
  see also economic insecurity; low income; poverty
materialism 101
McCoy, M. 89
McLuhan, M. 70, 88
Mexican-American women 203
migrant workers 76–7, **83**, 267
  see also labour migration
migration
  East to West 195 (*see also* Lebanese Canadians)
  forced 167–8, 197
  see also family reunification migration; immigrants; labour migration; older immigrant women

Milan, A. and Gagnon, V. 82
Mills, S. 121
minimal group paradigm 97
minority groups 47
  see also ethnic minorities; Indigenous peoples; marginalised groups
mobility needs 232
Modlich, R. 25
monitoring devices *see* Fitbit; wearable technology
Moore, S. 101
Moorman, S.M. 21
Morley, C. 102
Moulaert, T. 242
multigenerational living arrangements 186, 201, 203
  see also familial co-housing; intergenerational living arrangements
music 217–18

N

Naples, N.A. 99
nation state actors 262
nation states 257–8, 264, 266–7
National Aged Care Census and Survey (NACWS), Australia 73, 76, 142–3
neo-liberal monitoring 248–9
neo-liberalism 259–61, 273
new market frontiers 265–6
Nordic welfare model 38–9
  critique 40–1
Norway
  age-friendliness 37–8, 41–5
  equality and equity 45–8
  long-term care (LTC) workforce
    age-equitable bargaining 151–2
    characteristics **89**, *139*
    data gaps 82–8, 148–9
    health and safety protections 146–8
    pension precarity 135–41
    retention 141–4
    skills and pay 151
  older adult care 39–40
  older population 37
  welfare regime 134
  see also Nordic welfare model
Novek, S. and Menec, V.H. 23
nurses 71–88, 89, 90, 137–8, 140, 148, 150, 151
Nursing and Residential Care Facilities, Canada 62

O

O'Connor, D. 100, 101–2
older adult care 39–40
  see also care work; long-term care (LTC)

older immigrant women 177, 178, 180–1, 190–1
  ethnocultural groups 188–90
  family care 181, 182
  immigration as family project 181–2
  language, loneliness and social isolation 185–8
  material conditions 183–5
  research studies 178–9
oppression 96

P

Panama and Paradise Papers 268
para-professional care work 71
  see also care workers
Para Transpo 227, 229, 232
Parekh, R. 22
Paris 270
Park, S. 22
part-time work 140, 142
pay and skills, long-term care (LTC) workforce 149–51
Pedell, S. 251–2
pension precarity 135–41
pensions 147, 152
Personal Support Workers (PSWs) 142
Phillipson, C. 25, 257
Piketty, T. 258, 259, 273
policy and practice decision-making 122–3
polite racism 188
political freedom 257, 259, 261, 263, 266–7, 269, 273
political insecurity 198–200
political rights 257–8, 260, 266, 267
post-structuralism 101
postmodernism 101
poverty 1, 21, 22, 135, 137, 165, 183, 259, 270
  see also economic insecurity; low income; material conditions; wealth gap
power 97, 98, 102
precarious work 135–41
Pride Week 126
professional privileging 71
Programme for the International Assessment of Adult Competencies 56
public accountability 69, 73, 83, 90
public transportation *see* transportation
Puhakka, R. 23

Q

queer older adults 120
queer representation 122–3, 124–5
queer workers 120–1, 123, 124–5
queering age-friendliness 114–17
  indicators 121–7
  next steps 127–8

Index

research outline 117–18
safety 118–21, 125–6

R

race 82, 103
racism 162, 165–6, 188
rapid ethnography 226
regressive taxation 268
relationships 168–71, 172
  see also friendships;
    intergenerational relations
religion 46, 60, 61
religious groups 199
religious institutions 205–6
Repetti, M. 26
representation 122–3, 124–5
research methods 4
  scoping review 18–19
Residential Aged Care (RAC),
  Australia 74, 75
residential care 132, 133
residential schools 170
resilience 172, 200
resistance 274
responsibilisation 250
responsibility 43, 44
retention 153
retention, long-term care (LTC)
  workforce 141–4
Ring, L. 22
risk 264–5
Rowe, J. and Kahn, R. 240–1

S

Sadana, R. 17
safety 118–21, 125–6, 169, 213
  see also health and safety protections
Sandberg, L.J. and Marshall, B.L. 116
SARS Commission, Canada 144–5, 146
scoping review 18–19
sectarian identities 199
segregation 213
seniors 56–7, 62, 122
senior centres 187–8, 233
settler colonialism 162–3, 171–2
  and ageing 163–8
sex 59, 60–1
sexual orientation 59, 61
  see also 2SLGBTQI
Silverman, M. 23
Sixsmith, J. 22
skills and pay, long-term care (LTC)
  workforce 149–51
Slobodian, Q. 267
smart cities 251–2
Smith, R.J. 22
Smylie, J. and Firestone, M. 161
social activism 104

social care workers 170–1
social cohesion 22
social determinants of health (SDoH) 54, 224, 252
social exclusion 224–6, 230
social identity 97–8
social inclusion 224
social inequities 214
social isolation 25, 184, 185–6, 187–8, 224–6, 229, 230
social justice 101
social locations 98, 99, 100
social media 269
social services 113–14, 200
social welfare programmes 37
  see also Nordic welfare model; welfare
    state programs
Soilemezi, D. 23
solidarity 268, 274
state support 200–1
statistics 55–6, 62–3, 70, 71, 161–2
Statistics Canada (StatsCan) 77–8, 81, 82
stigma 212–13, 215–16
storytelling *see* counter-storytelling
Strange, S. 263
Streeter, C. 117, 119, 121
substance use 256
successful ageing 204, 241–2, 252
superannuation pension fund 141
surveillance capitalism 239, 243–5, 252–3, 266
  and age-friendly cities 251–2
  see also Fitbit
survey data 57, 58
Survey of Ageing and Independence,
  Canada 61–2
Survey of Older Workers, Canada 61–2
Survey of Persons Not in the Labour Force,
  Canada 56
Sussman, T. 126
sustainability discourse 39–40
Swaffer, K. 215
Swiss Grannies 271–2, 274
Syed, M.A. 25

T

Tamburri, N. 218
Target 244
taxation 268
technology 240, 243–5, 252–3, 265–6
  see also Fitbit; surveillance capitalism
Thunberg, G. 274
trade agreements 262–3
trade barriers 259
training 125–6
transgender persons 100, 120, 124
transnational ageing 196–8, 203, 206
transnational families 196, 203

transport disadvantage 225
transportation 184–5, 223–4
  age-equitable 230–2, 234
  community-based transportation
    232–4
  Ottawa case study 226–30
  social exclusion, social isolation
    and 224–6
trauma 170
Trump, D. 96
Turner, N. and Morken, L. 213
Turrell, G. 22
Turtiainen, K. 104

U

United Nations 1, 17
universal welfare state 37, 38, 40, 45

V

value chains 263
van Hoof, J. 23
van Vliet, W. 23
volunteers 40, 124, 182, 189, 233

W

Walker, A. 240, 242
Wang, Y. 25
Waterfront Toronto 251–2
wealth gap 2
  see also poverty
wealth hiding 268
wearable technology 240, 243–5,
    252–3
  see also Fitbit; surveillance capitalism

welfare regimes 134, 200, 204
  see also Nordic welfare model
welfare state programs 258–9, 260–1, 265
welfare state 38–41, 134, 257
  Norwegian 41–5
Wilson, S. 163
women 1, 80, 81, 87, 227–8, 259
  see also Mexican-American women;
    older immigrant women
Wood, T. 7
workforce data gaps 68, 69–70, 71–91,
    148–9
  Australia 73–7, 148–9
  Canada 77–82
  Norway 82–8
World Alzheimer's 2012 Report 216
World Health Organization (WHO)
  active ageing 242
  age-friendly framework 19, 25,
    37–8, 53–5, 59, 63–4, 114–15, 117,
    131–2, 239
  Decade of Healthy Ageing 17, 54–5
  health equity 27
World Trade Organization 262

X

Xie, L. 22

Y

Young, I.M. 96
Ysseldyk, R. 89, 97

Z

Zuboff, S. 243–4, 266

www.ingramcontent.com/pod-product-compliance
Lightning Source LLC
Chambersburg PA
CBHW051530020426
42333CB00016B/1857